THE ROLE OF LEGAL PRECEDENT IN PRIVATE LAW

THE ROLE OF LEGAL PRECEDENT IN PRIVATE LAW

A Comparative Study

Edited by
Christina Ramberg

INTERSENTIA
Cambridge – Antwerp – Chicago

Intersentia Ltd
8 Wellington Mews
Wellington Street | Cambridge
CB1 1HW | United Kingdom
Tel: +44 1223 736 170
Email: contact@larcier-intersentia.com
www.larcier-intersentia.com

Distribution for the UK and
Rest of the World (incl. Eastern Europe)
NBN International
1 Deltic Avenue, Rooksley
Milton Keynes MK13 8LD
United Kingdom
Tel: +44 1752 202 301 | Fax: +44 1752 202 331
Email: orders@nbninternational.com

Distribution for Europe
Lefebvre Sarrut Belgium NV
Hoogstraat 139/6
1000 Brussels
Belgium
Tel: +32 (0)2 548 07 13
Email: contact@larcier-intersentia.com

Distribution for the USA and Canada
Independent Publishers Group
Order Department
814 North Franklin Street
Chicago, IL 60610
USA
Tel: +1 800 888 4741 (toll free) | Fax: +1 312 337 5985
Email: orders@ipgbook.com

The Role of Legal Precedent in Private Law. A Comparative Study

ISBN 978-1-83970-536-6
D/2024/7849/63
NUR 822

British Library Cataloguing in Publication Data. A catalogue record for this book is available from the British Library.

CONTENTS

LIST OF CONTRIBUTORS

Luisa Antoniolli is Professor of Private Comparative Law at the Faculty of Law and the School of International Studies of the University of Trento (Italy). She earned a PhD in Comparative Law at the University of Florence (Italy), and is a member of the European Law Institute (ELI) and of the Italian Society for Comparative Law Research (Società italiana per la ricerca nel diritto comparato, SIRD). Her main research interests concern comparative law and European private law.

Leo Boonzaier is a Senior Lecturer in the Department of Private Law at the University of Cape Town (South Africa). He studied Social Science and Law at UCT and then did his graduate work at Oxford (United Kingdom).

John Cartwright is Emeritus Professor of the Law of Contract, University of Oxford (United Kingdom), and Research Fellow (formerly Director) of the Institute of European and Comparative Law, Oxford. He was also Professor of Anglo-American Private Law at the University of Leiden (the Netherlands) from 2007 to 2017; and for more than twenty years he has taught at Paris-Panthéon-Assas University (France), (first as visiting Professor, and since 2019 as contractual Professor of Private Law (Common Law)). His research focuses on English and comparative private law, especially contract and property law.

Fabiano Carvalho is a Civil Procedure Professor at Fundação Armando Álvares Penteado, São Paulo (Brazil). He has a PhD from Pontifícia Universidade Católica of São Paulo and has published several books and papers on private law, civil procedure, arbitration and precedents. Fabiano also works as a lawyer, assisting clients in complex litigation, both before courts and arbitral institutions.

Guillaume Leroy is Associate Professor of Private Law at Paris-Panthéon-Assas University (France). He is the author of a thesis on the practice of precedent in French law. Specialising in legal theory, he is particularly interested in legal argumentation and legal reasoning. His research also focuses on contract law.

Qiao Liu is currently Professor and Deputy Director of the Centre for Chinese and Comparative Law, School of Law, City University of Hong Kong. He is also an Honorary Professor at the TC Beirne School of Law, University of Queensland (Australia) and an Adjunct Chair Professor at the School of Law of Xiamen University (China). He serves as co-Editor-in-Chief of *The Chinese Journal* *of Comparative Law* (OUP). He teaches and researches in contract law (both Anglo-Australian and Chinese), comparative Chinese law and commercial law (both domestic and international) and has published in leading law journals including the *Modern Law Review*, *American Journal of Comparative Law* and the *Cambridge Law Journal*.

Christina Ramberg is Professor of Private Law at Stockholm University (Sweden). She has published many books and papers on general and specific contract law, electronic commerce and precedents. She participated in the Study Group for a European Civil Code and has represented Sweden and ICC in the UNCITRAL work on electronic commerce. She frequently acts as an arbitrator.

Marvin Straub is an assistant at the chair of Professor Jörg Neuner at the University of Augsburg (Germany) (civil law, labour and commercial law and philosophy of law).

Roman Zykov specialises in international arbitration with a particular emphasis on mergers and acquisitions, shareholders, construction, energy, mining, oil & gas, aerospace, trade-related disputes, investor-state dispute settlement (ISDS) and international public law. Dr. Zykov frequently acts as arbitrator under the ICC, SCC, VIAC, CIETAC, UNCITRAL and other arbitration rules. He also acts as counsel in arbitration and as an expert witness on Russian, CIS, arbitration and international law before arbitral tribunals and national courts. Since 2013 Dr. Zykov has acted as the Secretary-General of the Russian Arbitration Association and is a lecturer at Gubkin Russian State University of Oil and Gas, Institute of Mining and Energy Law.

COMPARATIVE INTRODUCTION TO THE ROLE OF PRECEDENT IN PRIVATE LAW

Christina RAMBERG

1. GENERAL INTRODUCTION

1.1. THE COMPARED JURISDICTIONS

This book is aimed at analysing how court decisions (precedents) function as a source of law in various jurisdictions. It compares jurisdictions from all over the world, from different legal families and with diverse legal traditions. Only the contribution from England and Wales represents a 'pure' common law jurisdiction. South Africa represents a mixed jurisdiction with a fairly new constitution. Traditional civil law jurisdictions are represented by the French legal family (Brazil, France and Italy) and the German legal family (Germany). The Nordic legal family is represented by Sweden. China and Russia are civil law systems that display interesting new developments.

The contributions provide stimulating materials for comparison since they are similar, yet different enough for a comparative analysis. Such similarities and differences comprise, for example, their traditional and modern attitudes towards precedent, their court systems as well as their division of the roles of the judiciary and the legislature.

1.2. WHY PRIVATE LAW?

This book focuses on private law. This is a particularly interesting area of law to compare for two reasons. First, precedents are less controversial in private law as the democratic deficit is less significant compared to other areas of law. Second, statutory private law often needs to be supplemented and developed by precedents due to a need to fill gaps or to interpret abstract statutory texts. The creative means of interpretation and gap-filling is more restricted in areas of law that are governed by the principle of legality (*nulla poena/tributum sine lege*), such as criminal law and tax law.

1.3. THE OVERALL COMPARATIVE CONCLUSIONS

The contributions to this book highlight the differences between the jurisdictions on a formal level, as well as differences in how precedents are considered as a source of law. Furthermore, and perhaps more interestingly, the contributions show that these differences do not necessarily entail any fundamental difference in the actual *de facto* importance of precedent. Finally, the contributions point to various difficulties in coping with precedents as a source of private law.

The doctrine of precedent has a well-established base in common law jurisdictions, such as England and Wales. Conversely, civil law jurisdictions have traditionally given precedents a lower significance. This has, however, been changing as both the pursuit of certainty and the ambition to treat like cases alike have pushed many civil law jurisdictions to grant precedents more importance as a source of law. It is quite clear that there is a global converging movement towards a common point regarding precedents.

Many of the ideas and concepts related to precedents have been developed by common law scholars. What is perceived as a precedent and how to find guidance by precedents are, to a large extent, inspired by common law scholarly works. As will be explained, it is complicated to fit some precedent-like phenomena into the common law system and vocabulary, such as proclamations by courts of an abstract summary nature.

The contributions to this book demonstrate that the move towards acknowledging precedents' increasing importance as a source of law is achieved by different means. By comparing the various aspects of dealing with precedents in many jurisdictions, the methodological understanding of precedents in each jurisdiction's national law is enhanced. By such understanding, one can be better equipped to cope with the implications for the future path in dealing with precedents.

1.4. SOME TERMINOLOGY

The notions of 'precedent' or 'case law' are hard to define and are used differently by different scholars. This contribution uses the terms 'precedent' and 'case law' to indicate a judicial decision regarding an actual case that may potentially influence later judicial decisions. When speaking of 'supreme courts' as a general term, this refers to the highest courts for private law matters within a range of jurisdictions, although the particular courts of individual jurisdictions are referred to where appropriate: the Supreme Courts of Brazil, China, Russia, South Africa and Sweden, the Supreme Court (formerly the House of Lords) of the United Kingdom for the law of England and Wales, the Cour de cassation for France, the Bundesgerichtshof for Germany, and the Corte suprema di cassazione for Italy.

2. THE HISTORY OF PRECEDENT IN PRIVATE LAW

The importance of precedents has varied over time in all the reporting jurisdictions. The trends throughout history are, however, surprisingly similar.

2.1. THE OLD TIMES

In many jurisdictions, precedents are the origin of private law. It has been claimed that a doctrine of precedent was familiar to South Africa's indigenous system of law. China, Germany, England and Wales, France and Sweden relied on judge-made private law in medieval times. In Brazil, precedents can be traced back to the colonial and imperial periods. Before the unification of Italy in 1861, judge-made law had a prominent role.

In quite a few jurisdictions the judges, at times in history, have made proclamations similar to statutory law. In Germany, courts were authorised to issue resolutions that qualified as substantive law. Also, in France, judges created rules in cooperation with the legislator.

Russia in the old times is different, as court decisions were not published and not recognised.

In the old times, most jurisdictions viewed judges as declaring already-existing law and not as actually creating new law.

2.2. THE EIGHTEENTH CENTURY

By the eighteenth century, many jurisdictions gradually became hostile towards precedent as a source of law and favoured statutory law. Some jurisdictions, such as Italy, France, and Prussia, formally limited the judges to the role of the mouthpiece of the legislator. One of the major aims of the French Revolutionaries was to abolish judicial power so that judges were confined to only apply statutory law, and instructed to address questions to the legislator whenever they deemed it necessary to interpret a statute or to enact a new rule to cover a statutory gap. China was perhaps an exception as during the Qing Dynasty (1636–1912) the role of precedent became both strengthened and systematised.

In England and Wales and Brazil in the eighteenth century, there was no strong hostility towards judges and precedents. Also, in Sweden, precedents remained important throughout the eighteenth century, probably due to the fact that the statutory private law mainly consisted of fragmented codified case law and customary law.

2.3. THE NINETEENTH CENTURY

In France, precedents already regained some recognition in the 1804 French Civil Code. In parts of Germany, precedents were important during most of the nineteenth century, whereas other parts of Germany continued to display a hostile attitude toward precedents.

By the late nineteenth century there was a development towards giving precedents increasing importance. This is very clear in England and Wales and in South Africa where the concept of *stare decisis* was established in the last decades of the nineteenth century. The increased importance was facilitated by the development of a modern case law reporting system and a modernisation of the court system. Likewise, in China, the system of precedent had by that time been well-established, with the central government starting to publish difficult criminal cases.

In France, precedents were an important tool to develop tort law and the law of unjust enrichment in the late nineteenth century. However, French scholarly works in the nineteenth century and in the beginning of the twentieth century considered precedents not as a source of law but merely as an authority in fact.

In other jurisdictions, such as Brazil, the importance of precedents in the late nineteenth century was less obvious but still strong. In Sweden, the Supreme Court was established in 1874. In Russia, the judiciary was separated from the government in 1864 and decisions from the highest court were published, although the general understanding was that they were not precedents.

Some jurisdictions were hostile towards precedents for a longer period, notably Germany and Italy. When the German Reich Court (Reichsgericht) was established in 1879, German court decisions became officially less important, but soon afterwards precedents were again unofficially acknowledged as necessary to interpret the statutory private law reform that was enacted in 1900. Italian judges had a strong position until the unification of the Italian state in 1861 when the powers of judges were radically restricted.

2.4. AFTER THE MID-TWENTIETH CENTURY

During the late twentieth century and the twenty-first century, precedents have gradually become increasingly important in most of the reporting jurisdictions. The main exception is in England and Wales, where a significant change was made to the doctrine of precedent in 1966, when the House of Lords (now the Supreme Court) acquired the power to depart from its own precedents; although this power is exercised cautiously, the doctrine of *stare decisis* became less strict in the second half of the twentieth century. South Africa may also represent an exception as a result of the country's new Constitution enacted in 1996.

Brazil has made many reforms aimed at strengthening the importance of precedents, mainly starting in the 1970s, and important large reforms starting in 2008 and 2015. Since the initiation of the Open and Reform policy in 1979, China has introduced reforms by the legislator as well as by the Supreme Court itself which have gradually enhanced the importance of case law, particularly after 1990. Italy has recently enacted a comprehensive reform which enhances the role of its highest court, the Corte suprema di cassazione, and aims at better managing its growing case load. The developments in France, Germany and Sweden are less obvious, without any major statutory reform, but it is nevertheless clear that precedents have lately become increasingly important with extensive debates about their function.

3. FORMAL SUPPORT FOR PRECEDENT AS A SOURCE OF LAW

3.1. THE NOTION OF A SOURCE OF LAW

The question whether precedents constitute a source of law depends on what constitutes a source of law. A broad notion of 'source of law' may encompass any argument which judges use to decide cases, and then it is easy to conceive precedents as a source of law. However, if 'source of law' means only sources that are expressly recognised in the constitution, precedents often do not qualify. While this distinction highlights the difference in importance between statutory law and precedents in a civil law system, it does not deny the possible role of precedents in the courts' adjudication of similar cases.

3.2. STATUTORY REGULATION OF PRECEDENT

The sources of law are formally regulated differently in the reporting jurisdictions.

According to the German Constitution, decisions by the Constitutional Court (Bundesverfassungsgericht) are binding on all courts and public authorities. There is, however, no corresponding statutory rule in Germany regarding decisions from the highest private law court (Bundesgerichtshof).

South Africa has a constitutional regulation regarding precedents, stating that courts have a duty to develop the common law to remove any inconsistency between the existing case law (common law) and the Constitution. This provision gives indirect legitimacy to precedents as a source of law, as it regulates an exemption from old precedents that are not in harmony with the new South African Constitution.

Statutory law in France and Germany lists sources of law without mentioning precedents (except regarding precedents from the German Constitutional

Court). An interpretation *e contrario* entails that precedents are not recognised as a source of law in these jurisdictions. But the picture is quite blurred. German statutory law stipulates that the highest court shall ensure a uniform application of the law, which indicates that precedent is a source of law. The blurred situation is quite similar in France. On the one hand, the French Civil Code prohibits judges from issuing rulings by way of general and regulatory provisions, and according to French statutory law, judicial rulings have effect only for the parties (*relative res judicata*). But, on the other hand, the French Civil Code states that a judge must provide a judgment in an actual case and that it is the task of the judge to interpret the text of statutory law and to extend its application according to its spirit. Furthermore, France has quite recently introduced a possibility for the highest court in private law matters (Cour de cassation) to give opinions to lower courts before they have rendered their decision.

Similarly to Germany and France, Italian statutory law lists sources of law without mentioning precedents and the Italian Constitution states that judges are subject only to the law. These provisions imply that precedent is not an Italian source of law. However, an Italian statute from 1941 states that the Corte suprema di cassazione, as the supreme court, ensures the exact compliance and the uniform interpretation of the law as well as the unity of national objective law which, in effect, gives precedent importance. Furthermore, a recent major reform in Italy is aimed at reinstating the guiding role of the Corte suprema di cassazione at the heart of case law, strengthening its role in leading case law evolution.

Brazil and China have legislative provisions regarding the sources of law but do not mention precedent as a source. Precedents are, however, perceived by many Brazilian scholars as a source of law. The Brazilian Code of Civil Procedure strengthens the authority of Supreme Court precedents as a source of law, considering that some types of decisions can bind all the lower courts, by imposing an obligation on the lower courts to explain why a given precedent governs the case or not. In China, statutory law gives the Supreme Court an explicit power to proclaim Judicial Interpretations and to issue Guiding Cases, which implies a right for that court to create binding norms.

Russia and Sweden have no statutory provision on the sources of law. The Swedish Procedural Act 1942 only vaguely states that the Supreme Court has a task to provide guidance for the application of private law.

Some jurisdictions have statutory rules expressing fundamental principles, which indirectly provide legitimacy for precedents as a source of law. The Brazilian Constitution, for instance, mentions the principles of efficiency, legal certainty, trust, stability of the law, continuity of the law, justice, and equity, which all support the importance of precedents. In Germany and Italy, the constitutional principles of equal treatment and protection of legitimate expectations are perceived by some scholars as indirect support for precedents as a source of law. The rule of law is a founding value in the South African Constitution, which is held as necessitating respect for precedents.

In England and Wales, the sources of law are not set out in a constitution or other statutory law. Case law is, however, clearly recognised as a formal source of law.

3.3. SELF-IMPOSED RULES BY COURTS

In the absence of statutory regulation of precedents as a source of law, in many jurisdictions the supreme courts have stated expressly that they take note of precedents and are more or less bound by them. Thereby, precedent as a source of private law has been established by the courts themselves, as a form of self-restraint by judges.

The supreme courts in Brazil, China, England and Wales, Germany, South Africa and Sweden have made statements regarding how precedents apply to their own jurisdictions. The Brazilian Supreme Court has stated that it must follow its own precedent, even when the precedent is against the Justices' personal interpretation of the law. According to the German Federal Constitutional Court, it is in the nature of the higher courts to develop general legal principles which may guide the lower courts, and the German Bundesgerichtshof has stated that it will deviate from its settled practice only where there are clearly predominant or compelling reasons. Similar statements have been made by the supreme courts in England and Wales and South Africa.

The Russian Supreme Court has not made any statement regarding how its own precedents apply to it but has encouraged lower courts to take the decisions of the Supreme Court into account. The South African Supreme Constitutional Court has made a stronger statement, requiring lower courts to accept the authority and the binding force of applicable decisions of higher tribunals.

3.4. A *DE FACTO* SOURCE OF LAW

Despite the lack of express statutory support for precedents as a source of law, all jurisdictions acknowledge precedents as an important source of law. In fact, lawyers in France, Italy and Germany acknowledge the fundamental role that case law plays in establishing private law, even though an *e contrario* interpretation of statutory provisions on sources of law indicates that precedents are not a formal source. What the French contributor to this book, Guillaume Leroy, states about French law apparently applies also to other states: 'The mystery that surrounds precedent in French law is thus the result of a significant gap between what is *said* and what is actually *done*.'

It is expected that judges take precedents into account when determining a case and judges are heavily influenced by case law in all the reporting jurisdictions. This is particularly clear in Brazil, where statutory law expressly reminds the judges about their duty to maintain stability and to safeguard coherence in the legal system.

3.5. INCENTIVES AND DISINCENTIVES ON JUDGES

Judges who do not adhere to precedents are not subject to any sanctions in most of the compared jurisdictions (Brazil, England and Wales, France, Germany, Italy, Russia and South Africa). However, in all these jurisdictions, there is an expectation that judges will take precedents into account and follow them, or at least be guided by them to strive for uniformity.

In some jurisdictions it is possible to impose administrative sanctions against judges who do not adhere to precedents. This is the case in Sweden where, at least in theory, judges may face administrative sanctions (for example a reduction in salary) if they openly deviate from a precedent without explaining why. In China, judges who do not search for and apply the relevant legal rules (including precedents) may be exposed to disciplinary consequences. Such consequences, which have fallen upon some judges on occasion, have important implications for how judges behave in discharging their judicial duties.

In Germany, a judge who constantly deviates from Bundesgerichtshof precedent could experience career setbacks. Some jurisdictions have measures to promote judges who refer to precedents, notably Brazil where it is a possible criterion for judges' promotion that they have referred to case law and complied with precedents.

Most jurisdictions, however, seem to rely on judges without having any formal incentives or disincentives to follow precedents. The expectations and the judges' concern for the legal order appear to function as sufficient incentives.

In England and Wales, Germany and Sweden, legal advisors are required to search for and analyse precedents or otherwise risk being liable for contractual damages for loss caused to their clients. Such contractual obligations would make no sense if precedents were, in fact, an unimportant source of law. In England and Wales and Germany, it is expected that legal counsel provides the courts with references to precedents as a support for their legal arguments. In Russia, it has become the norm that counsel extensively rely on case law in their pleadings.

3.6. SUMMARY

To sum up, the statutory regulation of precedents differs and there are often no clear statutory rules about how precedents operate as a source of law. It appears, however, that all the compared jurisdictions acknowledge precedents as relevant and important and expect judges to take precedents into account.

Therefore, while many of the reporting jurisdictions refrain from openly and officially recognising 'precedent' as a formal 'source of law', they all acknowledge the importance of precedents. Whether or not case law belongs to the sources of law depends on the definitions of 'source' and 'law'. Whether to categorise precedents as a source of law is, therefore, essentially only an ontological question.

4. THE BINDING NATURE OF PRECEDENT

4.1. CONFUSING TERMINOLOGY

Precedents are described in many ways: as binding, mandatory, fully or absolutely binding, *de facto* binding, having limited binding force, qualifying, presumptive, persuasive, guiding, inspirational, important, influential, subsidiary, educational, illustrative, models, ancillary decision tools, interplay between reflection and decision, etc. Not only are various terms used to describe precedents, what is meant by each term may also vary. An explanation for the imprecise terminology and the difficulty in understanding the intended level of bindingness may be the need to hide the judges' role as lawmakers.

China's Guiding Case system is an example of confusing or ambiguous terminology. While the name 'Guiding Case' indicates only a 'guiding' effect on future adjudication, Guiding Cases are in effect more than merely guiding as they must be followed by courts on all levels when deciding a similar case – and what is meant by 'followed' is also quite uncertain.

Also, the reform in Brazil is an example of vague terminology. According to Brazilian statutory law, the courts must consider precedents raised by the parties and analyse analogical arguments that support the application of the precedent in the case at hand, but precedents are still labelled as only persuasive. Also, in Sweden, it is said that precedents are only persuasive, but their status is in effect stronger.

Irrespective of how precedents are functionally described and labelled, there seems to be universal agreement among the reporting jurisdictions that precedents have effect and are important. However, in none of them are precedents absolutely binding.

4.2. WHERE ARE PRECEDENTS STRONGLY BINDING?

It is impossible to compare to what extent precedents are binding and to rank the reporting jurisdictions on a scale of bindingness. The reason is that it is not sufficiently clear in all jurisdictions how to identify legal rules in precedents nor under what circumstances it is allowed to deviate from a precedent.

It may appear that precedents in England and Wales are more binding than, for instance, precedents in France, Italy or Germany. This may, however, only be the appearance on the surface. England and Wales have developed sophisticated methods of identifying the *ratio decidendi* rules relating to the binding force of precedents, but these methods provide only limited certainty. There is uncertainty also regarding Guiding Cases in China as, on the one hand, they are binding but, on the other hand, this bindingness only implies that they might be departed from with an explanation of how the case at hand differs from the Guiding Case.

4.3. ABSTRACT SUMMARY STATEMENTS

In some jurisdictions, the supreme courts produce summary statements that are based on many cases, detached from the facts of a case and phrased in an abstract way. Examples are the legal theses (*súmulas*) in Brazil, the Judicial Interpretations and Guiding Cases in China, and the resolutions from the Russian Supreme Court. Such summary statements have a strong binding effect. The main goal of creating such summaries is to clarify to the lower courts and to the public how the courts have interpreted a point of law in order to overcome inconsistencies and in order to avoid new claims and appeals about that legal issue.

It is disputed whether to categorise such abstract summary statements as precedents and case law or rather as a *sui generis* source of law. The detachment from the factual context of an original case deprives the summary statements of the essential characters of common law precedents and the methods used in England and Wales to identify rules in precedents cannot be applied to such summary statements. For the purposes of this comparative analysis, the summary statements are categorised as precedents as they are made by courts and relate to case law.

The primary purpose of the summarising institutions in Brazil was not to enhance the status of precedent as a source of law. However, the Brazilian summaries have an indirect effect of reinforcing precedent, as they provide guidance to similar situations. Likewise, the resolutions from the Russian Supreme Court are intended to provide guidance to lower courts. On the contrary, the Chinese Guiding Cases were introduced with the purpose of producing binding legal rules to apply in future cases.

General statements of law, detached from their factual context, are also often made by the French Cour de cassation, and have a strong impact on later cases. Likewise, in Germany, Bundesgerichtshof decisions often include an abstract headnote. In Italy, the so-called *massime*, i.e. formulations which aim to report the *ratio* of judicial decisions in a short form, often have a highly abstract nature.

In jurisdictions that lack a formal institution that is tasked with summarising precedents, there is sometimes a kind of corresponding summary of past precedents in the actual reasoning in individual cases which can be described as 'embedded summaries'. When making a comparison with 'official' summaries totally detached from factual circumstance, the embedded summaries do not as clearly demonstrate that the judges function as lawmakers, and the embedded summaries are thus probably seen as less controversial. Nevertheless, such embedded summaries within a particular reasoning seem to be highly influential, although are often criticised for being *obiter dicta*.

In essence, the problem whether embedded summary statements qualify as precedent is similar to the problem of whether general broad statements in the reasonings of an individual case constitute *obiter dicta*.

4.4. WHAT TYPE OF CASES ARE PRECEDENTS?

A common feature in all the reporting jurisdictions is that lower courts are influenced by precedents from higher courts. There are differences with respect to which type of courts are influential and to what extent they are influential.

The courts in England and Wales are, to some extent, influenced also by other courts at the same level (horizontal effect), in particular the Court of Appeal is normally bound to follow its own earlier precedents, although the really significant precedents in England and Wales are the comparatively few cases of the Supreme Court and the (much more numerous) cases of the Court of Appeal. In South Africa precedents also have horizontal effect. In Brazil, China, France, Germany, Italy, Russia and Sweden, only decisions from the highest courts are relevant as precedents, although there is no prohibition against taking into account decisions from courts at the same or lower levels. Some reporters indicate that new legal databases and new software that facilitate the collection and structuring of many cases may in the future lead to an increased importance of cases from lower courts.

Some jurisdictions make a distinction between binding and persuasive precedents. In Brazil, certain procedures make it possible to establish precedents that must mandatorily be observed in future cases, as opposed to all other cases that are only persuasive. China distinguishes between three categories: cases that must be followed, cases that have strong implicit bindingness, and cases that have weak implicit bindingness. The French Cour de cassation has an imprecise hierarchy among cases, depending on the conditions in which the ruling is formulated and how it is received by those who interpret it.

In Italy, the focus lies not on the decision in an individual case, but rather rules that can be identified from a coherent line of judicial decisions, which may be hard to find due to the large number of cases and the many conflicting decisions. A special body within the Italian Corte suprema di cassazione is responsible for collecting and drafting the *rationes* of cases for publication (the so-called *massime*). The *massime* are a crucial source of law in practice, even if their quality is sometimes criticised. The *de facto* importance of *massime* is clear because they are cited, used and applied both by judges and lawyers.

4.5. *RATIONES DECIDENDI, OBITER DICTA* AND GENERALISATION

The methods of interpreting and applying precedents are substantially different from those applied to the interpretation of statutory law. It is quite clear in all the reporting jurisdictions that there is uncertainty how to distil legal rules from precedents. In England and Wales and South Africa there seems to remain uncertainties regarding how to precisely understand precedents – despite the long history of methodically analysing precedents as a source of law in these jurisdictions. Not surprisingly, there is even greater diversity of opinion on how to understand precedents in jurisdictions where precedents are a less established source of law.

All the reporting jurisdictions seem to be aware of and interested in the distinction between *obiter dicta* (i.e. statements that are not necessary to solve the case) and *rationes decidendi* (i.e. necessary statements about the law). Another similarity is that there seems to be a common uncertainty about the boundaries between the two. Furthermore, there seems to be common confusion about why it is relevant to make a distinction between *rationes* and *obiter dicta*. The Brazilian abstract general legal theses (*súmulas*) are categorised as *rationes decidendi*, despite their all-encompassing nature, and therefore have a stronger binding effect than other *obiter dicta* which are only persuasive.

In some jurisdictions *obiter dicta* are probably almost as influential as statements qualifying as *rationes decidendi* (for instance in Italy and Sweden). The reason why *obiter dicta* are influential is probably the striving for predictability and consistent application of the law (see, for example, Brazil and Sweden). Another reason may be that some jurisdictions are not experienced in distinguishing *obiter dicta* from *rationes decidendi* (see, for example, France and Sweden). In Germany, *obiter dicta* are sometimes used as a means for the court to indicate that it is likely that the court will deviate from a precedent in future cases where the facts are rather alike the facts in the precedent. In some jurisdictions, notably England and Wales and South Africa, *obiter dicta* are clearly less relevant than *rationes*, even though *obiter dicta* are often very influential.

There is general awareness about the problem regarding to what extent it is possible to generalise from the facts of a precedent to a later case and to extend its application to similar circumstances. In England and Wales and South Africa, it is common to see in-depth discussions in the courts' reasonings about the scope of precedents and how far they can be extended. In Brazil, China, Italy and Sweden, references can often be found to precedents in the supreme courts' reasoning, but only rarely do these reasonings make in-depth analyses of the facts in the precedent for the purpose of comparing it with the present case.

4.6. DEPARTURE (DEVIATION) FROM PRECEDENTS

All the reporting jurisdictions allow departure from earlier precedents under more or less the same conditions. Generally, departures are rare and are only to be made in exceptional situations and for good reasons. China has introduced safeguards that require detailed reasons by the adjudicating judge before making a deviation from a Guiding Case. Also, Germany has special procedures for deviations from precedents, which seem to create incentives for German courts to make hidden instead of transparent deviations.

In most jurisdictions the judges are expected to explain the reasons for a departure from an earlier precedent. In Brazil this is not only an expectation; the parties have an express statutory right to require judges to analyse and compare the facts between a present case and a precedent.

Many jurisdictions have rules that, in effect, entail hurdles for deviating from precedents. In Germany and Sweden, it is easier to get access to an appeal from a first-instance court when the first-instance court has deviated from a precedent.

4.7. DISTINCTION OR DEPARTURE (DEVIATION)?

There is an interesting debate in South Africa and Sweden regarding whether it is permissible or desirable to distinguish the case from a precedent or to transparently express that a decision is a departure from an earlier precedent. Some argue that departures should be disguised in order to safeguard the court's legitimacy. Others argue that it is better to communicate transparently that an old rule is replaced in order to avoid confusion and uncertainty.

The Supreme Court in England and Wales is reluctant to depart from its own precedents, but if it does so it will state this explicitly in its judgment. The French Cour de cassation has recently decided routinely to state explicitly when it overrules a precedent.

In South Africa the recently established Constitutional Court has tended to avoid direct conflict with prior judgments by creative acts of distinguishing. The South African contributor to this book, Leo Boonzaier, warns that:

> strained and unpredictable reinterpretations of prior decisions may themselves produce uncertainty, confusion, and perhaps a loss of legitimacy; and in due course the Court may require express flexibility to adapt constitutional law to changing conditions.

4.8. CONSEQUENCES WHEN PRECEDENTS ARE NOT FOLLOWED

In all the reporting jurisdictions a decision from a lower court that has disregarded precedents may be appealed. Otherwise, most of the reporting jurisdictions have no legal sanctions against not following precedents (see above regarding incentives and disincentives on individual judges).

Brazil, however, has a special remedy: a decision may be declared void if the lower courts fail to observe a binding precedent without distinguishing the case at hand or giving reasons for a deviation from the relevant precedent.

Also, Russia has a special sanction: a final lower court decision may be reopened if it later turns out that it is not in line with a resolution from the Supreme Court.

In England and Wales and South Africa, a case that has failed to consider an earlier precedent is named '*per incuriam*' and courts are generally not bound to follow such a decision.

4.9. PRECEDENT IN SCHOLARLY WORKS

How precedents are addressed by scholarly works is an indication of the importance of precedents. In some of the reporting jurisdictions, precedents used to be ignored by legal scholars or were used only as explanatory illustrations (notably Sweden). On the contrary, in England and Wales and South Africa, precedents have always been referred to by scholars as an authoritative source of law.

Nowadays, scholars in most of the reporting jurisdictions give precedents increased importance as a source of law, although it is less common to see in-depth analysis of precedents as a phenomenon in itself or its methodological use. In Brazil, China, France, Germany, Italy, Russia and Sweden, there is, however, a general awareness among scholars of the increased importance of precedents and also an increase in the study of precedents, sometimes with efforts to devise methods on how to use them. There seems to be a general growing awareness of the need to develop a coherent approach to precedents.

5. STYLE OF REASONING

The style of reasoning is important in order to understand how precedents operate. The courts in some jurisdictions employ reasoning that is very abstract in nature but in other jurisdictions the reasoning relates more closely to the facts of the case. In some jurisdictions the type of reasoning varies between different court levels.

5.1. ABSTRACT OR FACT-RELATED REASONINGS

In France and Italy, the reasoning of the highest courts is largely detached from the facts of the case and is expressed in a way resembling the style of statutory texts. Before the late eighteenth century, French courts did not give reasoned decisions.

Also, the Brazilian legal theses (*súmulas*) and the Chinese Guiding Cases are abstract in nature and resemble legislative texts. The Russian Supreme Court's plenum resolutions are also abstract in nature and detached from the facts of an individual case. By contrast, the Russian resolutions do not resemble statutory texts but are more comparable to an academic commentary on statutory text. As mentioned above, it is questionable whether these abstract summary statements qualify as precedents. However, it is undoubtedly easier to identify the legal rule when it is expressed as an abstract rule. As said by Luisa Antoniolli in the Italian contribution to this book:

> Consequently, all the complex legal techniques used for interpreting and applying judicial precedents (such as the distinction *ratio/obiter*, distinguishing and overruling) are radically different in this setting.

The courts of England and Wales, Germany, Russia, Sweden and South Africa employ reasoning that strongly connects to the facts of the case. The reasoning in these jurisdictions is often quite lengthy with references to general principles of law, and some jurisdictions also make references to precedents. Within this type of reasoning, there are often statements of a general character, resembling statutory language. Sometimes such statements also clarify the holding of the case, i.e. the rule established by the case. In Germany the federal courts frequently include headnotes that resemble statutory rules.

The question raised above regarding abstract summary statements by some high courts is equally relevant for abstract statements made within reasonings that describe the facts of a case. The difference is only a question of structure. It does not really matter whether the entirety of an abstract statement qualifies as precedent or whether isolated statements within reasonings qualify as an *obiter dictum*. The substance of the matter is fundamentally the same, namely that both abstract summary statements and *obiter dicta* are important as sources of law since they heavily influence courts in subsequent decisions.

5.2. REFERENCES TO PRECEDENTS IN REASONINGS

In Brazil, it is often necessary to demonstrate expressly in the court's reasoning how the case under consideration aligns with precedents, and Brazilian judges would violate the duty of substantiation if they failed to follow a precedent cited by a party without demonstrating either the existence of a distinction in the case under consideration or the overruling of the precedent. Similarly, in China lower courts are obliged to address cases cited by the parties, to search for and cite similar cases and to explain in their reasoning how similar cases are relevant and if there is reason to distinguish the case under consideration from previous similar cases.

In Russian reasonings there are no references to precedents. On the contrary, in the reasons given by the highest courts in England and Wales and South Africa it is practically a mandatory obligation to refer to relevant precedents and explain how they relate to the case under consideration and respond in the reasonings to a party who has invoked a precedent, as the decision may otherwise be *per incuriam* (i.e. inaccurate).

In most of the reporting jurisdictions the courts have no obligation to refer to previous cases, but it is often expected that they make such references. The German and Swedish supreme courts generally provide increasingly extensive explanations of how a case relates to precedents, but sometimes relevant precedents are not mentioned. France has recently reformed the style of reasonings in the Cour de cassation to become more explanatory. The French court has allowed itself the possibility to give references to precedents, although it is quite rare to find such references.

In Italy it is normal to see references to a line of precedents in the reasoning from the Corte suprema di cassazione. However, due to the many conflicting precedents there are often several different lines of precedents and, consequently, the references in the reasoning are often made only to precedents that the judges consider the most reasonable or expedient.

5.3. LEVEL OF EXPLANATORY REASONING

There seems to be a general trend towards more transparent and explanatory reasoning. This is clearly so in Brazil, China, France, Germany, Russia, and in Sweden. In France, the quite recent reform regarding the Cour de cassation's drafting style is expected to provide better guidance for future cases and thereby strengthen the importance of precedents. The reasoning of the Italian Corte suprema di cassazione is generally long and complex with limited reference to the facts of the case, and, consequently, it may be hard to understand. In England and Wales and South Africa the courts' reasoning has been quite lengthy and explanatory for a long time.

5.4. MULTIPLE OPINIONS

Brazil, England and Wales, Germany, Russia, South Africa and Sweden allow multiple opinions in court decisions. A common feature in these jurisdictions is that the reasoning generally provides detailed explanations of the facts and how the courts have reached their conclusion. In jurisdictions that do not allow dissenting or multiple opinions (such as Italy), reasoning gives limited explanations. It would be interesting to further explore whether there is any correlation between a prohibition against multiple opinions and non-explanatory reasonings. Probably, it could be anticipated that a prohibition against multiple opinions entails less explanatory reasonings, which in turn entails that precedent is a less prominent source of law. Of course, another explanation for the differences in style is that some appellate courts are limited to decide only whether the lower court applied the law correctly. It would, however, be interesting to examine further how a prohibition against multiple opinions affects the style of reasoning and how precedents operate as a source of law.

6. REPORTING SYSTEMS

How case law is accessible and reported is crucial for the relevance of precedents as a source of law. In all the reporting jurisdictions, records of cases from the supreme courts are nowadays easily available. The modern means of reporting cases is probably a crucial explanation for the increasing importance of precedents. Future development of software and artificial intelligence (AI) to handle cases will most likely further increase the importance of precedents as they will enable: (1) understanding of how the courts apply the law; (2) information about whether an individual judge applies the law in harmony with other judges; and (3) a greater accessibility of the substance of case law.

In England and Wales and South Africa, precedents first became a strong source of law in the nineteenth century when the reporting system became more developed. In Russia the introduction of commercial legal databases contributed enormously to the importance of precedents. Sweden has had an efficient law report system since the late nineteenth century, but precedents did not really become important until 100 years later when the Supreme Court's reasoning gradually became more explanatory, and the reporting was made easily accessible through databases. Likewise, in France the modern reporting systems have contributed to an increase in the importance of precedents.

The reporting differs with respect to structure. Some jurisdictions report in chronological order, whereas others are structured by subject.

In Italy the most important reporting system of case law (through the so-called *massime*, see above) is based on a synthetic statement of the rules that the Corte suprema di cassazione has applied in deciding the cases, with a limited focus on the material facts of the cases. This reporting system, which is often criticised for being misleading about the true content of the precedents, in fact makes it hard to apply, in a correct way, judicial precedent as a source of law. More recently, an Italian electronic retrieval system has made access to Italian case law easier and more comprehensive.

The differences in the reporting systems will probably be of less importance in the future due to the improved search possibilities in databases and AI tools enabling the identification of patterns on how the law is applied. An exciting development is anticipated, due to the AI solutions, that will likely soon facilitate the use of precedents as a source of law. Steps have already been taken in Brazil in order to enable AI in this respect.

7. PRECEDENT INFLATION

Some jurisdictions grapple with the problem of precedent inflation, notably Brazil, China, France and Italy. In such states it is hard to find the important and significant precedents among the many thousand decisions of the supreme courts each year.

Whether and how abundant case law is consolidated varies in the reporting jurisdictions. In Italy the enormous amount of case law from the Corte suprema di cassazione – more than 30,000 private law cases per year to be decided by more than 400 judges – entails many conflicting outcomes. Italy has no system for consolidating the many cases. This is probably one reason why precedents are less important in Italy. Rules for limiting the possibility for appeals have recently been enacted in Italy, and the recent comprehensive reform of the judicial system has introduced a new special procedure, which allows the Corte suprema di cassazione to grant binding precedential value to the rules applied in its decisions.

Brazil has remedied the problem with precedent inflation by *inter alia* introducing different types of cases with various binding effects. The most significant Brazilian precedents are published by the Supreme Court in a special record. China also makes a distinction between different types of Supreme Court decisions by a system of Guiding Cases and a special publication of both Supreme Court and lower court decisions (the *Gazette*) that the Supreme Court considers significant.

England and Wales, Russia, South Africa and Sweden effectively limit the number of significant precedents by filtering cases to be decided by the appellate courts.

France, which does not effectively limit the number of cases brought to the Cour de cassation (30,000 a year), has introduced systems to select important decisions. The French Cour de cassation also publishes the cases it considers the most important in official reports and on their website.

8. JUDGES AS LAWMAKERS

The role of judges as lawmakers depends on whether it is asked what formal power the judges have to make law, or whether they are perceived as lawmakers, or to what extent judges function in fact as lawmakers.

In some jurisdictions the judges are acknowledged and welcomed as lawmakers, such as in England and Wales and South Africa. In these jurisdictions judge-made law is uncontroversial, although there is an ongoing vivid debate in South Africa about the relationship between the legislators' and the courts' powers. Also, in Sweden, the Supreme Court judges acknowledge that they are lawmakers, and this seems rather uncontroversial nowadays. It is rarely openly acknowledged in Sweden that judges are lawmakers, although they in fact act as such.

The Brazilian legal theses (*súmulas*), the Chinese Guiding Cases and the Russian Supreme Court resolutions demonstrate how the legislature and the judge-made law interact. In China it is clear from express legislation that the judges' task is not only to interpret legislation, but also to issue Judicial Interpretations and Guiding Cases, which implies that the judges in the Chinese Supreme Court are implicitly acknowledged as lawmakers.

The Russian Supreme Court's resolutions demonstrate even more clearly that judges are lawmakers, as the resolutions are made in a style that is comparable to an academic commentary on statutory texts. Empirical studies show that the Russian Supreme Court is very active as a lawmaker by sometimes interpreting statutory rules even against the literal meaning of the rules.

In France it has long been acknowledged that the judges have the power to create law and to adapt the law to changing circumstances, as demonstrated by the development of tort law and the law on unjust enrichment in the nineteenth century and by the development of rules on termination of employment at the beginning of the twenty-first century. However, French judges often conceal their normative powers behind abstract reasoning, referring to statutory texts and the legislator's intentions.

In Germany the judges are clearly not seen as lawmakers, as that is seen as being against the principle of separation of powers between the legislator and judges. When judges determine a case by specifying legal norms by way of interpretation, they do not claim a legislative role but to fulfil only a supplementary function. However, it is acknowledged in Germany that judges in fact act as lawmakers, especially when there are gaps in the statutory law.

Italy appears to be the most hesitant jurisdiction to acknowledge judges as lawmakers, emphasising the judges' role of deciding a specific case. Yet even in Italy judges *de facto* operate as lawmakers.

8.1. RETROACTIVE AND PROSPECTIVE EFFECTS

The retroactive and prospective effects of precedents illustrate a fundamental problem with judges as lawmakers. The problem relates to judge-made law that alters a rule established in a former precedent which individuals have relied on and adopted their behaviour to. The legislator handles problems related to retroactive and prospective effects by promulgation of statutes regulating how a new statutory rule relates to actions made before the new rule comes into force. Judges who decide a case and introduce a new rule (either by deviating from an earlier precedent or by interpreting a statutory rule against the general understanding) usually cannot stipulate anything in their decision about the effects for parties outside the individual case at hand.[1]

Brazil's Constitution allows judges the power to give their decision in a case only prospective effects (and not retroactive effects). The judges thereby can prevent adverse effects for persons who have acted in reliance on the 'old' rule so that the new rule applies only to transactions made after the judges' decision.

Quite similarly to Brazil, the French highest court (the Cour de cassation) has introduced the possibility for judges to assess the disadvantages of retroactivity and to make exceptions on a case-by-case basis. By giving judges the possibility to decide that a case shall have effect only for future transactions, it is clear in both Brazil and France that the judges have law-making powers.

In Germany courts have made some rare prospective rulings – i.e. implemented a change of the legal position without applying the new findings to the case at hand – using the argument that a retroactive effect would have been disproportionately burdensome considering the parties' legitimate expectations based on previous precedents. The German prospective rulings have been heavily criticised in the legal literature.

Traditionally, South African courts are not permitted to give precedents prospective effect only, but there are some arguable recent exceptions.

Except for Brazil, France, Germany and South Africa, none of the reporting jurisdictions provide the judges with a corresponding power regarding prospective rulings. Such a power was denied in a case in 1998 by a judge of the Supreme Court in England and Wales, and, although in 1966 the judges of the House of Lords declared that they were allowed to depart from their previous decisions, they specifically mentioned the need to exercise caution in doing so because of 'the danger of disturbing retrospectively the basis on which contracts, settlements of property and fiscal arrangements have been entered into'.[2]

---

1 The French contribution to this book gives an interesting example of the retroactivity problem.

2 Practice Statement (Judicial Precedent) [1966] 1 WLR 1234.

8.2. REFRAINING FROM MAKING LEGAL REFORMS THROUGH PRECEDENTS

In England and Wales and Sweden, the supreme courts have sometimes pointed to the need for legal reform but refrained from making it through case law, as it would be more suitable for the legislator to deal with the problem.

When the legislator is too slow in making legal reform, there are examples of the courts intervening. For instance, the French Cour de cassation in the 1970s made a provocative ruling regarding tort liability in traffic accidents, whereafter the legislator introduced statutory revisions. Also, the Swedish Supreme Court intervened in a famous case when the old Promissory Notes Act from 1936 was not aligned to the use of electronic credit agreements.

8.3. DECLARATIONS OF EXISTING LAW OR CREATIONS OF NEW LAW?

The borderline is not sharp between, on the one hand, declaring (or revealing) a discovery of the pre-existing law and, on the other hand, creating new law. Whether judges are perceived as only declaring existing law or as creating new law differs between the reporting jurisdictions.

In England and Wales there has long been discussion about this matter and nowadays a realistic approach prevails: judges do create law. Swedish Supreme Court judges transparently admit that their decisions create new law and do not seem afraid of jeopardising their legitimacy by this. The Swedish Supreme Court's growing tendency to acknowledge transparently that it creates new law has contributed to its legitimacy as a lawmaker.

Chinese judges generally do not openly regard their role as creating legal norms. In Brazil, France, Germany, Russia and Italy, the judges are not seen as creating new law, but merely as discovering and declaring already-existing law. The reason is probably that a declarative conception conceals that judges are in fact something more than merely the mouthpiece of the legislator.

It is uncontroversial that judges are lawmakers in the sense of conducting creative interpretation in the light of new situations and creating norms applicable to future similar situations. Whether such law-making is labelled as declaring existing law or as creating new law is of minor importance in practice.

Nowadays, there is general agreement among lawyers in all the reporting jurisdictions that judges in effect create new law by filling legal gaps and by interpreting statutory law – albeit not necessarily in the same manner as legislators – even though the courts do not always openly state that they make law.

8.4. JUDGES' SUITABILITY FOR LAW-MAKING

There is a general distrust of judges as lawmakers. The reasons differ. Some emphasise the argument that judges are ill-suited to making law (notably in China and, for some situations, South Africa). Others point to the problem that judge-made law is anti-democratic as it interferes with the legislator's powers (notably in France, Germany, Italy, Russia and Sweden). The anti-democratic argument is naturally less prominent within the area of private commercial law as compared to more politically controversial areas of law.

The debates about judges' suitability as lawmakers and the distribution of powers between legislators and judges do not derogate from the general trend, in jurisdictions that have not traditionally recognised precedents as a source of law, that precedents are becoming increasingly important, and that fear of judicial power has been gradually decreasing. One sign of this is the French contract law reforms in 2016 and 2018 which were prompted more by the desire to make the law accessible than to avoid judge-made law.

The challenge is to find a proper balance between statutory law and judge-made law. The general attitude seems to be similar: judge-made law is not a problem *per se*, but the proper limits of the judicial power to make law must be carefully scrutinised.

In all reporting systems the judge-made law is subordinate to statutory law. All reporting jurisdictions seem to acknowledge that judicial law-making should supplement and not supersede legislative law-making. Most debates conclude that the legislator always has the upper hand because of the power to change unwanted precedents through new legislation which the courts must and will follow.

The room for judges' creative law-making reduces as the law is gradually clarified by precedents, which is interestingly pointed out by John Cartwright in the contribution to this book for England and Wales:

> The creative power of the common law within private law appears rather less vigorous now than it was in, say, the nineteenth century. This is not surprising. In the earlier periods, the courts were instrumental in developing the core areas of private law; and since then … it has become more natural for major new developments either to fill perceived gaps or to change the existing common law rules, to be undertaken by legislation.

9. IMPORTANCE OF PRECEDENT IN AREAS OF PRIVATE LAW

Precedents have less importance in areas of law covered by statutory law. In all jurisdictions, on matters of private law where there is legislation the role of precedents is only to supplement the legislation. However, even in jurisdictions with many statutory rules, it is impossible to get an accurate understanding of the law without also analysing precedents.

Not only the understanding of private law but the whole functioning of society is jeopardised if precedents are not applied. Luisa Antoniolli provides the following picture in the Italian contribution to this book:

> In the following decades [after 1980] the debate focused more generally on the crisis of justice, particularly of civil justice, the structural dimension of which threatens the stability of the whole Italian legal system, where the role of precedents is an issue inextricably connected to the working of the machinery of justice.

In the old times the courts were instrumental in developing the core areas of private law. Thereafter, the legislator has generally been more active within the area of private law. Tort law serves as an example of a private law area that has, in many jurisdictions, developed through case law (notably England and Wales, France, Italy, South Africa and Sweden) which has thereafter, in some jurisdictions, been turned into statutory law (France and Sweden).

In France the interaction between the courts and the legislator is interesting: the Civil Code of 1804 limited the relevance of precedents for contract law as it clarified many issues. Thereafter, contract law gradually developed through case law. The French reform of contract law in 2016 was, to a large extent, aimed at consolidating the case law and making contract law more accessible by turning case law into legislation.

Precedents play a significant role by interpreting abstract legislation using general and elastic concepts in private law, such as 'fair', 'fundamental', 'reasonable', 'negligence', 'gross', etc. As said by the Russian contributor to this book, Roman Zykov:

> There seems to be a universal understanding that statutory law, being abstract, does not always produce uniformity and predictability. In such circumstances, precedents enable the statutes to be applied in a uniform and predictable manner.

Precedents also fulfil a role in keeping the private statutory law relevant and up to date through a dynamic interpretation.

In Brazil and China, much statutory private law is relatively new. Such new statutory law often consists of broad and vague legal principles and undefined legal concepts which require the courts to provide concrete interpretations.

Precedents may also function as a means to facilitate coherence when the statutory law is fragmentary. In jurisdictions lacking systematic and coherent private law codes, the fragmentised statutory law necessitates case law to fill the statutory gaps (lacunas). Therefore, it is probably fair to conclude that precedents are more important in England and Wales, South Africa and Sweden compared to Brazil, China, France, Germany, Italy and Russia.

Italian private law is characterised by the fact that the Italian Civil Code has gradually lost its capacity to regulate legal relations comprehensively and systematically, leading to a plethora of special legislation. This makes the application of Italian private law complicated, which, in turn, frequently leads to conflicting case law.

Contract law (for example the interpretation of contracts) is an important example of an area that has been developed by precedents. This is very much so in Sweden where the general contract law is only partly laid down in statutory law, as is also the case in England and Wales and South Africa.

Also, property law is an area where precedents are important (e.g. in England and Wales, Russia, South Africa and Sweden). Some jurisdictions have developed parts of employment law through precedents (e.g. in France and South Africa). In Italy family law has developed through case law, *inter alia* with respect to the rights of children of same-sex couples, the right to maternal surnames, and protection of vulnerable parties in family relations.

10. FINAL REMARKS

All the contributors to this book demonstrate how the use of precedents as a source of law is well-suited to accommodating what all jurisdictions aspire to, namely a legal order that promotes certainty and efficiency by a coherent application of the law and a law that is in harmony with legitimate expectations. The importance of precedent and the converging development in all reporting jurisdictions is not surprising, as the use of precedent is necessary for the universal interests of foreseeability, treating like cases alike, continuity, stability, uniformity, legitimacy, confidence in the law and trust in court adjudication.

It is uncontroversial in all reporting jurisdictions that precedent contributes to efficiency and certainty. Once a legal uncertainty is clarified by precedent, it need not be considered again. Efficiency is promoted when judges rely on prior decisions instead of making a new independent analysis in later similar cases. Furthermore, precedent leads to coherent application of the law, which in turn clarifies disputing parties' legitimate expectations and thereby facilitates amicable settlements and decreases the inclination to take disputes to court.

Many argue that precedents do not create predictability in the same way as statutory law. Against this, some argue that statutory law does not provide any real predictability due to the language being either too general or too casuistic. The courts and scholars in the reporting jurisdictions generally acknowledge that predictability is best achieved through a combination of statutory law and precedent.

The formal obstacles and uncertainties relating to the use of precedent are gradually overcome by an understanding of how various precedents enrich the legal system and how precedent operates as a supplement to statutory law. However, all the contributors to this book report how their jurisdictions struggle with how to deal with precedent. As stated by the French contributor, Guillaume Leroy:

> The mystery that surrounds precedent in French law is thus the result of a significant gap between what is *said* and what is actually *done*, a gap that has nevertheless tended to narrow in modern times.

This statement seems to be true also for England and Wales where it is stated that precedent is strongly binding, but in practice there are many ways of deviating from precedent.

There seems to be a common ambition in all reporting jurisdictions to achieve a better understanding of how precedents function as a source of law. England and Wales and South Africa have long had a keen interest in how precedent functions. Scholars in the other reporting jurisdictions formerly focused on how to interpret statutory texts (exegetic interpretation), but they appear to now give more attention to how consolidated rules can be extracted from precedent.

Hopefully, this book will provide a deeper knowledge and understanding of how precedent functions in national laws by drawing attention to how problems regarding precedent – for example how rules are identified and the interaction between the legislator and judges – are discussed and dealt with in a range of different jurisdictions.

PRECEDENT IN BRAZILIAN PRIVATE LAW

Fabiano CARVALHO

1. INTRODUCTION

Precedent is rooted in the doctrine of *stare decisis*,[1] which in fact corresponds to the reduction of the legal maxim *stare decisis et non quieta movere* ('to stand by

[1] On the various meanings of the term *stare decisis*, see R. CROSS and J.W. HARRIS, *Precedent in English Law*, 4th ed., Clarendon Press, Oxford 1991, pp. 100–02. The evolution of this doctrine can be explored in J. HASNAS, '*Hayek, the Common Law, and Fluid Drive*' (2005) 1 *NYU Journal of Law & Liberty* 79, 92–93. The study of *stare decisis* was popularised and developed in Brazil by J.R.C. E TUCCI, 'Parâmetros de eficácia e critérios de interpretação do precedente judicial' in *Direito Jurisprudencial*, (eds) Teresa Arruda Alvim Wambier, Revista dos Tribunais, São Paulo, 2012, no. 3, pp. 101–07. It is also worth noting the contributions of G.S. NOGUEIRA, *Precedentes vinculantes no direito comparado e brasileiro*, 2nd ed., JusPodivm, Salvador, s/d, nos. 4.8 and 4.9, pp. 177–81.

and adhere to decisions and not disturb what is settled').[2] In Brazil, this doctrine has been embraced to express the idea that the courts, through their decisions, are expected to convey certainty, confidence, equality, and efficiency.

In a broad sense, a precedent is commonly referred to as a judicial decision rendered to address a legal dispute, which may potentially serve as a basis for resolving future cases based on the factual similarities between the cases.[3]

The use of precedent does not require that the facts – between the two cases, previous and subsequent – are absolutely identical, as no legal proceeding is entirely identical to another. The use of precedent presupposes the identification of pertinent factual similarities between the two cases. It is essential to discern what is important and what can be disregarded in order to resolve the dispute, employing precedent techniques.[4]

In Brazil, the assertion that precedent serves as a source of law has gained prominence.[5] For this reason, precedent is equated with other formal sources of law (such as statutes, decrees, regulations, etc.). Consequently, whenever a judicial body is called upon to decide a similar legal issue, it cannot depart from the precedent to apply a *different* rule. However, this does not imply that the court should *mechanically* apply the precedent. The judge is required to engage in analogical reasoning to establish a relationship of factual-legal similarity between cases.

When deciding on a case within a specific factual context framed by legal text, the court formulates a rule that constitutes the solution to the case at hand. This rule may be used to resolve another similar dispute to the previous one.[6]

The rationale behind precedents rests on the values and principles that promote them. These values include efficiency, legal certainty, trust, stability of the law, continuity of the law, justice or equity, legitimacy, and the improvement

---

2 *Stare decisis* is the policy of the court to stand by precedent; the term is but an abbreviation of *stare decisis et non quieta movere* – 'to stand by and adhere to decisions and not disturb what is settled'. Consider the word '*decisis*'. The word means, literally and legally, 'the decision'. Under the doctrine of *stare decisis* a case is important only for what it decides – for the 'what', not for the 'why', and not for the 'how'. Insofar as precedent is concerned, *stare decisis* is important only for the decision, for the detailed legal consequence following a detailed set of facts (*United States Internal Revenue Serv. v. Osborne (In re Osborne)* 76 F.3d 306 (9th Cir. 1996), 96-1 U.S. Tax Cas. (CCH), para. 50,185).

3 The well-known formula *ubi eadem ratio, ibi eadem dispositio* (where the reasoning is the same, there should be the same provisions) is applied (N. Bobbio, *Teoría general del derecho*, Trad. E. Rozo Acuña, Debate, Madrid, 1996, pp. 246–48).

4 F. Schauer, 'Precedent' (February 1987) 39(3) *Stanford Law Review* 571, 577.

5 J.R.C. e Tucci, *Precedente judicial como fonte do direito*, Revista dos Tribunais, São Paulo, 2004, n. 2, pp. 18–26. The same conclusion is drawn from the philosophy of law: K. Larenz, *Metodologia da ciência do direito*, 7th ed., Fundação Calouste Gulbenkian, Lisboa, 2014, n. 5, p. 612.

6 F. Didier Jr., P.S. Braga and R.A. de Oliveira argue that 'when deciding on a case, the judge necessarily creates (reconstructs) two legal rules (Curso de direito processual civil, 11th ed., JusPodivm, Salvador, 2016). The first, of a general nature, is the result of their interpretation/understanding of the facts involved in the case and their alignment with positive law'.

of judicial decisions.[7] Such values and principles governing precedents find support in the Brazilian Constitution[8] and non-constitutional legislation.[9]

In 2015, with the enactment of the Brazilian Code of Civil Procedure, the doctrine, in general, acknowledged the significance of precedent in the Brazilian judicial system.[10] The doctrine's stance received substantial support in Brazilian courts, which recognise the need to respect precedent 'as a general means of obtaining the protection of rights'.[11]

2. A BRIEF HISTORY OF PRECEDENTS IN BRAZILIAN LAW

Precedent is not a new concept in the Brazilian legal system. There are studies that trace its presence back to the colonial and imperial periods.[12] Perhaps, with the current Code of Civil Procedure, dogmatically, precedent has found its valuation.[13]

---

7 S. Brenner and H.J. Spaeth, *Stare Indecisis*, Cambridge University Press, Cambridge 1995, pp. 2–3.

8 For example, legal certainty, in turn, is included in the Preamble of the Constitution ('Democratic Rule of Law intended to ensure legal certainty') and is guaranteed by the heading of Art. 5 of the Brazilian Constitution ('All are equal before the law, without any distinction of any kind, Brazilians and foreigners residing in the country being ensured legal certainty'). Doctrine focuses on justifying the constitutionality of precedents. In this regard, L.B. de Macêdo, *Precedentes judiciais e o direito processual civil*, 2nd ed., JusPodivm, Salvador, 2017, Ch. 3, pp. 109–48, addresses this issue.

9 For example, Art. 927 of the Code of Civil Procedure is explicit in stating that all judges and all courts are to follow the precedents.

10 This statement can be confirmed through various footnotes.

11 Federal Supreme Court (STF), Extraordinary Appeal (RE) 655.265, General Repercussion (Theme 509), Rapporteur: Justice Luiz Fux; drafter of the appellate decision: Justice Edson Fachin, published in the Court Gazette (DJ) of 5 August 2016. The decision of the Supreme Court makes reference to D. Mitidiero, *Cortes superiores e cortes supremas: do controle à interpretação, da jurisprudência ao precedente*, Revista dos Tribunais, São Paulo, 2017, which can be considered a doctrinal reference on the subject of precedents.

12 M.S. Souza, *Os precedentes na história do direito processual civil brasileiro: colônia e império*, Dissertação de Mestrado, Universidade Federal da Bahia, Salvador, 2014, especially Chs. 2 and 3. Didier Jr. and Souza further elucidate precedents during the republican period in F. Didier Jr. and M.S. Souza, 'O respeito aos precedentes como diretriz histórica do direito brasileiro' (2015) 2 *Revista de Processo Comparado* 99, 106–20.

13 Civil law systems have always recognised the effectiveness of precedent. In a relatively old work, Tullio Ascarelli asserted that 'practically in France, Italy, Germany, Belgium, the Netherlands, etc., lawyers and judges, in their daily work, attribute fundamental and generally decisive importance to judicial precedents. In this regard, the difference from the English system, in private law, perhaps lies in the fact that, whereas in England judicial precedent holds general authority, in continental European systems, it is the overall direction of case law that ultimately carries virtually decisive weight. Even doctrinal works from the last forty years increasingly emphasise case law and often, it is this aspect that predominates, especially in French works. There are chapters of fundamental importance in European

Under the 1973 Code of Civil Procedure (CPC/1973), any judge, when pronouncing a decision within a collective body of judges, could request the prior opinion of the court 'regarding the interpretation of the law' if he/she verified a divergence on this matter or if the interpretation given in the judgment differed from that provided by another collective body (Article 476, items I and II of the CPC/1973). Scholars noted that this set of rules aimed to:

> prevent, to the extent possible, that the fate of the litigants and, ultimately, the unity of the legal system from depending solely on the assignment of the case or the appeal to one or another body of judges.[14]

The procedure for standardising case law aimed to produce a holding in the form of a 'legal thesis'.[15] In this regard, it is worth noting that Article 479 of the CPC/1973 stated that the judgment would be the subject of a case law summary and would constitute a *precedent* in the standardisation of case law.

In the previous system, according to the original wording of Article 542 of the CPC/1973, the extraordinary appeal played a significant role in standardising case law. Subsequent to the enactment of the 1988 Constitution, this function was attributed to the special appeal (Article 105, item III, *c* of the Constitution).

Numerous legal reforms have served to reinforce the importance of case law in the legal process, especially for expediting panel judgments (Article 120, sole paragraph; Article 518, paragraph 1; Article 544, paragraph 4; and Article 557 of the CPC/1973), establishing a technique for the judgment of appeals of same subject matter (Article 543-C, paragraph 2 of the CPC/1973), requiring the party who files an extraordinary appeal to demonstrate that it has broad impact (Article 543-A, paragraph 3 of the CPC/1973), and preventing the mandatory review of judgments against the Government (Article 475, paragraph 3 of the CPC/1973). To prevent or settle case law divergences, Law No. 10,352/2001 amended Article 555 of the CPC/1973 in order to establish the procedure for a judicial body with higher hierarchy assuming jurisdiction.

From the administrative perspective of a judge's career, under the CPC/1973, case law also took on interesting contours. For instance, Article 5, *d* of Resolution

---

private law, whose development is based on case law, and it would not be possible to present them without recalling the subsequent development of case law' (T. Ascarelli, *Problemas das sociedades anônimas e direito comparado*, 2nd ed., Saraiva, São Paulo, 1969, fn. 146, pp. 82–83).

14 J.C.B. Moreira, *Comentários ao código de processo civil*, vol. V, 17th ed., Forense, Rio de Janeiro, 2013, n. 3, p. 5. In the same vein, but with a concern that the statement of the standardisation procedure might become stratified or perpetuated, S. Sanches, *Uniformização da jurisprudência*, Revista dos Tribunais, São Paulo, 1975, p. 8. On the importance of this concept, including its mandatory nature, see J.I. Botelho de Mesquita, 'Da uniformização da jurisprudência – uma contribuição para seu estudo' in *Teses, estudos e pareceres de processo civil*, vol. 2. Revista dos Tribunais, São Paulo, 2005, n. 1, p. 228.

15 J.A. Rocha, *O procedimento da uniformização da jurisprudência*, Ch. II, Revista dos Tribunais, São Paulo, 1977, pp. 63–89.

No. 106 of 6 April 2010 from the National Council of Justice (CNJ)[16] – which provides for objective criteria for assessing merit in the promotion of judges and access to appellate courts and is currently in force – establishes that the assessment of the quality of decisions rendered will take into account the relevance of case law citations and compliance with the precedents of the Federal Supreme Court and Superior Courts.

However, with the advent of the 2015 Code of Civil Procedure, the doctrine of precedent took on a new dimension. There are two provisions that arc important to understand this significance.

The first of them is the heading of Article 926 of the Code of Civil Procedure (CPC). This legal provision enumerates four duties of the courts: (i) to standardise their understanding; (ii) to maintain stable understanding; (iii) to maintain integral understanding; and (iv) to maintain consistent understanding. When considered together, these duties materialise the principles of equality and legal certainty.

The second provision is Article 927 of the CPC, which establishes that, in the exercise of their judging function, all judges and all courts must comply with certain 'decisional standards'.[17] These decisional standards include: (i) judicial decisions rendered in specific proceedings (decisions of the Federal Supreme Court in concentrated control of constitutionality; appellate decisions in the assumption of jurisdiction or resolution of demands of same subject-matter incidents and in the judgment of extraordinary and special appeals of same subject matter); (ii) case law summary statements (binding precedent statements and case law summary statements of the Federal Supreme Court in constitutional matters and the Superior Court of Justice in non-constitutional matters); and (iii) judicial decisions originating from the highest bodies of Brazilian courts (the full court or special body to which they are bound).

The CNJ issued Recommendation No. 134/2022, which provides for the treatment of precedents in Brazilian law.

3. NATURE OF PRECEDENT

3.1. BINDING PRECEDENTS

In the Brazilian legal model two types of precedents coexist: *persuasive* and *binding* precedents.

---

16 The National Council of Justice (CNJ) is a public body, provided for in the Constitution, composed of judges, prosecutors, lawyers, and individuals with notable legal knowledge, aimed at improving the activities of the Judicial Branch.

17 The term 'decisional standards' (*padrões decisórios*) was coined by Alexandre Freitas Câmara, in A.F. Câmara, *Levando os padrões decisórios a sério: Formação e Aplicação de Precedentes e Enunciados de Súmula*. 1st ed., São Paulo: Atlas, 2017.

Any decision that does not fit within the enumerated items of Article 927 of the CPC will be classified as a persuasive precedent. Although not mandatory, the precedent can be used as an argumentative element to resolve similar cases. The persuasive component of the precedent does not originate from the judicial body that handed down the decision, the proceeding in which it was produced, or from the hierarchy of the court. Its power of persuasion stems from the legal basis adopted to justify the decision.[18]

Freedom of argumentation, inherent to the judicial process, presupposes the free expression of arguments deriving from judgments in cases with similar factual contexts.

In a certain way, albeit with less intensity, the use of precedents contributes to the consistency and integrity of the law.

As for binding precedents, the items of Article 927 of the CPC enumerate precedents and other decisional standards (case law summaries and binding precedents) that must be observed by judges and courts.

With respect to doctrine, there is a significant debate about the constitutionality of the binding nature stated in the Code. However, within the courts, there is no debate: the text of the law is accepted with tranquillity, reaffirming the mandatory nature of the decisional standards listed in the items of Article 927 of the CPC.

In any case, it seems indisputable that all bodies of the Judicial Branch must respect the precedents outlined in the items of Article 927. This statement applies also to the top-level bodies. Therefore, a Justice of the Federal Supreme Court will comply with the guidance of the Full Court. A different understanding would render the precedent model ineffective. A judge who realises that other judges – including Justices – do not follow the Federal Supreme Court's precedent may wonder why he or she should bother to do so.[19]

Pursuant to item I, decisions of the Federal Supreme Court in the concentrated control of constitutionality serve as mandatory precedents.

It should be noted that concentrated control of constitutionality, through the principal pathway, involves the Federal Constitution as its paradigm. It is carried out by the Federal Supreme Court through direct actions for the declaration of unconstitutionality against federal or state laws or normative acts, direct action for the declaration of constitutionality for federal laws or normative acts (Article 102, item I, *a* of the Federal Constitution), and actions for the declaration of constitutionality by omission to enforce a constitutional rule (Article 103, paragraph 2 of the Federal Constitution). On the other hand,

[18] STF, Objection to Investigation 4,703/DF, Rapporteur Justice Luiz Fux, published in the Electronic Court Gazette of 1 October 2018.

[19] The question is raised by R.A. Posner, *How Judges Think*, Harvard University Press, Cambridge, 2020, p. 144.

at state level, with the Constitution of a state as a backdrop, the State Appellate Court assumes a similar function through representations of unconstitutionality against state or municipal laws or normative acts (Article 125, paragraph 2 of the Federal Constitution).[20] Finally, special instances of concentrated control include the argument of non-compliance with a fundamental precept and direct intervention actions.

The provision in question is slightly different from the one stipulated in paragraph 2 of Article 102 of the Federal Constitution:

> The final judgments on the merits, rendered by the Federal Supreme Court, in direct actions for the declaration of unconstitutionality and in actions for the declaration of constitutionality will be effective against all and have a binding effect on other bodies of the Judiciary Branch and the direct and indirect government, at federal, state, and municipal levels.

The binding effect provided for in the constitutional provision arises from *res judicata*, which has *erga omnes* effect. In this case, what binds is the provision portion of the appellate decision handed down in the concentrated control of constitutionality proceedings (e.g. the declaration of unconstitutionality of Law No. 18,909/2016 of the state of Paraná).[21] In contrast, pursuant to item I of Article 927 of the CPC, the binding element of the decision made in the control of constitutionality is the *ratio decidendi*, which is derived from the grounds of the ruling (e.g.:

> the protection of the consumer does not legitimise the potential jurisdiction of the states to legislate on rules applicable to telecommunications service providers, even under the pretext of consumer protection or user health).[22]

Items II and VI of Article 927 of the CPC establish obligations to observe binding precedents and case law summaries of superior courts.[23] The text aims to convey that the judiciary bodies must adhere to the legal doctrine contained in the case

---

20 cf. L.R. Barroso, *O controle de constitucionalidade no direito brasileiro*, 8th ed., Atualizada com a colaboração de Patrícia Perrone Campos Mello São Paulo, Saraiva, 2019, n. 3, p. 223.

21 The Federal Supreme Court (STF) declared Law 18,909/2016 of the state of Paraná unconstitutional, and its *ratio decidendi* is explicitly stated in the text (Adim 5,725/PR, Rapporteur Justice Luiz Fux, decided on 6 December 2028).

22 According to Alexandre Freitas Câmara, the constitutional provision alone would have sufficed (A.F. Câmara, *Levando os padrões decisórios a sério: Formação e Aplicação de Precedentes e Enunciados de Súmula*, 1st ed., Atlas, São Paulo, 2017, 5.1, p. 182).

23 A case law summary is the synopsis of a given legal thesis, separate from concrete cases, which contains the court's stance on the interpretation of the law regarding a particular material or procedural legal issue. It consists of a brief text that encapsulates the court's 'position'. The case law summary is not a judgment, a precedent, or case law. A case law summary is not a precedent.

law summary reflecting the prevailing case law of the court. By and large, a case law summary represents a norm derived from the interpretation provided by the court's case law. However, despite its general and abstract nature, merely reproducing the case law summary without elucidating the factual context in which it was issued is insufficient to fulfil the duty.

On the other hand, as per item III of Article 927 of the CPC, the appellate decisions rendered in the incident of assumption of jurisdiction (Article 947 of the CPC), the incident of resolution of demands of same subject matter (Articles 976–87 of the CPC), and in the judgments of extraordinary and special appeals of same subject matter (Articles 1,036–41) are also to be observed by judges and courts. There is a strict relationship between the first part of paragraph 3 of Article 947 ('The appellate decision rendered in the assumption of jurisdiction shall be binding on all judges and division courts'), items I and II of Article 985:

> Once the incident is judged, the legal thesis will be applied:
>
> I – to all individual or collective cases that deal with the exact same legal matter and are pending within the jurisdiction of the respective court, including those pending in the small claims courts of the respective State or region;
>
> II – to future cases that deal with the exact same legal matter and are to be tried within the territory of jurisdiction of the court,

and Article 1,039:

> Once the affected appeals are decided, the panels shall declare other appeals dealing with the same controversy to be moot or shall render a decision by applying the established thesis,

all reflecting the concept of binding precedent outlined in item III of Article 927.

What is common among all the decision-making standards aligned in items I–IV of Article 927 is the fact that they are formed through procedures with defined adversary proceedings and processed by the most representative bodies within the courts.

Lastly, item V provides that the position of the full court or special body must be followed by all the bodies to which they are linked. The word 'position' carries the meaning of a collective pronouncement, i.e. an 'appellate decision'. Within the organisational structure, the full court and special body are *overlapping* bodies, as they are the upper echelons of the court, with highly qualified compositions. For example, the Full Court of the Federal Supreme Court is composed of the two Panels and the President. In the Superior Court of Justice, the Special Body (or Special Court) will be composed of the 15 most senior Justices and be presided over by the President of the Court (Article 2, paragraph 2 of the Rules of Superior Court of Justice.

However, despite this superlative conception of jurisdiction – 'the body from which the precedent originates' – some assert that the appellate decision originating from the full court or special body, based on the breadth of its adversary proceedings, would not have a binding character.[24]

Although appealing, the reasoning seems to be unsustainable under the Brazilian procedural model.

The first problem with this argument is the fact that the legal system does not establish any degree of obligation among the decisional standards listed in the items of Article 927. Furthermore, it would be difficult to mathematically determine the desirable *degree* of adversary proceedings developed in the previous process to apply the precedent to the subsequent case.

The application of precedent is based on the similarity of the factual context between the previous and subsequent cases, and, in principle, not through the *degree* of adversary proceedings that occurred in the proceeding or procedure in which the decision intended to be used as a *precedent* was rendered. If the thesis that adversary proceedings are a fundamental element for applying precedent were to prevail, it would be necessary to investigate the actions of the parties and everyone who in some way participated in the proceeding in which the decision that potentially serves as a precedent was handed down.

In this line of thought, it is accepted as possible that other procedures that create mandatory precedents, such as the incident of assumption of jurisdiction, may not have the *desirable* adversary proceedings, and yet the appellate decision rendered therein will not cease to be mandatory.

However, this does not mean that the adversary proceedings are not important for the technique of applying precedents. In fact, the issue is more related to the method of distinction than to the *binding nature* specified in item V of Article 927.

It should be noted that precedents and case law summaries, in some situations, may lose their *binding* nature.

The binding effect would cease to exist according to the position of the court within the structure of the Brazilian Judicial Branch. Here, some events are conceived. Initially, precedents established at the appellate level are not binding on bodies of higher courts. Therefore, a decision rendered in an incident of assumption of jurisdiction arising from a state court or a federal regional court is not binding on the bodies of the Superior Court of Justice or the Federal Supreme Court.

In addition, courts that are at the same hierarchical level are not required to follow each other's precedents. Therefore, for instance, a precedent arising from an incident of resolution of demands of same subject matter within the jurisdiction of the Appellate Court of the state of Rio de Janeiro is not binding

---

24 A.F. Câmara, *Levando os padrões decisórios a sério*, 5.1 and 5.2, pp. 182–204.

on the judicial bodies of another unit of the Federation. Additionally, there is no requirement to follow precedents from courts in different *systems*. Thus, for example, a thesis established in a special appeal of same subject matter is not binding on bodies of labour courts, even if the decided matter is common to both *systems* (such as procedural law).

However, this does not mean that the precedent cannot be used. Its use, however, will be persuasive.

There are other decisions that are not aligned with the provisions of Article 927 – thus, there is no binding effect – that can serve as persuasive precedents. For instance, a decision rendered by a foreign court.[25]

3.2. OVERTURNING A PRECEDENT AND APPLICATION OF PROSPECTIVE EFFECTS

In Brazil, the notion of the retroactive effect (*ex tunc*) of unconstitutional decisions has always been accepted. This idea of retroactivity ended up influencing the issue of the overturn of precedents.[26] Thus, when a precedent is overturned, the new position can be applied to ongoing cases.

However, in cases from the past where decisions were rendered based on the repealed precedent and are protected by *res judicata*, the new position cannot be applied. In such cases, it is not possible to file an action for relief from judgment[27] to try to overrule the decision that applied the precedent that was subsequently overturned.[28]

Overturning the precedent can cause disruptions for those who relied on the position established by the court and adjusted their behaviour according to the case law.

This statement is based on the premise that the non-retroactivity principle of the law does not apply to precedents, and the court, when establishing its (new) understanding, plays a significantly declaratory role in defining the law, and its decisions are based on legal and social sources that allow for the anticipation of a

---

25 For an overview of the use of foreign precedents by the Federal Supreme Court, see G. Abboud, *Processo constitucional brasileiro*, 3rd ed., Revista dos Tribunais, São Paulo, 2019, s. 6.11.1, pp. 1151–60. On the advantages of using international precedents, from the same author and work, s. 6.11.2, pp. 1160–61. Richard A. Posner criticises the use of foreign precedents to justify decisions. According to the University of Chicago professor, 'foreign decisions arise from a complex social, political, historical, and institutional context that most judges are unaware of.' (*How Judges Think*, Harvard University Press, Cambridge, 2020, p. 144. p. 351).

26 R. Peixoto, *Superação do precedente e segurança jurídica*, 4th ed., JusPodivm, Salvador, 2019, pp. 291–308.

27 An action for relief from judgment is a procedural institute intended to disregard *res judicata*.

28 cf. STF, RE 590.809 (Theme 136), Rapporteur Justice Marco Aurélio, judged on 22 October 2014.

jurisprudential change. The declaratory effect of the renewed position produces retroactive efficacy, encompassing, in most cases, pre-existing situations.

This statement is based on the premise according to which the non-retroactivity principle of the law does not apply to precedents,[29] and the court, when establishing its (new) position, 'plays a significantly declaratory role in defining the law, and its decisions are based on legal and social sources that allow for the anticipation of a case law change'.[30] The declaratory effect of the renewed position produces *ex tunc* effects, encompassing, in most cases, pre-existing situations.[31]

Within this context, a change in position can have unexpected consequences for sectors of society that legitimately relied on court guidance and aligned their behaviour with the interpretation provided by the precedent.[32]

The legislator, inspired by constitutional control rules (especially Article 27 of Law No. 9,868/1999),[33] granted the court the power to apply prospective effects of the new stance, focusing on social interest and legal certainty. Paragraph 3 of Article 927 literally states:

> [I]n the event of a change in the prevailing case law of the Federal Supreme Court and the superior courts or that arising from the judgment of cases of same subject matter, prospective effects may be applied to the change in the interest of social welfare and legal certainty.[34]

---

29 R. Peixoto, *Superação do precedente e segurança jurídica*, n. 4.4.1, pp. 314–23.

30 P.P.C. Mello, *Precedentes – o desenvolvimento judicial do direito no constitucionalismo contemporâneo*, Renovar, Rio de Janeiro, 2008, n. 2.5.2, p. 263.

31 The retroactive effect (*ex tunc*) seems to be clear because, otherwise, para. 3 of Art. 927, which grants the court the power to apply prospective effects of the new stance, would make no sense. However, it is worth noting the position of the STF: 'In accordance with the *prospective overruling* concept, case law change must have *ex nunc* effects because, otherwise, it surprises those who complied with the case law of that time. Alongside the importance of precedent, there is the importance of legal certainty, a principle whereby case law cannot cause a surprise to the parties to a dispute due to a change in the legal landscape.' (AR 2422/DF, Rapporteur Justice Luiz Fux, judged on 25 October 2018).

32 The term '*case law mutation*' is inspired by the constitutional doctrine that established the concept of '*constitutional mutation*'. For more on this topic, see C.P. de Souza Neto and D. Sarmento, *Direito constitucional – teoria, história e métodos de trabalho*, 2nd ed., Fórum, Belo Horizonte, 2014, particularly Ch. 8, pp. 341–59.

33 Law No. 9,882/1999, which governs the argument of the breach of a fundamental precept in its Art. 11, also regulates the retroactive effectiveness of the Federal Supreme Court's decision. The Code also refers to the application of prospective effects in para. 13 of Art. 525 and para. 6 of Art. 535. Here, the application is carried out by the Federal Supreme Court in the context of constitutionality control. Arts. 23 and 24 of the Law of Introduction to the Rules of Brazilian Law (Law No. 13,655) also regulate said application. Decree No. 9,830/2019 has regulated the mentioned provisions.

34 This matter has already been discussed in legal doctrine: A.P.S. Nogueira, *Modulação dos efeitos das decisões no processo civil*, Tese de doutorado: Faculdade de Direito da USP, São Paulo, 2013, n. 3.4, pp. 80–160; T S. Ferraz Jr., 'Irretroatividade e jurisprudência judicial' in T.S. Ferraz Jr., R.A. Carrazza and N. Nery Jr., *Efeito ex nunc e as decisões do STJ*, 2nd ed., Barueri, Manole 2009, pp. 1–32; R.A. Carrazza, 'Segurança jurídica e eficácia

In the theory of precedents, 'application of prospective effects' refers to the technique applied by courts to impose a restrictive model of the effects resulting from the new precedent that could affect past situations. The purpose of this institute is to limit the retroactivity of the new understanding, as it seeks to influence the effects of the new precedent on facts that occurred before it was established.

The technique of prospective effects can be applied to cases involving issues of substantive law or procedural law.[35]

The application of prospective effects of a decision that changes the previous stance aims to protect the legal sphere of the citizen. This technique seeks to protect the individual who placed their trust in and managed their behaviour based on the precedent. For this reason, it is said that the prospective effects should be examined from the perspective of the *present* projected into the *future*,[36] that is, at the exact moment when the individual conducted their behaviour in accordance with the court's guidance.

This is why the technique of prospective effects is fundamentally rooted in trust, here understood as a means to reduce uncertainties about the future.[37]

It is worth adding that this technique can serve as a norm of efficiency for the judiciary (Article 8 of the CPC), for example, by avoiding new disputes or the review of previously resolved disputes.

---

temporal das alterações jurisprudenciais – competência dos tribunais superiores para fixá-la – questões conexas' in T.S. Ferraz Jr., R.A. Carrazza and N. Nery Jr., *Efeito ex nunc e as decisões do STJ*, 2nd ed., Barueri, Manole 2009, pp. 32–71; N. Nery Jr., 'Boa-fé objetiva e segurança jurídica – eficácia da decisão judicial que altera jurisprudência anterior do mesmo tribunal superior' in T.S. Ferraz Jr., R.A. Carrazza and N. Nery Jr., *Efeito ex nunc e as decisões do STJ*, 2nd ed., Barueri, Manole 2009, pp. 75–104. And with a focus on tax law: M.A.M. Derzi, *Modificações da jurisprudência no direito tributário*, 1st ed., Noeses, São Paulo, 2009, especially n. 8, pp. 498–562 and Ch. V; and T.A.R. Lima, *Precedentes judiciais civis no Brasil*, Saraiva, São Paulo, 2013, n. 3.5.4.1.1, pp. 219–22. In civil law countries, this issue also has implications; cf., G. Drouot, *La rétroactivité de la jurisprudence*, LGDJ, Paris, 2016, with a particular focus on Title III, Ch. 2, pp. 243–64.

35 The application of prospective effects in procedural matters can be exemplified in the case of Same Subject-Matter 988, in which the Superior Court of Justice stated that: 'Although there is no risk that parties who relied on the absolute decisiveness will be surprised by the legal thesis established in this special appeal of same subject-matter, as there will only be preclusion when the appeal filed by the party is accepted by the Court, the application of prospective effects of this decision is necessary so that the legal thesis may apply only to interlocutory decisions rendered after the publication of this appellate decision'.

36 Teresa Arruda Alvim writes that, 'the institute should be approached from a perspective focused on the *present*, which concerns the need to know what the *conduct guidelines* (= what is the law) to which my action must conform is and the *future*: once the conduct guideline changes, my action must be assessed down the road, *not* based on the new guidelines, *but* the one that existed before, the one I submitted to in good faith because I trusted it' (T.A. Alvim, *Modulação na alteração da jurisprudência firme ou de precedentes vinculantes*, Revista dos Tribunais, São Paulo, 2019, p. 36).

37 The idea of trust should be timeless. In Niklas Luhmann's view, '*[m]ostrar confianza es anticipar el futuro. Es comportarse como si el futuro fuera cierto*' (N. Luhmann, *Confianza*, Trad. Amada Flores. 1st ed., Editorial Anthropos, Mexico, 1996. p. 15).

Paragraph 3 of Article 927 of the CPC imposes two prerequisites for the possibility of application of prospective effects of the new precedent: 'social interest' and 'legal certainty'. These are terms that are difficult to conceptualise, and both are based on the Constitution.[38]

The term 'social interest'[39] is associated with 'social rights'. According to Article 6 of the Federal Constitution, social rights include education, health, food, work, housing, transportation, leisure, security, social security, protection of motherhood and childhood, and assistance to the needy, as defined by the Constitution. In theory, if the change relates to any of these rights, it could potentially justify the application of prospective effects of the recent case law position. Furthermore, it is accepted that the realisation of a fundamental right protected by the Constitution may be considered an element to be incorporated into the concept of 'social interest', thereby limiting the effectiveness of the new understanding.[40]

Legal certainty, in turn, is enshrined in the Preamble of the Constitution ('Democratic Rule of Law intended to ensure *legal certainty*') and is guaranteed by the heading of Article 5 of the Constitution ('All are equal before the law, without any distinction of any kind, Brazilians and foreigners residing in the country being ensured *legal certainty*'). Furthermore, the idea of legal certainty is also set forth in paragraph 1 of Article 103 of the Constitution, which states that, in order to prevent legal *uncertainty*, the Federal Supreme Court may issue a binding precedent, whose purpose is to establish the validity, interpretation, and effectiveness of specific rules that are subject to controversy among bodies of the judiciary or the Government.

It should be noted that legal certainty should be viewed from both an *objective* and *subjective* standpoint. Objectively, it aims to ensure the integrity of the legal system in light of both interpretations (*old* and *new*). Subjectively, it concerns

---

[38] In France as well, cf. G. Drouot, *La rétroactivité de la jurisprudence*, LGDJ, Paris, 2016, n. 23, p. 13. Teresa Arruda Alvim suggests that the principle of trust is the subjective dimension of legal certainty (T.A. Alvim, *Modulação na alteração da jurisprudência firme ou de precedentes vinculantes*, Revista dos Tribunais, São Paulo, 2019, n. 8.4.4, p. 155).

[39] Daniel Mitidiero criticises the term 'social interest'. According to the author from Rio Grande do Sul, this requirement 'is entirely irrelevant. What matters for the prospective overruling of the precedent is the protection of legitimate trust (an element that is part of the conceptual core of the principle of legal certainty) and the equality of all before the law' (D. Mitidiero, *Precedentes – da persuasão à vinculação*, 2nd ed., Revista dos Tribunais, São Paulo, 2017, n. 6, (electronic version)).

[40] In this regard, Rafael Rott de Campos Velho, in his work on unconstitutionality in tax matters and the application of prospective effects based on exceptional social interest, adds that the author rejects the idea that the supremacy of public interest can be used as a means to assess public interest and that pragmatic or consequentialist arguments can be used (exclusively) to justify social interest (R.R.C. Velho, Inconstitucionalidade em matéria tributária e modulação de efeitos com lastro no excepcional interesse social, *Revista do Instituto do Direito Brasileiro*, Ano 2 (2013), no. 5, p. 4487–4495).

the beneficiary of the prospective effects application, i.e. the individual who has legitimately placed their trust in and adjusted their behaviour in accordance with the altered or revoked position.[41]

The prospective effects application is a duty of the court. Therefore, it is unnecessary for a request from the party or interested party (e.g. *amicus curiae*) to be made in order to have the court grant a restrictive effect to the new case law orientation, although such a request may be made. Naturally, any request for the court to apply the prospective effects technique should be substantiated. Generic, vague, imprecise and indeterminate arguments should be dismissed by the court.

When revoking the precedent and imposing the application of prospective effects of the new position, the court must provide a reasoned decision (Article 927, paragraph 4). The rationale will incorporate the prerequisites required to minimise the effects of the new case law direction. Empty phrases, such as 'serious situation', 'very serious consequences for society' or 'exceptional case with serious consequences for the litigant' are entirely unacceptable.[42] The decision must be adequately and rationally justified, with a comprehensive examination of the social interest and/or the principle of legal certainty. This means explicitly stating the reasons why the change in case law adversely impacts established or ongoing legal situations of the potential subjects affected by the court's new decision.[43]

Paragraph 4 of Article 927 adds further prerequisites that were previously undisclosed by paragraph 3 of the same provision: 'protection of trust' and 'equality':

> The modification of a summary statement, of well-established case law, or of a thesis adopted in the judgment of cases of same subject matter will adhere to the need for adequate and specific reasoning, considering the principles of legal certainty, protection of trust, and equality.

In a way, 'trust' and 'equality', broadly speaking, can be encompassed within the broader concepts of 'social interest' and 'legal certainty'.[44]

---

41 Regarding these dimensions of legal certainty, refer to H. Ávila, *Segurança jurídica*, 6th ed., Malheiros, São Paulo, 2021, specifically pp. 156–78.

42 The wording of para. II of Art. 489, para. 1, is relevant: '[A]ny judicial decision, whether interlocutory, judgment, or ruling, shall not be considered reasoned if it employs indeterminate legal concepts without explaining the specific reason for their application in the case'.

43 One must justify using legal arguments and 'not exclusively pragmatic' ones (T.R. de Bustamante, *Teoria do precedente judicial*, Noeses, São Paulo, 2012, n. 3.4.4.7, p. 465).

44 In France, for instance, doctrinal discussions suggest that when arguing for the application of prospective effects, trust is usually linked to the grounds of legal certainty, as it is considered

Although the law explicitly imposes the duty to provide reasoning in cases of 'change' of case law orientation (Article 927, paragraph 4), the court, likewise, particularly when there is a request from any interested party, must justify its position when rejecting the application of the prospective effects.[45]

3.3. LEGAL CONSEQUENCES IF THE PRECEDENT IS NOT FOLLOWED

In Brazilian law, interested parties are allowed to challenge decisions that do not adhere to binding precedents through two procedural mechanisms: (i) appeals; or (ii) autonomous actions.

First and foremost, considering the alignment between the means of challenging and the judicial decision, the law establishes a rather extensive list of remedies (Article 994 of the CPC) that can be employed to challenge decisions that fail to adhere to precedents. For instance, if a trial court decision does not follow a binding precedent, the party concerned has at its disposal the remedy of an appeal, which will lead to an appellate court.

Secondly, the remedy of claim – which has the nature of a legal action – can be employed when the court does not follow a binding precedent established through specific procedures (such as the incident of resolution of claims of same subject matter or the incident of assumption of jurisdiction, as per Article 988, item IV of the CPC).

Thirdly, if the decision that did not follow the precedent is final and supported by *res judicata*, the interested party may file an action for relief from judgment (Article 966, item V, and paragraphs 5 and 6 of the CPC).[46] In this case, the purpose of said action is to annul the decision that violated the precedent and initiate a new judgment. The time frame to file the action for relief from judgment is two years as of the final and unappealable decision that one intends to annul.

more generic (G. Drouot, *La rétroactivité de la jurisprudence*, LGDJ, Paris, 2016, n. 19, p. 11). Luiz Guilherme Marinoni mentions 'justified trust' to prevent 'unfair surprise' (L.G. Marinoni, *Precedentes obrigatórios*, 4th ed., Revista dos Tribunais, São Paulo, 2015, n. 9.3, p. 360).

45 When justifying the inapplicability of the application of prospective effects based on the assumption of 'social interest' and 'legal certainty', see STF RE 929.670, Rapporteur for the Appellate Decision, Justice Luiz Fux, published in the Electronic Court Gazette on 12 April 2019.

46 On the matter: W.Q. dos Santos, *Ação Rescisória por Violação a Precedente*, Revista dos Tribunais, São Paulo 2021; J.C.F. Bizarria, *Ação Rescisória e Precedentes*, Revista dos Tribunais, São Paulo 2021.

4. HOW TO IDENTIFY A LEGAL RULE IN A PRECEDENT

4.1. TO WHAT EXTENT CAN ONE GENERALISE FROM A PRECEDENT?

The generalisation of a precedent should be considered in the light of the rule in the heading of Article 926 of the Brazilian Code of Civil Procedure, which states that 'courts must standardise their case law and keep it uniform, stable, integral, and consistent'.

This provision lists four duties of the courts in relation to their case law: a) to standardise their understanding; b) to keep their understanding stable; c) to keep their understanding integral; and d) to keep their understanding consistent.[47] When considered together, these duties materialise the principle of equality.[48]

4.1.1. To Standardise the Understanding

Judicial activity is exercised by judges and courts, which, among other functions, are responsible for resolving disputes submitted to them through the application of the legal system. Given the plurality of judicial bodies and cultural, economic, legal, social, and political variations, it is conceivable that different solutions may arise for similar legal issues.

Within the context of courts, the variability of decisions on the same legal issue results in case law dispersion, breaking the logical-legal unity. The consequence of this is instability, legal uncertainty and inequality.

This is why making the court's understanding regarding a specific legal issue uniform constitutes a duty. Eliminating the divergence among the judicial bodies is to assign the normative meaning by the court.

4.1.2. Duty to Maintain Stable Understanding

It can be said that the duty of stability derives from the well-known Latin adage *stare decisis et non quieta movere*. Stability is the objective dimension of legal

[47] 'The duty of the Courts to keep their case law uniform, stable, integral, and consistent serves the purpose of ensuring material equality and protecting the trust and legitimate expectations of the litigant, providing them with a secure model of conduct to make the consequences of their actions predictable.' (STJ, Motions to Clarify (EDcl) in Special Appeal (REsp) 1.634.851/RJ, Rapporteur Justice Nancy Andrighi, published in the Electronic Court Gazette of 22 March 2019).

[48] In this regard, Lenio Luiz Streck specifically discusses consistency and integrity in L.L. Streck, 'O que é isto – A exigência de coerência e integridade no novo Código de Processo Civil' in G. Leite. *Hermenêutica e Jurisprudência no Novo Código de Processo Civil*, Saraiva, São Paulo, 2016, p. 160.

certainty.[49] The solidified understanding requires a minimum level of continuity, so that society may plan its behaviour based on the interpretive line defined by the court.

It is worth noting that stability strengthens the Judiciary as an institution, compelling all bodies (judges and courts) to identify themselves as part of the system. The duty of stability inhibits isolated violations of the court's guidance.[50] Therefore:

> a judicial body cannot decide on a matter for which there is constant case law simply by ignoring this line of decisions, promoting fluctuations in interpretations that contradict the requirement of certainty.[51]

The duty to maintain a stable understanding seeks to prevent the overruling or change of the court's understanding.[52] However, stability should not be understood as immutability.[53] The stability of precedents, legal theses, case law summaries and case law does not prevent the established understanding from being modified. The evolution of societal, legislative, economic, political, social and technological changes, or even those to correct errors,[54] among many others, can influence the way the court thinks.[55]

4.1.3. Duty to Maintain Integral Understanding

In the Brazilian legal model, broadly speaking, integrity pertains to the entirety of legal interpretation regarding the same legal issue, taking into account the set of rules, principles, values and precedents.[56]

---

49 L.G. Marinoni, *Precedentes obrigatórios*, 4th ed., Revista dos Tribunais, São Paulo, 2015, n. 2.1.3, p. 103.

50 Case law summary 316 of the Fórum Permanente dos Processualistas Civis (FPPC) 'The stability of the court's case law also depends on following its own precedents, including by its division courts.' Case law summary 453 of the FPPC: 'The stability referred to in the heading of Article 926 consists of the duty of the courts to follow their own precedents.'

51 A.F. Câmara, *O novo processo civil brasileiro*, 3rd ed., Atlas, São Paulo, 2017, n. 23.1, p. 433.

52 R. Cramer, *Teoria dos precedentes judiciais no direito processual civil*, Forense, Rio de Janeiro, 2016, n. 4.8.1.1, p. 125.

53 Antonio do Passo Cabral explains that 'On the other hand, Article 926 mentions the duty of consistency and integrity of the courts in the system of binding precedents, determining that they must maintain their case law "stable." It is beyond doubt that the stability resulting from precedents is also a form of procedural stability, yet another innovation of the CPC/2015.' (A.P. Cabral, *Novas tendências nos limites objetivos e temporais da coisa julgada*, Ano I no. 00, Associação Académica da Faculdade de Direito da Universidade de Lisboa, 2020, n. 4.1, p. 40).

54 The same is true in English law: D. Kelly, *Slapper and Kelly's English Legal System*, Trad. Marcílio Moreira de Castro, Forense, Rio de Janeiro, 2011, n. 3.6.3, pp. 100–01.

55 Luiz Guilherme Marinoni mentions 'loss of social congruence and the emergence of systemic unconsciousness' (L.G. Marinoni, *Precedentes obrigatórios*, 4th ed., Revista dos Tribunais, São Paulo, 2015, n. 5.1, p. 254).

56 From a philosophical perspective – which can also be applied to civil procedure – Ronald Dworkin states that integrity and consistency metaphorically serve as a 'chair novel' (*romance*

The duty to maintain integral understanding means that the court cannot disregard their uniformising activity in order to decide from a different perspective from the uniform understanding.[57] At this point, integrity serves as a 'guarantee against interpretative arbitrariness'.[58]

Integrity, as a duty, means the transition from an individualistic decision model to an institutional model, in which uniform case law is the result of the court's activity as an institution.

The duty of integrity is realised by applying the understanding consolidated by the court to future cases with similar factual situations.[59] Casuistic deviations infringe upon the duty of integrity.[60]

It is important to note that the duty of integrity does not conflict with the techniques regarding overruling or distinction.[61] Such techniques can shape

---

em cadeira) guide (R. Dworkin, *O império do direito*, Trad. Jefferson Luiz Camargo, Martins Fontes, São Paulo, 1999, pp. 275–79). This expression is well-known and used in Brazilian legal doctrine, for instance, T.S. da Silva, *Escrevendo um romance em cadeira: pressupostos teóricos da teoria dos precedentes*, n. 3.4, pp. 1254–61. Ronaldo Cramer asserts that '*integrity* requires that case law be built upon previous precedents to avoid uncertainty regarding the understanding of the norm and, consequently, of the law as a whole' (R. Cramer, *Teoria dos precedentes no direito processual civil*, Forense, Rio de Janeiro, 2016, n. 4.8.1.1, p. 126). Case law summary 456 of the FPPC: 'One dimension of the duty of integrity is that courts must decide in accordance with the unity of the legal system'.

57 'A judge is not free to choose according to their mood, sympathies, or life strategic options. A true judge, especially a constitutional judge, has duties of integrity and consistency.' (L.R. Barroso, 'A razão do voto: o Supremo Tribunal Federal e o governo da maioria' (2015) 5 *RBPP* 24, 35).

58 L.L. Streck, Comments on Article 926, in *Comentários ao código de processo civil*, 2nd ed., Org. Lenio Luiz Streck, Dierle Nunes e Leonardo Carneiro da Cunha. Saraiva, São Paulo, 2017, n. 2.1, p. 1186.

59 Lenio Luiz Streck writes that 'integrity also means making the application of the Law a "fair game" (fairness – which also means treating all cases equitably)' (L.L. Streck, *Dicionário de Hermenêutica: Quarenta Temas Fundamentais da Teoria do Direito à Luz da Crítica Hermenêutica do Direito*, Casa do Direito, Belo Horizonte, 2017, entry 4, p. 34). This doctrinal position is echoed in case law: 'The CPC/2015 establishes in its Article 926 that it is the duty of the courts to standardise their case law and keep it stable, integral, and consistent. The integrity and consistency of case law require that the binding and persuasive effects of determinative grounds (Articles 489, paragraph 1, V; 927, paragraph 1; 979, paragraph 2; 1,038, paragraph 3) be applied not only to cases that address the same issue, but also to cases dealing with different issues where the same determinative grounds can be applied. Such is the case in these proceedings.' (STJ, REsp 1.71.4361/SP, Rapporteur Justice Mauro Campbell Marques, Published in the Electronic Court Gazette of 17 October 2019).

60 STJ, Internal Interlocutory Appeal (AgInt) in Interlocutory Appeal in Special Appeal (AREsp) 1.410.406/RS, Rapporteur Justice Og Fernandes, Published in the Electronic Court Gazette of 22 October 2019.

61 Case law summary 457 of the FPPC: 'One dimension of the duty of integrity provided in the heading of Article 926 consists of following the techniques of distinguishing and overruling precedents, whenever necessary to adapt this understanding to the contemporary interpretation of the legal system.' This has already been acknowledged in case law. See STJ AgInt in AREsp 986.300/GO, Rapporteur Justice Og Fernandes, Published in the Electronic Court Gazette of 22 May 2019.

the integrity of the law from new perspectives (legal, social, political, economic, technological perspectives, etc.). If necessary, the technique for the application of prospective effects can lend a more static character to integrity.[62]

4.1.4. *Duty to Maintain Consistent Understanding*

Consistency is the logical, legal and harmonious relationship between the understanding established by the courts and the judgment of future cases involving similar factual and legal issues. Conversely, consistency prohibits contradiction.[63] This is why it is a *relational* concept.

The duty of consistency is connected to applying the *ratio decidendi* to similar situations. Consistency helps reduce uncertainties about the outcomes of future judgments.[64]

Such duties determine to what extent a precedent can be generalised.

4.2. RELEVANCE OF *OBITER DICTA*

By force of the Constitution (Article 93, item IX of the Constitution), reinforced by the Civil Procedure Code (in Article 11 and Article 489, item II and paragraph 1), all decisions of the judiciary must be substantiated, under penalty of nullity.

Especially in the precedent-based model, it is from the reasoning that the legal thesis (*ratio decidendi* or holding) is extracted, which is essential for resolving the dispute.

However, often, within a judicial decision, reasons that do not directly impact the resolution of the specific case are included therein. These legally irrelevant or unimportant arguments that are not necessary prerequisites for resolving the dispute, inserted in the decision's reasoning, are referred to as *obiter dictum* (*obiter dicta* in the plural) or simply *dictum*.[65]

---

62 On the compatibility between overruling and the duty of integrity, refer to F.V.F. Monnerat, *Súmulas e precedentes qualificados*, Saraiva, São Paulo, 2019, n. 1.3.2, p. 104.

63 F. Didier Jr., 'Sistema brasileiro de precedentes judiciais obrigatórios e os deveres institucionais dos tribunais: uniformidade, estabilidade, integridade e coerência da jurisprudência' in F. Didier Jr., L.C. da Cuhna, J.R. de Ataide Jr. and L.B. de Macêdo (eds), *Precedentes*, 2nd ed., JusPodivm, Salvador, 2016, n. 5.2.1, p. 390.

64 H. Ávila, *Teoria da segurança jurídica*, 6th ed., Malheiros, São Paulo, 2021, p. 354.

65 L.B. de Macêdo, *Precedentes judiciais e o direito processual civil*, 2nd ed., Salvador. JusPodivm, 2017, n. 5.5.3, p. 253; D. Mitidiero, *Precedentes – da persuasão à vinculação*, 2nd ed., Revista dos Tribunais, São Paulo, 2017, n. 5, pp. 90–91. In foreign doctrine: N. MacCormick, *Rhetoric and the Rule of Law*, Oxford University Press, New York, 2010, p. 145; A.F. Garay, *La doctrina del precedente em la corte suprema*, Abeledo Perrot, Buenos Aires, 2013, n. 4.6, pp. 134–36.

Literally, *obiter dictum* means 'saying incidentally'[66] or 'saying in passing'.[67] It therefore refers to an incidental reason or argument presented by the court without relevance to the resolution of the dispute. It can also be described as a mere opinion expressed in the reasoning but irrelevant to the solution of the case.[68]

Legal, moral, economic, social, political and various other arguments can fall into the *obiter dictum* category.[69] However, its identification is made in retrospect, based on the potential and future use of the precedent, although some court decisions in Brazil may explicitly mention the *obiter dictum* technique in their reasoning to simplify the process.[70]

Similar to the *ratio decidendi*, *obiter dictum* is an integral element to the precedent.

For this reason, the legal thesis and *ratio decidendi* are unmistakably distinct from *obiter dictum*. Some argue for a 'negative concept': everything that is not *ratio decidendi* is *obiter dictum*.[71] Fundamentally, the distinction arises from the principle of adversary proceedings. In reality, it can be said that *obiter dictum* is not an integral element of the adversary proceedings maintained by the parties[72] and, therefore, is something additional that is not under the direct consideration of the judicial body.[73] The *obiter dictum* is not directly related to the facts of the litigation or any issue that the party sought to argue during the course of the proceedings.[74]

It is claimed that *obiter dictum* has no binding effect.[75] However, this assertion does not mean that *dicta* are legally irrelevant for argumentation in other

66 N. Duxbury, *The Nature and Authority of Precedent*, Cambridge University Press, Cambridge 2008, p. 68.

67 T.A.A. Wambier, 'Estabilidade e adaptabilidade como objetivos do direito: civil law e common law' (2009) 34 *Revista de Processo* 121, 131.

68 N. MacCormick, 'Why cases have rationes and what these are' in L. Goldstein (ed), *Precedent in Law*, Clarendon Press, Oxford 1987, pp. 156–57.

69 Ibid.

70 STF, RE 651.703/PR, Rapporteur Justice Luiz Fux, Published in the Electronic Court Gazette of 25 April 2017.

71 O.V. Motta, *Justificação da decisão judicial*, Revista dos Tribunais, São Paulo 2016, s. 3.3.3, p. 182.

72 R. Cramer, *Precedentes judiciais: teoria e dinâmica*, Editora Forense, Rio de Janeiro 2016, s. 4.6.2, p. 107.

73 F. Schauer, *Thinking Like a Lawyer: A New Introduction to Legal Reasoning*, Harvard University Press, Cambridge (Massachusetts) 2009, s. 3.5, pp. 55–56.

74 Neil Duxbury affirms that: 'In judicial opinions, passages which are *obiter* come in various forms – they might be unnecessary to the outcome, or unconnected to the facts of the case or directed to a point which neither party sought to argue – and may have been formulated by the judge with less care or seriousness than would have been the case had the passage been part of the reason for the decision' (N. Duxbury, *The Nature and Authority of Precedent*, Cambridge University Press, Cambridge 2008, p. 68).

75 T.M. Benditt, 'The rule of precedent' in L. Goldstein (ed), *Precedent in Law*, Clarendon Press, Oxford 1987, pp. 99–100.

cases.[76] It is possible to extract persuasive efficacy[77] from them, so that *obiter* can be used in an argumentative manner by all parties to the proceedings.[78] The degree of persuasion depends on the arguments presented in the grounds of the judicial pronouncement, the depth of the argumentation, and the authority of the issuing body.[79]

Note that the use of the *obiter dictum* technique by the judicial body can indicate a court's policy and provide 'clues' as to how it will decide cases in future proceedings.[80]

Another function of *obiter dictum* is to signal significant distinctions or possible overruling of precedents.[81] However, legal doctrine notes that this technique can be risky because, as mentioned, *dicta* are not part of the arguments put forth by the parties or the subject matter of the case, and the 'incidental' arguments are not always presented with the necessary clarity in order to be understood. For these reasons, when there is an indication of an overruling or a change of a precedent through the *obiter dictum* technique, it is necessary for the judicial body to adequately document this indication and ascribe greater transparency to the reasoning section.[82]

---

76 P.P.C. Mello, *O Supremo e os precedentes constitucionais: como fica a sua eficácia após o novo Código de Processo Civil* (2015) 26(2) *Universitas JUS* 41, 49.

77 J.R.C. e Tucci, *Precedente judicial como fonte do direito*, São Paulo: Revista dos Tribunais, 2004, n. 8, p. 177; P.P.C. Mello, *Precedentes – o desenvolvimento judicial do direito no constitucionalismo contemporâneo*, n. 2.2, p. 126; Jaldemiro Rodrigues de Ataíde Júnior, *Precedentes vinculantes e irretroatividade do direito no sistema processual brasileiro*, n. 2.2.7, p. 88. Depending on its degree of persuasiveness, legal doctrine acknowledges that *obiter dictum* can approach *ratio decidendi* (L.G. Marinoni, *Precedentes obrigatórios*, 4th ed., Revista dos Tribunais, São Paulo, 2015, n. 2.2, p. 171).

78 Kenneth J. Vandevelde shows the persuasion technique with the *obiter dictum*, K.J. Vandevelde, *Thinking Like a Lawyer: An Introduction to Legal Reasoning*, 2nd ed., Westview Press, USA, 2011, pp. 106–08, 121.

79 With specific regard to the authority of the body, Kent Greenawalt writes that there is a tendency for the hierarchically lower body to follow what was recorded in *obiter dictum* by the higher body (K. Greenawalt, 'Reflections on holding and dictum' (1989) 39 *Journal of Legal Education* 431, 432). In a similar perspective, R. Cross and J.W. Harris, *Precedent in English Law*, 4th ed., Clarendon Press, Oxford 1991, n. 7, p. 77. Frederick Schauer records that in the famous *Marbury v. Madison* case (5 U.S. (1 Cranch) 137 (1803)), the Supreme Court declared, *obiter dictum*, that it upheld the power to exercise jurisdiction over the President of the United States (F. Schauer, *Thinking Like a Lawyer: A New Introduction to Legal Reasoning*, Harvard University Press, Cambridge (Massachusetts) 2009, s. 3.5, p. 53). For further details in the historical context, see S. Breyer, *Making Our Democracy Work: A Judge's View*, Knopf, New York 2010, pp. 12–21. Robert S. Barker seeks to explain the difference in legal thesis and *obiter dictum* based on the emblematic case mentioned above (R.S. Barker, *El precedente y su significado en el derecho constitucional de los Estados Unidos*, Ediciones Olejnik, Santiago 2018, pp. 33–40).

80 Kenneth J. Vandevelde shows the persuasion technique with the *obiter dictum*, K.J. Vandevelde, *Thinking Like a Lawyer: An Introduction to Legal Reasoning*, p. 51.

81 L.B. de Macêdo, *Precedentes judiciais e o direito processual civil*, 2nd ed. Salvador. JusPodivm, 2017, n. 5.5.3, p. 255.

82 A.P. Cabral, 'Estabilidade e alteração de jurisprudência consolidada: proteção da confiança e a técnica do julgamento-alerta' *O papel da jurisprudência no STJ*, Revista dos Tribunais,

4.3. COURTS THAT CAN SET PRECEDENTS

Brazilian law, decisions from higher courts (the Federal Supreme Court[83] and Superior Court of Justice)[84] and appellate courts (state appellate courts and regional federal courts) can potentially establish mandatory precedents.

This assertion can be substantiated by the procedures outlined in Article 927 of the CPC. For example, the incident for resolving demands of same subject matter is within the jurisdiction of appellate courts. The decision rendered in this procedure is a potential precedent. However, this precedent will be binding on all judicial bodies associated with the court that processed and heard the incident for resolving demands of same subject matter. In concrete terms, consider that a precedent was created in the Court of Appeals of the state of São Paulo. This precedent is mandatory for all judicial bodies associated with that court. The precedent is not binding, for instance, on the bodies of the Court of Appeals of other states (such as Rio de Janeiro, Paraná, Bahia, Amazonas, etc.).

On the other hand, if the decision is handed down by the Federal Supreme Court through the procedure of an extraordinary appeal of same subject matter, all branches of the Brazilian judiciary must follow the precedent.

4.4. CASES THAT CAN GENERATE A PRECEDENT

Brazilian law does not limit the types of issue that can constitute a precedent. Any area of law (private, public or criminal law) can lead to the establishment of a precedent.

There can be an interchange of precedents between these areas. For example, it is acceptable for a precedent originating in the field of private law to justify a decision rendered in a criminal case.

5. PRECEDENTS AND REASONING IN THE DECISION

In Brazilian law, pursuant to constitutional norms, all judicial decisions must be substantiated under penalty of nullity (Article 93, item IX of the Constitution).

São Paulo 2014, n. 10, p. 50. In the same sense is A.P. Cabral, 'A técnica do julgamento-alerta na mudança de jurisprudência consolidada' in *Revista de Processo* no. 221, n. 8, pp. 42–43. The lack of transparency is demonstrated by C.R.B. Moreira, 'Ação rescisória no STJ: exame de algumas questões' in I. Gallotti, B. Dantas, A. Freire, F.F. Gajardoni and J.M.G. Medina (eds), *O papel da jurisprudência no STJ*, Revista dos Tribunais, São Paulo 2014, n. 7.3, pp. 611–12. Georges Abboud, although in another context, also seems to remark on the difficulty in transparency of the *obiter dictum* (G. Abboud, *Discricionariedade administrativa e judicial*, Revista dos Tribunais, São Paulo 2014 (electronic version), n. 32).

83 Art. 102 of the Constitution determines the jurisdiction of the Federal Supreme Court.

84 Art. 105 of the Constitution determines the jurisdiction of the Federal Supreme Court.

Federal legislation explicitly states that a decision that merely invokes a precedent without identifying its determining grounds or demonstrating how the case at issue aligns with those grounds will not be deemed substantiated (Article 489, paragraph 1, item V of the CPC).

In practice, despite not being acceptable, it is very common for judicial decisions to be based solely on the decision synthesis. This summary is a mandatory requirement for full panel decisions of the courts and summarises the judgment in a few lines. It serves as a tool to facilitate research on topics addressed by the courts but does not suffice to justify judicial decisions.[85]

Moreover, a judge would violate the duty of substantiation if they failed to follow a precedent cited by the party without demonstrating either the existence of a distinction in the case under consideration or the overruling of the position (Article 489, paragraph 1, item VI of the CPC). When rejecting the application of the precedent cited by the party, the judge must provide an analytical demonstration that the factual context between the cases is distinct.

Should the judge fail to comply with their duty to substantiate decisions with precedents, the interested party may file a motion known as 'motion for clarification'. This motion is directed to the actual judge who rendered the decision and gives them the opportunity to supplement their decision.[86]

6. PRECEDENTS AND ARTIFICIAL INTELLIGENCE

While the concept is a subject of debate, there is a relatively accepted notion that artificial intelligence results from the endeavour to enable computers to perform tasks akin to those achievable by the human mind.[87] In this context, several authors acknowledge that artificial intelligence can have a beneficial role in the use of legal precedents.[88]

In order to create legal precedents from specific judicial procedures, some Brazilian courts have developed artificial intelligence models.

For instance, in June 2019, the Superior Court of Justice, the highest court responsible for providing the final interpretation of federal law, introduced the 'Athos' system. The primary purpose of this system is to identify cases that may

---

85 A. Alvim, L. Schmitz, 'Função indexadora. (Ab)uso mecanizado. Problema hermenêutico' in D. Nunes, A. Mendes, F.G. Jayme (eds), *A nova aplicação da jurisprudência e precedentes no CPC/2015*, Revista dos Tribunais, São Paulo, 2017, n. 3, p. 660.

86 L.G.A. Bondioli, *Comentários ao código de processo civil*, vol. XX, 2nd edn, Saraiva, São Paulo, 2017, n. 142, pp. 170–71.

87 M.A. Boden, *Inteligência artificial: uma brevíssima introdução*, Trad. Fernando Santos, Editora da Unesp, São Paulo, 2020, p. 13.

88 M. Mazzola, *Processo e novas tecnologias: utilização de QR Code em petições judiciais, atuação de robôs e as contribuições da inteligência artificial para o sistema de precedentes*, pp. 708–10.

be suitable for allocation to judges of the court for judgment under the procedure for appeals of same subject matter,[89] even before they are assigned to the judges. In addition, the 'Athos' system monitors and identifies cases with converging or diverging opinions among the judges of the Superior Court of Justice, cases involving legal issues of significant relevance, and potential distinctions or overruling of legal precedents. Judge João Otávio de Noronha, the President of the Superior Court of Justice, has stated that the tool streamlines the enormous caseload arriving at the Court, reduces the workload in the Justices' chambers, and enhances the quality of decisions, always in accordance with established legal precedents.[90]

Recently, in June 2023, the Federal Supreme Court – Brazil's constitutional court – introduced its own artificial intelligence model, named 'VitorIA'. This technological tool automatically identifies cases within the Court's docket that pertain to the same subject matter and groups them together. This simplifies the application of existing legal precedents or enables the creation of a procedure to set a new precedent for addressing cases of the same subject matter.

7. FINAL CONSIDERATIONS

Although in a very timid way, it is undeniable that Brazilian legislation has tried to value precedents in order to bring them closer to the precedent model of countries where the common law tradition prevails, all with the aim of guaranteeing predictability and legal certainty.

In Brazil, the precedent model has encouraged the legislator to create techniques to speed up the judgment of ongoing cases, which could be described as the management of cases dealing with repetitive issues.

In addition, precedents discourage the filing of lawsuits involving issues that have already been examined by the courts and are obsolete.

Looking to the future and thinking about the evolution of precedents in Brazil, there are major challenges that will require great efforts to overcome. Among them, two stand out: a) improving the quality of the reasoning stated in the decision that will potentially be used as a precedent, as well as the reasoning in the decision that applies the precedent; and b) encouraging a culture of respect for precedents among all legal operators (lawyers, judges, prosecutors, etc.).

---

89 On the procedure of appeals of same subject matter, please refer to Section 3.1 above.

90 'Revolução tecnológica e desafios da pandemia marcaram gestão do ministro Noronha na presidência do STJ' (2020) *stj.jus.br* <https://www.stj.jus.br/sites/portalp/Paginas/Comunicacao/Noticias/23082020-Revolucao-tecnologica-e-desafios-da-pandemia-marcaram-gestao-do-ministro-Noronha-na-presidencia-do-STJ.aspx>. There are academic studies that show this reality: G.S. Figueiredo, 'Projeto Athos: um estudo de caso sobre a inserção do Superior Tribunal de Justiça na era da inteligência artificial' (2022) University of Brasilia (Master's thesis).

PRECEDENT IN CHINESE PRIVATE LAW

Qiao Liu*

1. INTRODUCTION

Does China embrace a 'case law system'? The title of this contribution suggests that an affirmative answer should be given. However, much seems to depend on how 'case law' or 'precedent' is defined. If generally understood as 'a past event – in law the event is nearly always a decision – which serves as a guide for present action'[1] or 'prior decisions that function as models for later decisions',[2] 'case law' or 'precedent' appears to have existed for a long time in the history of China. It is commonplace that even in today's Chinese courtrooms, judges routinely look at past cases when adjudicating the dispute at hand.[3] However, if a stronger common law sense is given to the term, such as by equating 'precedent' with 'any past constitutional opinions, decisions, or events which the Supreme Court

* This contribution contains excerpts from the author's earlier publications, which are here reprinted with permission and fully acknowledged: Q. Liu, 'Chinese "Case Law" in Comparative Law Studies: Illusions and Complexities' (2019) 14(S1) *Asian Journal of Comparative Law* 97; R. Barioni, B. Fauvarque-Cosson, Q. Liu and C. Ramberg, 'The Emergence of Binding Precedents in Brazil, China, France and Sweden: A Comparative Study' (2022) 40 *Wisconsin International Law Journal* 1.

1 N. Duxbury, *The Nature and Authority of Precedent*, Cambridge University Press, Cambridge 2008, p. 1.

2 N. MacCormick and R.S. Summers, 'Introduction' in N. MacCormick and R.S. Summers (eds), *Interpreting Precedents: A Comparative Study*, Ashgate Publishing, Aldershot 1997, p. 2.

3 e.g. J.Z. Liu, L. Klöhn and H. Spamann, 'Precedents and Chinese Judges: An Experiment' (2021) 69(1) *American Journal of Comparative Law* 93.

or nonjudicial authorities invest with normative authority',[4] then it is clear that 'case law' in the Chinese context is dissimilar to and much broader than what 'precedent' strictly connotes.

The present contribution intends to offer an overview of the Chinese 'case law' system, attempting at times a deeper exploration into some of its key features. By 'case law', the more relaxed definition above is preferred but it is envisaged that two preconditions must be met. First, 'case law' is predicated on a court rendering an effective decision (including judgment and ruling/award) in the adjudication of a real-life dispute. Any other sense in which the term 'case' or 'precedent' is used, such as an example set by any other body or in any other process, however authoritative it might be, is not accommodated here. 'Case law' can, therefore, only be created out of an identifiable real case. However, it does not have to be in the full or original form of that case. As will be seen, it is possible that 'case law' may reside in a derivative, such as summarised, form of the original decision of the case. That 'case law' is incontrovertibly connected with a real case sets it apart from an abstract norm created by either a legislative or (if appropriate) judicial body. Second, 'case law' must, by definition, have influence on the judicial determination of a future like case. In the above definitions, such influence has been variously described as 'guide', 'model' or 'normality authority'. Indeed, there may be a broad spectrum of influence that 'case law' is likely to exert on a future case. Some cases with weak influence, such as those serving merely illustrative or educational purposes, may not aptly be regarded as 'case law'. For a past decision to form part of 'case law', a certain level of influence must be achieved.

2. BUILDING A CASE LAW SYSTEM IN CHINA

To place the Chinese case law system into its proper context, it is first necessary to note a series of steps that have, to date, been taken by the Supreme People's Court (hereafter the SPC), the highest court in China, in laying down some essential groundwork for such a system. The SPC has, over the years, made the following streamlined attempts to promote transparency and fairness and to instil public trust in court adjudication.

First, considerable progress has been made to enhance legal reasoning in court decisions. In the SPC's First Five-Year Outline Plan for Reform,[5] the enhancement as well as publication (online or in print) of the reasons of adjudication is considered a major reform measure to improve the quality of

4 M.J. Gerhardt, *The Power of Precedent*, Oxford University Press, Oxford 2008, p. 3.

5 SPC, 20 October 1999, Fa Fa [1999] No. 28, Art. 13 in (1999) 6 *Gazette of the Supreme People's Court (GSPC)* 185. Unless otherwise stated, all English translations of Chinese texts in this contribution are by the author of this contribution.

court decisions. This would enable litigants to understand better why court adjudication is just and fair and would help to improve judges' skills for writing decisions.[6] The SPC further provides that court decisions which fail to drive home the reasons for adjudication or that contain literal defects or errors are unsuited for publication.[7] With notable improvements in more recent cases on these aspects, the emphasis at the next stage will be placed on: further enhancing legal reasoning in appellate and retrial decisions and controversial, complex, socially influential first-instance decisions; encouraging more attention to counsel's opinion with reasons clearly stated in the decision where such opinion is not endorsed; and establishing proper standards for assessing the quality of legal reasoning and incorporating the result into judges' promotion and selection process.[8]

Second, according to the Fourth Five-Year Plan, all decisions handed down by the four levels of court (SPC, High People's Court (HPC), Intermediate People's Court (IPC) and Basic-level People's Court (BPC)) are, in principle, to be published on a unified online platform and only in defined exceptional cases is a decision exempted from this requirement.[9] The Fifth Five-Year Plan reinforces this requirement by emphasising the need to enhance transparency by strictly implementing an approval procedure for the above exemption and by avoiding selective uploading of decisions.[10] In 2016, the SPC designated the 'China Judgments Online' (CJO) website as the official platform for publishing court decisions.[11] All decisions except those involving state secrets or privacy issues or those resulting from a mediation shall be published on the CJO website within seven working days of them taking effect.[12] Aside from some technical alterations, a decision published on the website shall be identical to the original decision.[13]

---

6 Z. Mingshan (then President of the SPC), 'Official Explanatory Notes to Five-Year Outline Plan for Reform' (1999) 6 *Gazette of the Supreme People's Court (GSPC)* 190.

7 SPC Regulatory Measures on the Publication of Decisions [最高人民法院裁判文书公布管理办法], Fa Fa Ban [2000] No. 4, issued and effective as of 15 June 2000, Art. 4(5)(6).

8 Opinions Concerning Comprehensive Deepening of Reform on People's Courts: the Fourth Five-Year Outline Plan for Reform (2014–2018), SPC, Fa Fa [2015] No. 3, issued and effective as of 4 February 2015, Art. 34.

9 Fourth Five-Year Outline Plan, ibid., Art. 39.

10 Opinions Concerning Comprehensive Deepening of Reform on People's Courts: the Fifth Five-Year Outline Plan for Reform (2019–2023), SPC, Fa Fa [2019] No. 8, issued and effective as of 27 February 2019, Art. 19.

11 SPC Provisions on the Publication of Decisions on the Internet by People's Courts [关于人民法院在互联网公布裁判文书的规定], Fa Shi [2016] No. 19, approved in meeting No. 1689 of the SPC Judicial Committee (SPCJC) on 25 July 2016, effective as of 1 October 2016, Art. 2.

12 ibid., Arts. 4, 7. In practice, the website has yet to achieve a full publication rate. An insider's estimation is that about 70% of all decisions delivered since the operation of the website are published.

13 ibid., Art. 15. Most recently, the SPC has imposed restrictions on the public accessibility to original court judgments: SPC, Notice Concerning the Construction of People's Case Database

In an earlier document, the SPC provided for three other channels of publishing its own decisions in addition to official websites: *People's Daily* or *Law Daily* for influential cases; *People's Court Daily* and/or the *Gazette* for paradigmatic cases with some guiding function; and annually published collections of cases (Article 2).[14] With the proliferation of published cases (the number of decisions available on the CJO website is astronomic), the increasing challenge for studying Chinese court cases is that one cannot read all searchable cases. While this vast body of court decisions might open up a fertile field for relatively new methodologies such as empirical and/or statistical analyses and even the use of artificial intelligence, such methodologies have not, as yet, proved able to replace doctrinal studies that creatively extract or construct a line of reasoning from contextualised cases.

Further, amongst more recent related efforts to advance judicial reform, the SPC has established a system of judicial responsibility which exposes adjudicating judges to disciplinary consequences where they, *inter alia*, apply the relevant legal rules incorrectly.[15] Most significantly, as part of this system of judicial responsibility, the SPC Fifth Five-Year Plan intends to strengthen a series of uniform application of law mechanisms including, particularly, a mandatory reporting system for adjudicating judges' 'search for similar cases' (类案检索).[16] The SPC subsequently lays down more detailed rules about the search and its reporting.[17] Similar cases are defined as effective court decisions (including both judgments and rulings) that are similar in terms of basic facts, points of controversy, and application of law etc.[18] A people's court is required to conduct a search for similar cases when dealing with certain categories of cases, which include cases that should be submitted to the judges' professional meeting or judicial committee for discussion, cases on which no clear or uniform legal rules have been established, and cases which, as demanded by the president or

[关于建设人民法院案例库的通知], August 2023; SPC, Notice Concerning Accelerating the Construction of People's Case Database [关于加快推进人民法院案例库建设的通知], November 2023.

14 SPC Regulatory Measures, above n. 7, Art. 2.

15 e.g., Notice by the Supreme People's Court of Issuing the Implementation Opinions on Deepening the Comprehensive Reform Supporting the Judicial Accountability System [最高人民法院印发《关于深化司法责任制综合配套改革的实施意见》的通知], 31 July 2020, Fa Fa [2020] No. 26. Also, Notice by the Supreme People's Court of Issuing the Opinions of the Supreme People's Court on the Implementation of the Judicial Accountability System (Provisional) [最高人民法院关于印发《最高人民法院司法责任制实施意见（试行）》的通知], 25 July 2017, Fa Fa [2017] No. 20 (SPC Provisional Opinion on Judicial Accountability).

16 Fifth Five-Year Outline Plan for Reform, above n. 10, Art. 26.

17 SPC, Guiding Opinions Concerning Strengthening Search for Similar Cases to Unify the Application of Law (Provisional) [关于统一法律适用加强类案检索的指导意见（试行)], effective on 31 July 2020 (hereafter SPC Opinions on Search for Similar Cases).

18 ibid., Art. 1.

divisional chief judges or otherwise, require such a search.[19] The scope of the search for similar cases generally includes:[20]

(1) Guiding Cases issued by the SPC;
(2) typical cases issued or effective decisions rendered by the SPC;
(3) referential cases issued or effective decisions rendered by provincial-level High People's Courts; and
(4) effective decisions rendered by the immediate superior court or the adjudicating court.

With the exception of category (1) (Guiding Cases), preference should be given to cases decided in the last three years from the time of adjudication (for categories (2) to (4)). The above list of different categories of cases is intended to delineate the scope (and limits) of sources from which similar cases may be found and hence does not of itself attach legal effect to the above categories of cases. In the meantime, however, the SPC also states that 'where a similar case is found within a category in prior order, no further search is required'. This implies that the four categories of cases follow an order of decreasing importance, which could be used as a basis for establishing a case law hierarchy of varying bindingness. For example, as things stand, the four categories of cases might be divided into three different levels of bindingness. At the highest level, Guiding Cases (category (1)) are given explicit formal bindingness – they must be *canzhao*'ed (or followed)[21] and people's courts must respond with reasons to reliance by one or both parties or their lawyers upon a Guiding Case.[22] For other cases, their bindingness, if any, is at best 'implicit' or *de facto* since they 'may be used as a reference' by or 'may elicit a response' from people's courts. Nevertheless, there seems to be a difference in how likely those other cases are to be so treated. For example, some cases, particularly *Gazette* cases and typical cases,[23] may have a 'strong implicit bindingness', whilst any implicit bindingness from other cases is relatively weak.[24] In any event, the search results, whether Guiding Case or otherwise, and their treatment by the adjudicating judge/panel must be recorded and explained in either the adjudication report or a special similar case search report.[25]

---

19 ibid., Art. 2. It has been suggested that such circumstances should be further specified and extended to eight categories, including new-type cases, cases on which there exist competing opinions etc., see Research Team at the Beijing No. 3 IPC, 'A Study on the Legality Criteria and Regulatory Mechanism of Similar Case Adjudication' [类案裁判的适法标准和规范机制研究] (2021) 6 *China Applied Law Science* [中国应用法学] 62, 66–67.

20 SPC Opinions on Search for Similar Cases, above n. 17, Art. 4.

21 See text to and after n 33.

22 SPC Opinions on Search for Similar Cases, above n. 17, Arts. 9–10.

23 See text to and after n 57.

24 L. Shude [刘树德] and H. Jixian [胡继先], 'Understanding and Applying the Guiding Opinion on Search for Similar Cases' (2020) 25 *People's Judicature* 38, 40.

25 SPC Opinions on Search for Similar Cases, above n. 17, Arts. 7–8.

Where any actual or potential discrepancy with searched 'similar cases' is identified, this may invoke certain responsive mechanisms. For example, any discrepancy between prior SPC decisions must be referred to, and ultimately resolved by, the SPC Judicial Committee (which is the final decision-making institution within the Court).[26] In fact, an adjudicating judge in the SPC is required to compile a report covering all similar or related cases decided or being decided by the SPC. Where the adjudication at hand differs from the outcomes in such prior cases or creates a new legal standard or where such prior cases adopt different standards, the case must be considered by both a divisional meeting of judges with expertise on the matter and the SPC Judicial Committee (SPCJC) before a decision is rendered.[27] Consequently, this mechanism makes it harder for the SPC to depart from or ignore its own prior decisions and a greater degree of consistency is attained amongst SPC decisions. In terms of all court cases not limited to SPC cases, where the adjudication of a case may lead to 'a decision that may conflict with prior decisions of the adjudicating court or its superior court in similar cases', this constitutes one of the 'four special types of cases' that require additional monitoring and possibly intervention by the leadership of the court.[28] These provisions or mechanisms do not confer directly any legal force on 'similar cases'; however, they build up procedural safeguards for facilitating an atmosphere of *stare decisis*.

3. GUIDING CASES

At the apex of the hierarchy of Chinese cases sits a newly created body of cases known as 'Guiding Cases'.[29] The Guiding Case system was formally established by the SPC in 2010 and has been the subject of considerable scholarly comments both in China and overseas.[30]

26 Notice by the Supreme People's Court of Issuing the Implementation Measures for Establishing the Mechanism for Resolving Differences in the Application of Laws [最高人民法院印发《关于建立法律适用分歧解决机制的实施办法》的通知], 11 October 2019, Fa Fa [2019] No. 23.

27 SPC Provisional Opinion on Judicial Accountability, above n. 15, Arts. 39, 40.

28 Notice by the Supreme People's Court of Issuing the Guiding Opinions on Further Improving the Regulatory Mechanism for 'Four Special Types of Cases' [最高人民法院印发《关于进一步完善'四类案件'监督管理工作机制的指导意见》的通知], Fa Fa [2021] No. 30, Arts. 2(3), 5.

29 Provisions of the Supreme People's Court on Case Guidance Work [最高人民法院关于案例指导工作的规定], Fa Fa [2010] No. 51, approved by the SPCJC on 15 November 2010, issued and effective as of 26 November 2010 (hereafter SPC Provisions on Case Guidance); Detailed Rules for the Implementation of the Provisions of the Supreme People's Court on Case Guidance [最高人民法院关于案例指导工作的规定实施细则], Fa [2015] No. 130, approved by the SPCJC on 27 April 2015, issued and effective as of 13 May 2015 (hereafter SPC Implementation Rules on Case Guidance).

30 e.g., P. Yu and S. Gurgel, 'Stare decisis in China? The newly enacted Guiding Case System' (Ch. 9) in M. Wan (ed), *Reading the Legal Case: Cross-Currents between Law and the*

Guiding Cases are case summaries edited by the SPC on the basis of legally effective decisions following a set procedure of recommendation, selection, compilation and review.[31] Any court or interested party may recommend that a court decision be elevated to the status of a Guiding Case, provided that the case meets the criteria of social impact, generality, typicality, complexity, etc.[32] Within the SPC, the Case Guidance Office reviews the recommended case and, if satisfied with the recommendation, requests the case to be submitted to the Judicial Committee of the SPC (SPCJC) for discussion and approval.[33] At the time of writing, there are in total 224 Guiding Cases spanning over divergent fields of law, with the latest 39th batch being issued on 7 December 2023.[34]

While the title indicates a 'guiding' effect on future trials, Guiding Cases are given a more narrowly defined effect when the SPC states that 'people's courts of all levels shall *canzhao* [Guiding Cases] when deciding like cases'.[35] The word '*canzhao*' (参照) tends to cause quite a bit of interpretative confusion. It does not make sense to confine it to 'refer to', which implies a duty only to consider Guiding Cases as a reference but not necessarily to follow them. Therefore, the Detailed Implementation Rules clarify that where the case being decided is similar to a Guiding Case in respect of both its 'basic facts' and 'application of law', the court, in making the decision, shall *canzhao* the 'essential points of adjudication' of the Guiding Case and, in such a case, shall cite the Guiding Case by its identification number and cite the 'essential points' as the reasons rather than as a legal ground (referring to an applicable formal source of law) in its decision.[36] Where a litigant or his/her counsel or a prosecutor cites a Guiding Case in their argument,[37] the court shall respond and explain in its legal reasoning whether it has *canzhao* the Guiding Case and if not, why it has

Humanities, Routledge, London 2012, pp. 142–58; M. Jia, 'Chinese Common Law? Guiding Cases and Judicial Reform' (2016) 129 *Harvard Law Review* 2213; D. Jingting [邓矜婷], *Comparative and Empirical Studies on Guiding Cases* [指导性案例的比较与实证], Renmin University of China Press, Beijing 2015.

31 See generally, G. Feng, 'The Compilation and Application of China's Guiding Cases' [中国法院指导性案例的编选与适用], 27 January 2017, Stanford Law School China Guiding Cases Project.

32 SPC Provisions on Case Guidance, above n. 27, Art. 2 (including cases involving the application of legislative provisions of a relatively general nature and new or complicated cases involving unprecedented or difficult issues concerning the application of law).

33 All approved cases are published on the *Gazette of the Supreme People's Court*, the website of the Supreme People's Court, and the *People's Court Daily* (SPC Provisions on Case Guidance, above n. 27, Art. 6).

34 See the SPC Notice on the Issuance of No. 37 Batch of Guiding Cases, 30 December 2022, Fa [2022] No. 277.

35 SPC Provisions on Case Guidance, above n. 27, Art. 7.

36 SPC Implementation Rules on Case Guidance, above n. 27, Arts. 9, 10, 11. It is not clear what 'application of law' refers to given that a Guiding Case has a 'basic facts' section but not one entitled 'application of law'. There is, however, a 'relevant legislative provisions' section.

37 This provision does not have a restricting effect and a judge has a duty to find and follow an applicable Guiding Case: G. Feng, above n. 29.

not done so (Article 11). It thus appears that by *canzhao*, the SPC clearly intends Guiding Cases not merely to be 'referred to' or 'considered', but 'followed' or 'imitated'.[38] Some suggest that a court may choose not to follow a Guiding Case as long as it states the reasons for not doing so.[39] But the better interpretation of the above SPC provisions is that a court may only do so where it is satisfied and explains clearly that the case at hand is not 'similar' to the Guiding Case. It is, however, still unclear whether failure to *canzhao* a Guiding Case in a similar case constitutes a ground for appeal or retrial.[40] Guiding Cases redacted by the SPC appear to resemble precedents in common law jurisdictions in that they produce legal rules suitable for direct application to future adjudications. However, there is great danger in treating a Guiding Case as a precedent in the common law sense.

One notable difference of Guiding Cases from precedents in a common law system is the former's detachment from a full account of material facts. At the core of a Guiding Case is a section named 'Essential Points of Adjudication' which comprises a set of simply stated rules stripped of their factual context. Such 'Essential Points', as the only binding components of a Guiding Case, acquire their binding force not from the actual court decision from which the Guiding Case originates, but from the editing and approval process undertaken by the SPC. In this respect, such 'Essential Points' resemble a provision in a Judicial Interpretation since both embody abstract rules supposedly derived from judicial practice. Guiding Cases can thus be seen as a retail form of Judicial Interpretations by which the SPC pronounces individual (as opposed to a set of) 'canonical norms' in a way congruent with the civil law tradition.[41] The

[38] Thus Guiding Cases are so-called 'normative cases' and the only category of cases formally recognised by the SPC as binding: S. Lei (石磊), 'The System and Categories of People's Court Judicial Cases' [人民法院司法案例体系与类型] (2018) 6(36) *Law Application* [法律适用] 36, 38.

[39] H. Yunteng and SPC Guiding Case Office (eds), *Understanding and Applying SPC Guiding Cases*, People's Court Press, Beijing 2012.

[40] Given that the SPC explicitly stipulates that a Guiding Case should not be cited as a legal ground, is it possible to say that such a failure amounts to an 'erroneous application of law' under the Civil Procedure Law [民事诉讼法] of the PRC (adopted at the 4th Session of the Seventh National People's Congress on 9 April 1991, last amended at the 32nd Session of the Standing Committee of the 13th National People's Congress on 24 December 2021) Art. 177(2)? A negative answer was given by Judge Guo Feng (G. Feng, above n. 29, Appendix (Q&A)). Notably, however, the High People's Court (HPC) of Liaoning Province ordered a retrial in a recent case on the ground that the courts below gave no response to one party's citation of Guiding Case No. 24: *Liu et al v. Liu and Huatai Property Insurance Co Ltd* [再审申请人刘阿立、牟居芬、李艳艳因与被申请人刘祺、华泰财产保险股份有限公司本溪中心支公司机动车交通事故责任纠纷案] (2021) Liao Min Shen No. 5273 Civil Ruling, Liaoning HPC, 17 December 2021. This is, however, a single sample.

[41] R. Camarena González, 'From jurisprudence constante to stare decisis: the migration of the doctrine of precedent to civil law constitutionalism' (2016) 7(2) *Transnational Legal Theory* 257, 276.

purpose is to promulgate binding legal rules to guide future adjudication of like cases. Although a Guiding Case contains a separate 'Basic Facts' section, the latter is not a part that has a legally binding effect. The facts are given not as a source from which the rules originate, but as an 'illustration' of how the rules can be applied to an actual scenario. The rules under the 'Essential Points of Adjudication' section are formulated in such a way as to lend themselves to easy apprehension and application by lower courts. As a result, the SPC often has to heavily edit and simplify the original case and even 'manufacture' a rule out of the original court decision. The detachment from the rich context of the original case deprives a Guiding Case of the essential characteristics of common law precedents. It is thus suggested that the issue of a Guiding Case marks only the beginning of a process of case law making. A Guiding Case starts by laying down basic rules and future cases develop those rules based on their own facts within the boundary of the broad principle or 'spirit' expressed by the Guiding Case.[42]

Currently, Guiding Cases have the same legal status as Judicial Interpretations, both issued by the SPC. As a result of a 2019 amendment of the Organic Law enacted by the National People's Congress (NPC), the SPC is explicitly given the power not only to 'conduct interpretation on issues concerning the concrete application of law in adjudicative work', but also to 'issue guiding cases'.[43] The former power to 'conduct interpretation' was recognised as early as in the 1979 Organic Law and a few other Laws or resolutions made by the Standing Committee of the NPC.[44] The SPC has long taken such a power as a licence to create binding norms in the form of Judicial Interpretations to guide lower courts in their adjudication of disputes.[45] Although Judicial Interpretations are not explicitly recognised by the NPC as a source of law, there is no doubt that they resemble statutory laws both in form and substance and operate similarly

42 The SPC thus requires all lower courts to 'accurately grasp the guiding spirit' of the Guiding Cases and to understand their 'spirit and substance': SPC Notice on the Issue of the First Batch of Guiding Cases, Fa [2011] No. 354.

43 Organic Law of People's Courts of the People's Republic of China [中华人民共和国人民法院组织法] (adopted at the 2nd session of the Fifth National People's Congress on 1 July 1979, last revised and adopted at the 6th session of the Standing Committee of the 13th National People's Congress on 26 October 2018, revision came into force on 1 January 2019) Art. 18.

44 Also, the Resolution on Strengthening the Work of Interpretation of Law [关于加强法律解释工作的决议] (adopted at the 19th Meeting of the Standing Committee of the Fifth National People's Congress on 10 June 1981); Law of the People's Republic of China on the Supervision of Standing Committees of People's Congresses at Various Levels [中华人民共和国各级人民代表大会常务委员会监督法] (adopted at the 23rd meeting of the Standing Committee of the 10th National People's Congress of the People's Republic of China on 27 August 2006, effective as of 1 January 2007), Art. 31.

45 Supreme People's Court Provisions on the Judicial Interpretation Work [最高人民法院关于司法解释工作的规定], Fa Fa [2007] No. 12, effective as of 1 April 2007, amended 16 June 2021. Notably, Art. 5 clearly states that Judicial Interpretations 'have legal force'.

as statutory laws in judicial practice.[46] Judicial Interpretations can be, therefore, regarded as a judicial source of law consciously established by the SPC and consolidated in the many years practice of people's courts at all levels. The 2019 amendment of the Organic Law suggests that Guiding Cases are to be treated in the same way as Judicial Interpretations. The core of a Guiding Case is in the 'Essential Points of Adjudication', which comprise one or more standalone statements of legal rules. Thus, contrary to common understandings,[47] the rules pronounced in a Guiding Case resemble provisions of a Judicial Interpretation in that they are intended to operate in a forward-looking manner and are not, in practice, by necessity anchored on any provision made by the legislature. Such 'Essential Points' differ from provisions of a Judicial Interpretation only in a formalistic or procedural aspect, namely that the former can only be cited in the reasoning part of a future decision,[48] whereas the latter should be cited as 'applicable law' (or legal ground) in the decision.[49]

As things stand, however, Guiding Cases are denied a greater role due to their limited number (only 224 in total at the time of writing). According to a study of the first 31 batches (178 in total) of Guiding Cases issued by 31 December 2021, Guiding Cases had not been appropriately distributed in terms of subject areas and had not, as yet, provided the desired guidance; subsequent cases applying prior Guiding Cases were actually on a slight decline, with 'latent'[50] rather than 'explicit' application featuring in most (60%) of such subsequent cases.[51] Nevertheless, the SPC has recently implemented a number of measures to uplift the quantity and quality of Guiding Cases.[52] These significant moves foreshadow

46 Generally, D. Hao [董椑], *On Judicial Interpretation* [司法解释论], China University of Political Science and Law Press, Beijing 1999; W. Cheng [王成], 'A Study on the Effect of SPC Judicial Interpretations' [最高法院司法解释效力研究] (2016) 28(1) *Peking University Law Journal* [中外法学] 263.

47 e.g. M. Jia, above n. 28, 2232–33.

48 SPC Implementation Rules on Case Guidance, above n. 27, Arts. 10 and 11.

49 SPC Provisions for the Citation of Such Normative Documents as Laws or Regulations in Court Decision [最高人民法院关于裁判文书引用法律、法规等规范性法律文件的规定] (adopted at the 1470th meeting of the SPCJC on 13 July 2009, effective as of 4 November 2009) Arts. 1, 2.

50 'Latent application' (隐性适用) of a Guiding Case refers to the situation where a judge, mainly driven by a desire to evade drafting burden and possible judicial responsibilities, adopts the reasoning or spirit (and hence the outcome) of the Guiding Case without displaying any outward link to it: see S. Haibo (孙海波), 'Latent Application of Guiding Cases and Its Correction' [指导性案例的隐性适用及其矫正] (2018) 2 *Global Law Review* [环球法律评论] 144, particularly 149–50.

51 G. Ye (郭叶) and S. Mei (孙妹), 'The 2021 Judicial Application Report on the Supreme People's Court Guiding Cases' (2022) 4 *China Applied Law* (中国应用法学) 199.

52 Notice by the Supreme People's Court of Issuing the Several Opinions on Promoting the High-quality Development of Case Guidance [最高人民法院印发《关于推进案例指导工作高质量发展的若干意见》的通知], Fa [2021] No. 294, 22 December 2021), Arts. 4, 5, 7, 12 (such measures include widening the scope of selection to *Gazette* cases, SPC decisions etc., increasing the frequency of the Judicial Committee meetings, and creating incentives for submitting or producing Guiding Cases).

a long process of slow evolution ahead, rather than a reversal of the current trajectory of Guiding Cases.

4. *GAZETTE* CASES

Prior to the introduction of Guiding Cases into the Chinese case law system, the most significant category of published cases in China probably comprised cases published in the *Gazette of the Supreme People's Court* (*Gazette* cases) since 1985.[53] A recent survey in Sichuan Province shows that the *Gazette* was regarded by judges and practicing lawyers alike as the publication with the greatest influence on their case work.[54] Normally, an adjudicating judge in a lower court submits the case to the *Gazette* and the editorial office of the *Gazette* decides whether the case should be published as 'cases' (案例). The editorial office of the *Gazette* also selects and publishes effective decisions rendered by the SPC as 'selected decisions' (裁判选登). Since 1999 Issue 12 of the *Gazette*, both 'cases' and 'selected decisions' in the *Gazette* have ceased to be submitted to the SPCJC for discussion or approval before publication. Currently, therefore, the editorial office has a broad discretion over the selection of *Gazette* cases. From 2016–20, the *Gazette* published, on average, 83 'selected decisions' and 187 'cases', in total 270 *Gazette* cases per year.[55] Compared to the astronomical number of court decisions published on the 'China Judgment Online' website,[56] the combined number of Guiding Cases and *Gazette* cases is still extremely small.

The fact that cases are published in the *Gazette* along with legally binding materials such as Judicial Interpretations gives them an appearance of authoritativeness. But are they truly 'authorities' binding upon lower courts? *Gazette* cases are said to be 'an important means through which the Supreme People's Court provides guidance to lower courts with regard to their adjudicative work'.[57] 'Guidance' is a magic word. The SPC provides guidance on adjudicative

---

53 All *Gazette* cases (in original text) are available at the official website of the *Gazette*: <http://gongbao.court.gov.cn/>. For conceptual clarity, *Gazette* cases in this contribution to this book do not include Guiding Cases, which are also published in the *Gazette*.

54 Z. Weimin and C. Mingguo (eds), *Studies on the Guiding Case System with Chinese Characteristics* [中国特色案例指导制度研究], Beijing University Press, Beijing 2014, p. 50. Also, N. Liu, '"Legal Precedent" with Chinese Characteristics: Published Cases in the Gazette of the Supreme People's Court' (1991) 5(1) *Journal of Chinese Law* 107, 118–19; S. Finder, 'China's Evolving Case Law System in Practice' (2017) 9 *Tsinghua China Law Review* 245, 250.

55 See the official website of the SPC *Gazette*: <http://gongbao.court.gov.cn/>.

56 A simple search for court decisions entered in the year of 2020 returns more than 22 million entries: <http://wenshu.court.gov.cn/>.

57 'Complete Collection of the Gazette of the SPC of the PRC' (1995), introductory note by the Editorial Department, cited from A. Chen, *An Introduction to the Legal System of the People's Republic of China*, 4th ed., LexisNexis Butterworth, Hong Kong, 2011, p. 167. Also, Xiao Yang's letter to editors of the *Gazette* of the SPC, X. Yang (1999) 1 *Gazette of the Supreme People's Court (GSPC)* 3.

work to lower courts through trials, Judicial Interpretations or other rule-making documents, Guiding Cases, professional meetings, judges' training etc.[58] Not all such means of guidance can be understood to carry a binding force. Thus, softer words such as *cankao* (consult) or *jiejian* (borrow), emphasising the role of a *Gazette* case as a reference for deciding cases, have been used. It is, however, argued that all such words must be understood in their political context and the choice of the softer word 'guidance' was intended to controvert possible questioning of the SPC's constitutional power to create binding precedents as well as to allay discomfort of other state organs.[59] Unfortunately, the SPC's true intention is never made clear. As stated above, there are two categories of *Gazette* case: 'cases' (*anli*) are submitted by lower courts and approved and rewritten or edited by the SPC, whilst 'selected decisions' (published since 2003 Issue 2) consist of 'exemplary' original decisions made by the SPC itself. Since Issue 9 in 2005, both of these categories have been prefaced with a paragraph of 'essential points of adjudication', which seems to be the part designated to play the guidance role.[60] But (in contrast to Guiding Cases) the SPC never spells out the legal effect of such 'essential points'. The persuasiveness of *Gazette* cases is further weakened by the fact that the selection of cases by the SPC is often driven by the financial or political instead of legal significance of a case and that, since the issue of Volume 12 in 1999, the *Gazette* cases have ceased to be submitted to the Judicial Committee for discussion or approval. At any rate, lower courts' reception is as important as the SPC's intention. Although lower courts are not allowed to cite *Gazette* cases directly in their decisions, such cases may feature in the Adjudication Report prepared by the main adjudicating judge and be considered and discussed in the internal deliberation process leading up to the final decision. In practice, some decisions have also adopted the legal reasoning in a *Gazette* case without referring to that case. The frequency with which such an 'implicit reference' is made to a *Gazette* case is yet to be ascertained empirically. But given the limited number and accessibility of *Gazette* cases (slightly over 1,300 in total at present), it would not be a surprise that lower courts resort to such cases only sparingly and in a random and unsystematic manner.[61] After all, *Gazette* cases are generally seen by lower courts as something that are of themselves non-binding and merely serve as a guidance or aid in deciding like

---

58 SPC's Opinions Concerning the Regulation of the Trial-related Relationship between Superior and Inferior Courts, Fa Fa [2010] No. 16, approved in No. 1493 Meeting of the SPCJC on 28 December 2012, Art. 8.

59 N. Liu, above n. 52.

60 X. Xi and the Second Civil Court of the SPC (eds), *Understanding and Applying SPC Interpretations on Sales Contracts: Texts, Interpretations, Reasons and Cases*, The People's Court Press, Beijing, 2012, p. 4.

61 C. Mingguo and Z. Weimin, 'Obstacles in the Application of Guiding Cases and Their Overcoming: A Preliminary Analysis of Case Application in Sichuan Courts' (2012) 5 *Journal of Law Application* 67, 69–70.

cases, unless the SPC unequivocally requires lower courts to follow the specific rule established on some rare occasions.[62]

The most remarkable example one could find as support for this view is perhaps the *Huang Muxing* case,[63] where a lender applied for a retrial of an appellate decision previously delivered by the SPC, alleging that the SPC failed to follow a prior *Gazette* case.[64] The lender argued that the SPC should have followed the *Gazette* case by declaring the disputed loan contract valid and allowing civil procedures to proceed despite the fact that one of the borrowers was being charged and prosecuted in separate criminal proceedings for taking out the loan. The SPC rejected the lender's application and stated that:

> the Gazette case cited by Huang Muxing is not a Guiding Case issued in accordance with our court's Provisions Concerning Case Guidance Work, therefore his claim that the present case should be dealt with by reference to the Gazette case is without foundation.

Notably, the SPC rejected the application without exploring whether the 'essential points of adjudication' outlined in the *Gazette* case might apply to the facts of the present case. The failure to refer to the case in the appellate decision was held not to constitute an error of law and hence the lender was denied a retrial of the case.

In contrast, there are circumstances in which it may be hard to justify a disregard for a prior court decision. It has been shown above that *Gazette* cases are not necessarily binding unless they are also Guiding Cases. Might non-Guiding Cases published in the *Gazette* be given a similar legal effect? At this juncture it is only possible to make some general preliminary observations. First, the influence of a case and the regard likely given to it by another court is a matter depending on a combination of complex factors and one that should be answered on a case-by-case basis. Sometimes the answer hinges on the potential influence on a specific court. Prior decisions of an immediately superior court, particularly those concerning an appeal from the decision of the lower court in question, may be most influential on that lower court.[65] Second, being published in the *Gazette* implies that the case is approved and edited by the SPC and easily accessible. This satisfies the minimum standards for a case to be properly

---

62 C. Guangzhong and X. Zhengquan, 'Reflections on the Question of Establishing a Judicial Precedent System in Our Country' (1989) 2 *China Legal Science* 86, 90.

63 *Li Yidong et al v. Huang Muxing* [李艺东等与黄木兴一般借款合同纠纷申请再审案] (2014) Min Shen Zi No. 441 Civil Ruling, SPC, 4 June 2014.

64 *Wu Guojun v. Chen Xiaofu et al* [吴国军诉陈晓富、王克祥及德清县中建房地产开发有限公司民间借贷、担保合同纠纷案] (2010) appellate decision by Huzhou IPC on 2 August 2010, (2011) 11 *Gazette of the Supreme People's Court (GSPC)*.

65 D. Hao, above n. 44, pp. 356–64. See also, C. Mingguo and Z. Weimin, above n. 59, 68 (in an experimental survey, the greatest proportion of cases referred to by the selected IPCs and BPCs in Sichuan Province in trials conducted in a certain period were: prior decisions made by the same court – 45.16%; HPC cases – 22.58%; SPC cases – 14.52%).

regarded as a binding or at least an influential precedent, namely accessibility and reasonable quality in legal reasoning and decision-writing. Whether the decision in the case must come from a court ranked high in the hierarchy (such as the Intermediate People's Court and above) is a question that can be debated. Third, although a *Gazette* case is not by itself binding, it can acquire a binding force or at least greater influence if it has been effectively followed on a number of occasions. A line of well-published cases may develop and reinforce a common principle, rule or point of law so that they enhance each other's authority and persuasiveness. For example, a decision of the SPC in 2000 had a devastating effect on the banking industry in China as a vast number of security/surety contracts entered into by banks were declared invalid on the ground that the security was set up upon company assets by the board of directors in favour of some of the shareholders.[66] In a series of *Gazette* cases the SPC clearly steered away from this troublesome position, holding that such contracts are valid and enforceable insofar as the third party has duly examined relevant documents.[67] Fourth, while in most of the *Gazette* cases the essential points of adjudication are no more than a reiteration of existing legal rules,[68] there are an increasing number of *Gazette* cases[69] that create new rules, fill existing gaps and settle uncertain points of law. The latter cases constitute more promising references

66 *Fujian Zhongfu Co Ltd v. Industrial and Commercial Bank of China Fuzhou Mindu Branch* [福建省中福实业股份有限公司等与中国工商银行福州市闽都支行借款担保纠纷案] (2000) Jing Zhong Zi No. 186, SPC, 17 November 2001 (a contract by which the board of directors of a company set up a security interest on company assets in favour of shareholders was held invalid by the SPC based on Art. 60(3) of the Company Law which prohibited a director or manager from so conducting). The decision put 270 billion RMB worth of bank loans in jeopardy, thus leading to a joint protest by the Industrial and Commercial Bank of China, Agricultural Bank of China, China Construction Bank, Bank of China and Bank of Huaxia (A Letter concerning certain Issues regarding the SPC's Application of the Interpretations on the Security Law, 15 June 2001).

67 *China Import and Export Bank v. Guangcai Investment Co Ltd et al* [中国进出口银行与光彩事业投资集团有限公司、四通集团公司借款担保合同纠纷案] (2006) Min Er Zhong Zi No. 49, SPC, 15 May 2006, (2006) 7 *Gazette of the Supreme People's Court (GSPC)*; after amendments Art. 16(1) and (2) of the current Company Law subject a security contract to strict approval procedures within the company – China National Building Materials Import & Export Group Co v. Beijing Lang & Overseas Trading Co Ltd et al [中建材集团进出口公司诉北京大地恒通经贸有限公司等进出口代理合同纠纷上诉案] (2009) Beijing HPC, 22 September 2009, (2011) 2 *Gazette of the Supreme People's Court (GSPC)*; *Dalian Donggang Sub-Branch of China Merchants Bank Co Ltd v. Dalian Zebon Fluorocarbon Paint Stock Co Ltd et al* [招商银行股份有限公司大远东港支行与大连振邦氟涂料股份有限公司等借款合同纠纷案] (2012) Min Ti Zi No. 156, SPC, 22 April 2014, (2015) 2 *Gazette of the Supreme People's Court (GSPC)*.

68 C. Mingguo and Z. Weimin, above n. 59, 54 (the authors' survey found that this was the case in 86% of all *Gazette* cases and only 11% of *Gazette* cases dealt with new issues not covered by existing law).

69 W. Qin, 'On the Establishment and Methods of Application of the Chinese Guiding Cases System – Taking the SPC Gazette as a Sample' (2007) 4 *Legal Methods and Legal Thinking* 205, 217.

for courts deciding future like cases. For example, a *Gazette* case clarifying that a contract clause excluding an employer's liability for industrial injuries is invalid is likely to be treated as law at a time when the legislation is silent on the matter.[70] Similarly, a *Gazette* case might exhibit an observably distinct approach from that adopted in similar non-Guiding Cases not published in the *Gazette* and it has happened that a court in a subsequent case chose firmly to follow the approach of the *Gazette* case because of its 'substantive persuasiveness'.[71] Therefore, *Gazette* cases are not legally binding. They are, generally speaking, easily observable and widely respected by Chinese judges; however, this does not necessarily lead to any actual influence. Some *Gazette* cases might wield greater influence than others. The extent of influence, if any, hinges on a variety of factors including but not limited to the persuasiveness of the reasoning adopted and elucidated in the *Gazette* case.

5. A WIDER WEB OF CASE LAW: CONCLUDING REMARKS

Going back to the four categories of 'similar cases' falling within the scope of search by an adjudicative judge or panel, the above discussion covers only category (1) – Guiding Cases and possibly the most important subcategory of category (2) – *Gazette* cases. Category (2) also consists of typical cases and SPC cases not published in the *Gazette*. Typical cases are selected from cases dealing with issues that are 'typical, significant and impactful on economic and social life' or 'attract wide attention from the public' and are issued by the SPC without the need to obtain approval from its Judicial Committee (SPCJC).[72] They aim to 'establish correct value orientation, disseminate correct judicial ideas and regulate judicial adjudication' and are treated as non-binding references akin to 'judicial guiding documents'.[73] As recently stated by the Chinese Government when responding to an inquiry by the European Union,[74] 'typical' cases are

70 *Zhang Lianqi and Zhang Guoli v. Zhang Xuezhen* [张连起、张国莉诉张学珍损害赔偿案] (1988) Tanggu District People's Court, 24 December 1988, (1989) 1 *Gazette of the Supreme People's Court (GSPC).*

71 C. Yue Feng (陈越峰), 'The Objective Influence of Gazette Cases on Similar Cases Decided by Lower Courts' [公报案例对下级法院同类案件判决的客观影响] (2011) 5 *China Law Science* 176, 186–88.

72 Opinion of the Supreme People's Court on Ameliorating the Work Mechanism for Unifying the Standards of Application of Law [最高人民法院关于完善统一法律适用标准工作机制的意见], Fa Fa [2020] No. 35, issued and effective as of 14 September 2020, Art. 5.

73 ibid. If not *Gazette* cases, typical cases are usually published on the SPC website: e.g. '2019 Typical Cases of Maritime Adjudication' <http://www.court.gov.cn/zixun-xiangqing-252691.html> (last accessed 15 March 2024).

74 WTO, 'Response to the European Union's Request for Information Pursuant to Article 63.3 of the TRIPS Agreement', IP/C/W/683, 7 September 2021, para. 4.

'cases for reference and have no legal effect of general application'.[75] Therefore, typical cases are similarly positioned as *Gazette* cases in that, despite bearing a notable SPC mark, the actual influence of each case must be assessed on an individual, circumstantial basis.

The current scope of the Chinese case law system can be further extended to at least align with the scope of the search for similar cases. Category (3), comprising referential (or typical/representative) cases selected and issued by the HPC, is likely to gain importance in the immediate future.[76] The SPC Fifth Five-Year Plan alludes to establishing a registration mechanism for such cases.[77] By involving a large number of HPC judges in the case law making process, this initiative will undoubtedly unleash a greater productive force and considerably alleviate the existing bottleneck problem restricting the number of cases produced by the SPC. For practical reasons, category (4), consisting of prior decisions of the immediate superior court or the adjudicating court (mainly HPC or IPC decisions), has long been and will continue to be an important reference for judges at the lower courts (particularly IPCs and BPCs). Compared to category (2) cases, cases in the last two categories do not have any formal legal force either. The general influence or importance of category (3) or (4) cases is seen as weaker than category (2) cases. However, when confined to a certain jurisdictional area or a certain court, category (3) or (4) cases may achieve a degree of influence comparable to or even higher than category (2) cases. Whether this is indeed so with respect to a particular category (3) or (4) case will be determined by applying the same circumstantial assessment outlined above.

Such is the existing frontier of the Chinese case law system. Understandably, this system is itself a thing in the making. With the many pro-case law measures and mechanisms initiated or approved by the SPC being made to work, it is foreseeable that the internal structure of that system will become clearer and more stable. A binding force that gradually increases towards its core (Guiding Cases) may be crystallised and reinforced. The frontier may be further extended. However, the shape of the system seems to be discernible and expected to last: a mixture (and possibly hierarchy) of cases of varying importance to ensure that useful guidance is available for resolving recurring problems in their respective context in a large country with diversified local circumstances.

---

[75] For potential useful roles such 'typical cases' may play in the context of the 'One Belt One Road' initiative, see Q. Liu, 'The Use of Case Law in China's Belt and Road Initiative' (2021) 29(1) *Asia Pacific Law Review* 129.

[76] A HPC may provide guidance to lower courts in the same hierarchy (province or autonomous prefecture) by issuing 'Referential Cases', see SPC Opinions on Trial-related Relationship between Superior and Inferior Courts, above n. 56, Art. 9.

[77] Fifth Five-Year Outline Plan for Reform, above n. 10, Art. 26.

PRECEDENT IN ENGLISH AND WELSH PRIVATE LAW

John CARTWRIGHT

1. A GENERAL INTRODUCTION TO LEGAL PRECEDENT

The doctrine of precedent is fundamental to the common law system, and therefore to English law – the law of England and Wales.[1] Other common law legal systems around the world, which have drawn their systems from English law, share an understanding of the need for a system of precedent as an inherent feature of the common law method, but their details are inevitably different,[2] and this contribution will discuss only the doctrine of precedent as it has been developed and now applies within English law.[3]

---

1 In private law, 'English law' refers to the law of the single legal jurisdiction of England and Wales. Within the United Kingdom there are also the jurisdictions of Scotland and Northern Ireland, separate legal systems which are not of concern here.

2 cf. R. CROSS and J.W. HARRIS, below n. 3, pp. 19–24.

3 The leading text, although now outdated on some details, is R. CROSS and J.W. HARRIS, *Precedent in English Law*, 4th ed., Clarendon Press, Oxford 1991, on which this contribution

There are two separate aspects to precedent. In its most general form, the doctrine of precedent is based on the principle that judicial decisions (case law) are a source of law, operating alongside but independently from legislative sources of law. However, once it is accepted that case law constitutes a formal source of law, a second question arises: how binding is the judicial decision given by a court in any particular case? The answer to this second question will lead to the detail of the doctrine of precedent, and its role within the English legal system, which will be discussed in the following sections. A general discussion of the issues will first be given here.

1.1. CASE LAW AS A SOURCE OF LAW IN ENGLISH LAW

It is of the essence of a common law system, such as English law, that judicial decisions are accepted to be a source of law – not only historically, but also in the modern, living law. This must have been true in the past, since there are many rules of law, including the fundamental rules of key areas of private law (contract, tort and property),[4] which cannot be traced to any legislative text but were first articulated and applied by judges in their decisions and, indeed, have been further developed and sometimes changed significantly by later decisions. Case law must, therefore, be a source of law – a formal source, in the sense that the courts are recognised as having the authority to create and develop these rules of law through their decisions in individual cases.[5] Some writers and judges have held the view that the common law is a body of pre-existing legal rules which the courts only reveal (or 'declare') through their decisions, rather than themselves creating or changing them. This is not, however, how the role of case law is now seen. In 1999, Lord Goff said:[6]

> Historically speaking, the declaratory theory of judicial decisions is to be found in a statement by Sir Matthew Hale over 300 years ago, viz. that the decisions of the courts do not constitute the law properly so called, but are evidence of the law and as such 'have a great weight and authority in expounding, declaring, and publishing what

---

draws generally, but particular references will be given where appropriate. See also N. Duxbury, *The Nature and Authority of Precedent*, Cambridge University Press, Cambridge 2008.

4 J. Cartwright, *Contract Law: An Introduction to the English Law of Contract for the Civil Lawyer*, 4th ed., Hart Publishing, Oxford 2023, pp. 20–21.

5 cf. the notion of case law as an 'authority' in fact, but not a legally binding rule, in the civil law: J. Carbonnier, 'Authorities in Civil Law: France' in J. Dainow (ed), *The Role of Judicial Decisions and Doctrine in Civil Law and in Mixed Jurisdictions*, Louisiana State University Press, Baton Rouge 1974, pp. 91, 97.

6 *Kleinwort Benson Ltd v. Lincoln City Council* [1999] 2 AC 349, 377 (HL). See also Lord Browne-Wilkinson at 358 (the declaratory theory 'is, as Lord Reid said in the article "The Judge As Law Maker" (1972–73) 12 *J.S.P.T.L. (N.S.)* 22, a fairy tale in which no one any longer

> the law of this Kingdom is:' see *Hale's Common Law of England*, 6th ed. (1820), p. 90. To the like effect, *Blackstone Commentaries*, 6th ed. (1774), pp. 88–89, stated that 'the decisions of courts are the evidence of what is the common law.' In recent times, however, a more realistic approach has been adopted, as in Sir George Jessel M.R.'s celebrated statement that rules of equity, unlike rules of the common law, are not supposed to have been established since time immemorial, but have been invented, altered, improved and refined from time to time: see *In re Hallett's Estate*; *Knatchbull v. Hallett* (1880) 13 Ch.D. 696, 710. There can be no doubt of the truth of this statement; and we all know that in reality, in the common law as in equity, the law is the subject of development by the judges – normally, of course, by appellate judges. We describe as leading cases the decisions which mark the principal stages in this development, and we have no difficulty in identifying the judges who are primarily responsible. It is universally recognised that judicial development of the common law is inevitable. If it had never taken place, the common law would be the same now as it was in the reign of King Henry II;[7] it is because of it that the common law is a living system of law, reacting to new events and new ideas, and so capable of providing the citizens of this country with a system of practical justice relevant to the times in which they live.

The declaratory theory appears to be based on a constitutional sensitivity, recognising a limitation on the power of the courts by contrast with the legislative power of Parliament. However, in the absence of comprehensive legislative texts laying down the rules of law in the manner of a codified system, the courts' role in developing the law is not a constitutional problem but a constitutional necessity.

The way in which the courts 'make law' through their decisions is fundamentally different from the legislative process. In deciding a case – and therefore in producing a decision which might constitute, for the future, a 'precedent' – the court can respond only to the particular facts of the dispute on which it is adjudicating, and can act only within the context of the law as it then exists: the court must respect any legislative rules which, by their nature, take a higher place within the hierarchy of norms which make up the sources of English law,[8] and the court must take account of existing case law – in particular, earlier case law which is binding under the rules of precedent, but also the general body of relevant English cases even if they are not formally binding, and even, sometimes, relevant cases from other jurisdictions, particularly within the common law world, which might indicate a possible path for the English

---

believes'); Lord Lloyd at 394 (the declaratory theory 'always was a fairy tale'). For a significant discussion by the current Deputy President of the UK Supreme Court see Lord Hodge, 'The Scope of Judicial Law-Making in the Common Law Tradition' (2020) 84 *Rabels Zeitschrift für ausländisches und internationales Privatrecht* 211.

7 [Henry II reigned from 1154–89. This is an oblique reference by Lord Goff to the time to which the 'common law' of England is generally traced by historians: J. Baker, *An Introduction to English Legal History*, 5th ed., Oxford University Press, Oxford 2019, p. 16.].

8 See Section 1.3. below.

common law to take.[9] In the modern law,[10] academic literature also forms a relevant (but not in any sense binding) part of the picture of the existing and developing common law for the purposes of the court's decision. Again, Lord Goff said:[11]

> When a judge decides a case which comes before him, he does so on the basis of what he understands the law to be. This he discovers from the applicable statutes, if any, and from precedents drawn from reports of previous judicial decisions. Nowadays, he derives much assistance from academic writings in interpreting statutes and, more especially, the effect of reported cases; and he has regard, where appropriate, to decisions of judges in other jurisdictions. In the course of deciding the case before him he may, on occasion, develop the common law in the perceived interests of justice, though as a general rule he does this 'only interstitially', to use the expression of O.W. Holmes J. in *Southern Pacific Co. v. Jensen* (1917) 244 U.S. 205, 221. This means not only that he must act within the confines of the doctrine of precedent, but that the change so made must be seen as a development, usually a very modest development, of existing principle and so can take its place as a congruent part of the common law as a whole.

This does not mean that the courts cannot make radical changes in the common law; they can, as long as the change would not be contrary to any binding legislative rule, and as long as the court in question is not constrained by binding precedent not to do so in the particular case.[12] However, even the Supreme Court is reluctant to break with long-standing established rules of the common law, sometimes even expressly urging the legislator to act to correct a perceived problem within the (judge-made) rules of the common law.[13]

---

9 For the rules of precedent, see Section 4. below, and for the relevance of case law from other jurisdictions, see Section 5. below.

10 Judges in the nineteenth century would generally refuse to admit evidence of academic writing (by living authors, at least), although nowadays the courts even encourage the presentation of relevant academic argument to assist them in novel cases: e.g. compare *Union Bank v. Munster* (1887) 37 ChD 51, 54 with *Linden Gardens Trust Ltd v. Lenesta Sludge Disposals Ltd* [1994] 1 AC 85, 112 (HL). See also A. Braun, 'Professors and Judges in Italy: It Takes Two to Tango' (2006) 26 *Oxford Journal of Legal Studies* 665, comparing Italy with England.

11 *Kleinwort Benson Ltd v. Lincoln City Council*, above n. 6, 378.

12 The Supreme Court (or, until 1 October 2009, its predecessor the [Judicial Committee of the] House of Lords: see below n. 69) is therefore most likely to take such a step: for the rules of precedent, see Section 4. below. In *Kleinwort Benson Ltd v. Lincoln City Council*, above n. 6, 378, Lord Goff gave the example of the development by the House of Lords of 'our modern system of administrative law' during the twentieth century. Within private law, one might think of cases decided by the House of Lords which provided key steps in the development of the tort of negligence (see *Donoghue v. Stevenson* [1932] AC 562 (HL(Sc)), or of a general law of restitution for unjust enrichment (see *Lipkin Gorman v. Karpnale Ltd* [1991] 2 AC 548 (HL)).

13 e.g. *Beswick v. Beswick* [1968] AC 58, 72 (HL) (Lord Reid, preferring legislative reform of the common law doctrine of privity of contract, but noting that the House of Lords could act).

1.2. CASE LAW AS BINDING PRECEDENT IN ENGLISH LAW

The common law system accepts not only that case law in general can be a source of law, but also that the decisions taken by the courts in individual cases can be sources of law. As Lord Goff made clear in the first passage quoted above,[14] there can be identified leading cases which have made, or changed, the law and, indeed, the judges responsible.[15] This acceptance of the potential authority of the decisions taken in individual cases raises the need for general rules to determine the *relative* authority of cases. This is where can be found, at the core of the doctrine of precedent, a set of rules to determine what, within the decision of a court, constitutes its binding rule, and on which courts that rule will be binding. The rules of precedent will be discussed in more detail later, but it will be shown: that they broadly require a court to follow the necessary legal reasoning (the '*ratio decidendi*') of an earlier court in a relevant, similar case, at least where the earlier court was of a higher jurisdiction, and sometimes even where it was at the same level in the jurisdictional hierarchy; that the rules of precedent have been developed and are policed by the courts themselves; and that they operate in a generally stable and ordered way with a high degree of compliance by the judges at all levels.

1.3. THE RELATIONSHIP BETWEEN THE COMMON LAW AND STATUTE

Recognising the common law, created by case law, as a source of law alongside legislation necessarily raises a question about the relationship between these two sources of law.[16] Legislative enactments take precedence over the common law, in the sense that an existing statute can be a constraint on the courts' freedom to develop the common law, and a new statute can override an established common law rule, although of course the courts are as involved in taking decisions on the application of legislation as they are in taking decisions on the common law. Indeed, the rules of precedent are not limited to the courts' decisions on questions of common law, but also extend to the binding force of their decisions on the interpretation and implementation of legislative texts. However, the power of the courts in relation to legislation is essentially the power to interpret the legislative text – a power which is exercised with some restraint, particularly

---

14 *Kleinwort Benson Ltd v. Lincoln City Council*, above n. 6, 377.

15 The individuality of judges in the English legal system is a hallmark which can be significant for the practical operation of the doctrine of precedent as regards the degree of influence to be attributed to their statements ('*obiter dicta*') even where they are not part of the formal decision (the '*ratio decidendi*'): see Section 4.1. below.

16 J. Cartwright, above n. 4, Ch. 2.

in relation to primary legislation by Parliament.[17] This is very different from their (potentially creative) power in relation to the common law, although the nature and scope of judicial law-making in the common law is very different from law-making by the legislator.[18] The force of a judicial decision – even one which constitutes a binding precedent – is also very different from a legislative text.[19]

2. A BRIEF HISTORY OF PRECEDENT IN PRIVATE LAW

Although the development of the common law through judicial decisions dates back some centuries,[20] the doctrine of binding precedent could not be developed until the later nineteenth century when the modern, reliable system of law reporting was in place, together with the modern court hierarchy with its appeal structure, including the House of Lords exercising its judicial role as a final appeal court. Indeed, the rules of precedent, in the form recognised today, were not settled until the middle of the twentieth century.[21]

The rules have been developed by the courts themselves, not imposed by legislation. The rule that a court is bound by certain previous decisions is therefore a form of self-restraint by the judges, in the interests of the principle of *stare decisis* – that fairness to litigants demands that like cases be treated alike.[22] One might expect that it would be the highest court, the House of Lords (until its replacement by the Supreme Court in 2009),[23] that would have imposed the rules of precedent, but lower courts have also played their part in acknowledging

---

17 The courts focus on finding the meaning of the words of the statute rather than what Parliament (subjectively) meant or ought to have provided for: see generally J. Bell and G. Engle, *Cross: Statutory Interpretation*, 3rd ed., LexisNexis Butterworths, London 1995; and in more detail, D. Bailey and L. Norbury, *Bennion, Bailey and Norbury on Statutory Interpretation*, 8th ed., LexisNexis Butterworths, London 2020. There is no general power of judicial review of primary legislation in English law: even a statute which is incompatible with the European Convention on Human Rights must be given effect (although under the Human Rights Act 1998, s. 4, the courts may make a declaration of its non-compliance). However, the courts have developed a broad jurisdiction to review secondary (delegated) legislation by the executive, which must act within the powers given by primary legislation.

18 Section 1.1. above.

19 cf. N. Duxbury, above n. 3, pp. 59–62, discussing the distinction made by R. Dworkin, *Taking Rights Seriously*, Duckworth, London 1978, pp. 110–23, between the 'enactment force' and the 'gravitational force' of a precedent.

20 J. Baker, above n. 7, pp. 206–12.

21 R. Cross and J.W. Harris, above n. 3, pp. 24–25. For a fuller discussion of the history, see N. Duxbury, above n. 3, Ch. 2.

22 The term *stare decisis* appears in the English case reports as early as the seventeenth century: *Hanslap v. Cater* (1673) 1 Ventris 243, although the doctrine of binding precedent was not yet established.

23 See below n. 69.

and defining the rules of their own limited power to depart from the law set out in earlier decisions. Once the principle of binding precedent is acknowledged, it is not surprising that the courts should recognise their duty to follow a relevant earlier decision of a higher court.[24] But some courts have also accepted that, in principle, they are bound by their own earlier decisions. In particular, in 1944 the Court of Appeal settled that it is generally bound by earlier decisions of the Court of Appeal.[25]

The point of the doctrine of precedent is to provide stability and predictability in decision-making by the courts.[26] This does not mean that the rules of precedent cannot be changed if the need arises, and one very significant change must be noted. In 1898, the House of Lords had made clear that it must follow its own earlier decisions: only an Act of Parliament could change the law as decided by the House.[27] However, this rule proved problematic, given the difficulty of securing legislative change to correct decisions of the House of Lords that were later perceived to be outdated or even erroneous,[28] and in 1966 the House of Lords itself softened the rule by declaring that, although they would continue to treat former decisions of the House as normally binding on them, they would now be prepared to depart from a previous decision when it appears right to do so, bearing in mind 'the danger of disturbing retrospectively the basis on which contracts, settlements of property and fiscal arrangements have been entered into'.[29] Although there was now a power at this highest level[30] to depart from

---

24 Subject to the question of what makes an earlier decision relevant (and thereby binding): see Section 4.1. below.

25 *Young v. Bristol Aeroplane Co Ltd* [1944] KB 718 (CA), below n. 79. The issue did not arise in the appeal to the House of Lords in the case, but one of the five Lords hearing the appeal expressed his agreement with the view stated by the Court of Appeal on the question of precedent: [1946] AC 163, 169 (Viscount Simon).

26 *Willers v. Joyce (No 2)* [2016] UKSC 44, [2018] AC 843 at [4]: 'Decisions on points of law by more senior courts have to be accepted by more junior courts. Otherwise, the law becomes anarchic, and it loses coherence, clarity and predictability' (Lord Neuberger, speaking for a court composed of nine Supreme Court Justices).

27 *London Street Tramways Co Ltd v. London CC* [1898] AC 375 (HL). The House of Lords had struggled with this question throughout the nineteenth century: N. Duxbury, above n. 3, p. 42.

28 For a good example, see the difficulties presented by privity of contract (the common law rule that a third party could not sue on a contract even if the contracting parties made it expressly for his/her benefit and intended him/her to have the right to sue in his/her own name to enforce it), which was accepted as fundamental doctrine by the House of Lords in 1915 (*Dunlop Pneumatic Tyre Co Ltd v. Selfridge & Co Ltd* [1915] AC 847 (HL)), but was later regretted by some members the House (see, e.g. *Scruttons v. Midland Silicones Ltd* [1962] AC 446 (HL), 473 (Lord Reid)); legislative reform was finally achieved in 1999. See J. Cartwright, above n. 4, pp. 29–30, 244–46.

29 Practice Statement (Judicial Precedent) [1966] 1 WLR 1234 (Lord Gardiner LC, on behalf of himself and the Lords of Appeal in Ordinary, i.e. the whole Judicial Committee of the House of Lords). They also noted 'the especial need for certainty as to the criminal law'.

30 The Practice Statement (Judicial Precedent), above n. 29, made clear that it was 'not intended to affect the use of precedent elsewhere than in the House', i.e. it did not change the rule

previous decisions, the general rule remained that the House would follow its own decisions, in the interests of certainty:[31]

> Their Lordships regard the use of precedent as an indispensable foundation upon which to decide what is the law and its application to individual cases. It provides at least some degree of certainty upon which individuals can rely in the conduct of their affairs, as well as a basis for orderly development of legal rules.

This power has been exercised from time to time, but the House of Lords and the Supreme Court, which in 2009 took over the same jurisdiction and the same rules of precedent,[32] have continued to emphasise that it is to be exercised sparingly.[33]

This change in the rules of precedent made by the House of Lords in 1966 has some remarkable features. It was a change – useful and welcome, no doubt, but still a major change in the rules governing judicial authority within the English common law – made by a simple announcement by the senior judges themselves.[34] But it was not an announcement made in the course of a judicial decision,[35] but a separate statement, under the guise of a statement of judicial practice,[36] and one which would therefore have effect for the future without affecting the decision in a case currently being heard.[37]

The only other formal change that has been made to the rules of precedent in recent years has been in consequence of the withdrawal of the United Kingdom (UK) from the European Union (EU). As long as the UK was within the EU legal order, one aspect of the rules of precedent was the extent to which UK domestic courts were required to follow decisions of the Court of Justice of the EU (CJEU). The answer to this question has now been changed by UK legislation, in two separate steps. First, at the end of 2020, on completion of the implementation period of the Withdrawal Agreement, much of the EU law as it then existed was retained within domestic UK law. This still raised a question about the role of the CJEU in relation to the interpretation of the retained EU law, and it was provided that English courts were not bound by any principles laid down, or decisions

established by *Young v. Bristol Aeroplane Co Ltd*, above n. 25, that the Court of Appeal is bound by its own previous decisions.

31 Practice Statement (Judicial Precedent), above n. 29.

32 See below n. 69.

33 See below n. 84.

34 For debate about the constitutional propriety of the change, see N. Duxbury, above n. 3, pp. 131–39.

35 cf. the cases in which the Court of Appeal and the House of Lords had declared the rules of precedent: above nn. 25, 27.

36 This is a curious title, since the rule of precedent is surely a legal rule, or at least a constitutional convention, rather than simply a matter of procedure: N. Duxbury, above n. 3, pp. 136–37.

37 There is no principle by which the decision of an English court can make changes in the law to take effect only for the future: see below n. 51.

made, by the CJEU after the end of 2020, although they could have regard to such later decisions, or to other relevant things done by other EU entities or by the EU itself. The courts below the Court of Appeal remained bound by the retained EU case law as it stood at the end of 2020 (and as long as it had not been modified in domestic law since then) but the Supreme Court and the Court of Appeal were not bound – although in deciding whether to depart from any retained EU case law, the Supreme Court and the Court of Appeal were required to apply the same test as the Supreme Court would apply in deciding whether to depart from its own case law (that is, under the 1966 Practice Statement).[38] A second step was taken when the UK Parliament legislated to remove from UK law, with effect from the end of 2023, a number of provisions deriving from EU law but also to assimilate the remaining retained EU law into UK domestic law by abolishing the application of the supremacy of EU law, and removing from domestic law the general principles of EU law, insofar as they had been retained in relation to the law enacted before the end of 2020. The power of domestic courts to depart from EU case law which had been retained since 2020 was also increased, giving priority to the development of domestic law.[39]

3. NATURE OF PRECEDENT

The legal rule within a precedent – the *ratio decidendi* – and the application of the rules of precedent within the court structure in England and Wales, are discussed in Section 4. below. But once the *ratio decidendi* has been identified, then it is binding on future courts within the terms of those rules of precedent. Precedent is a rule, not simply guidance: a court can be criticised on appeal for having failed to follow a binding precedent, although there is no personal (disciplinary) sanction against the judge or judges who failed to follow the rule of precedent, nor does there appear to be any other (informal or social) sanction. Indeed, whether the court hearing the appeal reverses the lower court's decision will depend on its own consideration of the earlier precedent: the mere failure of the lower court to follow a binding precedent does not lead to reversal on appeal, since it is for the appeal court to decide the appeal on its general merits, and the appeal court may itself be in a position to overrule the earlier precedent.[40] The failure – even deliberate – of a lower court to follow a precedent by which

[38] The European Union (Withdrawal) Act 2018, s. 6, amended by the European Union (Withdrawal Agreement) Act 2020, and supplemented by the European Union (Withdrawal) Act 2018 (Relevant Court) (Retained EU Case Law) Regulations 2020 (SI 2020/1525).

[39] The Retained EU Law (Revocation and Reform) Act 2023, further amending the European Union (Withdrawal) Act 2018, above n. 38. After the end of 2023 the 'retained' case law is referred to as 'assimilated': see s. 5 of the 2023 Act.

[40] e.g. *Miliangos v. George Frank (Textiles) Ltd* [1976] AC 443 (HL).

it was technically bound does not in itself generally affect the binding force of the earlier precedent on later cases, although where the Court of Appeal takes such a step and thereby creates a conflict of authorities, the rules of precedent require the later court to accept the most recent decision unless and until the conflict is resolved by the Supreme Court.[41] But in practice the lower courts do generally regard themselves as bound by relevant precedents, to the point where – if they cannot find a way round a binding precedent, such as by 'distinguishing' the present case from the earlier case which created the precedent[42] – they will sometimes openly express their unhappiness with the precedent whilst faithfully following it.[43] No doubt this is sometimes done to encourage a higher court to exercise its power to review the earlier precedent and to overrule it, either on appeal in the present case, or in a future case.[44] It has even been said recently that, in the interest of legal certainty, the technique of distinguishing earlier cases should be used with restraint, and only where there is a sound reason, rooted in legal principle, for doing so: the solution to a precedent which is perceived to be unfair is by appeal to a higher court with the power to decide on whether it should be overruled.[45] There is also a special procedure for an appeal to be brought directly to the Supreme Court from the first-instance decision – to 'leapfrog' the Court of Appeal – where the trial judge certifies that he/she was bound, and the Court of Appeal would similarly be bound, by a point of law in an earlier case which should be (re)considered by the Supreme Court, and if the Supreme Court itself gives permission for the appeal.[46]

One of the higher courts – the Court of Appeal or the Supreme Court – may act within its powers to overrule an earlier precedent.[47] The effect of

---

41 Section 4.2. below.

42 N. Duxbury, above n. 3, pp. 113–16.

43 e.g. *South Caribbean Trading Ltd v. Trafigura Beheer BV* [2004] EWHC 2676 (Comm), [2005] 1 Lloyd's Rep. 128 at [108] (Colman J: 'But for the fact that *Williams v. Roffey Bros Ltd* … was a decision of the Court of Appeal, I would not have followed it').

44 The style of judgments in English law facilitates this: each judge in the court is entitled to give a fully reasoned judgment, expressing not only his or her own view on the law to be applied, but also any doubts and reservations on the law or on the outcome of the case. The judgments are public and can be used in argument in any appeal or in later cases – and the identity of the judges in earlier cases can be relevant in the degree of influence that their statements might have. For a recent example where the Court of Appeal said expressly that it must follow a binding precedent of the Court of Appeal, but would be prepared to grant permission for an appeal to the Supreme Court, see *Paul v. Royal Wolverhampton NHS Trust* [2022] EWCA Civ 12, [2023] QB 149 at [99], [106].

45 *Sevilleja Garcia v. Marex Financial Ltd* [2018] EWCA Civ 1468, [2019] QB 173 at [67]–[69] (Lewison LJ).

46 The Administration of Justice Act 1969, ss. 12–15; the Tribunals, Courts and Enforcement Act 2007, ss. 14A–14C; the Employment Tribunals Act 1996, ss. 37ZA–37ZC; the Special Immigration Appeals Commission Act 1997, ss. 7B–7D; the Supreme Court Practice Direction 3.6. For a recent example of a 'leapfrog appeal', see *FirstPort Property Services Ltd v. Settlers Court RTM Co Ltd* [2022] UKSC 1, [2022] 1 WLR 519.

47 Section 4.2. below.

overruling has been explained by the House of Lords.[48] The decision of a court which overrules an earlier precedent changes the law; the new law is effective for the future – binding other courts, within the rules of precedent, in their future decisions; but it does not change decisions which were already taken on the basis of the old precedent, except, of course, where the decision of the lower court in the present case is itself reversed by the appeal decision. But there is also a limited retrospective effect of the decision, since the new law applies to the case in hand (and therefore the parties to the case could not have known that it was the law when they acted in such a way as to give rise to the dispute in question), and it applies to any other case which is still to come before the courts, even if its facts have already occurred. This is the inevitable effect of a decision in the common law system, by contrast with statute which will normally apply only with prospective effect.[49] The risk of instability in the law by overruling an established precedent can sometimes be a reason for a court to be reluctant to change the law, even if it has power to do so and considers that the law as it is reflected by the earlier precedent ought to be changed.[50] But the English courts have not developed a system of prospective overruling.[51]

4. HOW TO IDENTIFY A LEGAL RULE IN A PRECEDENT

The rules comprising the doctrine of precedent in English law are established by the cases.[52] The first question is how to identify *what*, within a judicial decision, is potentially binding on future courts (as opposed to statements made in the

---

48 *Kleinwort Benson Ltd v. Lincoln City Council* [1999] 2 AC 349 (HL) at 358–59 (Lord Browne-Wilkinson), 378–79 (Lord Goff), 393 (Lord Lloyd), although Lord Browne-Wilkinson and Lord Lloyd dissented in the final decision in the case: see below n. 50). The House of Lords decided by a majority that money paid under a mistake of law should be recoverable, overruling long-standing cases which had held that only money paid under a mistake of fact could be recovered.

49 Legislation will normally make this clear by a provision defining the date at which the legislation comes into effect; see, e.g. the Contracts (Rights of Third Parties) Act 1999, s. 10(2), (3) (the Act does not apply to a contract entered into within six months from the date when the Act was passed, except where such a contract expressly provides for the Act to apply). However, in the absence of express provision there is also a presumption of statutory interpretation that legislation is not intended to be retroactive: J. Bell and G. Engle, above n. 17, pp. 187–90.

50 In *Kleinwort Benson Ltd v. Lincoln City Council*, above n. 48, Lord Browne-Wilkinson (at 364) and Lord Lloyd (at 397–98) dissented on the basis that a change in the 'mistake of law' rule should be made by Parliament, not by a decision of the House of Lords with its retroactive effect at common law.

51 *Kleinwort Benson Ltd v. Lincoln City Council*, above n. 48, 379 (Lord Goff: 'such a system, although it has occasionally been adopted elsewhere with, I understand, somewhat controversial results, has no place in our legal system').

52 See also J. Cartwright, above n. 4, pp. 24–29, much of which is summarised here.

course of the decision which might be influential, though not binding, in future cases). The second question is *which courts* are bound by such precedents.

4.1. WHAT IS THE BINDING ELEMENT OF A CASE? THE '*RATIO DECIDENDI*', AND THE RELEVANCE OF '*OBITER DICTA*'

The rules of precedent apply not to a case in general but to its '*ratio decidendi*': the 'reason for deciding'. This means the point of law that was applied by the court (or by a majority of the judges in the court, in the case of disagreement between the judges in a multi-judge court) in order to decide the case as it did on its facts. This may sound straightforward, but the search for the *ratio decidendi* of a case can be open to interpretation, particularly where the deciding court has not itself made it explicit.[53]

Broadly speaking, the *ratio* can be found by identifying, first, the dispute between the parties on the facts of the case, then which party prevailed according to the decision of the court, and then the legal reason(s) given by the court for that decision. The *ratio decidendi* is the point of law that determined the decision, but it is inevitably grounded in and, indeed, defined by the facts as they are presented to the court by the parties.[54] There may be more than one legal issue in question in a case and more than one point of law decided (and therefore more than one *ratio decidendi*), and on any relevant point of law the judges within a court may not always agree. In a single-judge court, such as a trial at first instance in the High Court, there is only one judgment to analyse. But to find the *ratio decidendi* it is necessary to analyse multiple judgments where they are given in a multi-judge court, such as the Court of Appeal, which is commonly composed of three judges, or the Supreme Court, which commonly sits as a panel of five Justices but in significant cases may sit as a panel of seven or even nine. The ease or difficulty in finding the *ratio decidendi* depends not only on the complexity of the case[55] but on the way in which the judges express themselves in their own judgments. Sometimes they set out clearly the legal rule that they propose to apply, particularly where they

---

53 For detailed discussion, see R. Cross and J.W. Harris, above n. 3, Ch. II; N. Duxbury, above n. 3, Ch. 3.

54 *Quinn v. Leathem* [1901] AC 495, 506 (HL). The facts may be determined by the court in response to the parties' pleadings, or they may sometimes be assumed to be true by the court as part of its decision, notably where the court decides a preliminary point of law, such as in striking out the claimant's or the defendant's statement of case which could not in law succeed on the pleaded facts, even if proved to be true: the Civil Procedure Rules 1998 (SI 1998/3132) r. 3.4(2)(a).

55 For a complicated example, see *Miller v. Jackson* [1977] QB 966 where a number of different points of law arose, on which the three judges of the Court of Appeal disagreed but decided the case in different pairs on the different points.

recognise the novelty of the legal issues and therefore the potential significance of their decision.[56] And sometimes the judges in a multi-judge court present their decision in a way that avoids later debate about differences between their individual opinions, such as where one member of the court gives a detailed judgment with which other judges expressly agree,[57] or where a single judgment is given in the name of a number of the judges,[58] or even as a judgment of the whole court.[59] The presentation of their judgments is, however, a matter for the judges in the court, and although sometimes there has been a fashion in the multi-judge courts (and, in particular in the House of Lords – now the Supreme Court) for simplified, single judgments which reduce later debate about the *ratio decidendi*, there have also been periods when the judges have chosen to give multiple judgments in order to avoid the idea that the court is laying down definitive legal rules, and to allow more flexible later interpretation of the scope of their own decision.[60]

The precedent – the *ratio decidendi* – is the *point of law* that determined the court's decision. The court's *findings of fact* are not in themselves part of the *ratio*, although they serve to define the scope of the precedent itself. But some points of a decision will not be pure questions of law but of the application of a broadly-stated legal test to the facts of the case, such as whether an exclusion clause in a contract satisfies the legal requirement that it be 'reasonable', or that a term in a consumer contract be not 'unfair'.[61] On some questions, the courts may also exercise more overt discretions, such as whether it is equitable to order specific performance of a contract, even if performance is possible and, according to the applicable general rules, the contract is one which would normally be enforced.[62] Such cases do not produce binding precedents as readily as decisions taken simply on pure questions of law, although the way in which a court has applied the (open-textured) legal test can become part of the *ratio decidendi* and therefore not only relevant but even binding in future cases.[63]

The nature of judgments in the English courts, in which the judges explain and discuss their reasoning, allows for much more to be said than is necessary to decide the case. Sometimes the judges will take the opportunity presented by

---

56 e.g. Lord Atkin in *Donoghue v. Stevenson* [1932] AC 562 (HL), 599.

57 e.g. *Co-operative Insurance Society Ltd v. Argyll Stores (Holdings) Ltd* [1998] AC 1 (HL).

58 This is currently common practice in the Supreme Court, e.g. *MWB Business Exchange Centres Ltd v. Rock Advertising Ltd* [2018] UKSC 24, [2019] AC 119.

59 e.g. *Great Peace Shipping Ltd v. Tsavliris Salvage (International) Ltd* [2002] EWCA Civ 1407, [2003] QB 679.

60 See, e.g. *Cassell & Co Ltd v. Broome* [1972] AC 1027 (HL), 1084–85; A. Paterson, *The Law Lords*, Macmillan, London 1982, pp. 183–84.

61 e.g. the Unfair Contract Terms Act 1977, s. 11; the Consumer Rights Act 2015, s. 63.

62 J. Cartwright, above n. 4, pp. 280–85.

63 See, e.g. *Ryan v. Mutual Tontine Westminster Chambers Association* [1893] 1 Ch. 116 (CA), 126 (Kay LJ: specific performance is discretionary, but 'confined within well-known rules').

the case before them in order to comment on other points of law which do not arise, or which, though they could form the basis of their decision, do not do so because they decide the case on the basis of some other legal point. Sometimes the judges, in explaining their decision in the actual case as it is presented, will seek to explain the limits of the decision by discussing a hypothetical alternative set of facts to which the decision would not apply.[64] Strictly speaking, all the discussion which is not itself a necessary explanation of the legal reason for the court's decision in the case does not form part of the *ratio decidendi*, but can be categorised as '*obiter dicta*' – things 'said along the way', incidental to the decision itself. But the line between *ratio decidendi* and *obiter dicta* can sometimes be debatable;[65] even statements which are clearly *obiter dicta* – and therefore not formally binding on future courts within the rules of precedent – can have great significance for future decisions, particularly where the statements are made by judges at a level of authority, either formal or personal, which carries weight in the eyes of later judges who are able to use the *obiter dicta* to assist them in their decisions. It is natural for a court (if it is free to do so within the rules of precedent) to be influenced by statements by a higher court indicating how it would decide a relevant point of law if presented with it. But the common law method of judging and law reporting, under which individual judges give judgments which are published in their own name, and build their reputations on their body of judgments, means that *obiter dicta* by particular judges can also carry a personal authority so that they will be taken seriously.[66]

All of this, however – finding the *ratio decidendi* of an earlier case; determining its limits (e.g. by the facts of the earlier case and so how far the decision can in future be distinguished); and determining also what other statements in the case are merely *obiter dicta* but may be persuasive in a later case – ultimately depends on the decisions of the later cases themselves. It can be said that, at least in complex or debatable cases, the authority of a case decided today is determined not by today's court but by the way it is interpreted by the later court which is asked to apply it.[67] This is true as a general proposition in the development of the common law, but particularly where the later court will be bound to follow the earlier case if its *ratio decidendi* applies to the facts of the new case. It is therefore necessary to understand the rules of the doctrine of precedent, and in particular to how the binding force of the *ratio decidendi* of a case, once decided, operates within the English court structure.

---

64 e.g. *Krell v. Henry* [1903] 2 KB 740 (CA), 750–51.

65 N. Duxbury, above n. 3, pp. 68–76.

66 e.g. *Enka Insaat ve Sanayi AS v. OOO 'Insurance Company Chubb'* [2020] UKSC 38, [2020] 1 WLR 4117 at [271] (Lord Sales: 'Lord Mustill's opinion in this area [i.e. arbitration law] carries great weight').

67 cf. N. Duxbury, above n. 3, p. 74.

4.2. THE PRECEDENT IS BINDING ON WHICH COURTS?

Understanding the rules of precedent in English private law requires an understanding of the civil court structure in England and Wales. In summary,[68] civil cases dealing with matters of general private law are heard at first instance in either the County Court (which has centres across the country) or the High Court (based in London, but High Court business can be heard also at centres around the country), depending on the type or value of the claim. Appeal from the County Court is to either a senior County Court judge, or the High Court or the Court of Appeal, depending on the nature of the claim; an appeal from a first-instance decision of the High Court is generally to the Court of Appeal. Appeals normally require the permission of either the trial court or the appeal court: there is no automatic right of appeal. There is a limited possibility of further appeal to the Supreme Court,[69] but only with permission of the Court of Appeal or the Supreme Court, and generally only where the case raises an arguable point of law of general public importance. This significantly limits the number of appeals heard by the Supreme Court.[70]

The general rule is that a court is bound to follow the *ratio* of an earlier relevant decision of a court which is higher in the court hierarchy, and the Court of Appeal is bound by its own previous decisions.[71] However, there are some nuances in the application of this general rule (and some uncertainties as to the rule).[72]

The County Court is bound to follow a decision of the High Court, the Court of Appeal or the Supreme Court (and older decisions of the House of Lords). It is not bound by its own decisions, although these are not generally published so there is no readily identifiable body of case law from the County Court.

A judge in the High Court is bound to follow a decision of the Court of Appeal or of the Supreme Court (and older decisions of the House of Lords), even if

---

68 For further detail and references, see J. Cartwright, above n. 4, pp. 26–29, from which this section is taken.

69 Until 1 October 2009, the final court of appeal was the House of Lords, which exercised its appeal functions through its Judicial Committee. The appeal jurisdiction was then transferred to the newly-created Supreme Court by the Constitutional Reform Act 2005, s. 40, but the general scope of jurisdiction is unchanged. See generally <https://www.supremecourt.uk>.

70 In the five-year period from 1 April 2018 to 31 March 2023 the Supreme Court heard an average of 64 appeals each year (the actual number varying between 50 and 74) – and this covers the whole of its appellate jurisdiction, including criminal cases and cases from Scotland and Northern Ireland – although each year it also determined a significant number of applications for permission to appeal (e.g. in 2022–23 it determined 273 applications, of which 196 were refused): 'Supreme Court and Judicial Committee of the Privy Council Annual Report and Accounts 2022–2023' (2023) HMSO, HC 11, pp. 29, 37, available on <https://www.supremecourt.uk/about/planning-and-governance.html>.

71 The Practice Statement (Judicial Precedent), above n. 29, reversed the rule that the House of Lords was also bound by its own previous decisions.

72 For detail see R. Cross and J.W. Harris, above n. 3, Chs. III, IV.

he/she believes that the earlier decision was wrong.[73] But the High Court judge in one case is not bound by an earlier decision of the High Court in another case, although the modern practice is that a judge should follow the earlier decision unless convinced it is wrong.[74] However, there is some uncertainty about how a High Court judge should deal with the situation where he/she considers that a decision of the Court of Appeal is inconsistent with an earlier decision of the Supreme Court or the House of Lords. It has been said that the duty of the judge is to follow the (more recent) decision of the Court of Appeal,[75] although there are examples of judges refusing to do this on the grounds that the Court of Appeal had failed properly to take into account a binding decision of the House of Lords – in other words, the judge discounts the decision of the Court of Appeal on the grounds that it was reached in error.[76]

The Court of Appeal is bound to follow a decision of the Supreme Court (and older decisions of the House of Lords). The House of Lords has emphasised the importance of adherence to the rules of precedent, and has made clear that the Court of Appeal should normally follow the domestic rules even in a case which raises an issue under the European Convention on Human Rights and where there is an argument that the House of Lords (or, now, the Supreme Court) might itself decide otherwise on the basis of the case law of the European Court of Human Rights.[77] The Court of Appeal is also bound by its own previous decisions[78] except where:[79] (1) there are conflicting decisions of the Court of Appeal, in which case it is free to decide which to follow; (2) a decision of the Court of Appeal is inconsistent with a *later* decision of the House of Lords, which therefore impliedly overrules the earlier decision; or (3) it decides that the previous decision of the Court of Appeal was given '*per incuriam*': it was in error because it failed to consider a binding legal rule (such as an earlier decision of the House of Lords) which would have affected the decision.[80] In its criminal jurisdiction, the Court of Appeal does not apply the rule that it must follow its

---

73 e.g. *South Caribbean Trading Ltd v. Trafigura Beheer BV*, above n. 43.

74 *Coral Reef Ltd v. Silverbond Enterprises Ltd* [2016] EWHC 3844 (Ch), [2018] 4 WLR 104 at [47].

75 *Miliangos v. George Frank (Textiles) Ltd* [1976] AC 443 (HL), 478.

76 *Uganda Co (Holdings) Ltd v. Government of Uganda* [1979] 1 Lloyd's Rep 481 (QB), 486–87.

77 *Kay v. Lambeth LBC* [2006] UKHL 10, [2006] 2 AC 465 at [40]–[45]. The rules of precedent in matters of EU law, since the UK completed withdrawal from the EU, are now regulated by statute: above nn. 38, 39. For the position during the period when the UK was still a Member State of the EU, see R. Cross and J.W. Harris, above n. 3, pp. 182–85.

78 e.g. *Re Selectmove Ltd* [1995] 1 WLR 474 (CA), 481.

79 *Young v. Bristol Aeroplane Co Ltd* [1944] KB 718 (CA), 729–30.

80 This third exception has been extended (controversially) to cover the case where the Court of Appeal decides that the previous decision was plainly wrong because it failed properly to give effect to a binding earlier decision even though it was considered: see *Great Peace Shipping Ltd v. Tsavliris Salvage (International) Ltd (The Great Peace)* [2002] EWCA Civ 1407, [2003] QB 679. For criticism of the decision in relation to the doctrine of precedent, see S.B. Midwinter, 'The Great Peace and Precedent' (2003) 119 *Law Quarterly Review* 180.

own previous decisions with the same rigidity as in its civil jurisdiction,[81] and it has recently been held, in the context of a point of criminal law, that, where the Justices of the Supreme Court unanimously direct that an otherwise binding decision of the Court of Appeal should no longer be followed, and propose an alternative test that they say must be adopted, the Court of Appeal is bound in later cases to follow that direction from the Supreme Court even though it was strictly made by way of *obiter dictum*.[82]

As has been already noted, since 1966 the Supreme Court regards itself as normally bound to follow its own previous decisions, or those of the House of Lords, but having a power to depart from those previous decisions.[83] However, it has been said (and repeated) by their Lordships that, in the interests of stability in the law, they will exercise that power cautiously, and only in the case of decisions which are impeding the proper development of the law or have led to results which were unjust or contrary to public policy.[84] Where the Supreme Court is being asked to depart, or may decide to depart, from one of its own previous decisions, it will normally sit as a panel of seven Justices (rather than the usual number of five), and the departure from a previous decision will be stated explicitly and explained in the new judgment.

5. MANDATE TO CREATE PRIVATE LAW

The nature of the common law, historically and in the modern law, necessarily carries the mandate for the courts to create private law through their case law.[85] Although clearly accepted by the whole legal system, including Parliament as sovereign legislator, the mandate was created by the courts themselves, and its limits are, for the most part, self-imposed by the courts in order to provide a stable, regulated context for the development of the law.[86]

The existing rules governing English-law cases as precedents have been discussed.[87] The impact of decisions made by courts in other jurisdictions varies, depending on the jurisdiction in question, although none are formal precedents – in the sense of having binding force within the doctrine of precedent as it is applied in English law. Only the *ratio decidendi* of an English-law decision is

---

81 *R. v. Gould* [1968] 2 QB 65 (CA), 68–69.

82 *R. v. Barton* [2020] EWCA Crim 575, [2021] QB 685 at [104].

83 Section 2. above.

84 See *Cassell & Co Ltd v. Broome* [1972] AC 1027 (HL), 1054; *Jones v. Secretary of State for Social Services* [1972] AC 944 (HL), 966; *Chartbrook Ltd v. Persimmon Homes Ltd* [2009] UKHL 38, [2009] 1 AC 1101 at [41]; *Kay v. Lambeth LBC* [2006] UKHL 10, [2006] 2 AC 465 at [42].

85 Section 1.1. above.

86 Section 2. above.

87 Section 4. above.

binding.[88] Even the decision of a court composed wholly or mainly of judges who also sit in the highest English courts is not formally binding as a matter of English law if, in giving their decision, the judges are sitting as the court of another jurisdiction – such as when the UK Supreme Court hears an appeal on a matter of Scottish law, or where the Judicial Committee of the Privy Council (in practice, largely made up of Justices of the Supreme Court)[89] hears an appeal from a UK overseas territory or Crown dependency, or from a Commonwealth jurisdiction which retains the right of final appeal in private law not to its highest national court, but to the King in Council. There have been notable cases, decided by the House of Lords for Scotland,[90] and by the Privy Council,[91] which have later been followed by the English courts not by way of formal precedent, but almost as such. Sometimes the court will indicate expressly that, although it is deciding a matter of (technically) foreign law, there is no distinction between that law and English law on the point in issue.[92]

Decisions taken by the national courts of other common law jurisdictions can be relevant for an English court where the context for the point of law addressed in the other jurisdiction – within the general scheme of the common law as it is shared by the common law jurisdictions – is similar to the context of the English case within English law. The common historical heritage of the modern common law systems – with not only their common links to the substantive English common law but also their shared assumptions as to the development of the law by judges – gives a certain affinity between the systems, but they can exercise the freedom to develop their own national law and therefore to depart from the approach taken in English law. Where the courts of another common law system have developed its law in a new direction, the English courts may be interested (but not bound) to consider whether a similar development could be accepted in England and Wales.[93]

One might expect that there would be less of a place in the English courts for consideration of decisions taken by the national courts of jurisdictions outside

---

88 Section 4.1. above.

89 See generally <https://www.jcpc.uk>.

90 e.g. *Donoghue v. Stevenson* [1932] AC 562 (House of Lords on appeal from Scotland).

91 e.g. *Overseas Tankship (UK) Ltd v. Morts Dock & Engineering Co (The Wagon Mound)* [1961] AC 388 (Privy Council on appeal from Australia). See also *Willers v. Joyce (No 2)*, above n. 26 at [12] (decisions of the Privy Council should 'normally be regarded by any Judge of England and Wales, and indeed any Justice of the Supreme Court, as being of great weight and persuasive value').

92 e.g. *Donoghue v. Stevenson*, above n. 90, 579 (Lord Atkin). cf. *Invercargill City Council v. Hamlin* [1996] AC 624, 640 (Privy Council on appeal from New Zealand declining to follow English authorities on the basis that conditions in New Zealand are different).

93 See, e.g. *Murphy v. Brentwood DC* [1991] 1 AC 398 (HL), 461, 466–68, 469–70, 473–74, 476–78, 481 discussing Commonwealth and American authorities before deciding to depart from the earlier decision of *Anns v. Merton LBC* [1978] AC 728 (HL) under the 1966 Practice Statement, above n. 29.

the common law tradition, such as the European civil law jurisdictions. There is certainly no assumption that English law should develop along the lines of the civil law on particular points as they arise within the English case law – which is right as a matter of comparative law technique: transplanting into one's own system individual rules from another legal system requires a careful understanding of how the rules fit within that other system and whether they would be an appropriate fit within one's own system.[94] However, there is a long tradition within the English courts of considering how other legal systems handle particular points of law, particularly where there is a lacuna in English law or where there is a perception that the existing law is unsatisfactory and should be reconsidered.[95] And in the modern era, the close link to the European civil law jurisdictions through membership of the EU, and in particular through European-wide attempts to harmonise areas of private law, has given an impetus to arguments being brought before the English courts in favour of rethinking some particular rules of English private law so as to align them with the approach taken elsewhere in Europe.[96] Such arguments can, however, only form an inspiration for the English judges, who are never bound to take such steps. Indeed, the inherent limitations on judicial development of the common law, taken together with the reluctance of even the Supreme Court to depart from previous law in a way which is too radical or would risk disturbing the stability of the law and transactions entered into under the law as it is already established or generally understood, act as a restraint on such development.[97]

6. IMPORTANCE OF PRECEDENTS IN PRIVATE LAW

Precedents have had great importance in the development of English private law, given the essential nature of the common law[98] and the fact that in the core

94 See generally M. Graziadei, 'Comparative Law, Transplants, and Receptions' in M. Reimann and R. Zimmermann (eds), *The Oxford Handbook of Comparative Law*, 2nd ed., Oxford University Press, Oxford 2019, Ch. 16.

95 For the influence of civil law on the development of the English law of contract in the nineteenth century, see D. Ibbetson, *A Historical Introduction to the Law of Obligations*, Oxford University Press, Oxford 2001, Ch. 12.

96 See, e.g. *Shogun Finance Ltd v. Hudson* [2003] UKHL 62, [2004] 1 AC 919 at [85]–[86] (Lord Millett, dissenting); *Yam Seng Pte Ltd v. International Trade Corp Ltd* [2013] EWHC 111 (QB), [2013] 1 CLC 662 at [125] (Leggatt J, *obiter*). Such judicial views have not, however, been unanimous: cf. *Shogun Finance Ltd v. Hudson* at [55] (Lord Hobhouse, rejecting an argument which would 'advocate [a reform of the common law] on the basis of continental legal systems which are open to cogent criticism'). It remains to be seen how the withdrawal of the UK from the EU affects the English courts' approach in relation to the development of the common law: cf. above nn. 38, 39.

97 Above nn. 13, 50.

98 Section 1.1. above.

areas of private law – contract, tort and property – Parliament has generally left the common law intact, or has at least intervened only sporadically to change some details. There has never been a general civil code, and a project to codify the law of contract which was begun by the Law Commission in the mid-1960s was abandoned in 1972.[99] Although there has been legislation on particular (and sometimes very significant) issues, the fundamental rules of the law of contract, as well as of the law of tort and property, remain within the common law – the law made by the courts through their cases, which the courts themselves continue to apply and develop.[100] The contemporary significance of precedents therefore remains strong. Although there are many new developments in society which necessitate new legal frameworks, and therefore new legislation – whether in the context of consumer law or commercial law – the authority of the old lines of cases remains in place insofar as they have not been superseded by legislation.

The creative power of the common law within private law appears rather less vigorous now than it was in, say, the nineteenth century. This is not surprising. In the earlier periods, the courts were instrumental in developing the core areas of private law,[101] and since then, they have developed the doctrine of precedent as a formal set of rules within the hierarchy of courts.[102] Taken together with the reluctance of even the Supreme Court to change fundamental doctrines of the common law, and their general view that significant change is better effected by the legislature than by the courts,[103] it has become more natural for major new developments, either to fill perceived gaps[104] or to change the existing common law rules,[105] to be undertaken by legislation. There is still a significant role for the courts in the general (if modest) development of existing common law principles,[106] and of course they still play a very significant part in interpreting and giving effect to legislation, where the case law on questions of statutory interpretation itself creates precedents and the judges can on occasion have a very significant role in keeping the legislation relevant through their dynamic interpretation of the language of a statute.[107]

The importance of individual precedents within English law might appear to present a very significant practical challenge, at least from the perspective

---

99 J. Cartwright, 'The English Law of Contract: Time for Review?' (2009) 17 *European Review of Private Law* 155, 168–69.

100 J. Cartwright, above n. 4, pp. 20–21.

101 Section 1.1. above.

102 Section 2. above.

103 See above nn. 13, 50.

104 e.g. the development through legislation of consumer law in the later twentieth century.

105 e.g. the reform of the common law doctrine of privity of contract: see above n. 28.

106 *Kleinwort Benson Ltd v. Lincoln City Council* [1999] 2 AC 349, 378, quoted above, text to n. 11.

107 J. Cartwright, above n. 4, p. 35; D. Bailey and L. Norbury, above n. 17, pp. 507–17, setting out the principles of the courts' 'updating construction' of statutes, including its limits

of a reader who comes from a legal system where the highest (and therefore most influential) courts produce very many decisions – sometimes even tens of thousands a year. This is not, however, generally perceived to be a problem within English law. The really significant precedents – those formally binding on the lower courts – are those of the Supreme Court and the Court of Appeal,[108] and the number of cases decided by these courts is not large by continental (civil law) standards.[109] It should also be remembered that it is for the parties' lawyers to support their arguments with appropriate citation of precedents, which the lawyers can find by searching electronic databases.

7. CONCLUDING REMARKS

In English law the courts have the power to create and develop the common law, and although in the modern law there is a great deal of legislation – which the courts have the power (and, indeed, the duty) to interpret and apply – there has been no systematic or complete legislative codification of the core areas of private law (contract, tort, property) and therefore the role of the courts in developing the law remains. It is also now recognised that the courts have power not only to fill lacunas in the existing law, but also to change the law to correct previous decisions or to respond to new issues as they arise. But this apparently broad power of the courts is limited in two significant respects – limitations which do not apply to the legislator.[110]

First, the courts can decide only cases as they are presented to them by the parties, and they must decide the case for the parties. This means that the scope of judicial law-making is limited by the facts of the case in hand; the courts can declare a new rule of law for the purposes of this case (and for other similar

(only where consistent with legislative intention) but also examples from the case law which have taken account of changes in social conditions, developments in technology and other changes.

108 Section 4.2. above.

109 For the (small) number of appeals decided by the Supreme Court, see above n. 70. The number of appeals decided by the Court of Appeal is not huge: in recent years the number of final appeals heard and decided in civil cases has reduced for various reasons, but between 2007 and 2018 the number was between 1,000 and 1,300 a year: see Ministry of Justice, 'Civil Justice Statistics Quarterly: January to March 2023' (1 June 2023) Royal Courts of Justice Annual Tables 2022, Table 2.5, available at <www.gov.uk/government/statistics/civil-justice-statistics-quarterly-january-to-march-2023>.

110 See also Lord Hodge, above n. 6, 223–27, discussing a range of constraints on judicial law-making, some self-imposed by the judges, others imposed by the nature of decision-making in the common law and the relationship between the courts and the legislative sovereignty of Parliament. He also notes at 227 that judicial law-making is 'a minority activity. The vast majority of judicial work, well over 90 percent, involves no law-making but is what Lord Devlin famously described as "the disinterested application of known law"'.

cases) but the rule they declare is law by reason only that it is necessary for their decision between the parties, on the facts (the '*ratio decidendi*') – they have no power to make general declarations of law for the future that do not apply to the case in hand.

Second, the courts are bound by the rules of precedent, which limit their freedom to act to change the law. The rules are self-imposed – created by the courts themselves – and are applied with a self-restraint that might seem quite remarkable: judges may criticise precedents by which they are bound, but still follow them. And although the Supreme Court is clearly in the best position to change the law, given its general authority within the English legal system and also its power (since 1966) to depart even from its own previous decisions, the fact that it expressly exercises caution in so doing, and more generally in taking radical decisions on well-established points of common law, sets the general tone for restraint on judicial development of the law. The courts of all levels are able to interpret earlier precedents, sometimes distinguishing them to avoid being bound by them – that is a consequence of the relatively open-textured form of many judicial decisions. But even the technique of distinguishing earlier cases is exercised with restraint, and once the scope of a precedent is clearly established, it can operate as a limit (or at least a constraint) on further judicial development. To this must be added the significant rule that, once a point of law has been decided by the Court of Appeal, only the Supreme Court (or legislation) can reverse it – which, given the limited number of appeals that the Supreme Court can hear each year, and the difficulties of obtaining legislative intervention to change the judge-made law, acts as a further general restraint on the development of the law.

Taking all this together, one can learn from studying the doctrine of precedent in the English common law not only the detailed rules of the law of precedent and their operation in practice, but also how the doctrine contributes to a restraint on judicial development and therefore to a relatively stable set of legal rules – but also to a difficulty for the courts in developing the law easily or quickly to adapt to new problems as they arise. The effect is to create a more conservative legal system than might be seen in another system which, whilst following the common law tradition in seeing judicial precedents as a formal source of law, adopts looser rules relating to the binding force of precedent, and so allows the courts greater latitude in the development of the law, or in a system (such as in the civil law tradition) which sees the role of the courts as not making the law but interpreting the will of the legislator, at least where the interpretative power of the courts can be used as a more flexible tool in developing the law stated in legislative texts than would be recognised by the English courts in the interpretation of legislation.

PRECEDENT IN FRENCH PRIVATE LAW

Guillaume Leroy

1. A GENERAL INTRODUCTION TO LEGAL PRECEDENT

In France, precedent is perceived as constituting a concept specific to *common law* systems. It is therefore usually equated with the French term *jurisprudence*.[1] However, what characterises *jurisprudence*[2] in French law is that it officially has no binding force,[3] since there is no principle of *stare decisis*. The status of precedent in the *civil* and *common law* systems thus constitutes their fundamental difference. The lack of *legal* authority of *case law* is essentially due to two provisions of the French Civil Code. Firstly, Article 5 of the Civil Code prohibits judges from issuing rulings by way of general and regulatory provisions. Secondly, judgments, whatever they may be, have effect only for the parties, in accordance with the principle of *relative res judicata*, enshrined in Article 1355 of the Civil Code. On the other hand, in the field of private law, case law, especially that emanating from the Cour de cassation, would be given genuine *de facto* authority,[4] which would take the form of two complementary rules, similar to the horizontal and vertical dimensions of precedent in *common law* countries. First, a 'law of continuity', whereby 'what the *Cour de cassation* has ruled in the past, it will rule in the future'.[5] Secondly, a 'law of imitation', according to which 'what the *Cour de cassation* has ruled, lower jurisdictions will rule'.[6] The mystery that surrounds precedent in French law is therefore the result of a significant gap between what is *said* and what is actually *done*,[7] a gap that has nevertheless tended to narrow in modern times. The official status of precedent is gradually evolving, with difficulty detaching itself from the history that has shaped it.

---

1 P. Malaurie, 'Les précédents et le droit' (2006) 58 *RIDC* 319: 'Precedents are judicial decisions handed down in similar cases; they constitute jurisprudence (in the French sense of the term)'.

2 The term 'jurisprudence' has multiple meanings and it is difficult to isolate a single definition. The broadest definition is as follows: 'All the solutions provided by judicial decisions in the application of the law … or even in the creation of the Law', G. Cornu and Association Henri Capitant, *Vocabulaire juridique*, 12th ed., PUF, Paris 2018.

3 G. Cornu, *Droit civil: Introduction au droit*, 13th ed., Montchrestien ('Domat/Droit privé' collection), Paris 2007, p. 229.

4 P. Deumier, 'Jurisprudence', *Répertoire de droit civil*, Dalloz, Paris 2017, §90.

5 H. Capitant, F. Terré and Y. Lequette, *Les grands arrêts de la jurisprudence civile*, 13th ed., vol. 1, Dalloz ('Grands arrêts' collection), Paris 2015, p. 84.

6 ibid.: 'They know that if they do not comply with the directives of the higher courts, their decisions will be censured'; M. Troper, *La théorie du droit, le droit, l'État*, PUF ('Léviathan' collection), Paris 2001, p. 171: '… because of the hierarchy of the courts, not only do judges in fact apply the rules laid down by the higher courts … but it is clear that if they fail to do so, their judgments could be set aside, *as if* they had violated a rule'.

7 M. Troper and C. Grzegorczyk, 'Precedent in France' in N. MacCormick and R.S. Summers (eds), *Interpreting Precedents. A Comparative Study*, Ashgate Publishing, Aldershot 1997, p. 112: 'the role of precedents in the French system can be considered either very small or very important, according to whether one looks at the justificatory material that is cited or the material that is in fact used by the courts'.

2. A BRIEF HISTORY OF PRECEDENT IN PRIVATE LAW

2.1. FROM THE *ANCIEN RÉGIME* TO THE *CODE CIVIL*

To understand the mistrust of case law in French legal thought, it is necessary to go back to the pre-Revolutionary period. Under the *Ancien Régime*, Parliaments[8] created law by issuing rulings (*arrêts de règlement*). These rulings had the distinctive feature of being disconnected from a particular dispute; the judges were creating a rule for the future. Not only did they participate in the legislative function,[9] but they also 'operated according to the system of precedent'.[10] Yet one of the major aims of the Revolutionaries was precisely to destroy judicial power.[11] This is what Robespierre had to say about *jurisprudence* during the debate on the role of the Tribunal de cassation:[12]

> This word *jurisprudence* – must be erased from our language. In a State with a constitution and legislation, the case law of the courts is nothing other than the legislation.[13]

In keeping with the ideas prevalent among the philosophers of the Enlightenment, it was during this period that the cult of statute law (*culte de la loi*) was established as the sole source of true law. Revolutionary texts reserved the power to enact the law to the legislature.[14] In this model of thought, judges must confine themselves to scrupulously applying legislation,[15] conceived as the expression of the general will.[16] The culmination of this desire to annihilate the creative power of the judge is probably to be found in the practice known as *référé-législatif*. Judges are required to refer to the legislature 'whenever they deem it necessary either to interpret a law or to make a new one'.[17] The judge, deprived of the right to interpret the law, is placed entirely under the dependence of the legislature.

8 The parliaments of the *Ancien Régime* were superior courts of justice responsible, from the time of the Capetians until the Revolution, for dispensing justice.

9 L. Josserand, *Cours de droit civil positif français*, 3rd ed., vol. 1, Sirey, Paris 1938, p. 23, §26.

10 C. Atias, *De la difficulté contemporaine à penser le droit*, PUAM ('Droits, pouvoirs et sociétés' collection), Aix-en-Provence 2016, p. 211.

11 C. Atias, above n. 10, p. 146: '... the revolution was made much more against judges than against the clergy or the king'.

12 Became the Cour de cassation by the *Sénatus-consulte* of 18 May 1804, adopted following the promulgation of the Civil Code.

13 Sitting of 18 November 1970, *Parliamentary Archives*, 1st series, vol. XX, p. 516.

14 *Loi du 16–24 août 1790 sur l'organisation judiciaire*, Art. 11: 'The courts may not directly or indirectly take part in the exercise of legislative power'.

15 Montesquieu, *Œuvres complètes: De l'esprit des lois*, Book XI, vol. II, Ch. VI, Les Belles Lettres, Paris, 1955, p. 72: 'The judges of the nation are ... only the mouth that pronounces the words of the law, inanimate beings who can moderate neither its force nor its rigour'.

16 Declaration of the Rights of Man and of the Citizen of 1789 (*Déclaration des Droits de l'Homme et du Citoyen*), Art. 6.

17 *Loi du 16–24 août 1790 sur l'organisation judiciaire*, Art. 12.

The Civil Code of 1804 was a partial break with the absolutism of the Revolution. In his famous preliminary speech, Portalis, one of the four drafters of the Civil Code, not only shook the fantasy of the perfection of statutes, but also rehabilitated *jurisprudence*. Affirming that it would be wrong to 'think that there could exist a body of statutes which would have provided in advance for all possible cases',[18] he considered that it was up to the judge, when the need arose, to 'branch them out, to extend them, by wise and reasoned application, to private hypotheses, to study the spirit of statutes when the letter kills'.[19] This vision is embodied in Article 4 of the Civil Code,[20] which marks the rehabilitation of judicial interpretation.[21]

For the first three quarters of the nineteenth century, case law remained 'under the legislation'.[22] Its role, however, went beyond literal analysis to identify the guidelines and coherence of the Civil Code.[23]

2.2. THE FIGURE OF THE JUDGE ALONGSIDE THE LEGISLATION

Subsequently, at the end of the Second Empire and the birth of the Third Republic, case law became a source of law in competition with statute law.[24] What some have described as the 'golden age of *jurisprudence*'[25] should be seen in the context of the ageing of the Civil Code, which was particularly affected by the changes brought about by the industrial revolution. One of the most striking examples of the emergence of a real creative power is the interpretation by the Cour de cassation of the first paragraph of Article 1384 (now Article 1242) of the Civil Code.[26] In the mind of the drafters of the Civil Code, this formula was limited to announcing the particular cases of vicarious liability (*responsabilité du fait d'autrui*) or liability for damage caused by things (*responsabilité du fait*

---

18 J.-E.-M. Portalis, *Discours préliminaire du premier projet de Code civil*, Editions Confluences, Bordeaux 2004, p. 19.

19 J.-E.-M. Portalis, above n. 18, p. 23.

20 Civil Code, Art. 4: 'A judge who refuses to give judgment, on the pretext of the silence, obscurity or inadequacy of the law, may be prosecuted as guilty of denial of justice'.

21 J. Chevallier, 'L'interprétation des lois' in G. Fauré and G. Koubi (eds), *Le titre préliminaire du Code civil*, Economica ('Études juridiques' collection), Paris 2003, p. 125: 'article 4 of the Civil Code recognises [the judge's] power, at least implicitly, to interpret the law; better still, it requires him to do so'.

22 P. Rémy, 'La part faite au juge' (2003) 107 *Pouvoirs* 22.

23 P. Malaurie, *Introduction au droit*, 8th ed., LGDJ ('Droit civil' collection), Paris 2020, p. 322.

24 P. Rémy, above n. 22, 30.

25 P. Malaurie, above n. 23, p. 323.

26 Art. 1384 of the Civil Code: 'A person is liable not only for the damage he causes by his own act, but also for that caused by the act of persons for whom he is responsible, or by things in his custody'.

des choses), i.e. animals and buildings, set out below.[27] The result was that, on the basis of this exegetical interpretation, the many victims of accidents at work caused by the development of machinery were deprived of compensation, as they were unable to attribute the cause of the accident to the fault of an identified person. It was at this point that the Cour de cassation, in its *Teffaine* ruling of 18 June 1896, established the general principle that a person is liable for the things in his or her care. In so doing, it renewed the interpretation of the first paragraph of Article 1384 of the Civil Code[28] in the light of a new context. As Philippe Rémy writes, '*the statute law has become the judge's mouth*'.[29] This prosperous period for the affirmation of judge-made law was not only characterised by a renewal of the interpretation of the texts of the Civil Code. The Cour de cassation also came to establish rules or principles in the absence of a textual basis. For example, in an 1892 decision, the courts established an action for unjust enrichment (*enrichissement sans cause*) based on 'the principle of equity which forbids enrichment at the expense of others'.[30] Whether case law proceeds by way of creative interpretation or creates a rule unrelated to a pre-existing normative text, it remains 'alongside the statute law' (*à côté de la loi*). *Jurisprudence* appears as a complementary body to legislation, which is reflected in the style of motivation of the rulings, which borrows its laconism from the statute law.[31]

2.3. THE FIGURE OF THE JUDGE ABOVE THE LEGISLATION

The position of a judge subject to the legislature, gradually becoming a potential co-author of the statute law, was to degenerate into 'the unheard-of figure of a civil judge censoring the law'.[32] How could a 'judge beside the law' become a judge 'above the law'? Article 55 of the Constitution of the Fifth Republic provides that 'treaties or agreements duly ratified or approved shall, upon publication, prevail over Acts of Parliament'. Pursuant to the aforementioned article, in a *Société des cafés Jacques Vabres* ruling of 25 May 1975, the Cour de cassation recognised its competence to review the conventionality of national legislation, the primacy of the treaty rule over it being accepted without discussion. Since then, it has been possible for the

27 F. Terré, *Les obligations*, 13th ed., Dalloz, Paris 2022, p. 1096, n° 974.

28 R. Saleilles, *D. (Recueil Dalloz)*, 1987, p. 439: '[The] function [of case law] is not to limit the statute law to the applications that it may have had in mind in the limited sphere of the economic state from which it was inspired, but to give it all the progressive vitality of a principle that operates and acts; the statute law, thanks to case law, must adapt to the progress of the times and to historical development itself'.

29 P. Rémy, above n. 22, 31.

30 Cass. Req., 15 juin 1892, *Patureau-Miran v. Boudier, publié au Bulletin.*

31 F. Zénati, *La jurisprudence*, Dalloz ('Méthodes du droit' collection), Paris 1991.

32 P. Rémy, above n. 22, 33.

courts, embodying the figure of the 'judge above the legislation'[33] to 'combat the statute law'.[34] In particular, the rise of fundamental rights has enabled national supreme courts to set aside legislation on the grounds that it is incompatible with a supra-legislative text.[35] Since, through the review of conventionality, the courts can repudiate provisions of a legislative nature while at the same time providing a legal basis for the solution they reach – making it possible to transgress legislation[36] without transgressing the *law* – the obvious result is a potential increase in their powers.[37] More recently, going beyond an *abstract* review of the conventionality of legislation, which would have the characteristic of focusing on the statute law independently of its application to particular circumstances, the judges, going further in the protection of fundamental rights, have accepted the possibility of a *concrete* review of the conventionality of the application of legislation to a particular case. The judgment that inaugurates this practice was handed down on 4 December 2013;[38] on the basis of Article 8 of the European Convention on Human Rights (ECHR),[39] the Cour de cassation ruled out the nullity of marriage between relatives, provided for in Article 161 of the Civil Code,[40] in a case where the marriage between a father-in-law and his daughter-in-law had lasted more than 20 years without being challenged. The Court clarified its methodology in two stages in a judgment handed down on 8 December 2016 in a similar case. It first reviewed the conventionality *in abstracto* of the legislative provision in question before:

> assessing whether, in the concrete circumstances of the case before it, the application of those provisions would not result in a disproportionate interference with the right to respect for private and family life guaranteed by the Convention in the light of the legitimate aim pursued.[41]

The 'concrete' review of conventionality extends to criminal matters, where strict legalism usually prevails;[42] surprising as it may seem, it can neutralise a criminal

---

33 P. Rémy, above n. 22.

34 P. Malaurie, 'La jurisprudence combattue par la loi, la loi combattue par la jurisprudence' (2005) 15 *Defrénois* 1205.

35 P. Deumier, 'Contrôle concret de conventionnalité: l'esprit et la méthode' (2016) *RTD Civ.* 578.

36 This hypothesis should be distinguished from the rare cases where the Cour de cassation has handed down a *contra legem* ruling, finding no justification in a supra-legislative rule or principle.

37 M. Cappelletti, *Le pouvoir des juges*, PUAM ('Droit public positif' collection), Aix-en-Provence 1990, p. 65.

38 Cass. civ. 1re, 4 décembre 2013, no. 12-26.066, *publié au Bulletin.*

39 ECHR, Art. 8.

40 Art. 161 of the Civil Code: 'In the direct line, marriage is prohibited between all ascendants and descendants and relatives in the same line'.

41 Cass. civ. 1re, 8 décembre 2016, no. 15-27.201, *publié au Bulletin.*

42 S. Pellé, 'Contrôle de proportionnalité et droit pénal: quelle "doctrine" de la chambre criminelle?' (2022) *Recueil Dalloz* 1186.

offence. In this respect, since 2016[43] and under the terms of the case law that has now become established, the Cour de cassation has ruled that:

> the criminalisation of conduct constituting a criminal offence may, in certain circumstances, constitute a disproportionate interference with the exercise of freedom of expression, having regard to the nature and context of the conduct in question.

At the same time, a final major trend is affecting the practice of precedent-setting before the Cour de cassation. Since 2016, the Court has allowed itself to cite its own precedents in a number of so-called rulings with *motivation enrichie*, in a bid to reform its motivation, which was considered outdated from both a formal and a substantive point of view. The traditional reasoning of the Cour de cassation is characterised by its terseness. The style of reasoning is marked by the conciseness of the reasons in support of the solution adopted by the Court, which usually does not make it possible to determine the real lines of argument that led to the choice made by the Court. The stated aim of the *motivation enrichie* is to compensate for what has proved to be a regrettable shortcoming. However, this kind of motivation only concerns certain types of judgments considered by the high court to be of prime importance. That is to say, judgments reviewing proportionality with regard to a fundamental right, judgments ruling on a question of principle, solutions of interest for the unity of case law, and judgments reversing case law. In addition to the reference to precedents, rulings with *motivation enrichie* should, where appropriate, also highlight the method used by the Court to interpret the relevant legislation, mention the alternative solutions that were rejected and, lastly, refer to the impact assessment (*études d'impact*) carried out where these played a significant role in the choice of the solution adopted.

Finally, it must be specified that, since 2019, the Cour de cassation has changed the formal style used to draft all its decisions. The Court has adopted what it calls a 'direct style' of motivation. Previously, an opinion of the Court consisted of a single sentence (*phrase unique*). The judgment now consists of several numbered paragraphs. Moreover, the main composite parts of the judgment are now clearly identified: 'facts and procedure', 'reviewing pleas' and 'Court's response'.

3. NATURE OF PRECEDENT

3.1. PRECEDENT IN THE SHADOW OF *JURISPRUDENCE*

In French law, it is traditionally held that the sources of law correspond to the *formal* sources of law, which take shape in texts and are the only ones capable

[43] Cass. crim., 26 octobre 2016, no. 15-83.774, *publié au Bulletin*.

of generating general binding legal rules. Legislation is the most topical embodiment of this. In addition to *formal* sources, there are *informal* sources or mere *authorities*. A major question that has animated French legal thought for over a century is whether case law is merely an authority, like *doctrine*, or whether it constitutes a source of law. Basically, for some authors, citing, in particular, the principle of the separation of powers,[44] case law can only constitute an authority.[45] On the other hand, for another part of the doctrine, based on a 'realist' conception,[46] case law constitutes a source of law in its own right. These authors note that case law plays a major normative role and accept that judges have the ability to create law outside the statute law.

Unfortunately, the Cour de cassation itself continues to fuel this debate. In a noteworthy ruling of 9 October 2001, it stated that:

> the interpretation given by the courts to the same rule at a given time cannot differ according to the period of the facts in question, and no one can claim an acquired right to a fixed body of case law.[47]

Case law solutions are, therefore, simply incorporated into the text being interpreted, even if the Cour de cassation's interpretation of the text changes. A declarative conception of case law is thus established even if this falls within the realm of fiction: the judge does not create law, but merely discovers a pre-existing state of the law that is supposed to have always existed. Moreover, case law is inherently retroactive, as the judge necessarily rules on facts that predate the judgment.

However, the natural retroactivity of case law can lead to deleterious consequences in the presence of an overruling.[48] The above-mentioned ruling is a perfect illustration of this. In this case, in 1974, a doctor monitoring a patient's pregnancy noted that the child was breech and recommended a vaginal delivery rather than a caesarean section. At the time, case law accepted that doctors were not at fault if they did not reveal exceptional risks to their patients. However, one of these risks materialised and the child was born with sequelae. When the child came of age, he sued the doctor for breach of his duty to inform (*obligation d'information*). His action was based on a change in case law in 1998, under which the Cour de cassation now requires doctors to inform their patients of the

---

44 R. David, *Le droit français*, vol. 1 (*Les données fondamentales du droit français*), LGDJ, Paris 1960, p. 162.

45 J. Carbonnier, *Droit civil: Introduction*, 1st ed., PUF ('Quadrige' collection), Paris 2004, p. 274: 'We can say [that case law] is an authority: it influences the decision more or less strongly, without ever imposing it in law'.

46 P. Esmein, 'La jurisprudence et la loi' (1952) *RTD Civ.* 20: 'It is to misunderstand reality too much to refuse to see [case law] as a source of law'.

47 Cass. civ. 1re, 9 octobre 2001, no. 00-14.564, *publié au Bulletin*.

48 The hypothesis in question is that of the Cour de cassation abandoning its own precedent.

exceptional risks involved. The Lyon Court of Appeal refused to hold the doctor liable on the grounds that he was not required to provide such information at the time of the events. However, the Cour de cassation overturned the appeal court's decision, applying the principle of retroactivity. As Pascale Deumier points out, 'in 2001, a doctor was found liable for failing to comply with a 1998 ruling during an operation in 1974'.[49]

This case caused such a stir in the legal community that the Cour de cassation gradually came to accept, on an exceptional basis, the possibility of modulating the effects of overruling its own decisions over time. Today, it summarises its position on the modulation of the effects of reversals over time as follows:

> While new case law applies ipso jure to everything that has been done on the basis and in reliance on old case law, the application of this principle may irremediably affect the situation of parties who have acted in good faith, in accordance with the state of the law applicable at the date of their action, so that the judge must assess the disadvantages justifying an exception to the principle of retroactive application of case law and determine, on a case-by-case basis, whether there is a manifest disproportion between the advantages and disadvantages.[50]

The paradox is striking: the very possibility of modulating the reversal over time implies recognition of the creative power of case law;[51] the Court accepts that judge-made law can only be valid for the future, thus contravening the provisions of Article 5 of the Civil Code.[52] This means that case law is, as a matter of principle, devoid of any normative authority, while by way of exception it is conceived as a source of law. Such a configuration is clearly nonsensical and logically untenable.[53]

Unsurprisingly, the Cour de cassation's citation of its own precedents has once again revived the debate on the status of *jurisprudence*. Some saw in it the Court's recognition of their binding nature, on the model of the *common law*, and its corollary, the weakening of the authority of the legislation.[54] Others have taken the view that this in no way confers on them the character of a

---

49 P. Deumier, *Introduction générale au droit*, 7th ed., Lextenso/LGDJ, Paris 2023, s. 377.

50 Cass. civ. 1re, 6 avril 2016, no. 15-10.552, *publié au Bulletin*.

51 N. Molfessis (ed), *Les revirements de jurisprudence: Rapport remis à Monsieur le Premier Président Guy Canivet*, LexisNexis, Paris 2005, p. 10.

52 Rémy Libchaber observes that 'everything is happening as if the Cour de cassation were not itself subject to article 5 of the Civil Code': R. Libchaber, 'Les articles 4 et 5 du Code civil ou les devoirs contradictoires du juge civil' in G. Fauré and G. Koubi (eds), *Le titre préliminaire du Code civil*, Economica ('Études juridiques' collection), Paris 2003, p. 143.

53 P. Jestaz, 'Les sources du droit: le déplacement d'un pôle à un autre' (1996) *RTD Civ.* 299: '[Jurisprudence] is treated ambiguously. On the one hand French jurists study case law extensively and sometimes idolatrously, in any case they teach it as positive law. But on the other hand, they officially deny it the status of an autonomous source'.

54 P.-Y. Gautier, 'Contre le visa des précédents dans les décisions de justice' (2017) 13 *Recueil Dalloz* 752.

binding norm, but that the exposition of precedents merely reveals the weight of its *de facto* authority, in a move towards transparency.[55] The debate continues because French legal thought is, to some extent, a prisoner of the legicentrism (*légicentrisme*) inherited from the Revolution.

However, it is now agreed that the question of whether or not case law belongs to the sources of law is insoluble insofar as it depends on the definition previously given to law. It is therefore essentially an ontological debate.[56]

3.2. PRECEDENT AS AN ARGUMENT

In order to transcend this debate, it seems necessary to conceive of sources as arguments, taking note of the fundamentally argumentative nature of law.[57] The focus then shifts from *jurisprudence* as a potentially normative object to precedent as an argument capable of constraining legal discourse.[58] It would then appear that, since there are very few novel legal issues that have not given rise to any precedent, the Cour de cassation follows its own precedents as a matter of principle, in order to ensure that like cases are treated alike.[59] It will only abandon a precedent in exceptional circumstances, if there are serious and good reasons to do so. One author has even observed that judges at the Cour de cassation were driven by a veritable 'cult of precedent'.[60] It is therefore interesting to observe that, beyond the divergence of doctrines between the civil law and common law systems, there is a convergence of practices with regard to the authority of precedent, which comparatists have not failed to reveal.[61]

---

55 P. Deumier, 'Et pour quelques signes de plus: mentionner les précédents' (2016) *RTD Civ.* 65.

56 F. Zénati, 'Clore enfin le débat sur la jurisprudence aujourd'hui' (1992) *RTD Civ.* 360: 'Whether case law is a source of law presupposes that we agree on what a source of law is and therefore on what law is. Depending on one's idea of the law, one will admit or refuse to admit case law as a source of law. The status of case law is a matter of ontology'.

57 N. MacCormick, *Rhetoric and The Rule of Law: A Theory of Legal Reasoning*, Oxford University Press, Oxford 2009, p. 14.

58 G. Leroy, *La pratique du précédent en droit français: Étude à partir des avis de l'avocat général à la Cour de cassation et des conclusions du rapporteur public au Conseil d'État*, LGDJ ('Bibliothèque de droit privé' collection vol. 365), Paris 2023.

59 ibid.

60 A. Bancaud, 'Une "constance mobile": la haute magistrature' (1989) 76–77 *Actes de la recherche en sciences sociales* (Droit et expertise) 31.

61 A. Gambaro, R. Sacco, L. Vogel, *Traité de droit comparé: Le droit de l'Occident et d'ailleurs*, LGDJ, Paris 2011, p. 50: '... between a system which, without declaring it openly, in fact respects precedents and another which, while proclaiming that it respects them, in fact attaches a large number of exceptions to the principle, the differences, which are nuanced, are ultimately more a matter of form than substance. In short, in none of its aspects does source theory establish a real dividing line between the *common law* and *civil law* systems'; see also J. Bell, 'English Law and French Law – Not So Different?' (1995) 48 *Current Legal Problems* 87.

4. HOW TO IDENTIFY A LEGAL RULE IN A PRECEDENT

4.1. COUR DE CASSATION'S PRECEDENTS AS QUASI-LEGISLATIVE RULES

It is customary for the Cour de cassation to formulate rules expressed in canonical terms, reminiscent of legislative language. It intends to impose these rules on the lower courts and on itself, so that in the minds of French jurists, the case law of the Cour de cassation has a *quasi-legislative* value.[62] These rules will then be applied to subsequent cases that fall within its scope: the precedent constitutes the major part of the syllogism, even though this is most often concealed in the reasoning. This effort at concealment is due to the fact that French judges, whoever they may be, officially derive their legitimacy from the legislation. However, all this is not without consequence. As judges of the Cour de cassation take refuge behind the letter of the statute, and even behind the will of the legislature[63] to give legitimacy to their normative choices, it is most often difficult to distinguish the creative element in their rulings.

In order to ensure the stability and uniformity of the law in France,[64] the Cour de cassation gives priority to its own precedents over those of lower courts. There seems to be unanimous agreement that, given the structure of the judicial system, only the Cour de cassation can create precedents. Thus, while it is true to say that lower courts are not legally obliged to comply with the precedents of the Cour de cassation, their rulings are subject to censure if they do not. Consequently, it is only in very rare cases that the appeal courts enter into 'rebellion'. In this context, either the rebellion is broken by the highest court, or the Cour de cassation abandons its own precedent and adopts that of one or more appeal courts.[65] While *open data* is likely to make the decisions of lower courts massively accessible and therefore potentially increase the attractiveness

---

62 F. Zénati, *La jurisprudence*, Dalloz ('Méthodes du droit' collection), Paris 1991, p. 177.

63 For a recent example, see Cass. ch. mixte, 21 juillet 2023, no. 21-15.809, *publié au Bulletin*.

64 *Code de l'organisation judiciaire*, Art. L. 411-1.

65 The Cour de cassation was, for example, reluctant to extend cases of vicarious liability outside the hypotheses set out in the first paragraph of Art. 1384 of the Civil Code. It was at this point that the lower courts began to resist and, in the case of damage caused by minors who had escaped from a re-education centre, ruled in favour of the existence of a general principle of vicarious liability. After 15 years of general resistance, the Cour de cassation reversed its position in the famous *Blieck* ruling of 29 March 1991 (Cass. ass. plén., 29 mars 1991, no. 89-15.231). On this occasion, it indicated that the legal list of 'persons for whom liability is incurred' was no longer exhaustive, D. Lanzara, *Le pouvoir normatif de la Cour de cassation à l'heure actuelle*, LGDJ ('Bibliothèque de droit privé' collection), Paris 2017, p. 205, no. 363.

of this *jurisprudence du fond*,[66] it is nevertheless likely that this will not overturn its authority due to the pre-eminence of vertical stability.

4.2. THE PROBLEM OF THE HIERARCHY OF COUR DE CASSATION PRECEDENTS

Does this mean that all the Cour de cassation's rulings have precedential value? The potential answer to this question is affirmative, insofar as all of them can undoubtedly be invoked as an argument. However, it is clear that they do not all have the same argumentative force. What makes the French Cour de cassation different from the UK Supreme Court, for example, is that it deals with several thousand cases every year.[67] Of these cases, the vast majority are of interest only to the parties to the dispute, in particular those where the Court exercises its *disciplinary* function, which some authors distinguish from its *normative* function. This raises the delicate issue of the hierarchy of the Cour de cassation's precedents. Basically, it can be said that the hierarchy depends on the conditions in which the ruling is formulated and how it is received by those who interpret it, in particular *legal doctrine*, one of whose fundamental tasks is to explain and criticise the Cour de cassation's precedents.

With this in mind, criteria are used to *classify* precedents according to their value, in order to prevent the Court's precedents from becoming a composite whole and their use from becoming impractical from an argumentative point of view. Firstly, it is often agreed that if the ruling emanates from *assemblée plénière* or a *chambre mixte*, i.e. the most solemn divisions of the Cour de cassation, weight should be given to that decision. Secondly, it can be established that the ranking of precedents from the Cour de cassation can be linked to the way in which they are situated in time. In this respect, French jurists, particularly practitioners, attach greater importance to recent precedents,[68] in the sense that they are supposed to reflect positive law. Nevertheless, some major rulings, even if they are old, have a high degree of attractiveness.[69] Lastly, the attractiveness of a ruling or decision will depend on the extent to which it has been published and the reactions of *doctrine* to it. In France, legal doctrine (*doctrine juridique*) is essentially the discourse on the law expressed by academics. Firstly, its purpose is to interpret and systematise the rules of positive law using a conceptualist approach, in particular by establishing legal categories. Secondly, beyond its

---

66 P. Deumier, 'Une autre jurisprudence?' (2020) 10 *JCP G.*, doctr. 277.

67 More than 16,000 civil appeals (*pourvois*), for example, were dealt with by the Court in 2021.

68 J. Carbonnier, *Droit civil: Introduction*, 1st ed., PUF ('Quadrige' collection), Paris 2004, pp. 274–75.

69 H. Le Berre, 'La jurisprudence et le temps' (1999) 30 *Droits* 71 and H. Le Berre, 'Temps, interprétation et droit' (1999) 30 *Droits* 73.

descriptive aspect, it inevitably includes a normative component insofar as it makes value judgments about the law. At the beginning of the last century, doctrine gradually abandoned the cult of the Civil Code which had been the distinctive feature of a doctrinal movement know as *l'école de l'exégèse*, and changed its object of fascination, focusing in particular on the case law of the Cour de cassation.[70] Since then, legal writers have contributed to knowledge of case law, in particular by selecting and promoting certain rulings; its mission is to extract the rules and principles derived from the rulings of the Cour de cassation and to bring them into coherence.[71] But, once again, doctrinal work cannot be reduced to a purely neutral and descriptive activity. Indeed, academic writers regularly criticise case law and propose alternative solutions. This raises the complex question of the impact of doctrinal discourse on the choices made by the Cour de cassation. It is agreed that legal doctrine is not a *source of law*, but only an *authority*;[72] authors are divided on the question of the extent of this authority.[73] Although this influence is inevitably difficult to measure, it should be noted that the *travaux préparatoires* regularly refer to the work of academic writers. With the advent of *motivation enrichie*, the Cour de cassation allows itself 'exceptionally' to refer to legal doctrine in its judgments.[74] The drafting guide published in 2023 states that 'neither the name of an author nor the references of a column or commentary should ever be indicated'. In this way, the Court seems to be endeavouring to perceive legal doctrine as an entity,[75] rather than as the work of individuals.[76]

It is necessary to return to the question of the hierarchy of precedents. In fact, it would be unreasonable to crystallise any position of principle regarding the possibility of ranking the precedents of the Court in absolute terms according to the criteria set out above. Any attempt at systematisation, particularly on the basis of criteria – which are more like indices – that are imprecise and therefore difficult to manipulate, would appear to be doomed to failure. Although it is undeniable that not all judgments have the same value, their ranking ultimately depends essentially on argumentative factors. From this point of view, the

---

70 P. Esmein, 'La jurisprudence et la doctrine' (1902) *RTD Civ.* 5 and following: 'The legal doctrine ... must take case law as its main object of study.'

71 It should be noted, however, that the *doctrine*'s historical disinterest in the case law of the lower courts is tending to decline under the impulse of their greater accessibility.

72 P. Deumier, *Introduction générale au droit*, 7th ed., Lextenso/LGDJ, Paris 2023, s. 385.

73 P.-Y. Gautier, 'L'influence de la doctrine sur la jurisprudence' (2003) 42 *Recueil Dalloz* 2839, 2839 and following; G. Canivet, 'La Cour de cassation et la doctrine. Effets d'optique' in C. Atias, C. Caillé, F. Collart Dutilleul, G. Goubeaux, F. Leduc, D. Mazeaud, A.M. Morales Moreno, E. Savaux, G. Vermelle and G. Viney, *Mélanges offerts à Jean-Luc Aubert*, Dalloz, Paris, 2005, p. 373 and following.

74 For an example, see Cass. ass. plén., 20 janvier 2023, n° 20-23.673, §9.

75 P. Jestaz and C. Jamin, 'L'entité doctrinale française' (1997) *D.* 167.

76 L. Aynès, P.-Y. Gautier and F. Terré, 'Antithèse de l'entité' (1997) *D.* 229.

ranking of precedents is less the result of a static conception according to which it would be possible to attribute an *a priori* value to them, than of a dynamic conception based on the value that the person arguing before the Court or the value that the Court itself wanted to attribute to them, through a relative subjectivity.

Today, however, it can be postulated that the judgments which are most significant, at least from the Court's point of view, are those which adopt *motivation enrichie*. In particular, before the introduction of *motivation enrichie*, it was sometimes difficult to determine whether the Court had abandoned one of its precedents or merely amended it.[77] This sometimes led to doctrinal disagreements about the real scope of the abstruse judgment. From now on, the Court undertakes to systematically state explicitly when it overrules a precedent.

As has been seen, it is extremely difficult to draw the line between what French legal writers refer to as *arrêts de principe* and *arrêts d'espèce*. The fact remains that an *arrêt de principe* can be defined as a ruling that sets out a rule or principle, which will certainly be applied to the case in point, but which will be called upon to cover other similar cases in the future. It is to be hoped that, in future, every *arrêt de principe* will benefit from *motivation enrichie*. If used properly,[78] this way of drafting judgments tends to reduce the mysterious nature of the lacunar judgments that the Court has tended to issue before the reform of its motivation, including in response to highly complex legal problems.

4.3. RELEVANCE OF *OBITER DICTA*

In this context, is there a place for *obiter dictum* in the case law of the Cour de cassation? French legal writers have recently developed a keen interest in this notion. Sébastien Tournaux defines *obiter dictum* as a rule of law set out in the decision, but outside the scope of the dispute.[79] In accordance with this definition, *obiter dictum* manifests itself in judgments by assuming either a pedagogical or a normative function. It is the latter function that is controversial because of the spectre of Article 5 of the Civil Code, according to which rulings must never be binding.

However, the work carried out on this concept shows that the contours of the notion of *obiter dictum* as it exists in *common law* systems cannot be transposed

---

77 J. Ghestin, 'De l'effectivité normative d'un arrêt de la Cour de cassation' (2015) *RTD Civ.* 1.

78 For an example of *motivation enrichie* that doesn't fully achieve its purpose, see G. Leroy, 'Dénouement sur la nature du délai de l'action en garantie des vices cachés' (2023) 18 *Gaz. Pal.* 18. The reasons given for a recent judgment (Cass. ch. mixte, 21 juillet 2023, no. 21-15809, *publié au Bulletin*) are intended to create the illusion that the solution is in some way linked to an interpretation of the law that complies with the will of the legislature, in order to conceal the Court's exercise of genuine judicial power.

79 S. Tourneaux, 'L'obiter dictum de la Cour de cassation' (2011) *RTD Civ.* 45.

to the French legal system, thus acknowledging the limits of borrowing terminology. In particular, legal scholars note that what they refer to as *obiter dictum is* binding.[80] This divergence in legal methods between common law and civil law can be attributed to the absence of a methodology of precedent in French national law. Above all, given that *obiter dictum* can be described as the argumentative context of the *ratio decidendi*[81] and that this context does not appear in French precedents because of the style of motivation, it is hardly surprising that the difference between *ratio* and *dicta* is not exploited by the arguments produced before the Court.[82] Time will tell whether this 'all-or-nothing French logic' will change under the impact of *motivation enrichie*.

5. MANDATE TO CREATE PRIVATE LAW

As has been seen, it appears that only the Cour de cassation is likely to generate precedents. Some of these precedents can be seen as creating law. A distinction can then be made between autonomous creation (see below Section 5.1.) and creation under external influence (see below Section 5.2.), of a more or less restrictive nature.

5.1. AUTONOMOUS CREATIONS

In the first place, creation takes place in the silence of the texts. For example, in three rulings handed down on 25 June 2003, the Cour de cassation created an autonomous method of terminating an employment contract, open only to employees, which was not provided for in any text of the *Code du travail*: the *prise d'acte*. This is a decision by the employee to terminate the employment contract on the grounds of misconduct on the part of the employer during the performance of the contract. This 'termination produces the effects either of a dismissal without real and serious cause [*licenciement sans cause réelle et sérieuse*] if the facts invoked justified it, or, if not, of a resignation'.[83] It should be noted, however, that while the 2003 rulings are undeniably innovative, they

80 S. Tourneaux, above n. 79. Most often, *obiter dicta* are set out in the form of a rule of law (S. Hortala, *Les obiter dicta de la Cour de cassation*, Dalloz ('Nouvelle bibliothèque des thèses' collection), Paris 2019, p. 256).

81 R. Siltala, *A Theory of Precedent: From Analytical Positivism to a Post-Analytical Philosophy of Law*, Hart Publishing, Oxford 2000, p. 65.

82 G. Leroy, *La pratique du précédent en droit français: Étude à partir de l'avis de l'avocat général à la Cour de cassation et des conclusions du rapporteur public au Conseil d'État*, LGDJ ('Bibliothèque de droit privé' collection vol. 635), Paris 2023, no. 138.

83 Cass. soc., 25 juin 2003, no. 01-42.679, *publié au Bulletin*.

in no way constitute a radical creation *ex nihilo*.[84] In fact, attention should be drawn to the fact that any effort at creativity in case law systematically stems from a gradual and sometimes more or less slow construction: 'instead of being an absolute innovation, it is a renovation'.[85]

Secondly, the creative activity of the Cour de cassation takes place on the basis of a text of statutory law, so that, in this case, the creation maintains a link with the text. In particular, it can flourish in a process of adapting the law to changing circumstances. Take an example from tort law. The question is as follows: can the keeper of a thing that has caused damage to another person be exonerated from liability by showing that the victim was at fault? The Cour de cassation has answered this question in the affirmative. In the 1930s, on the basis of the first paragraph of Article 1384 of the Civil Code, it ruled that the victim's fault was partially exonerating when it did not have the characteristics of *force majeure*.[86] 40 years later, this solution was strongly criticised in the case of motor vehicle accidents. How could it be acceptable for the victim to suffer a reduction in his or her compensation as a result of carelessness or negligence, even though the perpetrator of the damage was not liable to pay compensation, since he or she is compulsorily insured? This is why many academics argued that the legislator should intervene to protect the victims of traffic accidents. The reform was so slow to be adopted that the Cour de cassation changed the interpretation of the aforementioned article of the Civil Code in a 'provocative' ruling designed to force through a reform of the law of liability for motor vehicle accidents. In the *Desmares* ruling, it stated that 'only an event constituting a case of force majeure exonerates the keeper of the thing from the liability incurred by him by application of article 1384, paragraph 1er of the Civil Code'. Consequently, 'the behaviour of the victim, even if it was not unforeseeable and irresistible for the guardian, cannot exonerate him, even partially'.[87] The Cour de cassation, through an evolving interpretation, made a major overruling, thereby abolishing the partial exoneration enshrined in 50 years of case law.[88] The legislature feared that the *Desmares* precedent was too far-reaching, as its scope extended beyond traffic accidents, and hastened to pass the Act of 5 July 1985 to improve the situation of traffic accident victims.[89] Henceforth, under this statute,

---

84 F. Géa, 'Prise d'acte de la rupture' in *Répertoire de droit du travail*, Dalloz, Paris 2019, §7.

85 S. Goyard-Fabre, 'L'innovation dans le champ juridique ou le passé recomposé' (2014) 3 *Revue de métaphysique et de morale* 322.

86 Cass. civ., 8 février 1938, *Bulletin des arrêts Cour de Cassation Chambre civile* no. 23 p. 49.

87 Cass. civ. 2e, 21 juillet 1982, *Desmares*, no. 81-12.850, *publié au Bulletin*.

88 H. Capitant, F. Terré, Y. Lequette and F. Chénedé, *Les grands arrêts de la jurisprudence civile*, 13th ed., vol. 2, Dalloz ('Grands arrêts' collection), Paris 2015, p. 413: 'The consequences of this reversal were considerable: the fault or act of the victim, however serious, lost all exonerating virtue if it was not unforeseeable and irresistible. It was an all-or-nothing policy'.

89 *Loi no. 85-677 du 5 juillet 1985 tendant à l'amélioration de la situation des victimes d'accidents de la circulation et à l'accélération des procédures d'indemnisation.*

only the inexcusable or intentional fault of the non-driver victim can exclude his or her right to compensation. Having achieved its objective, the Cour de cassation abandoned its *Desmares* precedent in three rulings of 6 April 1987, once again recognising the partially exonerating effect of the victim's conduct, thereby returning to the initial solution. These rulings were welcomed by legal scholars, who argued that the denial of this partially exonerating effect could only be admissible in a system of compulsory insurance.[90]

5.2. CONSTRAINED CREATIONS

Case law creations must now be situated in their environment, which exerts a weight of varying intensity on the Cour de cassation.

5.2.1. The Influence of Conseil d'État Precedents

At the very least, the Cour de cassation is careful to ensure that its precedents, as far as possible, comply with those handed down by the Conseil d'État, the highest jurisdiction in the administrative judicial order. This is particularly apparent in labour law, where the case law of the Conseil d'État in civil service law (*droit de la function publique)* influences the case law of the social chamber (*chambre sociale*) of the Cour de cassation, and vice versa. This is a privileged influence and by no means an absolute constraint, which was only perceptible in the *travaux préparatoires* of the rulings until a ruling on 20 January 2023.[91] In this judgment, the Cour de cassation stated for the first time, in matters of social security law, that a precedent set by the Conseil d'État was an element that it had taken into account to justify the development of its own case law.[92]

5.2.2. The Influence of Precedents Set by the Cour de cassation's Counterparts

Where foreign courts are concerned, the degree of influence is probably even weaker. Although it remains rare, the *conseiller-rapporteur* or the *avocat general à la Cour de cassation* may make use of comparative law. Nevertheless, as F. Haid points out, 'the references to comparative law in these documents seem to be intended primarily to add emphasis to the presentation without claiming to have any argumentative significance'.[93] In other words, the comparative law argument is never, as it stands, decisive; it cannot override the reference to the national statutes or to case law. Until a ruling on 13 May 2023, the Cour de

---

[90] H. Capitant, F. Terré, Y. Lequette and F. Chénedé, above n. 88, p. 415.

[91] Cass. ass. plén., 20 janvier 2023, no. 20-23.673, *publié au Bulletin*.

[92] See also Cass. ass. plén., 8 mars 2024, no. 21-12.560, *publié au Bulletin*, §16.

[93] F. Haid, 'Les classes ou sous-classes d'arguments utilisables pour répondre à une problématique juridique de droit privé' (2021) 3 *RRJ* 1605, 1676.

cassation had never included in its motivation elements taken from precedents handed down by its counterparts at European or world level. In this ruling, in order to ensure a stronger premise, the Court noted that the interpretation it was about to adopt was in line with that previously adopted by the UK Supreme Court.[94] The comparative law argument, while not binding in any way, unlike the precedent set by the Court itself, nevertheless reinforces the strength of the argumentation.[95]

More radical is the constraint emanating from the European Court of Human Rights (see below Section 5.2.3.), the Court of Justice of the European Union (see below Section 5.2.4.) and the Conseil constitutionnel (see below Section 5.2.5.). These will each be briefly assessed in turn.

However, it should be noted at the outset that the case law of these various courts is contributing to a clear trend towards the 'fundamentalisation' of French private law (*fondamentalisation du droit privé*). This phenomenon refers to the rise of fundamental rights in the field of private law. This reflects the horizontal nature of the fundamental rights that can be invoked in relations between individuals.[96] For example, in contract law, the development of fundamental rights contributes to limiting the role of the will of the contracting parties, so that a clause that would unjustifiably infringe one of these rights could be neutralised by the judge.[97]

5.2.3. *The Constraint Emanating from the Precedents of the European Court of Human Rights*

This section will start with the precedents of the European Court of Human Rights (ECtHR). Article 46(1) of the European Convention on Human Rights (ECHR) provides that the 'High Contracting Parties undertake to abide by the final judgment of the Court in any case to which they are parties'. It follows from these provisions that the Court's judgments are binding on the state concerned. This is known as *res judicata*. The condemnation of France by the Strasbourg Court has thus led to changes in French private law. For example, the Cour de cassation refused to allow an individual to change sex, whatever the reasons.[98] However, the ECtHR condemned France in a ruling on 24 March 1992, stating that the Cour de cassation's precedent was incompatible with the right to respect

94 Cass. ass. plén., 12 mai 2023, no. 22-82.468, *publié au Bulletin*, §22–24.

95 C. Perelman and L. Olbrechts-Tyteca, *Traité de l'argumentation*, 6th ed., Éditions de l'Université de Bruxelles, Brussels 2008, p. 628.

96 C. Drouiller, *Ordre public et droits fondamentaux: Contribution à l'étude de la fondamentalisation du droit privé interne*, Institut francophone pour la Justice et la Démocratie, Bayonne 2021, p. 26.

97 R. Cabrillac, *Droit des obligations*, 15th ed., Dalloz ('Cours' collection), Paris 2022, p. 26.

98 Cass. civ. 1re, 21 mai 1990, no. 88-12.829, *publié au Bulletin*: 'transsexualism, even when medically recognised, cannot be analysed as a genuine sex change, as the transsexual, although having lost certain characteristics of his original sex, has not acquired those of the opposite sex'.

for private life, protected by Article 8 of the Convention.[99] As a result, the Cour de cassation abandoned its precedent in a ruling of 11 December 1992,[100] henceforth admitting that a transgender person, whose altered morphology and social behaviour give them an appearance that brings them closer to the sex they claim, could obtain a change of status.

What about the ECtHR's rulings that do not concern France? Can the Cour de cassation ignore them? Not at all, because they benefit from interpretative authority (*res interpretata*). In this regard, the Cour de cassation stated in a 2011 ruling that: 'States that have adhered to the ECHR are bound to respect the decisions of the ECtHR, without waiting to be challenged before it or to amend their legislation'.[101] Thus, for example, the Cour de cassation usually ruled that the unlawfulness of a piece of evidence should lead to its rejection in court. An employer who wished to rely on information collected by an automated personal data processing system prior to its declaration to the CNIL,[102] in defiance of the Act of 6 January 1978 on Data Processing, Data Files and Individual Liberties,[103] was denied the benefit of the right to evidence.[104] The Court reversed its position in a judgment of 25 November 2020, in the light of the *Lopez Ribalda v. Portugal* ruling handed down by the ECtHR on 17 October 2019. The Cour de cassation now holds that:

> the unlawfulness of a means of proof ... does not necessarily entail its rejection in the proceedings, the court having to assess whether the use of that evidence undermined the fairness of the proceedings as a whole, by balancing the right to respect for the employee's personal life against the right to evidence, which may justify the production of material infringing an employee's personal life provided that such production is essential to the exercise of that right and that the infringement is strictly proportionate to the aim pursued.[105]

This example shows that the Cour de cassation is obliged to bring its case law into line with that of the European Court of Human Rights.

5.2.4. *The Constraint Emanating from the Precedents of the Court of Justice of the European Union*

With regard to the judgments of the Court of Justice of the European Union (CJEU), the Cour de cassation has had occasion to state that 'CJEU precedents are

99 *B. v. France*, 25 March 1992, no. 13343/87, ECtHR.
100 Cass. ass. plén., 11 décembre 1992, no. 91-11.900, *publié au Bulletin.*
101 Cass. ass. plén., 15 avril 2011, no. 10-17.049, *publié au Bulletin.*
102 *Commission nationale de l'informatique et des libertés* (National Commission for Data Protection and Liberties).
103 *Loi no. 78-17 du 6 janvier 1978 relative à l'informatique, aux fichiers et aux libertés.*
104 Cass. soc., 8 octobre 2014, no. 13-14.991, *publié au Bulletin.*
105 Cass. soc., 25 novembre 2020, no. 17-19.523, *publié au Bulletin*, §16.

binding on national courts'.[106] In particular, a ruling in response to a request for a preliminary ruling binds all national courts that apply the provision interpreted by the CJEU, insofar as the CJEU constitutes *the authentic* interpreter of European law.[107] If necessary, this may lead the Cour de cassation to overturn a precedent.

Take the example of a case recently decided by the *chambre commerciale* of the Cour de cassation. Articles L134-12 and L134-13 of the *Code de commerce* transpose respectively Articles 17(3) and 18 of Council Directive 86/653/EEC of 18 December 1986 on the coordination of the laws of the Member States relating to self-employed commercial agents ([1986] OJ L382/17). Under the first of these texts, in the event of termination of his relationship with the principal, the commercial agent is entitled to compensation for the loss suffered. According to the second, the compensation provided for in Article L134-12 is not due in particular when the termination of the contract is caused by the commercial agent's gross negligence. The question arose as to whether breaches discovered by the principal after termination of the contractual relationship were such as to deprive the commercial agent of his right to compensation. The Cour de cassation answered this question in the affirmative.[108] However, on a question referred by a German court for a preliminary ruling, the CJEU adopted a position contrary to that adopted by the Cour de cassation.[109] Surprisingly, the Cour de cassation maintained its solution, disregarding the interpretation adopted by the CJEU.[110] The turnaround did not come until a ruling on 16 November 2022, in which the Cour de cassation referred to the *Volvo* ruling[111] to justify abandoning its established precedent.[112]

5.2.5. *The Constraint Emanating from the Precedents of the Conseil Constitutionnel*

Finally, with regard to the *jurisprudence* of the Conseil constitutionnel, it should be noted at the outset that it is responsible for reviewing the conformity of statutes with the Constitution, whether *a priori*, i.e. before they are promulgated by the President of the Republic,[113] or *a posteriori*. *A posteriori* control of the

---

106 Cass. civ 1re, 15 juin 2016, no. 15-16.356.

107 All the courts are bound by the interpretation given to a Union rule in a reference for a preliminary ruling, the judgment of the CJEU having general *erga omnes* effect (Case C-28/62, *Da Costa en Schaake NV and Others v. Administratie der Belastingen*, ECLU:EU:C:1963:6; Case C-453/00, *Kühne & Heitz NV v. Produktschap voor Pluimvee en Eieren*, ECLI:EU:C:2004:17, [2004] *ECR* I-837).

108 Cass. com., 1 juin 2010, no. 09-14.115.

109 Case C-203/09, *Volvo Car Germany GmbH v. Autohof Weidensdorf GmbH*, ECLI:EU:C:2010:647.

110 Cass. com., 24 novembre 2015, no. 14-17.747; Cass. com., 19 June 2019, no. 18-11.727.

111 Cass. com., 16 novembre 2022, no. 21-17.423, *publié au Bulletin*, §11, 12.

112 ibid., §13.

113 *Constitution du 4 octobre 1958*, Art. 61.

constitutionality of statutes has only existed since the constitutional reform of 2008. It is provided for in Article 61-1 of the Constitution, which states that:

> Where, in proceedings pending before a court, it is claimed that a legislative provision infringes the rights and freedoms guaranteed by the Constitution, the matter may be referred to the Conseil constitutionnel by the Conseil d'État or the Cour de cassation.

In accordance with Article 62 of the Constitution,[114] the decisions of the Conseil constitutionnel have the force of *res judicata*.[115] Thus, a decision of the Conseil constitutionnel is binding on a court as soon as it applies a statute that has been the subject of a constitutionality review. However, it is common ground that the Conseil constitutionnel is not the *authentic* interpreter of the Constitution, but only a *privileged* interpreter.[116] Apart from the authority of *res judicata*, the Cour de Cassation, in its *Breisacher* ruling of 10 October 2001,[117] refused to recognise the binding authority of *res interpretata* of the decisions of the Conseil constitutionnel. It must be understood that only what the Conseil has affirmed with regard to statute's text referred to is *res judicata*. By contrast, the Conseil's interpretations of the Constitution itself have only moral authority.[118]

As regards the interaction between constitutional case law and the case law of the Cour de cassation, it is worth noting that the Conseil constitutionnel accepts that 'by raising a priority constitutionality issue, any individual has the right to challenge the constitutionality of the effective scope conferred by settled case law on the provision whose compliance with the rights and freedoms guaranteed by the Constitution is being challenged'.[119] This is an application of the 'living law' doctrine enshrined by the Italian Constitutional Court. Under these conditions, the Conseil may sanction a settled case law interpretation, in particular by the mechanism of reservation of interpretation (*reserve d'interprétation*) going against the interpretation emanating from the Cour de cassation, which has been the subject of the review.[120] The interpretation of the Conseil constitutionnel replaces that of the Cour de cassation. By arrogating to itself the power to assess

---

114 ibid., Art. 62 *in fine*: 'No appeal shall lie from the decisions of the Constitutional Council. They shall be binding on public authorities and on all administrative authorities and all courts'.

115 Cons. const., 16 janvier 1962, no. 62-18 L. It is now admitted that the authority of *res judicata* extends to 'reservations of interpretation' formulated in a decision (Cons. const, 2 décembre 2004, no. 2004-506 DC), only if they are issued directly on the statute referred to the Conseil constitutionnel (Cass. Civ. 1re, 22 mars 2005, no. 04-50.024, *publié au Bulletin*).

116 M. Disant, *L'autorité de la chose interprétée par le Conseil constitutionnel*, LGDJ ('Bibliothèque constitutionnelle et de science politique' collection vol. 135), Paris 2010, p. 68.

117 Cass. ass. plén., 10 octobre 2001, no. 01-84.922, *publié au Bulletin*.

118 M. Verpeaux and M. Heitzmann-Patin, 'Contentieux constitutionnel: actes administratifs – compétences juridictionnelles' in *Répertoire de contentieux administratif*, Dalloz, 2022, s. 94.

119 See in particular, Cons. const., 6 octobre 2010, no. 2010-39 QPC.

120 M. Haulbert, *L'interprétation normative par les juges de la QPC*, Dalloz ('Nouvelle bibliothèque des thèses' collection), Paris 2020, p. 358.

the constitutionality of the Conseil d'État and the Cour de cassation's precedents, the Conseil constitutionnel adopts a position that shows little respect for their power to interpret legislation.[121]

6. IMPORTANCE OF PRECEDENTS IN PRIVATE LAW

The importance of the Cour de cassation's precedents in the development of private law can be understood by considering the pressure on its choices of the courts around it (see below Section 6.1.) and the Court's relationship with the legislator (see below Section 6.2.).

6.1. RELATIONS BETWEEN THE COUR DE CASSATION AND ITS JUDICIAL ENVIRONMENT

As regards relations with its judicial environment, the overall trend is towards the potential transformation of private law under external impetus, particularly from the CJEU or the ECtHR. The application by the Cour de cassation of the ECHR as interpreted by the Strasbourg Court is not fundamentally a *horizontal* dialogue, but rather a *vertical* one, in which the Cour de cassation yields to the injunctions of the ECtHR. This has been particularly apparent in the case of surrogate motherhood.

Under the terms of Article 16-7 of the French Civil Code, 'any agreement concerning procreation or surrogate motherhood is null and void'. Given the existence of this prohibition in domestic law, couples wishing to have a child have travelled to foreign countries where this practice is legal, to enter into surrogacy agreements. They then applied to have the child's foreign birth certificate transcribed into French civil status registers. Disputes arose on this issue. Initially, and in particular in three rulings of 6 April 2011[122] and two rulings of 13 September 2013,[123] the Cour de cassation, invoking the concepts of unavailability of personal status and fraud, refused to allow foreign civil status records to be transcribed in France. As a result, the transcription and establishment of filiation in France was refused in respect of both the biological parent and the intended parent. These solutions were condemned by the ECtHR in two judgments of 26 June 2014.[124] The Strasbourg Court in fact found a violation of Article 8 of the ECHR with regard to the right to respect for the

121 M. Haulbert, above n. 119, p. 359.

122 Cass. civ. 1re, 6 avril 2011, no. 09-66.486, 10-19.053 and no. 09-17.130, *publié au Bulletin*.

123 Cass. civ. 1re, 13 septembre 2013, no. 12-18.315 and no. 12-30.138, *publié au Bulletin*.

124 *Lebassée v. France*, 26 June 2014, no. 65941/11, ECtHR and *Mennesson v. France*, 26 June 2014, no. 65192/11, ECtHR.

private life of children. More specifically, it recognised that France had gone beyond what its national margin of appreciation allowed by obstructing, in a situation where the father of intention is also the child's biological father, the recognition and establishment, under domestic law, of the child's parentage with his biological father.[125] A few months later, the Cour de cassation overruled its precedent to bring it into line with that of the Strasbourg Court.[126]

6.2. RELATIONS BETWEEN THE COUR DE CASSATION AND THE LEGISLATOR

The relationship between the Cour de cassation and the legislator is usually one of constructive cooperation. Their relationship is best described as a back-and-forth movement. The reform of the French *droit des obligations* in 2016 is illustrative of such a movement; the content of the reform, with the aim of making the law more accessible, is largely confined to codifying the interpretations that the Cour de cassation had made of the provisions of the Code of 1804, through which it had significantly developed the law of contracts. It is therefore essentially a matter of consolidating case law by reintegrating it into the legislation.[127] However, a number of new statutory provisions have been introduced. These include the introduction of a provision in general contract law prohibiting any clause in an adhesion contract that creates a significant imbalance (*déséquilibre significatif*).[128] As this is a new provision, observers were eagerly awaiting the interpretation that the Cour de cassation would give to it, particularly with regard to the question of its relationship with the special law prohibiting unfair terms. The statute law is thus clarified, supplemented and sometimes adapted by case law.[129] And in a constant balancing act, the legislature may enshrine case law, without this necessarily resolving the problems of interpretation that surround the texts that pursue this objective.

More rarely, however, the legislator may intervene to break a precedent. Take the example of surrogate motherhood to illustrate the *bris de jurisprudence*. On the question of the transcription of filiation established abroad in respect of the parents of intention, the Cour de cassation forwarded a request for an advisory opinion to the ECtHR, on the basis of Protocol No. 16 to the ECHR.[130] In its opinion, the Strasbourg Court states that the child's right to respect for his or her private life requires domestic law to offer the possibility of recognising

---

125 *Mennesson v. France*, 26 June 2014, no. 65192/11, ECtHR, §100.

126 Cass. ass. plén., 3 juillet 2015, no. 14-21.323 and no. 15-50.002, *publié au Bulletin*.

127 F. Terré, P. Simler, Y. Lequette, and F. Chénedé, *Droit civil: Les obligations*, 13th ed., Dalloz ('Précis' collection), Paris 2022, p. 52.

128 Civil Code, Art. 1171.

129 See, cass. com., 26 janvier 2022, no. 20-16.782, *publié au Bulletin*.

130 Cass. ass. plén., 5 octobre 2018, no. 10.19.053, *publié au Bulletin*.

a parent-child relationship between the child and the mother of intention, designated in the birth certificate legally established abroad as the 'legal mother'. However, it does not require this recognition to be made by transcription into the civil status registers of the birth certificate legally established abroad. According to the ECtHR, it may take another form, such as the adoption of the child by the mother of intention, provided that the procedures laid down by domestic law guarantee that it is carried out effectively and promptly.[131] However, in two rulings of 18 December 2019, the Cour de cassation decided to 'change case law' by now allowing the transcription of all birth certificates that have been duly drawn up in accordance with foreign law and are free from fraud, regardless of the gender of the intended parent.[132] It thus went further than the ECtHR had required, deciding that transcription would henceforth be automatic. In the Bioethics Act (*loi de bioéthique*) of 2021, the legislature amended Article 47 of the Civil Code relating to foreign civil status records. The text states that such a record is authentic unless it is 'irregular, falsified or the facts stated therein do not correspond to reality'. It is now completed as follows: 'This is assessed in the light of French law'. This addition neutralises the case law of the Cour de cassation.

7. CONCLUDING REMARKS

It can be anticipated that, in the future, precedent will cease to be a collateral victim of the ambiguity surrounding the status of *jurisprudence* in France. It will henceforth usually be studied for what it is: a legal argument, the force and scope of which must be assessed without taking an ontological stance. However, it cannot be ruled out that precedent may, in rare cases, degenerate into a political instrument. This raises the question of the limits of precedent, which it will be up to the Cour de cassation to determine, taking into account its jurisdictional and institutional environment in a relationship of collaboration, deference, or opposition. In any event, there is no doubt that the future of private law will largely depend on the future of precedent and its limits.

131 ECtHR, Grand Chamber, Advisory Opinion, 10 April 2019, Application No. P 16-2018-00.

132 Cass. civ. 1re, 18 décembre 2019, no. 18-11.815, *publié au Bulletin*; Cass civ. 1re, 18 décembre 2019, no. 18-12.327, *publié au Bulletin*.

PRECEDENT IN GERMAN PRIVATE LAW

Marvin STRAUB

1. A GENERAL INTRODUCTION TO LEGAL PRECEDENT

A precedent is a court decision on a legal issue which is raised anew in a subsequent case.[1] In the German legal usage, the term *precedent* (*Präjudiz*) does not imply any statement as to its binding force because German law does not recognise the principle of *stare decisis*. In the absence of explicit legal requirements, the role of precedents in private law has, due to the importance of legal decisions, always been controversial in jurisprudence. Related to the question of their binding nature is the question of their legal source quality. From a constitutional perspective, any binding effect can be disputed, for example, because the judge is bound only by law and statute, but not by precedent.

1.1. CONCEPTUAL DELIMITATION

Among the sources of law, precedent must be distinguished from statutory law and customary law.

1.1.1. Statutory Law and Precedent

The most important source of German private law is statute. Unlike past codifications, today's statutes lay down the legal position using *abstract* rules rather than casuistry.[2] Being *bound* by the rule of law under Article 20(3) of the German Constitution (GG), courts must apply these abstract rules in their decision-making. Due to the abstract and general character of statute, a rule of the German Civil Code (BGB), for instance, applies to a multitude of different cases, whereas judicial precedent applies only to the *specific* circumstances.

1 See K. Larenz, *Methodenlehre der Rechtswissenschaft*, 6th ed., Springer, Berlin 1991, p. 429.
2 J. Neuner, *Allgemeiner Teil des Bürgerlichen Rechts*, 13th ed., C.H. Beck, Munich 2023, §7, nos. 21–26.

1.1.2. *Customary Law and Precedent*

Customary law is recognised as a second source of law beside statutory law.[3] Customary law may be created by both those who are subject to the law and those who apply the law.[4] The latter case refers to the so-called judicial customary law which evolves from *precedent* and must therefore be distinguished from precedent itself.[5] The key difference is that a customary norm has the same effect *as* statutory law by which the judiciary is *bound* under Article 20(3) of the GG.[6]

The formation of customary law not only requires a long-standing, consistent practice (*longa consuetudo*) but the concerned parties must also be convinced that this practice is legally necessary (*opinio necessitatis*).[7] For example, academic titles may be recorded in the German commercial register. Though this practice lacks statutory basis, it is recognised by customary law because the registration courts have been recording these titles for years and this practice finds the unanimous approval of scholars.[8] However, a constant and undisputed judicial practice of long standing alone is not sufficient[9] because without the subjective conviction of the concerned parties that this practice reflects a legal necessity, there is no effectual legitimisation for its quasi-statutory application.[10] The unwritten rule of law must correspond to the general sense of justice on the basis of a long-standing practice and thus be recognised and *consented to as a rule of law* by the persons concerned.[11]

Judicial decisions that fall short of this kind of consented practice qualify only as precedent and do not possess the binding force of customary law; the distinction is necessary in order to not overly restrict the determination

---

3 F. Bydlinski, *Juristische Methodenlehre und Rechtsbegriff*, 2nd ed., Springer, Vienna 1991, pp. 213–14; K.F. Röhl and H.C. Röhl, *Allgemeine Rechtslehre*, 3rd ed., Carl Heymanns, Cologne 2008, pp. 544–45; J. Neuner, above n. 2, §4, no. 5; for a critical view, see P. Raisch, 'Zur Abgrenzung von Gewohnheitsrecht und Richterrecht im Zivil- und Handelsrecht' (1986) 150 *Zeitschrift für das gesamte Handelsrecht und Wirtschaftsrecht* 117, 119–20 and M. Bertelmann, *Die ratio decidendi zwischen Gesetzesanwendung und Rechtssatzbildung an Hand höchstrichterlicher Rechtsprechung*, Diss. Bonn 1975, pp. 14–26 with further references.

4 In detail, M. Klose, 'Modernes Gewohnheitsrecht' (2017) 8 *Rechtswissenschaft* 370; S. Meder, *Ius non scriptum – Traditionen privater Rechtsetzung*, 2nd ed., Mohr Siebeck, Tübingen 2009.

5 Contrary to that, M. Bertelmann, above n. 3, p. 214.

6 See *BVerfGE* vol. 78, 214, 227; H.D. Jarass in H.D. Jarass and B. Pieroth, *Kommentar zum Grundgesetz*, 17th ed., C.H. Beck, Munich 2022, Art. 20 no. 53.

7 See *BVerfGE* vol. 122, 248, 269; *BVerfGE* vol. 28, 21, 28–29; *BVerfGE* vol. 22, 114, 121; K. Larenz, above n. 1, p. 433; J. Neuner, above n. 2, §4, no. 5 with further references.

8 See BGH 04.04.2017, *NZA* 2017, 734, 735–36.

9 Explicit *BVerfGE* vol. 122, 248, 269; see also F. Bydlinski, 'Richterrecht über Richterrecht' in C.-W. Canaris and A. Heldrich (eds), *50 Jahre Bundesgerichtshof: Festgabe aus der Wissenschaft, Band I. Bürgerliches Recht*, C.H. Beck, Munich 2000, pp. 3, 22; contrary to that, L. Enneccerus and H.C. Nipperdey, *Allgemeiner Teil des Bürgerlichen Rechts*, 15th ed., vol. 1, Mohr Siebeck, Tübingen 1959, p. 267.

10 See K. Larenz, above n. 1, p. 433.

11 See F. Bydlinski, above n. 3, p. 215; J. Neuner, above n. 2, §4, no. 7; M. Klose, above n. 4, 371–72 with examples and references.

of the legal position by the courts because it is only possible to deviate from customary law by an act of parliament or by a contrary practice of long standing (*desuetudo*).[12] Even the Federal Constitutional Court (Bundesverfassungsgericht or BVerfG) exercises restraint and holds the view that, for instance, the Grand Criminal Panel of the Federal Court of Justice (Bundesgerichtshof or BGH) may deviate from a court practice that has been recognised for decades in case this respective practice 'were only known to few people even in legal specialist circles'.[13] Due to the lacking *opinio necessitatis*, in these cases it is the task of the judicature to *review* the rules it laid down and develop them further where necessary.[14]

1.2. CONSTITUTIONAL IMPLICATIONS

As will be discussed later, there are different concepts to establish the binding effect of precedents. All of them are exposed to three constitutional objections: firstly, that any binding effect of precedents would contravene the rule of law to which the judiciary is bound; secondly, that it would conflict with the judicial independence; and lastly, that it would not be compatible with the doctrine of the separation of powers.[15]

1.2.1. Obligation of the Judiciary under Article 20(3) of the Constitution to Respect the Rule of Law

Except in a few cases,[16] precedent has no strong binding effect under German law. Sporadic and ever-isolated views that seek to provide court decisions with quasi-statutory effects have not prevailed because they lack a normative basis, apart from being constitutionally untenable. A contrary view negates even a restricted binding force of precedent by pointing out that the judiciary is bound to the rule of law under Article 20(3) of the GG.[17] However, this very obligation to respect

---

12 J. Neuner, above n. 2, §4, no. 8; see also BGH 04.09.2013, *NJW* 2014, 387, 389.

13 *BVerfGE* vol. 122, 248, 265, 269.

14 See *BVerfGE* vol. 122, 248, 267; also reserved J. Neuner, above n. 2, §4, no. 8; J. Esser, 'Richterrecht, Gerichtsgebrauch und Gewohnheitsrecht' in J. Esser and H. Thieme (eds), *Festschrift für Fritz von Hippel zum 70. Geburtstag*, Mohr Siebeck, Tübingen 1967, pp. 95, 121–22; E. Schlüchter, below n. 26, p. 49.

15 A. Ohly, 'Generalklausel und Richterrecht' (2001) 201 *Archiv für die civilistische Praxis* 1, 33–36.

16 For these, see in the text at below n. 91 and following.

17 See esp. F. Müller and R. Christensen, *Juristische Methodik*, 11th ed., vol. I, Duncker & Humblot, Berlin 2013, pp. 139–40 and F. Müller, 'Richterrecht – rechtstheoretisch formuliert' in *Richterliche Rechtsfortbildung – Festschrift der Juristischen Fakultät zur 600-Jahr-Feier der Ruprecht-Karls-Universität Heidelberg*, C. F. Müller, Heidelberg 1986, pp. 65, 78–79.

the rule of law is an explicit rejection of statutory positivism. Moreover, judge-made law[18] is indeed subsumed under the binding legal standards referred to in the rule of law.[19]

The decisive question is not whether the judiciary is bound by statute *or* precedent[20] but rather to what extent the judiciary must *comply* with legal interpretations contained in precedent. As a rule, the German judiciary is free to either adopt the prevailing opinion or to deviate from the views of a superior court,[21] which is why there is no *quasi-statutory* binding force of precedent. However, according to the Federal Constitutional Court, an explanation is mandatory 'when a court … wants to deviate from a *legal interpretation of a norm by the highest courts*'.[22] As a consequence, the obligation of judges to reflect the content of precedent does not prevent them from respecting the rule of law under Article 20(3) of the GG; instead, the rule of law actually requires judges to reflect on precedent of the highest courts for the purposes of preventing arbitrariness.[23]

1.2.2. Judicial Independence under Article 97(1) of the Constitution

The second constitutional objection against any binding effect of precedent could be seen in Article 97(1) of the GG. According to Article 97(1) of the GG, judges are independent and subject only to the law. The historical regulatory purpose of Article 97(1) of the GG does not preclude a binding force of precedent because the ambition of the drafters of the constitution aimed exclusively at 'not subjecting judges to any directive'.[24] This means that Article 97(1) of the GG relates merely to 'the relationship of the judges to the carriers of non-judiciary power'[25] for which reason the norm neither hinders an *intra-judicial* binding force nor does it even contain a statement in this regard.[26]

---

18 See BVerfG 14.02.1973, *NJW* 1973, 1221, 1222 – *Soraya*; J. Neuner, *Die Rechtsfindung contra legem*, 2nd ed., C.H. Beck, Munich 2005, p. 7 with further references.

19 W. Fikentscher, *Methoden des Rechts in vergleichender Darstellung*, vol. 4, Mohr Siebeck, Tübingen 1977, pp. 327–30 and M. Reinhardt, *Konsistente Jurisdiktion*, Mohr Siebeck, Tübingen 1997, pp. 461–67; for a critical view M. Bertelmann, above n. 3, pp. 54–58.

20 Convincing A. Ohly, above n. 15, 1, 34.

21 See only C. Hillgruber in G. Dürig, R. Herzog and R. Scholz, *Kommentar zum Grundgesetz*, 98th ed., C.H. Beck, Munich 2022, Art. 97 no. 49; therefore the judicature is 'constitutionally irregular' (*BVerfGE* vol. 87, 273, 278).

22 BVerfG 24.09.2002, *NJW* 2003, 501, 502 (emphasis added) with further references.

23 ibid., 501, 502.

24 (1951) 1 *Jahrbuch des öffentlichen Rechts der Gegenwart* 717; in detail with further references J. Neuner, above n. 18, pp. 8–9.

25 *BVerfGE* vol. 31, 137, 140; *BVerfGE* vol. 12, 67, 71; for a critical view K. Larenz, 'Über die Bindungswirkung von Präjudizien' in H.W. Fasching and W. Kralik (eds), *Festschrift für Hans Schima zum 75. Geburtstag*, Manzsche Verlags- und Universitätsbuchhandlung, Vienna 1969, pp. 259–60.

26 Controversial, see E. Schlüchter, *Mittlerfunktion der Präjudizien*, de Gruyter, Berlin 1986, p. 115; M. Payandeh, *Judikative Rechtserzeugung*, Mohr Siebeck, Tübingen 2017, pp. 166–72 and A. Ohly, above n. 15, 1, 35–36, each with references.

1.2.3. *The Doctrine of the Separation of Powers*

The third constitutional objection refers to Article 92 of the GG, according to which the judicial power is exclusively vested in the judges, whereas the task of law-making is awarded to the legislative power under Articles 77 and 78 of the GG. On this basis, it is claimed that a somehow binding effect of precedent would risk an entanglement of competences[27] and turn court decisions into 'magistrate edicts', thus overriding democratically developed principles of legislation.[28]

The argument is unconvincing for several reasons: *firstly*, the parliament has but a prerogative of law-making and not a monopoly;[29] *secondly*, the cases decided by the judiciary do not affect this legislative prerogative in any way because even assuming a binding force of court decisions, they are never issued in the form of abstract and general rules of law;[30] and furthermore, the usual headnotes in the decisions of German Federal Courts do not call into question the principle that any possible binding effect is limited to the *ratio decidendi*.[31] *Thirdly*, the implementation of the doctrine of the separation of powers under German law is not absolute.[32] §132(4) of the Courts Constitution Act (GVG), for instance, provides that an adjudicating panel of the BGH is to submit its decision to the Grand Panel[33] when this is 'necessary for the development of the law or in order to ensure a uniform application of the law'. More generally speaking, when the judiciary issues *praeter legem* decisions or specifies legal norms by way of interpretation, it does not claim a legislative role[34] but rather fulfils its *complementary function* resulting from its obligation to respect the *rule of law* under Article 20(3) of the GG.[35]

However, the judiciary shall not disregard the legal provisions issued by the parliaments; a court decision therefore violates Article 20(3) of the GG when 'the considerations forming the reasons given for the decision reveal that the court transcended its function of applying the law by assuming the role of a lawmaker'.[36] As long as the decisions adhere to these statutory provisions, a

27 To this objection in detail, J. Neuner, above n. 18, pp. 55–59 with references.

28 So indeed F. Müller and R. Christensen, above n. 17, p. 140.

29 M. Kriele, *Theorie der Rechtsgewinnung*, 2nd ed., Duncker & Humblot, Berlin 1976, pp. 60–63; A. Ohly, above n. 15, 1, 35 with further references.

30 J. Neuner, above n. 18, p. 57.

31 Closer on this aspect below in the text at n. 72 and following.

32 H. Honsell in J. von Staudinger, *Kommentar zum BGB*, Otto Schmidt/de Gruyter, Berlin 2018, introduction before §1, no. 212; A. Ohly, above n. 15, 1, 34.

33 See in more detail in the text at below n. 203 and following.

34 See already G. Radbruch, 'Rechtswissenschaft als Rechtsschöpfung: ein Beitrag zum juristischen Methodenstreit' (1906) 22 *Archiv für Sozialwissenschaft und Sozialpolitik* 355, esp. 363–64.

35 See C.-W. Canaris, *Die Feststellung von Lücken im Gesetz*, 2nd ed., Duncker & Humblot, Berlin 1983, pp. 37–38, fn. 95; in detail J. Neuner, above n. 18, pp. 47–84, esp. p. 56; contrary to that, F. Müller, 'Richterrecht – rechtstheoretisch formuliert', above n. 17, pp. 80, 84.

36 *BVerfGE* vol. 87, 273, 280.

binding effect of *legally induced* precedent strengthens the principle of the separation of powers because the reference to arguments contained in precedent ensures that subsequent decisions are tied in with these legal provisions as well.[37]

In summary, the constitutional objections against any binding force of precedents are not convincing for the reasons stated. Before looking at the various conceptions used to justify the binding effect, the following section will turn to history.

2. A BRIEF HISTORY OF PRECEDENT IN GERMAN PRIVATE LAW

Legal precedent has a changeful history in Germany. Based on (contradictory) passages of the Roman *Corpus Iuris Civilis*, medieval scholars qualified court decisions as customary law and consequently recognised them as a binding source of law.[38] Later on, in the Holy Roman Empire, the decisions of the Imperial Chamber Court, founded in 1495, were recorded in numerous collections and therefore gained considerable importance as a source of knowledge for the development of the law.[39] From the Chamber Court Code of 1555, the coeval literature concluded the authority of the Imperial Chamber Court to issue *conclusa pleni* (decisions of the whole court) with general binding force regarding unclear procedural and substantive questions.[40] Until the eighteenth century, the court was authorised to issue resolutions by means of majority vote; these resolutions qualified as substantive law as long as they complied with common law or imperial law and were not subsequently abrogated by the Visitation or the Imperial Diet. The decisions of the *single senates* also acquired force of law and were therefore binding, insofar as another senate was not allowed to take a contrary decision on similar circumstances.[41]

With respect to the sixteenth and seventeenth centuries, legal historians attribute the practical role of precedent to the coexistence of town law, state law and imperial law, and the corresponding lack of priority of any type of positive law.[42] However, at the beginning of the eighteenth century, critical voices emerged reproving the virtually legislative practice of the Imperial Chamber

---

37 See K. Langenbucher, *Die Entwicklung und Auslegung von Richterrecht*, C.H. Beck, Munich 1996, p. 25.

38 U. Müßig, 'Geschichte des Richterrechts und der Präjudizienbindung auf dem europäischen Kontinent' (2006) 28 *Zeitschrift für Neuere Rechtsgeschichte* 80, 81–82; in detail M. Payandeh, above n. 26, pp. 71–73.

39 U. Müßig, above n. 38, 80, 82; F. Diedrich, *Präjudizien im Zivilrecht*, Kovač, Hamburg 2004, pp. 45–48.

40 U. Müßig, above n. 38, 80, 83.

41 To the whole issue U. Müßig, above n. 38, 80, 84–85.

42 U. Müßig, above n. 38, 80, 86; M. Payandeh, above n. 26, p. 84.

Court, which at times took decisions in contrast to the law in order to then obey these decisions as precedent.[43]

While the territorial legislations in Kurhessen and Bavaria were quite open to a binding effect of precedent, Saxony and Prussia strictly delimited this effect. In Prussia in particular, the very critical attitude of Frederick II led to a statutory ban on interpretation and an obligation of the courts to direct an inquiry to the Department of Justice in case of doubts concerning the interpretation.[44] The scepticism towards judge-made law reached its peak in §6 of the Introduction of the General State Laws for the Prussian States: 'Academic opinions and previous court decisions shall not be taken into account for further decisions.' Any interpretative doubt had to be 'reported to the Legal Committee requesting its appraisal', but since the committee was found to be prone to error, this procedural obligation was mitigated only shortly thereafter.[45]

The nineteenth century is marked by the impact of the German Historical School of Law; therefore, the customary law resulting from the convictions of both the public and legal practitioners was deemed as the leading source of law, while disappointment regarding the expected codifications re-enhanced the standing of court decisions.[46] Some territorial statutes on precedent declared court decisions to be generally binding, while others provided an obligation to submit the case to the Secret Supreme Tribunal, however, only in those cases in which a court wished to deviate from its own former decision.[47] In territories without such statutes on precedent, both literature and jurisprudence established the prevailing opinion that the court practice already generates customary law and thereby acquires binding force.[48]

This concept of binding court practice ended up with the establishment of the Reich Court of Justice in 1879: 'This particular court practice … cannot rightfully pretend to be adhered to … because it is solely based on an incorrect notion of the decisive legal rule.'[49] In this regard, the German Civil Code (BGB), which came into force in 1900, did not establish any uniform paradigm regarding the effect of precedent because it made *no statement* on the role of court decisions in the interpretation of statute.[50] In view of the increasing number of court decisions and their high practical and factual relevance, it seems contra-indicated not to make a legal statement. This initial situation explains why so much has been written in the twentieth and twenty-first centuries on the question of whether

43 U. Müβig, above n. 38, 80, 86.
44 M. Payandeh, above n. 26, pp. 74–77; U. Müβig, above n. 38, 80, 87–88, 88–90.
45 U. Müβig, above n. 38, 80, 90, 92.
46 U. Müβig, above n. 38, 80, 96.
47 M. Payandeh, above n. 26, pp. 78–83; U. Müβig, above n. 38, 80, 97.
48 U. Müβig, above n. 38, 80, 98–100.
49 *RGZ* vol. 1, 313; more examples at U. Müβig, above n. 38, 80, 101.
50 H. Honsell, above n. 32, introduction before §1, no. 202; M. Payandeh, above n. 26, p. 81.

and under what conditions judicial decisions can be binding. Thus, there is a detailed jurisprudential dispute on the question of the role of precedents in private law.

3. HOW TO IDENTIFY A LEGAL RULE IN A PRECEDENT

Before turning to the different concepts on how to justify binding effect of precedent, the questions of *which part* of a decision can have binding effect at all and which courts are competent to create such precedent, are considered.

3.1. THE INTERMEDIARY FUNCTION OF PRECEDENT

Although §313(3) of the German Code of Civil Procedure (ZPO) dictates that the reasons given for the decision shall contain only the considerations 'of the facts and the legal aspects on which the decision *is based*'[51] at times the courts use the occasion to complement some considerations *beside* the contentious issue. Yet, the *warranted correctness* of the decision refers exclusively to the *ratio decidendi* which therefore is to be distinguished from *obiter dicta*.[52]

The *ratio decidendi* refers to the decisive rule which connects the statutory norm and the relevant facts of the specific case.[53] This rule must feature the degree of abstraction strictly necessary in order to decide similar circumstances in an equal manner.[54] In Germany one speaks of the 'intermediary function of precedent'[55] because a judicial decision not only serves to regulate the specific case but also provides a maxim[56] or, more precisely, a possible model for the reasoning of subsequent decisions.[57] According to the Federal Constitutional Court, it is:

> in the very nature of the higher courts that they will emphasise the general principles in their decisions of specific cases and that they try to develop general legal principles which may guide the lower courts … when deciding similar cases.[58]

---

51 Emphasis added.

52 See H.-M. Pawlowski, *Methodenlehre für Juristen*, 3rd ed., C.F. Müller, Heidelberg 1999, nos. 1028–75, esp. 1034; C. Schönberger, 'Höchstrichterliche Rechtsfindung und Auslegung gerichtlicher Entscheidungen' (2012) 71 *Veröffentlichungen der Vereinigung der Deutschen Staatsrechtslehrer* 296, 322 with further references; contrary to that, K.F. Röhl and H.C. Röhl, above n. 3, p. 568.

53 E. Schlüchter, above n. 26, p. 123.

54 J. Neuner, above n. 18, p. 59.

55 E. Schlüchter, above n. 26, pp. 123–26; J. Neuner, above n. 18, p. 59; K. Langenbucher, above n. 37, p. 93 and more often.

56 M. Kriele, *Recht und praktische Vernunft*, Cologne 1979, s. 98.

57 See E. Schlüchter, above n. 26, p. 123.

58 *BVerfGE* vol. 18, 224, 237–38.

3.2. FEDERAL SUPREME COURT PRECEDENT

This peculiar function of the federal supreme courts justifies their sole authority to issue binding precedent. The following refers only to the *courts of last resort*, in civil proceedings, that is to say, the Federal Court of Justice (BGH) under §133 of the GVG and the Federal Labour Court (BAG) under §72(1), sentence 1 of the Labour Courts Act (ArbGG). Due to the limited territorial jurisdiction of the Higher Regional Courts (OLG), they are not in the position to fulfil the task of harmonising jurisdiction on a federal level, and therefore not included in the notion of 'federal supreme court'.[59]

In spite of this limitation, the decisions of the courts of first instance (local court (AG) and district court (LG)) are of practical importance insofar as they serve as a *reference* for new developments. For instance, if a lawyer filing a suit with the District Court of Hamburg refers to a pertinent decision of the District Court of Munich, experience shows that the judge in Hamburg will look into the reasoning of the judiciary in Munich. However, these references never qualify as binding precedent granting legitimate expectations because even with regard to unclear legal questions, the decisions of lower courts may always be set aside by the competent superior court.[60] Instead, if a judicature of a federal supreme court already exists, any *deviating* decision cannot be a basis of legitimate expectations because the deviating lower court *must* by all means admit the applicable appeal.[61] Lawyers, too, may rely on decisions of the federal supreme courts, and usually do not need to point out deviating decisions of lower courts to their clients.[62]

3.3. HOW TO DETERMINE THE *RATIO DECIDENDI*

In Germany, two approaches are discussed for the determination of the *ratio decidendi*: the first one is based on *formal criteria* originating from the Anglo-American legal practice, the second one on the methodological means of *interpretation*.

3.3.1. *Formal Criteria*

A *purely* formal determination of the main reasons by means of fixed assessment patterns is unfeasible because the attempt to remove all *obiter dicta* by logical

59 See D. Olzen, 'Die Rechtswirkungen geänderter höchstrichterliche Rechtsprechung in Zivilsachen' (1985) 40(4) *Juristenzeitung* 155, 155.

60 See K. Larenz and C.-W. Canaris, *Methodenlehre der Rechtswissenschaft*, 3rd ed., Springer, Berlin 1995, p. 257.

61 See also in the text at below n. 196 and following.

62 See BGH 06.11.2008, *NJW* 2009, 1593, 1594 with further references.

deductions cannot be completely successful.[63] Goodhart's Test[64] may be helpful to gather the relevant facts, but the monocausal perspective neglects other aspects, such as, for instance, the reasoning of the judge or his or her referring to relevant precedents.[65] Wambaugh's Test[66] uses formal logic in order to abstract the obvious idea that only the reasons that 'caused the decision' can be part of the *ratio*: if A then B, in which B is the effective result and A is an excerpt of the reasons of the decision. Whether A is also a part of the *ratio decidendi* must be asserted by negating A. If non-A still results in B, then A was only an *obiter dictum* according to Wambaugh's Test because it obviously did not affect the decision. This approach may help to exclude absolutely incidental statements of the court from the *ratio decidendi*, but most arguments will affect the result to a greater or lesser extent. This is why this test does little to identify the really essential aspects of a decision.[67] Therefore, the formulation partially encountered in the German debate defining *ratio* as a condition '*sine qua non*' of the specific decision is not suitable as a sole criterion. It is also not convincing to abandon the whole distinction between *ratio* and *obiter dictum* just because a non-ambiguous distinction seems impossible.[68]

3.3.2. *The Interpretation of the Decision*

The more convincing way to determine the *ratio decidendi* is to use the methodology of legal interpretation.[69] The exclusive source of insight is the court decision as recorded in writing, thus making literal sense and giving contextual meaning to the decisive elements which separate the *ratio decidendi* from any 'decorative attachment'.[70] Since precedents are not abstract or general norms, the lower courts do not interpret them as they would interpret statute but 'on the basis of their implicit knowledge as to *how* court decisions are to be understood.'[71]

The German Federal Courts in particular frequently precede their decisions with headnotes. These headnotes appear as legal rules, yet they are mere *abstracts of the reasons given for the decision.* They do not contain rules that would be

63 K. Langenbucher, above n. 37, pp. 68–71; also critical M. Payandeh, above n. 26, p. 463–64.

64 A.L. Goodhart, 'Precedent in English and Continental Law' (1943) 50 *Law Quarterly Review* 40; A.L. Goodhart, 'Determining the Ratio Decidendi of a Case' (1930) 40 *Yale Law Journal* 161.

65 Convincing K. Langenbucher, above n. 37, p. 71 with further references.

66 E. Wambaugh, *The Study of Cases*, Little Brown, Boston 1894, pp. 8, 17 and following.

67 K. Langenbucher, above n. 37, p. 69.

68 See to that opinion K. Langenbucher, above n. 37, pp. 71–75 with references.

69 See e.g. K. Larenz and C.-W. Canaris, above n. 60, pp. 178–80; K. Langenbucher, above n. 37, pp. 75–93 and M. Payandeh, above n. 26, pp. 460–63.

70 K. Larenz and C.-W. Canaris, above n. 60, p. 178.

71 M. Albers, 'Höchstrichterliche Rechtsfindung und Auslegung gerichtlicher Entscheidungen' (2012) 71 *Veröffentlichungen der Vereinigung der Deutschen Staatsrechtslehrer* 257, 270 (emphasis added).

equably applicable to other cases[72] but can only be understood in light of the specific decision, which is why a headnote may not be equated with the *ratio decidendi*.[73] The recently emerged academic opinion that judicial headnotes must invariably be interpreted and applied as abstract and general statutory rules is, therefore, not convincing.[74] One should not be blinded by the formal appearance of the headnotes as abstract and general rules but, at the most, use them as a hint to the decisive legal aspects considering the context of the respective case at hand and the reasons given by the court.[75] The German courts would misconceive their function if they 'wished to establish general rules by deciding a specific case'.[76]

3.3.2.1. Limitation and Generalisation of Precedent

When interpreting court decisions, one must distinguish between the first decision on a certain topic and an established jurisprudence. An isolated decision is not an appropriate basis for a judge-made rule because the scope for interpretation is much larger than it is with a settled wording which is constantly and literally applied and quoted by the judiciary.[77] Moreover, courts tend to enunciate conceptions that go beyond the decision of the specific case when they encounter *new legal issues*.[78] Without a thorough enquiry of the underlying facts, there is a risk of hastily *over-interpreting* a precedent on a new matter,[79] which is often followed by frustration in case the Federal Court of Justice substantiates its previous decision by defining certain restrictions and exceptions in later cases.[80]

Developments towards generalisation are certainly present in judicial practice,[81] as was the case with contractual liability claims of third parties which the Reich Court of Justice originally recognised exclusively within lease agreements, and which were afterwards extended to other contract types as well.[82]

---

72 K. Larenz, above n. 1, p. 359.

73 H.-M. Pawlowski, above n. 52, nos. 80–80a.

74 T. Lundmark and S. Herrmann, 'Auslegung von Rechtsprechung' (2020) 1–2 *Neue Juristische Wochenschrift* 28, 30, 31, explicitly assert that 'statutory norms are in no way different than judge-made norms [!]' and 'subject not only to a similar but to the identical methodology', further claiming that this insight is 'as simple as it is hitherto unknown.' Such equivalences have already been rejected by H. Coing, 'Zur Ermittlung von Sätzen des Richterrechts' (1975) *Juristische Schulung* 277, 278: 'The treatment of judicial decisions as if they were statutory norms … is inadmissible because it contrasts the peculiarity of judge-made law.'

75 See for the limits of the interpretation of the wording, K. Langenbucher, above n. 37, pp. 77–78.

76 J. Esser, *Grundsatz und Norm in der richterlichen Fortbildung des Privatrechts*, 4th ed., Mohr Siebeck, Tübingen 1990, p. 268.

77 See K. Langenbucher, above n. 37, pp. 77, 82 with examples.

78 K. Larenz, above n. 1, p. 358.

79 C. Schönberger, above n. 52, 296, 322.

80 Example at K. Larenz, above n. 1, p. 359; see also M. Payandeh, above n. 26, p. 462.

81 See for the analogous application of precedents, K. Langenbucher, above n. 37, pp. 94–95, 101.

82 See K. Larenz, *Lehrbuch des Schuldrechts*, 14th ed., vol. I (*Allgemeiner Teil*), C.H. Beck, Munich 1987, pp. 224–31.

This kind of gradual expansion and solidification of precedent is a particular feature of the judge-made norm-concretisation. Therefore, in a chain of precedents, one must always interpret the specific decision in the context of all precedents.[83] This is why judicial headnotes often contain comments in brackets defining their relation to former decisions; for instance, the decision BGHZ 69, 95 adds the comments 'clarification of BGHZ 63, 45' to its first headnote and 'confirmation of BGHZ 61, 59' to the fourth headnote. One can also find comments such as 'in continuation of the decision ...' or 'supplementing the decision ...'.[84] For persons applying and interpreting the law, this self-referential process of concretisation is very useful in order to correctly grasp the core of a decision.

3.3.2.2. Example Case

As a conclusion, the matter can be illustrated by analysing[85] the decision BGHZ 44, 321 and following, in which the *underlying facts* were essentially the following: the plaintiff had leased a piece of land from the testatrix. He had built a restaurant on the property, thus effecting an increase in the value of the land of 74,000 DM. The basis for the construction was a promise of the testatrix to bequeath the piece of land to the plaintiff by means of a disposition by will. In truth, the testatrix revoked the respective will and subsequently appointed the defendants as her heirs. Consequently, the plaintiff demanded from the defendants the payment of 74,000 DM because the result the plaintiff intended to secure by his performance was not achieved (*condictio causa data causa non secuta* under §812(1), sentence 2, 2nd alternative of the BGB).

The *reasons given for the decision* contained the following clauses: a claim under §812(1), sentence 2, 2nd alternative of the BGB requires that the parties agreed on an intended result of the contract, which does not necessarily have to be contractually binding, especially because a binding agreement would already lead to a contractual claim for restitution. This agreement must always be asserted in the respective case at hand; it may also be a tacit one, and especially, if the recipient knew and approved of the result intended by the performing party, the silence of the recipient must be deemed as consent. All these clauses are part of the *ratio decidendi* because they are of the essence for interpreting and applying §812(1), sentence 2, 2nd alternative of the BGB in the case at hand. In contrast, the further clause that 'a unilateral expectation of the performing party' does not suffice[86] is an *obiter dictum*, for the court assumed that in fact, there was a bilateral agreement.

---

83 K. Langenbucher, above n. 37, p. 81.

84 BGH 07.10.1994, *NJW* 1994, 3346 (headnotes).

85 According to H. Coing, above n. 74, 277, 282.

86 *BGHZ* vol. 44, 321, no. 13.

This distinction between *ratio decidendi* and *obiter dictum* would also have been the logical result using only the formal criteria described in Section 3.3.1., yet the BGH provides a distinction between the current and previous decisions, thus giving a more detailed shape to the current one. The senate of the BGH, especially, does not want to follow the former statements of the Reich Court of Justice regarding tacit agreements, insofar as their meaning differed from the reasons given for the current decision.[87] Ultimately, the BGH positions this current decision within a chain of precedents,[88] so that one has to look into the referenced findings in order to correctly comprehend the *ratio decidendi*.[89] However, the interpretative context may lose significance once a precedent is constantly applied because in this case, its content will be gradually shifted to an abstract level.[90]

4. THE NATURE OF PRECEDENT

This contribution has already discussed the constitutional implications and will now set out the difficulties regarding legal theory and methodology when establishing a binding force of precedent within a system that does not recognise the general principle of *stare decisis*. The following section will begin with the specific provisions that exceptionally design a binding force of precedent.

4.1. STATUTORY BINDING FORCE OF PRECEDENT

According to §31(1) of the BVerfGG, the decisions of the Federal Constitutional Court (BVerfG) are binding on *all* courts and public authorities. This extensive binding force is due to the status and function of the BVerfG which, according to §1(1) of the BVerfGG, is an 'autonomous and independent federal court' and therefore stands *beyond* the stages of appeal; it has the final say on the interpretation of the Constitution.[91] As to the binding force under §31(1) of the BVerfGG, this means, *inter alia*, the following:

> If, within the so-called constitution-conformant interpretation of a non-constitutional norm, the Federal Constitutional Court declares that certain per se possible interpretations of this norm would conflict with the constitution, no other court may deem these interpretations constitutional.[92]

---

87 ibid.
88 ibid.
89 So in the result also H. Coing, above n. 74, 277, 283.
90 A. Ohly, above n. 15, 1, 41.
91 *BVerfGE* vol. 48, 40, 45; *BVerfGE* vol. 70, 134, 136–37.
92 *BVerfGE* vol. 40, 88, 94.

Also, *within* the stages of appeal, there may be a statutory binding force of a decision from a higher court. For instance, in the event a decision is reversed by the court of last resort and remitted to the court of appeal for further proceedings, the court of appeal, according to §563(2) of the ZPO, 'must base its decision on the legal assessment on which the reversal of the decision was based'. This provision prevents a situation in which 'the final decision is delayed or even circumvented by a constant shifting between lower and higher court because neither of them will change their legal opinion'.[93] As this rule only applies to an individual case, it is not a matter of binding precedents in relation to other cases.

Ultimately, the binding force may be based on *substantive res judicata* under §322(1) of the ZPO. In German civil procedure, this is the case when an *incidental question* relevant to the case has already been answered by a final decision. For example, the court deciding on vindication of property under §985 of the BGB[94] is not authorised to recheck the ownership situation which has already been assessed in a former and now final decision, as long as the factual circumstances have remained unaltered (*non bis in idem*); the judicial assessment in this case therefore has binding force.[95] As this rule also only applies to an individual case, it is not a matter of binding precedents in relation to other cases. This brief overview was only intended to show in which cases German law grants a court decision binding effect for subsequent decisions. The following section will now turn to the legal source quality of precedents.

4.2. PRECEDENT AS A SOURCE OF LAW

There is a broad academic discussion on the question of whether precedent may be recognised as a *source of law*. The German term for precedent (*Präjudiz*) is ambiguous. The classic methodology only qualifies statutory and customary law as sources of law.[96]

Some claim that statutes and court decisions have the *same rank* because they are an expression of the same objective law.[97] Where this is supposed to postulate a *norm-like* binding of the judiciary to precedent, the binding to the statutory laws would dissolve over time. Such a classification of court decisions

93 Gemeinsamer Senat der obersten Gerichtshöfe des Bundes 06.02.1973, *NJW* 1973, 1273, 1274 to the old version of the identical wording of §565, sentence 2 of the ZPO.

94 Wording: 'The owner may require the possessor to return the thing.'

95 See only P. Gottwald in T. Rauscher and W. Krüger, *Münchener Kommentar zur Zivilprozessordnung: ZPO*, 6th ed., C.H. Beck, Munich 2020, §322, no. 52.

96 K. Larenz, above n. 1, p. 432, and the references above n. 3.

97 Explicit G. Less, *Vom Wesen und Wert des Richterrechts*, von Palm & Enke, Erlangen 1954, p. 66; H. Kruse, *Das Richterrecht als Rechtsquelle des innerstaatlichen Rechts*, Mohr Siebeck, Tübingen 1971, pp. 7 and following; see also W. Fikentscher, above n. 19, p. 317.

as a norm-like source of law lacks any legal basis and is therefore rejected by the prevailing opinion.[98]

Court decisions can either fulfil or fail the obligation to comply with the law in accordance to Article 20(3) of the GG, but can never themselves serve as a binding legal norm within the meaning of this provision.[99] In fact, it is one of the fundamental functions of the judiciary to review former decisions and renounce interpretations formerly deemed as correct where necessary.[100] Therefore, scattered and even more radical views doubting that statute had any significance for the judicial decision[101] or claiming that court decisions were the primary rules of law while statute was more of a formality,[102] did not prevail.[103] On the other end of the spectrum, some argue that precedent is a mere 'source of cognition of the legal position'[104] and a 'subjective ancillary tool for deciding'[105] without any full or limited binding force. They claim a binding force would lead to a 'cementation of law'[106] and therefore judges, even in cases of doubt, would *not* have to follow the established judicature of the federal supreme courts;[107] in this view, court decisions are placed on the same level as legal literature.[108] According to this, previous decisions would only represent actual practice and not that which should be rightly practiced.[109] In the end, all of those positions fall short of the mark because the question whether or not court decisions have binding force cannot be answered by the formal classification as a source of law.[110] Quite conversely, the scope of the factual and legal validity of court decisions sum up to a *limited binding force* and therefore, court decisions are best described as a subsidiary source of law.

---

98 See only *BVerfGE* vol. 131, 20, 42; J. Neuner, above n. 18, p. 58; H.D. Jarass, above n. 6, Art. 20 no. 53 with further references.

99 M. Bertelmann, above n. 3, p. 58.

100 See *BVerfGE* vol. 122, 248, 267.

101 H. Isay, *Rechtsnorm und Entscheidung*, Scientia, Neudruck Aalen 1970; critical to his opinion E. Forsthoff, *Recht und Sprache*, Niemeyer, Halle (Saale) 1940, p. 27.

102 H. Rottleuthner, *Richterliches Handeln*, Athenäum Fischer, Frankfurt am Main 1973, p. 152 with fn. 116.

103 F. Bydlinski, above n. 3, p. 503.

104 See e.g. K. Larenz, above n. 1, p. 432; K. Larenz, above n. 25, p. 262.

105 H. Köhler, 'Gesetzesauslegung und "gefestigte höchstrichterliche Rechtsprechung"' (1985) *Juristische Rundschau* 45, 48; alike W. Schlüter, *Das Obiter Dictum*, C.H. Beck, Munich 1973, pp. 50, 51.

106 R. Fischer, *Die Weiterbildung des Rechts durch die Rechtsprechung*, C.F. Müller, Karlsruhe 1971, p. 28; J. Esser, above n. 14, pp. 95, 121.

107 H. Köhler, above n. 105, 45, 48.

108 Thus the criticism of A. Ohly, above n. 15, 1, 20.

109 See C.-W. Canaris, 'Die Stellung der "UNIDROIT Principles" und der "Principles of European Contract Law" im System der Rechtsquellen' in J. Neuner and H.C. Grigoleit (eds), *Gesammelte Schriften*, vol. 1, de Gruyter, Berlin 2012, pp. 491, 494.

110 W. Grunsky, *Grenzen der Rückwirkung bei einer Änderung der Rechtsprechung*, C.F. Müller, Karlsruhe 1970, p. 14; W. Schlüter, above n. 105, p. 51; R. Riggert, *Die Selbstbindung der Rechtsprechung durch den allgemeinen Gleichheitssatz (Art. 3 I GG)*, Duncker & Humblot,

4.2.1. *Factual Validity of Precedent*

In the academic debate, the factual 'validity' of precedent can be considered undisputed;[111] even scholars considering court decisions as a mere source of cognition do not deny their high factual importance.[112] In terms of legal philosophy, a factual validity of *precedent* without legal validity is by all means possible because even the factual application of a *statute* is only a mandatory[113] but not sufficient basis of its legal validity.[114]

In the German legal praxis, the factual importance of precedent is illustrated by the fact that an essential part of the work of any legal practitioner consists of searching, evaluating, and finally 'applying' the 'appropriate' court decisions.[115] Especially the lower courts do not see decisions of federal supreme courts as a mere ancillary tool, but more or less obey them without further ado.[116] The federal supreme courts, for their part, use sequences of references that can be rather long and in which they quote their own previous rulings to motivate a subsequent decision. The BGH also grants *de facto* validity to the prevailing judicial practice.[117] Legal advisers conform their activity to high court decisions, for instance, by aligning the general terms and conditions of their clientele to the latest decisions of the BGH.[118] In this way, the legal practitioner also aims to prevent liability for negligence that a notary, for example, could face if he or she neglects to evaluate the judicature of the federal supreme courts when assessing a legal issue.[119] In the views of the BGH, the current rulings of the federal supreme courts are of:

> outstanding significance for the contractual performance of lawyers and tax advisors. That is why, as a rule, they have to align their notes, instructions, and recommendations with these rulings, even if they deem them incorrect.[120]

Berlin 1993, p. 24; B. Rüthers, C. Fischer and A. Birk, *Rechtstheorie mit juristischer Methodenlehre*, 11th ed., Munich 2020, no. 243; contrary to that, H. Kruse, above n. 97, p. 20.

111 See only B. Rüthers, C. Fischer and A. Birk, above n. 110, no. 244; M. Kriele, above n. 29, p. 253; terminological criticism at F. Bydlinski, above n. 9, p. 23.

112 See H. Köhler, above n. 105, 45, 48.

113 H. Henkel, *Einführung in die Rechtsphilosophie*, 2nd ed., C.H. Beck, Munich 1977, p. 545.

114 See S. Meyer, *Juristische Geltung als Verbindlichkeit*, Mohr Siebeck, Tübingen 2011, p. 20 with further references.

115 F. Bydlinski, above n. 3, p. 502; F. Bydlinski, 'Hauptpositionen zum Richterrecht' (1985) 40(4) *Juristenzeitung* 149, 150.

116 W. Schlüter, above n. 105, p. 25; C. Schönberger, above n. 52, 296, 319; A. Ohly, above n. 15, 1, 42.

117 See, e.g. BGH 29.01.1957, *NJW* 1957, 949, 950.

118 See K. Larenz, above n. 25, p. 247; see also H.-J. Koch and H. Rüßmann, *Juristische Begründungslehre*, C.H. Beck, Munich 1982, p. 186.

119 BGH 09.07.1992, *NJW* 1992, 3237, 3239.

120 BGH 28.09.2000, *NJW* 2001, 146, 148.

Some scholars even claim that an unbiased reader of German court decisions would never come to the conclusion that 'under common law, precedent is binding, whereas under German law, it shall not be binding'.[121] Following the surveys of the American 'Realistic School', a hit rate of 80% is predicted for lawyers in Germany who forecast the court decision of an everyday case on the basis of precedent.[122] Consequently, the *reason* of the factual validity of precedent is apparently the same as it is for the validity of statute and lies in its *recognition* by the legal community.[123]

Without going into detail, it is worth noting that the sporadic disregard of precedent does not annul their factual validity.[124] One example of such an 'outlier' is the decision of the District Court of Stuttgart (ref. 21 O 519/95) which explicitly states:

> This court does not misconceive that ... due to the above considerations ... and in the light of the rulings of the BGH ... the contract would not result in a violation of public policy. However, the respective rulings of the BGH are obsolete for this court. The BGH is a tendentious enterprise dominated by judges with party-cards of the current governing coalition, and all too often, it functions as the extended arm of the rich and powerful by primarily considering and thus promoting their interests with its decisions ...[125]

This polemic against the rulings of the federal supreme courts may be seen as an *exception that proves the rule* and has no impact on the factual validity of precedent. Due to this practical significance of court decisions, scholars often speak of a 'de facto source of law'.[126]

4.2.2. Legal Validity of Precedent

Much more controversial is the question of whether there is a *legal basis* which gives validity to court decisions under German law. Now it is by no means admissible to deduct the legal basis from the factual circumstances or, more generally, to deduct what ought to be from what is.[127] Hence, the question in point is not whether precedent is to be observed without any further conditions,[128]

---

121 W. Fikentscher, 'Präjudizienbindung' (1985) *Zeitschrift für Rechtsvergleichung* 163, 173–74.

122 See M. Kriele, above n. 29, pp. 259–60.

123 See to this theory H. Welzel, *Die Frage nach der Rechtsgeltung*, Westdeutscher Verlag, Cologne 1966, pp. 10–22; H. Henkel, above n. 113, pp. 546–49 with further references.

124 This is also the case with the validity of law, see only H. Henkel, above n. 113, p. 545.

125 LG Stuttgart 12.6.1996, AG 1996, 561, 562 with a negative note from H.-J. Mertens.

126 e.g. J. Neuner, above n. 18, p. 57; C.-W. Canaris (1972) *Sammlung Arbeitsrechtlicher Entscheidungen* 22, 22; different B. Rüthers, C. Fischer and A. Birk, above n. 110, nos. 244, 217 ('sociological source of law').

127 K. Larenz and C.-W. Canaris, above n. 60, p. 258.

128 Applicable F. Bydlinski, above n. 9, p. 32 with fn. 57.

but whether there is a *substantive legal command* which constitutes a binding force of precedent.[129] The debate offers essentially two ways to constitutionally motivate the binding force: the first one infers a principle of equal application of the law from the general principle of equal treatment under Article 3(1) of the GG, and the second one resorts to the principle of protection of legitimate expectations which is rooted in the rule of law and shaped by the principle of legal certainty.[130]

4.2.2.1. Equal Application of the Law under Article 3(1) of the Constitution

The judiciary is directly bound by the general principle of equal treatment via Article 1(3) of the GG; some scholars see this as a legal basis for an obligation to duly consider precedent.[131] According to an isolated and contrasting view, Article 3(1) of the GG is limited to a merely *formal criterion* which would only prohibit a different treatment based on personal characteristics,[132] and consequently, the general principle of equal treatment would not be suitable for substantively determining the prerequisites of a possible deviation from precedent.[133]

In the practice of the Federal Constitutional Court, the respective impact of the general principle of equal treatment is limited to a review for arbitrariness, meaning that there is no general binding force of precedent and a court must justify only deviations from the interpretation of a legal rule by a federal supreme court.[134] Only in this case, the deviating decision must evince that the court thoroughly considered the legal situation; however, citing an academic statement that does not even mention the disregarded precedent of the federal supreme court is not sufficient proof.[135] The review for arbitrariness in its function as an expression of the general principle of equal treatment therefore does not 'prohibit deviating decisions' but 'demands a corresponding justification'.[136] In this way, federal supreme court precedents substantively shape the requirements

---

129 See A. Ohly, above n. 15, 1, 29; R. Zimmermann, *Die Relevanz einer herrschenden Meinung für Anwendung, Fortbildung und wissenschaftliche Erforschung des Rechts*, Duncker & Humblot, Berlin 1983, p. 86; similarly M. Payandeh, above n. 26, pp. 136–50, esp. p. 138.

130 See H. Maurer, 'Kontinuitätsgewähr und Vertrauensschutz' in J. Isensee and P. Kirchhof, *Handbuch des Staatsrechts der Bundesrepublik Deutschland*, 3rd ed., vol. IV, C.F. Müller, Heidelberg 2006, §79, no. 156.

131 So esp. C. Gusy, 'Richterrecht und Grundgesetz' (1992) 45(11) *Die Öffentliche Verwaltung* 461; F. Bydlinski, above n. 9, pp. 23–24, 45–50; H.-M. Pawlowski, above n. 52, nos. 60, 217, 520–30; monographic R. Riggert, above n. 110.

132 K. Langenbucher, above n. 37, p. 108.

133 ibid., pp. 108, 109.

134 e.g. BVerfG 24.09.2002, *NJW* 2003, 501, 502.

135 BVerfG 19.07.1995, *NJW* 1995, 2911, 2912.

136 Applicable A. von Ungern-Sternberg, 'Normative Wirkungen von Präjudizien nach der Rechtsprung des Bundesverfassungsgerichts' (2013) 138 *Archiv des öffentlichen Rechts* 1, 51; C. Bittner, 'Höchstrichterliche Ankündigungsrechtsprechung – Rechtsfortbildung ins Ungewisse?' (2013) 68(13) *Juristenzeitung* 645, 646.

for justifying deviations under the principle of equal treatment[137] because in order to substantively motivate a *deviation*, the judge of the lower court[138] must attentively examine the precedent by looking into the underlying facts and their legal assessment by the federal supreme court.[139]

Some scholars object to the mandatory justification of deviating judgments with the argument that the principle of equal treatment would only demand a uniform application of legal norms, not of precedent as well.[140] This objection seems inadequate because firstly, the underlying assumption[141] is dubious since Article 3(1) of the GG shall not secure equal results but equal justifications of court decisions,[142] and secondly, the question is not if the judges are bound by the legal rule *or* the precedent but only in which manner they have to consider the precedent *within* their interpretation of the legal rule. It would also be unconvincing, for instance, if a judge of the first instance were free to reinterpret statutory blanket clauses (*Generalklauseln*), disregarding the respective established jurisprudence of the Federal Court of Justice.[143]

Thus, the principle of equal treatment allows only motivated deviations, unless the precedent proves to be *incorrect*, in which case the principle 'no equal treatment in breach of the law' applies.[144] Apart from these minimum standards guaranteeing equal treatment and banning arbitrariness that are necessary under the rule of law, a further 'self-binding' by the judiciary on the basis of Article 3(1) of the GG is excluded.[145]

4.2.2.2. Protection of Legitimate Expectations under Article 20(3) of the Constitution

An obligation to justify deviating decisions may also be derived from the doctrine of protection of legitimate expectations, which is an expression of the rule of law secured by Article 20(3) of the GG. The protection of legitimate expectations is the subjective aspect of legal certainty and safeguards *individual expectations of continuity*.[146] The rule of law is binding on any governmental

137 See F. Bydlinski, above n. 9, p. 24, no. 42 with further references; see also K. Röhl and H. C. Röhl, above n. 3, p. 604.

138 See to the disputable addressee problem C. Gusy, above n. 131, 461, 468–70 and M. Payandeh, above n. 26, pp. 174–77.

139 Detailed R. Riggert, above n. 110, pp. 48–56.

140 H. Köhler, above n. 105, 45, 47.

141 ibid., 45, 47.

142 See also J. Esser, *Vorverständnis und Methodenwahl in der Rechtsfindung*, Athenäum Verlag, Frankfurt am Main 1970, p. 185.

143 See M. Kriele, above n. 29, pp. 263–64; probably contrary to that, H. Köhler, above n. 105, 45, 47.

144 See *BVerfGE* vol. 19, 38, 47; A. Ohly, above n. 15, 1, 30; K. Langenbucher, above n. 37, pp. 108–09.

145 In detail on the whole topic, M. Payandeh, above n. 26, pp. 173–77.

146 See only B. Grzeszick in T. Maunz and G. Dürig, above n. 21, Art. 20 VII no. 69.

authority, yet it is questionable if the protection of legitimate expectations may constitute a legal basis for a binding force of precedent. Now, the question is *not* whether the protection of legitimate expectations results in an absolute binding force,[147] especially because there is no general legitimate expectation as to the continuation of either statute or judicial practice.[148] The key question is rather the same as it was under Article 3(1) of the GG, namely under what conditions courts may *deviate* from an established jurisprudence. Two additional questions revolve around whether legitimate expectations of a continuing judicial practice effect a *retroactive* binding force, and if so, whether courts are required to announce a change in their practice. Such a retroactive protection of legitimate expectations would indeed produce a *limited* binding force of preceding legal opinions. Regardless of these questions, expectations that were frustrated in civil proceedings shall primarily be compensated under civil law rather than under constitutional law.

Non-constitutional compensation of legitimate expectations

Precedent-based expectations that have been manifested in concrete transactions may be protected in different ways, be it by the supplementary interpretation of the contract, by an application of the principle of good faith under §242 of the BGB,[149] by the provisions on the frustration of contract under §313 of the BGB,[150] or by the negation of fault in liability claims.[151] The last two examples illustrate this matter.

If a settlement is agreed on the basis of a unanimous extra-contractual expectation of the continuance of a certain judicial practice, and if this practice subsequently changes, then, according to §313(1) of the BGB, the parties may adapt the content of the agreement to the changed judicial practice,[152] as long as neither of the parties is unreasonably burdened by this adaptation.[153]

---

147 See H. Köhler, above n. 105, 45, 47.

148 See A. von Ungern-Sternberg, above n. 136, 1, 48 with further references.

149 See *BGHZ* vol. 132, 119, 130–31; C. Höpfner, 'Vertrauensschutz und Richterrecht – Zur Zulässigkeit rückwirkender Rechtsprechungsänderungen im Zivilrecht' (2006) *Recht der Arbeit* 156, 164–65.

150 §313(1) of the BGB: 'If circumstances which became the basis of a contract have significantly changed since the contract was entered into and if the parties would not have entered into the contract or would have entered into it with different contents if they had foreseen this change, adaptation of the contract may be demanded to the extent that, taking account of all the circumstances of the specific case, in particular the contractual or statutory distribution of risk, one of the parties cannot reasonably be expected to uphold the contract without alteration.'

151 F. Maultzsch, 'Das Zeitelement in der richterlichen Fortbildung des deutschen Rechts' (2015) 79 *Rabels Zeitschrift für ausländisches und internationales Privatrecht* 322, 348–50; K. Langenbucher, above n. 37, pp. 134–36; K. Larenz and C.-W. Canaris, above n. 60, p. 259; H. Maurer, above n. 130, §79 no. 153.

152 See BGH 02.05.1972, *NJW* 1972, 1577, 1579; K. Larenz and C.-W. Canaris, above n. 60, p. 259.

153 BGH 02.05.1972, *NJW* 1972, 1577, 1580.

In a decision on 'aerial lift safety', the BGH rejected a tort liability claim for *lack of fault* because:

> neither are there German court decisions on the safeguarding of aerial lift pylons … nor can such an obligation of safeguarding be readily derived from hitherto existing decisions on the obligation to safeguard the slope.[154]

Consequently, the injuring party was not at fault because a change in the judicial practice was not foreseeable at the moment of the incident.[155]

Constitutional compensation of legitimate expectations

In cases of lacking applicable civil statutory law, the legitimate expectation of a continuing judicial practice is protected by an *analogous application* of the constitutional doctrine prohibiting 'genuinely retroactive legislation' which 'subsequently modifies the legal assessment of bygone and completed facts'.[156] In contrast, the so-called 'artificial retroactivity' is allowed in principle, meaning that new statutory rules may apply to ongoing circumstances that have begun but are not yet completed.[157] A limitless application of this doctrine to changing court practices would be quite complicated because court decisions mostly refer to bygone facts, and decisions deviating from precedent would therefore be impossible in view of legitimate expectations of continuity.[158]

Some argue that for the citizen, it makes no difference whether a claim fails due to a changing statute or a changing judicial practice.[159] This pragmatic objection may have a point, yet the comparable result should not lead to overlooking the differing *modus operandi*[160] because the legislator can always abstain from extending new regulations on bygone facts, whereas a denial of justice is prohibited to the judiciary, meaning that the decision on the presented cases is mandatory.[161] According to the Federal Constitutional Court, a judicial protection of individual expectations is necessary on rare occasions only,[162] especially because a changing judicial practice would also be 'harmless when in line with a foreseeable development'.[163]

---

154 BGH 23.10.1984, *NJW* 1985, 620, 621.

155 See K. Langenbucher, above n. 37, p. 135.

156 *BVerfGE* vol. 57, 361, 391; *BVerfGE* vol. 72, 175, 196; B. Grzeszick in T. Maunz and G. Dürig, above n. 21, Art. 20 VII nos. 80 and 83–87 to the exceptions.

157 See *BVerfGE* vol. 109, 96, 122 with further references.

158 See A. von Ungern-Sternberg, above n. 136, 1, 49–50; K. Langenbucher, above n. 37, p. 138.

159 W. Knittel, *Zum Problem der Rückwirkung bei einer Änderung der Rechtsprechung*, Ernst und Werner Gieseking, Bielefeld 1965, p. 22.

160 H. Maurer, above n. 130, §79, no. 147.

161 See K. Langenbucher, above n. 37, p. 122.

162 *BVerfGE* vol. 126, 369, 394–95; *BVerfGE* vol. 122, 248, 277–78; see also F. Maultzsch, above n. 151, 322, 341–42.

163 *BVerfGE* vol. 122, 248, 277; *BVerfGE* vol. 84, 212, 227–28.

The only remaining possible basis of legitimate expectations is an *established* jurisprudence of a federal supreme court whose continuity must seem settled.[164] For instance, the plaintiff may not legitimately expect the continuance of a favourable judicial practice which has been 'disputed among courts and scholars for several years'.[165] If instead, there is a basis of legitimate expectations in the form of a settled jurisprudence that forms the basis of the expectation, this jurisprudence needs to be *attributable* to the parties of the concrete proceeding in order for the expectation to be legitimate; although the parties did not 'create' the precedent themselves, it is generally attributable to them due to the democratic origination of the decision.[166] Very much like expectations regarding statute, an expectation of the continuance of judicial practice in general is sufficient in order to be legitimate.[167]

Protection of legitimate expectations regarding past circumstances (prospective overruling)

As a rule, changes in the judicial practice operate retroactively and can thus be applied to bygone facts.[168] In only a few decisions, the federal supreme courts have applied the doctrine of prospective overruling to protect hitherto legitimate expectations.[169]

The Federal Labour Court (BAG), for instance, has deemed a works agreement to be effective, although the parties, 'under current law, had no right to … change existing regulations to the detriment of the employees'.[170] Yet, the expectation that the agreement would be permissible was legitimate because for over 25 years, the courts had considered the type of modifications made by the works agreement to be permissible, and the parties had no knowledge of the upcoming change in the judicial practice.[171]

The BGH maintains a very reserved attitude in this context,[172] yet found it also necessary to protect existing expectations after changing its conception of the liability regime in the civil law partnership under §705 and following of the BGB. Since its 2003 decision, newly entered partners are liable for existing

---

164 See *BVerfGE* vol. 126, 369, 395; *BVerfGE* vol. 84, 212, 217–18.

165 BGH 21.12.1972, *NJW* 1973, 364; see also K. Langenbucher, above n. 37, pp. 133–34.

166 J. Neuner, above n. 18, p. 172; see also F. Maultzsch, above n. 151, 322, 343.

167 W. Grunsky, above n. 110, pp. 26–27; K. Langenbucher, 'Rechtsprechung mit Wirkung für die Zukunft' (2003) *Juristenzeitung* 1132, 1136 with further references; for a critical view see F. Bydlinski, 'Gegen die "Zeitzündertheorien" bei der Rechtsprechungsänderung nach staatlichem und europäischem Recht' (2001) 123 *Juristische Blätter* 2, 13.

168 See only F. Maultzsch, above n. 151, 322, 346 with further references.

169 In detail, ibid., 322, 350–54.

170 BAG 20.11.1990, *NZA* 1991, 477, 481.

171 ibid., 477, 479, 480; F. Maultzsch, above n. 151, 322, 350–51 with further references.

172 Closer with examples K. Langenbucher, above n. 167, 1132, 1137–39 and F. Maultzsch, above n. 151, 322, 351–54.

commitments according to §130 of the Commercial Code (HGB) applied by analogy.[173] For partners that had entered prior to that decision, the BGH kept applying its previous and contrary judicial practice because a retroactive extension of liability would have been disproportionately burdensome and their expectation not to be liable was therefore considered legitimate.[174]

Both decisions *implement* a change of the legal position without applying the new findings to the case at hand. In the German academic debate, the doctrine of *prospective overruling* was harshly criticised because the plaintiff would lose the case in spite of having successfully enforced the correct legal position with great effort and at high risk.[175] It was claimed that the limited retroactivity would dissuade potential plaintiffs from taking action against incorrect developments of the judicial practice, since they would fear losing the case in spite of being right.[176] The critics rightly rejected the proposition of a mitigating counter-exception that would disregard the legitimate expectation only in the case at hand,[177] because such an exception would involve massive problems in terms of justice and equal treatment.[178]

Notwithstanding these special issues, the main objections against the doctrine of prospective overruling are already unconvincing: the overruling decision is not 'intentionally incorrect'[179] because the judge truly pronounces the new legal finding and consequently rejects the previous opinion. The fact that the protection of legitimate expectations results in the dismissal of the action neither renders the decision incorrect nor qualifies the new finding as an *obiter dictum*.[180] More precisely, it is not a case of *obiter dictum* because the pronunciation of the new legal position is as formative an element for the dogmatic justification of the legitimacy of the expectation under the new position as is the reasoning regarding legitimate expectations in general.[181] The causality which is indeed lacking between the new legal position and the overruling decision demonstrates only that the *ratio decidendi* cannot be fully comprehended using formal criteria.[182] As a result, the 'rightness' of the overruling decision cannot be

---

173 BGH 07.04.2003, *NJW* 2003, 1803, 1804.

174 See ibid., 1803, 1805.

175 F. Bydlinski, above n. 9, pp. 17, 50–56 and F. Bydlinski, above n. 167.

176 F. Bydlinski, above n. 9, p. 51.

177 C. Ziegler, *Selbstbindung der Dritten Gewalt*, Peter Lang, Frankfurt am Main 1993, pp. 209–11; in detail F. Maultzsch, above n. 151, 322, 354–55 with further references.

178 F. Bydlinski, above n. 167, 2, 9.

179 L. Brocker, 'Rechtsprechungsänderung und Vertrauensschutz' (2012) *Neue Juristische Wochenschrift* 2996, 2999 with further references.

180 But so, F. Bydlinski, above n. 167, 2, 9, 14–15.

181 Alike, C. Bittner, above n. 136, 645, 649; this must be distinguished from cases in which, for example, only an indeterminate legal term is redefined without any effect on the concrete result; there is no reliance on the retention of the original reasoning, see L. Kähler, *Strukturen und Methoden der Rechtsprechungsänderung*, 2nd ed., Nomos, Baden-Baden 2011, pp. 59–63.

182 See already in the text at above n. 63 and following.

assessed on the basis of non-constitutional norms but only in due consideration of the pertinent constitutional principles in the specific case.[183]

Expectations foiled by obiter dicta

Many changes of the judicial practice are announced only by *obiter dicta* when the respective issue is not decisive for the case at hand, but the court feels the need to express its doubts in regard to the previous practice. These legal opinions expressed only *on the occasion* of the decision, and not in order to support it, are usually pronounced in a very reserved manner;[184] the BGH, for instance, stated incidentally: 'There is much to suggest that ... the contrasting view of the Reich Court of Justice ... might have to be rejected',[185] and the BGH did indeed reject it four years later.[186] Yet, at times, the court dispels its doubts and keeps up the former practice.[187] The academic literature consequently asserts that *obiter dicta* may foil the expectation of continuing practice but cannot be a basis of legitimate expectations themselves.[188]

Result

Under German law, the validity of precedent cannot only be factual but also based on a statutory principle in the form of the protection of legitimate expectations.[189] In individual cases, that might lead to a decision *consistent* with the previous legal position even though the courts have changed this very position in the meantime. The extent of statutory validity is but very small because the underlying constitutional compensation of legitimate expectations is only suitable when a change in the settled practice of a federal supreme court would represent an unreasonable burden for the concerned person as a result. On the other hand, there can be no legitimate expectation of a continuing practice if the judiciary has already pronounced an *obiter dictum* doubting this practice and thus rendering the change *foreseeable*. Though immediately applicable only on the level of the federal supreme courts, the constitutional protection of legitimate expectations is not irrelevant for lower courts but serves as a guiding principle clarifying the prerequisites for *deviating* from federal supreme court precedents.[190]

---

183 K. Langenbucher, above n. 37, p. 137.
184 See L. Kähler, above n. 181, pp. 75–78 with further references.
185 BGH 16.02.2000, *NJW-RR* 2000, 1108.
186 See BGH 14.07.2004, *NZM* 2004, 738, 740.
187 F. Maultzsch, above n. 151, 322, 356 with fn. 178.
188 C. Bittner, above n. 136, 645, 650; F. Maultzsch, above n. 151, 322, 356; C. Höpfner, above n. 149, 156, 159.
189 Explicit, F. Bydlinski, above n. 9, p. 21; F. Bydlinski, above n. 115, 149, 152.
190 H. Maurer, above n. 130, §79, no. 144.

4.2.2.3. Conclusion: The Doctrine of the Subsidiary Source of Law

The said features render precedent a *subsidiary source of law* for later decisions;[191] though that does not make them one of the binding legal standards under Article 20(3) of the GG, neither may they be disregarded as insignificant 'legal opinions'. This differentiated conception of precedent gives priority to the judicial interpretation of statute and points out that a judge must deviate from precedent once he or she has methodologically formed the conviction that the specific precedent is incorrect in the context of the current legal order.[192]

Consequently, judges shall not blindly obey precedent, yet in the face of equally strong arguments for and against its application ('*non liquet*'), the principles of equal treatment and the protection of legitimate expectations commit them to continuity.[193] In practice, the classification as a subsidiary source of law implies that the judge shall give reasons if he or she deviates from a precedent.[194] In this point, the doctrine of the subsidiary source of law corresponds to Alexy's doctrine of argumentation which states: 1) if a precedent may be invoked for or against a certain decision, it must be invoked; and 2) the person who wants to deviate from precedent bears the argumentative burden.[195]

4.3. CONSEQUENCES OF DECISIONS DEVIATING FROM FEDERAL SUPREME COURT PRECEDENT

In terms of civil procedure, a court of *first instance* deviating from precedent must admit the appeal under §511(4), sentence 1, no. 1 of the ZPO,[196] if the deviation has an impact on its decision.[197] Likewise, the deviating court of *second instance* must admit the appeal on points of law under §543(2), sentence 1, no. 2 of the ZPO. Both provisions shall expressly 'ensure a uniform adjudication' and serve not only to rebuke deviating judges of the first two instances but also

---

191 F. Bydlinski, above n. 3, pp. 501–15; F. Bydlinski, above n. 9, pp. 33–45; K. Larenz and C.-W. Canaris, above n. 60, pp. 256–60; C.-W. Canaris, 'Richtigkeit und Eigenwertung in der richterlichen Rechtsfindung' in J. Neuner and H.C. Grigoleit (eds), above n. 109, pp. 423, 428; contrary to that, E. Picker, 'Richterrecht oder Rechtsdogmatik – Alternativen der Rechtsgewinnung? – Teil 2' (1988) 43(2) *Juristenzeitung* 62, 71–72 with fn. 133; L. Kähler, above n. 181, pp. 334–40 with further references.

192 F. Bydlinski, above n. 3, p. 511.

193 See F. Bydlinski, above n. 9, p. 33.

194 K. Larenz and C.-W. Canaris, above n. 60, p. 257.

195 R. Alexy, *Theorie der juristischen Argumentation*, 7th ed., Suhrkamp, Frankfurt am Main 2012, pp. 334–41, esp. p. 339; in result probably also P. Krebs, 'Die Begründungslast' (1995) 195 *Archiv für die civilistische Praxis* 171, 185.

196 In detail, B. Rimmelspacher in T. Rauscher and W. Krüger, above n. 95, §511, nos. 75–77; M. Payandeh, above n. 26, pp. 290–93.

197 See BGH 27.03.2003, *NJW* 2003, 1943, 1945; W. Schlüter, above n. 105, pp. 41–42.

to question the federal supreme court practice and adjust it when necessary. If the court of second instance does not admit the appeal on points of law, the parties can enforce the implementation of the appeal procedures by raising a complaint against the denial under §544 of the ZPO. There is no such possibility between first and second instance but in the academic writing, the appeal is considered permissible if a denial is arbitrary or violates the guarantee of judicial protection.[198] Regardless of this, these provisions prove the above-mentioned argumentative burden of the deviating court[199] and the system-inherent interest to ensure the unity of the legal order while further developing the law.[200]

In terms of criminal procedure, a judge may be liable for 'perversion of justice' under §339 of the German Criminal Code (StGB) in case his or her decision deviates in an extreme manner from a constant judicial practice and therefore forms an arbitrary act.[201] If, on this basis, a judge has been sentenced to imprisonment for a term of at least one year, his or her civil service status terminates immediately under §24(1) of the German Judiciary Act (DRiG). Apart from these *very rare* and extreme cases, a judge who constantly deviates from or disregards federal supreme court precedents could encounter career setbacks;[202] however, they cannot be held personally liable.

5. MANDATE TO CREATE PRIVATE LAW

As far as there are gaps in codified law, the supreme courts play an important role in supplementing and developing private law. For example, in the absence of comprehensive codification, a large part of German labour law is based on case law. In general, there is no doubt that the courts are authorised to *develop* the law within the framework of the applicable laws and the constitutional limits.

There is also an interesting specific mandate to establish a uniform judicial practice.

5.1. NATIONAL HARMONISATION OF THE JUDICIAL PRACTICE

A particular remit in ensuring a *uniform judicial practice* is carried out the by the 'Joint Senate' of the federal supreme courts under Article 95(3), sentence 1

198 See B. Rimmelspacher in T. Rauscher and W. Krüger, above n. 95, §511, no. 87 with further references.
199 See M. Payandeh, above n. 26, p. 296.
200 See B. Rimmelspacher in T. Rauscher and W. Krüger, above n. 95, introduction to §511, no. 3.
201 BGH 06.10.1994, *NJW* 1995, 64, 67.
202 D. Olzen, above n. 59, 155, 157 points this out.

of the GG. According to §2 of the RsprEinhG,[203] it must convene when a single senate of one of the federal supreme courts wants to deviate from a decision of another federal supreme court (so-called 'external deviation').[204] This body must be distinguished from the 'grand panels' of each of the federal supreme courts which are to resolve 'internal deviations'; in civil matters, for instance, §132(2) of the GVG dictates that the Grand Civil Panel of the BGH is competent to decide when a single senate of the BGH wants to deviate from the adjudication of another senate or of the Grand Civil Panel itself.[205] According to §132(5), sentence 1 of the GVG, the Grand Civil Panel is composed of the president and one member from each of the civil panels. Lastly, there are the United Grand Panels which, according to §132(1) and (2) of the GVG, have to decide when a civil panel wants to deviate from a criminal panel[206] or *vice versa*. If any senate deviating from the *ratio decidendi* of a decision of another senate omits to turn to the Grand Panel or to the Joint Senate as would be its duty, this is to be considered a removal from the jurisdiction of the lawful judge under Article 101(1), sentence 2 of the GG,[207] which can be challenged by constitutional complaint.[208]

As early as during the period of the Reich Court of Justice, the term *horror pleni* emerged and is still used today to describe the general aversion and scepticism of the judges against the involvement of the greater panels.[209] This aversion is reflected by the fact that the Grand Civil Panel had to pronounce only four decisions in the last ten years of which only *one (!)* regarded the submission of a deviation issue under §132(2) of the GVG. Two of the decisions concerned issues of fundamental importance under §132(4) of the GVG whose submission is advisable when a single senate is entrusted with a new legal issue and expects that another senate might adopt a deviating position in a subsequent case.[210] The last of the four decisions was based on a submission under §132(3) of the GVG, which provides the senate who pronounced the precedent with the possibility of a preliminary ruling abandoning its position before the Grand Panel or the United Grand Panels are involved.

---

203 Act on the preservation of the uniformity of the jurisprudence of the federal supreme courts.

204 H. Schultze-Fielitz in H. Dreier (ed), *Grundgesetz-Kommentar*, 3rd ed., vol. 3, Mohr Siebeck, Tübingen 2018, Art. 95 no. 35 with further references.

205 H. Schultze-Fielitz in H. Dreier, above n. 204, Art. 95 no. 36.

206 As to precedent in criminal law, see P. Hünfeld 'Die Bedeutung der Präjudizien im Strafrecht' in U. Blaurock (ed), *Die Bedeutung von Präjudizien im deutschen und französischen Recht*, Alfred Metzner Verlag, Frankfurt am Main 1985, pp. 105–28.

207 Art. 101(1), sentence 2 of the GG: 'No one may be removed from the jurisdiction of his or her lawful judge.'

208 See M. Jachmann-Michel in T. Maunz and G. Dürig, above n. 21, Art. 95 no. 160 with further references.

209 In detail, C. Jungmann, 'Ein neuer "horror pleni" in den Zivilsenaten des Bundesgerichtshofs?' (2009) 64(8) *Juristenzeitung* 380.

210 ibid., 380, 381.

In quite a similar way as the submission of deviating decisions *within* the stages of appeal, the mentioned provisions illustrate the interest of the German legal order in a preferably homogeneous judicial practice in order to promote legal certainty and an equal application of the law. At the same time, the provisions demonstrate the ability to adapt to new circumstances under due consideration of the argumentative burden. In this way, any continuity already involves the idea of change.[211]

5.2. INTERNATIONAL HARMONISATION OF THE JUDICIAL PRACTICE

It finally remains an issue of dispute, though, whether courts should more strongly consider foreign case law in order to harmonise the judicial practice on an international level.

Comparative law issues are rarely dealt with by German courts;[212] the necessity of considering foreign court decisions is essentially limited to the scope of application of international treaties, as was stressed by the BGH with regard to Article 3 of the Hague Protection of Minors Convention: 'First of all, the *judicial practice of the other contracting states* is to be duly considered in order to achieve a uniform interpretation of the convention.'[213] Apart from the scope of application of international treaties, foreign decisions can be used as a *source of cognition of the legal position* at most,[214] especially because the in-depth comparison of legal systems required by Conventions such as the Convention on Contracts for the International Sale of Goods (CISG) is preferably dealt with by scholars rather than by those who apply the law.[215]

6. IMPORTANCE OF PRECEDENTS IN PRIVATE LAW

In legal practice, the reception of precedents mostly serves the purpose of shortening and simplifying since otherwise, a new and complex process of weighing and concluding would be required each time an abstract legal rule is applied.[216] Frequently, the citation of federal supreme court precedent replaces

---

211 See A. Leisner, *Kontinuität als Verfassungsprinzip*, Mohr Siebeck, Tübingen 2002, pp. 632–36.

212 See T. Möllers, *Juristische Methodenlehre*, 4th ed., C.H. Beck, Munich 2021, §3 nos. 88–93a.

213 *BGHZ* vol. 111, 199, 209 (emphasis added).

214 See B. Großfeld, 'Vom Beitrag der Rechtsvergleichung zum deutschen Recht' (1984) 184 *Archiv für die civilistische Praxis* 289, 295.

215 D. Magnus in J. von Staudinger, above n. 32, Art. 7 CISG no. 37; R. Bodenheimer in B. Gsell, W. Krüger, S. Lorenz and C. Reymann, *beck-online.Großkommentar*, C.H. Beck, Munich 2024, Art. 7 CISG no. 17.

216 F. Bydlinski, above n. 3, p. 504; see also M. Payandeh, above n. 26, p. 13.

the argumentation, and this applies not only to the lower instances, but also to the BGH itself.[217]

This impact on work efficiency[218] may be reversely illustrated by looking at a decision of the Administrative Court of Berlin. Herein, the chamber expressly *deviated* from both the practices of the Federal Administrative Court (Bundesverwaltungsgericht or BVerwG) and of the Federal Court of Justice (BGH) and therefore deemed it necessary to justify its legal considerations in entirely unusual depth.[219] One can hardly assume that the reasoning would have been as extensive if the decision had been compatible with the precedents,[220] especially because such a decision complying with the federal supreme court practice would most probably have been confirmed.[221]

Finally, the hierarchic structure of 'lower', 'higher' and 'highest' courts may have a psychological impact insofar as the expertise and the number of staff of the BGH will, in cases of doubt, result in the loyalty of the lower and higher courts.[222] The federal supreme courts are quite aware of their authority and tend to reverse the decisions of the second-instance courts by pointing to an 'erroneous assumption' or 'wrongful legal opinion' of the court of appeal, or by stating that 'the court of appeal misconceived that ...'.[223] It would also be quite unrealistic to expect the BGH not to reverse a hypothetical decision which negates the personality rights that the BGH itself developed, because otherwise the BGH would be forced to admit that the recognition of personality rights does not follow from the 'only correct interpretation' of Articles 1 and 2 of the GG.[224]

In general, the BGH underlines that it will only deviate from its settled practice in the presence of 'clearly predominant or per se compelling reasons.'[225] The statement is unfounded when formulated in such absolute terms because at times the court abandons a practice of long standing without giving any reasons,[226] occasionally even by using the same formulation as before but with a different meaning.[227] Yet another possibility is the 'hidden change' in which the

---

217 See D. Olzen, above n. 59, 155, 157; for the development of the style see in detail, J. Lashöfer, *Zum Stilwandel in richterlichen Entscheidungen*, Waxmann, Münster 1992, pp. 81 and following.

218 More detailed M. Kriele, above n. 29, pp. 258–61; C. Schönberger, above n. 52, 296, 319.

219 VG Berlin 01.12.2000, *NJW* 2001, pp. 983–89.

220 L. Kähler, above n. 181, pp. 46–47.

221 R. Zimmermann, above n. 129, p. 150; H. Köhler, above n. 105, 45, 45.

222 See *BVerfGE* vol. 126, 369, 395; BGH 28.9.2000, *NJW* 2001, 146, 148; K. Larenz, above n. 25, p. 262; D. Olzen, above n. 59, 155, 157.

223 J. Lashöfer, above n. 217, p. 108, fn. 1 with references.

224 See M. Kriele, above n. 29, p. 252.

225 *BGHZ* vol. 85, 64, 66; to this K. Langenbucher, above n. 37, pp. 116–17 and the analysis of F. Bydlinski, above n. 9, pp. 9–15, esp. pp. 11–12.

226 See W. Fikentscher, above n. 121, 163, 171–73 and L. Kähler, above n. 181, pp. 49–51, both with examples.

227 L. Kähler, above n. 181, p. 50.

BGH suggests continuity by citing precedent while in truth deviating from the previous practice.[228]

7. CONCLUDING REMARKS

As this contribution has shown, precedent has great practical and theoretical significance for German private law. Since German law does not recognise the doctrine of *stare decisis*, there are only very few rules regulating a binding force of precedent, and any plea for a general binding force encounters issues in terms of constitutional law, legal theory, and methodology. All these issues can be addressed by the doctrine of the subsidiary source of law that manages to emphasise the obligation of the judges to respect the rule of law and, at the same time, to grant great theoretical significance to the *factual* validity of precedent. The doctrine is backed by the constitutional principles of equal application of the law and of the protection of legitimate interests. In sum, it can be stated that the judicial rule-making and the reception of these rules are vital aspects of the legal order which is designed with a focus on continuity, and that they are indispensable in a conception of law as a system of rules because only with their help can the uniformity and certainty of law be ensured.[229]

---

228 ibid., pp. 51–53 with examples.

229 See J. Neuner, above n. 18, p. 59; on the system idea in detail, C.-W. Canaris, *Systemdenken und Systembegriff in der Jurisprudenz*, 2nd ed., Duncker & Humblot, Berlin 1983.

PRECEDENT IN ITALIAN PRIVATE LAW

Luisa Antoniolli

1. A GENERAL INTRODUCTION TO JUDICIAL PRECEDENTS IN ITALIAN LAW

Under Italian law, judicial precedents are formally not recognised as an independent source of law. In fact, the hierarchy of legal sources established by the Civil Code[1] does not recognise case law as an independent source, in line with a formalistic and positivist approach rooted in the theory of the separation of powers: judges, who are not democratically selected and accountable, can only interpret and apply the law, but not make it. The declaratory theory of case law formally still applies, but in fact all lawyers, both academics and practitioners, as well as the general public, are acutely aware of the fundamental role that case law plays in establishing the law.[2] There is no legal area where it is possible to understand the law only through the applicable statutory rules; in most areas, case law is a crucial component, and this is definitely true also in private law.

---

[1] Art. 1 of the general provisions of the Civil Code (the so-called '*Preleggi*') lists as sources (*fonti*) of law: statutes (*leggi*), statutory instruments (*regolamenti*) and customs (*usi*).

[2] See A. Pizzorusso, *Fonti del diritto*, 2nd ed., Zanichelli, Bologna-Roma, 2011; M. Taruffo, 'Legalità e giustificazione della creazione giudiziaria del diritto' in M. Taruffo, *Sui confini: Scritti sulla giustizia civile*, Il Mulino, Bologna 2002, pp. 195 and following.

The law in the books/law in action cleavage in case law also affects the position of judicial precedents among the sources of law. The specific features of the Italian legal (and particularly the judicial) process, and more generally the structural features of the Italian legal system, tend to stress the importance, rather than of individual judicial decisions (i.e. a judicial precedent in its proper meaning), of a coherent line of judicial decisions that establish a rule (*giurisprudenza consolidata* or *conforme*). This feature implies a very different role of case law compared to other systems (of which the English one is the quintessential example),[3] where every precedent establishes a rule that must (under certain conditions) be followed by other judges. This means that no system of *stare decisis*, or binding precedent, exists. Yet, although a theory of binding precedents in Italian law does not exist, precedents are very relevant. But, due to the large number of decisions, particularly of the Italian supreme court (Corte suprema di cassazione), the impact of judicial precedents tends to be more a matter of quantity than of quality. Moreover, due to the frequency of contrasting precedents, the discretion and margin of manoeuvre at the disposal of following judges is very wide, and usually it is possible to decide and follow a different line (*orientamento giurisprudenziale*). Finally, Italian judicial decisions tend to have a strong emphasis on legal rules, rather than on the match between legal rules and material facts.[4]

All these features, and the mechanisms devised over time to remedy some of the most dysfunctional distortions and deficiencies, shape the role of judicial precedent in Italy. This contribution will analyse in more detail the fundamental elements of the Italian legal system that explain this situation, which revolve around three essential features: first, the extremely high number of cases decided by the highest civil court of the Italian legal system, the Corte suprema di cassazione, which amounts to several tens of thousands each year (compared to a number of hundreds, or even less, in many legal systems), and frequently leads to conflicting precedents, causing a severe problem of legal uncertainty and unpredictability. Second, the chronic state of crisis of the Italian judicial system, characterised by an excessive duration and a heavy backlog of judicial decisions, which started in the 1950s and gradually but steadily worsened in the following decades.[5] Third, the predominance of the legal elements, as opposed

---

3 See R. Cross and J.W. Harris, *Precedent in English Law*, 4th ed., Clarendon Press, Oxford 1991; L. Antoniolli Deflorian, 'Il precedente giudiziario come fonte di diritto: l'esperienza inglese' (1993) I *Riv. dir. civ.* 157 (and following).

4 See M. Taruffo, 'Precedents in Italy' in E. Hondius (ed.), *Precedent and the Law: Reports of the XVIIth Congress of the International Academy of Comparative Law (Utrecht, 16–22 July 2006)*, Bruylant, Brussels 2007, pp. 179 and following; M. Taruffo, 'Note sul precedente giudiziale' in A. Carleo (ed), *Il vincolo giudiziale del passato*, Il Mulino, Bologna 2018, pp. 109 and following; M. Taruffo, 'Precedente e giurisprudenza' in (2007) *Riv. trim. dir. proc. civ.* 709 (and following).

5 See S. Chiarloni, 'Civil Justice and its Paradoxes: An Italian Perspective' in A. Zuckerman (ed), *Civil Justice in Crisis: Comparative Perspectives of Civil Procedure*, Oxford University

to the factual ones, in the reporting system of case law, based on the so-called *massime*, i.e. the formulation of the legal rules applied in each case, which are generally used by lawyers as the main source to find relevant precedents.

1.1. THE JUDICIAL SYSTEM IN ITALY

The current Italian judicial model is largely based on the French model, which was already applied in parts of Italy before the unification of the country in 1861.[6] The judiciary is organised in a hierarchical way, staffed by bureaucratic career judges, separate from the legal profession.[7] After the fascist period, which strengthened the hierarchical features and the control of the executive over the judiciary, a new democratic system emerged in the aftermath of World War II, built around the new Constitution enacted in 1948, which strengthens the independence of the judiciary and focuses on fundamental rights, among which the right to judicial protection (Article 24 of the Constitution) plays a fundamental role.[8]

The fundamental guarantees for the judiciary are established by two articles of the Constitution: Article 101 rules that judges are subject only to the law, guaranteeing also the internal side of independence of any judge from interference by any other judge (even those at a higher level in the hierarchy of courts).[9] This principle is often interpreted as providing the foundation for the

Press, Oxford 1999, pp. 263–89: 'The Italian civil process is largely useless for citizens who ask for justice. … the original mechanism of the civil process has been replaced by "complex celebration of obscure and often indecorous rituals" which delay justice' (p. 264). The author underlines that under the previous Code of Civil Procedure of 1854, the average duration of proceedings was considerably shorter than after the 1940 CPC. From the 1950s onwards, the number of cases lodged systematically exceeded the number of cases concluded, causing an increasing backlog. See also M. Bin, *Il precedente giudiziario: Valore e interpretazione*, CEDAM, Padua 1995.

6 See S. Benvenuti, 'The Italian Machinery of Justice' in A. De Luca and A. Simoni (eds), *Fundamentals of Italian Law*, Giuffrè, Milan 2014, pp. 143 and following; V. Varano, 'Machinery of Justice' in J.S. Lena and U. Mattei (eds), *Introduction to Italian Law*, Kluwer Law International, The Hague 2002, pp. 99 and following. For an old, but penetrating account of the fundamental features of the Italian legal system, see M. Cappelletti and J.H. Merryman, *The Italian Legal System – An Introduction*, Stanford University Press, Stanford 1967.

7 S. Chiarloni, above n. 5, writes of 'A cult of authority, passive obedience, and routine activity', where 'Excessive importance is given to formalities' (p. 278).

8 According to Art. 24(1) of the Constitution, everyone is entitled to judicial protection of his/her rights and legitimate interests (*interessi legittimi*). The rule also envisages the establishment of legal aid instruments for people in need, in order to guarantee access to justice.

9 The selection, appointment, assignment, promotion and sanctioning of judges are decided exclusively by the High Council of the Judiciary (Consiglio Superiore della Magistratura, CSM, Art. 105 of the Constitution), which is the independent regulatory body of judges presided by the President of the Republic (Art. 107 of the Constitution). Judges (as well as

lack of binding force of judicial precedents: if judges are only subject to the law, it is not possible to tie them to previous decisions of other judges, even if they are in a higher hierarchical position. Second, Article 104 of the Constitution defines the judiciary as a branch which is autonomous and independent from all other powers, ensuring the external dimension of its independence. Moreover, the organisation of the judiciary must be regulated by statute ('*riserva di legge*', Article 108 of the Constitution), which is a guarantee of independence from the executive. The constitutional guarantee of individual rights rests on the principle of due process (*equo processo*), which also requires regulation by statute ('*regolato dalla legge*', Article 111 of the Constitution). Further elements that are constitutionally guaranteed in the judicial process are: the equal position of the parties and their right to participate in the proceedings, in accordance with the adversarial principle (*principio del contraddittorio*); the impartiality and neutrality of the judge; and the reasonable duration of the process.[10]

The fundamental values underpinning the Constitution, which build a solid democratic system of checks and balances and a comprehensive catalogue of fundamental rights, are still not fully implemented in several aspects of civil justice, such as the right to access to justice and defence, although many gaps have been gradually filled by subsequent legislation, often pushed by the case law of the Constitutional Court.[11]

The Italian justice system is based on a dual hierarchy of courts: ordinary courts, which decide civil and criminal cases on three levels; and administrative courts, with two levels of courts (the Tribunali amministrativi regionali (TAR) and the Consiglio di Stato (Council of State)).[12] A special position is occupied by the Constitutional Court, which is entrusted with the task of judicial review, i.e. of checking the compatibility of statutes with the Constitution, quashing those that are conflicting (which are declared null and void from the time of publication of the decision: Article 136 of the Constitution).[13]

---

public prosecutors, who in Italy are considered part of the judiciary) are selected through a '*concorso pubblico*', i.e. a public competitive examination (Art. 106 of the Constitution).

10 Art. 111(2) of the Constitution: '*Ogni processo si svolge nel contraddittorio tra le parti, in condizioni di parità, davanti a giudice terzo e imparziale. La legge ne assicura la ragionevole durata.*'

11 See M. Taruffo, *La giustizia civile in Italia dal '700 ad oggi*, Il Mulino, Bologna 1980, pp. 310–18.

12 Other independent courts are the Court of Auditors (Corte dei conti) for cases concerning public finance, tax courts (*commissioni tributarie*) and military courts. Art. 103 of the Constitution prohibits the establishment of special courts, as a guarantee for the protection of fundamental rights of citizens.

13 The Constitutional Court, which is an institution established by the 1948 Constitution (and two further constitutional laws: Law 1/1948 and Law 1/1953) starting its work in 1956, is composed of 15 judges, with a non-renewable nine-year term: five judges are appointed by the President of the Republic, five by Parliament, and five by the higher courts (Art. 135 of the Constitution). The Court can be accessed by ordinary judges when they consider that there

Ordinary courts, which deal both with civil and criminal matters, are structured on a three-tiered system: the Tribunali are the courts of first instance of general jurisdictions,[14] and are complemented by courts with limited (but in practice quite extensive) jurisdiction (*Giudici di pace*, Justices of the Peace);[15] the Corti d'appello (courts of appeal);[16] and the Corte suprema di cassazione (Court of Cassation),[17] which is the supreme court for civil and criminal cases.[18] The right to appeal a first-instance case in front of the court of appeal is not established by the Constitution, but it is usually considered as part of the fundamental judicial guarantees, and consequently, until recently, no effective system of filter existed. Only since 2012, due to the serious problems of overload and the backlog of cases, has the court been able to reject the appeals that do not have a 'reasonable probability' of success (Law 134/2012).

The increasing workload of courts and the extended time required for reaching a final decision, and the growing cost of civil justice and the rise of new types of disputes have also led to a veritable explosion of ADR (arbitration, mediation, conciliation) in the last decades, a phenomenon that is common to many other Western legal systems. ADR has several advantages: it is less formal and quicker than ordinary justice, it can be tailored to the features of specific sectors (consumer disputes, family matters, housing, etc.) and is usually less expensive. Yet, these advantages must be balanced with potential drawbacks, such as limited procedural guarantees, lack of legal and technical expertise of the deciding bodies, limited neutrality. Moreover, citizens may have recourse to

---

is a conflict between a statutory rule and the Constitution (the so-called *rinvio incidentale*), since ordinary judges do not have a power of judicial review; and by institutions in case of constitutionally relevant conflicts among them (*rinvio in via principale*).

14 Most cases in the Tribunali are adjudicated by a single judge (*giudice unico di primo grado*), except serious and complex cases. The Tribunali are divided in sections based on the type of cases (civil, criminal, labour, social security, commercial, etc.). There is no jury, apart from in the most serious criminal cases, which are tried by a special section of the tribunale, the Corte di assise. There are currently 135 Tribunali across the country (Law 148/2011).

15 The Justices of the Peace were established in 1991, replacing the former *giudici conciliatori*, to administer simple and speedy justice for minor cases (although for civil cases involving a sum above a very low threshold, parties need to be assisted by a professional lawyer). Their jurisdiction has steadily increased, in order to diminish the backlog of cases of ordinary courts and decrease the duration of cases. See V. Varano and A. De Luca, 'Access to Justice in Italy' (2007) 7(1) *Global Jurist*. There are currently 179 offices of Justices of the Peace across the country (Law 148/2011).

16 The Court of Appeal usually sits in panels composed of three judges, and the review of the first-instance decision covers both legal and factual aspects.

17 'Cassazione' literally means quashing: the supreme court has the task of quashing decisions of lower courts that have wrongly applied the law.

18 Since 2001, a new '*processo civile telematico*' (PCT) has been introduced (Decree 123/2001) allowing the use of telematic and informatic instruments in the civil process. Since 2014 (Law 114/2014), the telematic process has become the standard procedure, and since March 2021 (partly as a consequence of the Covid-19 emergency) it applies also to the Cassazione.

them only because they have been dissuaded from taking their cases to court due to their excessive length, uncertainty and costs.[19]

The framework of Italian civil procedure is provided by the Code of Civil Procedure (*Codice di procedura civile*, CPC) of 1940,[20] with many other important statutes complementing it, establishing a legal setting that often requires a complex work of coordination by interpreters.[21] The guiding prainciples of the civil process in the Code are orality, immediacy and concentration ('*oralità, immediatezza e concentrazione*'). Despite having been enacted during the fascist period, there were only a few essential features of the Code that were closely linked to its ideology, mainly concerning the rules on labour disputes.[22] In fact, its structure was mainly the result of a compromise between different academic and practice positions.[23] As a consequence, the Code of Civil Procedure (similarly to the 1942 Civil Code) has survived the demise of the fascist regime, although it has been significantly revised by numerous extensive reforms.

1.2. JUDICIAL PRECEDENTS AND THE CORTE SUPREMA DI CASSAZIONE

The Corte suprema di cassazione (Cassazione), the highest court for civil (as well as criminal) affairs, is a '*giudice di legittimità*', i.e. it decides on the correct

19 In general, the Italian legal system does not allow self-help and self-enforcement concerning individual rights.

20 The Code is based on a draft made by a commission composed of prominent legal scholars (Redenti, Carnelutti, Calamandrei), and is heavily influenced by the theories of the most important scholar of the time, Giuseppe Chiovenda, whose theories and conceptual framework were extensively modelled on German civil procedure. See M. Cappelletti and J.M. Perillo, *Civil Procedure in Italy*, Martinus Nijhoff, The Hague 1965.

21 See G. Costantino (ed), *La riforma della giustizia civile: Prospettive di attuazione della legge 26 novembre 2021, n. 206*, Cacucci, Bari 2022: '*La disciplina processuale è, ormai, da tempo un tessuto profondamente lacerato, nell'ambito del quale, l'incubo degli interpreti e degli operatori consiste nello scioglimento delle contraddizioni in funzione di una necessaria opera di coordinamento*' (p. 31).

22 It is interesting to note that after the fall of the fascist regime, many lawyers strongly advocated the repeal of the Code of Civil Procedure, but mainly for various interests rather than for its value or ideological features. On the contrary, the Code was generally backed by legal doctrine, which suggested only the reform of specific parts, leading to the first extensive reform of the Code in 1950 (Law 581/1950). See M. Taruffo, above n. 11, Ch. 6.

23 Among the novelties modifying the previous Code of 1854 is the establishment of the *giudice istruttore* (judge of the preliminary phase), a member of the court who is tasked with the preparation of the trial and the admission of evidence, sending the case to the full panel (which can check and review the measures decided) when he/she considers it ready for the decision. This mechanism mediates between the proposals for a single judge and those stressing the need of collegiality. At the same time, although the new procedural system grants wider power to the *giudice istruttore* (who also has significant discretion in adjusting the phases of the procedure to the specific features of each case), in line with the public dimension of private litigation, the role of private autonomy of the parties (according to the so-called '*principio dispositivo*') remains paramount, rejecting an inquisitorial model.

interpretation and application of the law, but not on the facts of the cases, which are left to the lower courts (*giudici di merito*). This is because its task is to guarantee the uniform and correct application of the law, performing a fundamental function of interpretation of the law (*funzione nomofilattica*).[24] The Cassazione, therefore, plays a major role in establishing judicial precedents. Yet, the evolution of its working methods and rules has led it over time to act as a sort of third-instance judge, adjudicating tens of thousands of cases each year. This has emphasised its role as a decision-maker of specific cases, rather than its role in steering case law, and has led to frequent and serious problems of conflicting precedents.[25] While in the 1960s the number of civil cases submitted to the Cassazione each year was around 3,000, the number increased to approximately 17,000 by the 2000s and has reached over 30,000 cases in recent years.[26]

The ever-increasing workload of the Cassazione, linked to a more general litigation explosion, also led to a gradual and significant increase in the number of judges (now over 400),[27] organised in several sections (*sezioni semplici*, which decide in five-judge panels). There are currently six civil sections and seven criminal sections, plus the 'Sezioni unite civili' (civil plenary session, composed of nine judges) and the corresponding 'Sezioni unite penali' (criminal plenary session), which are tasked with solving conflicts among the case law of the sections and other matters of particular importance. This complex pattern has led to a sharp increase of conflicts in their decisions, which risks nullifying the unifying function (*nomofilachia*) of the court. The need to manage the flood of cases has led to the introduction of several mechanisms in a sequence of reforms (some of which are unfolding at present), none of which seem to have been fully successful.[28] In 2009, an important reform of the Code of Civil

24 Even after the unification of Italy, five regional Courts of Cassation survived (Turin, Florence, Naples, Palermo and Rome), and consequently conflicts among their case law was frequent. A single national Corte suprema di cassazione was introduced only in 1923 (Royal Decree of 24 March 1923, no. 601) in order to unify case law. P. Calamandrei, 'La Cassazione civile, II' in P. Calamandrei, *Opere giuridiche*, vol. VII, Naples, 1976, defined *nomofilachia* as the power of the Cassazione to check case law in order to protect 'objective' law, i.e. statutory law, by aligning its interpretation.

25 See M. Taruffo, 'La Corte di cassazione tra legittimità e merito' in M. Taruffo, *Il vertice ambiguo: Saggi sulla cassazione civile*, Il Mulino, Bologna 1991, pp. 101 and following; A. Proto Pisani, 'Su alcuni problemi organizzativi della Corte di cassazione: contrasti di giurisprudenza e tecniche di redazione della motivazione' (1988) V *Foro it.* 27; S. Chiarloni, 'Efficacia del precedente giudiziario e tipologia dei contrasti di giurisprudenza' (1989) *Riv. trim. dir. proc. civ.* 118 (and following); G. Moneta, 'Contrasti nella giurisprudenza della Cassazione civile e certezza del diritto' (1990) *Contratto e impresa* 1009 (and following).

26 See S. Chiarloni, above n. 5, p. 267. See below Section 5.

27 There are 417 judges in the staff of the Corte suprema di cassazione and 50 auxiliary judges (*giudici ausiliari*); 67 judges work at the Ufficio del massimario della Cassazione. In fact, the actual working staff is normally significantly smaller (currently there are 73 judge vacancies at the court, 33 at the Massimario, and 37 auxiliaries).

28 For an overview of the reforms of civil justice between the end of World War II and 1980, see M. Taruffo, above n. 11, Ch. 7, who underlines that while the draft for reforms of the 1950s

Procedure established the inadmissibility of appeals to the supreme court when the decision appealed is in line with the existing case law of the Cassazione, and parties do not raise new elements justifying its revision, and also when the appeal is manifestly groundless (*inammissibile*) (Article 360bis of the CPC).[29] Yet, neither the significant extension of the powers of the Sezioni unite, nor the strengthening of the mechanisms for selecting cases, have been fully successful in harmonising case law, nor in limiting the duration of judicial processes.[30]

This phenomenon has been partly caused and reinforced by the increasing complexity and heterogeneity of statutory law: the Codes (particularly the Civil Code in the area of private law) have gradually lost their capacity to regulate legal relations comprehensively and systematically, and a plethora of special legislation, sometimes poorly drafted and frequently inspired by conflicting aims, makes their interpretation and application by judges much more complex and difficult. Finally, rapid social and technological changes lead to legal gaps, which take time to regulate by statute, but often require an immediate response by judges. The interaction of all these elements impacts the nature and character of case law and implies a serious risk of judicial conflicts.

While these elements are not unique to the Italian legal experience, they are particularly serious in Italian law.[31] Moreover, the fact that this problem has been going on for many decades tends to foster a passive and pessimistic attitude among lawyers, as well as entrenching a dysfunctional behaviour by both judges and lawyers, which is only reinforced by the failure of piecemeal and limited reforms of the judicial process.[32]

---

and 1960s were mostly technical, those of the 1970s acknowledged the social and policy implications of civil justice as a mass social phenomenon, also thanks to the input by several important comparative studies (such as those of Cappelletti and Denti).

29 Law 69/2009. The Sezioni unite of the Cassazione (case nos. 19051/2010 and 7155/2017) have decided that also precedents decided after the appeal can be considered for establishing inadmissibility.

30 See S. Chiarloni, above n. 5, p. 267: 'the Corte di Cassazione is no longer able to guarantee the equal treatment of parties throughout the country, the predictability of its decisions, and the high prestige of its members as supreme judges. Instead, the court has become a sort of judicial supermarket, wherein lawyers can often be sure to find any precedent they need to plead the case of their client'. Another aspect that has been often criticised is the lack of comprehensive empirical work and statistical data, which is essential for devising any successful reform. This is partly linked to the traditional lack of empirical and quantitative skills of lawyers and highly abstract character of legal education.

31 Common law systems have much stronger and effective systems of leave, in order to ensure that their supreme courts only decide a small number of cases, namely those related to important and controversial issues of law. Due to fundamental constitutional principles, in civil law systems courts are not supposed to be able to decide autonomously which cases to hear and which to reject, because this amounts to a discretionary power and may be considered a denial of justice. Yet, if one moves away from rhetorical claims, many civil law countries (such as Germany and France) have introduced effective mechanisms to limit the number of cases decided by supreme courts, granting them selecting powers.

32 Subsequent reforms of civil justice have taken place in 1950 (Law 581/1950), 1973 (Law 533/1973 on labour disputes), 1990 (Law 353/1990) and 1991 (Law 374/1991, establishing

1.3. THE NEW REFORM OF THE ITALIAN CIVIL PROCESS

A comprehensive reform of the whole judicial system, covering also criminal law,[33] ADR (*risoluzione alternativa delle controversie*), arbitration, family and personal status justice, and other important areas, has recently taken place in Italy.[34] The part of the reform concerning civil justice was drafted by a governmental commission presided by Francesco Paolo Luiso, a prominent academic scholar. After a lengthy discussion, Parliament approved the reform in November 2021: Law 206/2021 establishes the guidelines for subsequent delegated legislation to be enacted by the Government in order to ensure the efficiency of civil justice.[35] The reform is based on the principles of simplification, speed and rationalisation (*semplificazione, speditezza, razionalizzazione*) of the civil process, and aims to provide a rational and coherent character to the plethora of piecemeal changes of the last decades.

---

the Justices of the Peace), together with several other sectoral but relevant reforms. A veritable 'tsunami' of judicial reforms (G. Costantino, above n. 21, p. 27) has taken place after 2005, touching on a number of issues: the reform of the procedure at the Cassazione (Legislative Decree 40/2006), the reform of the judiciary (Law 150/2005), the reform for the decrease and simplification of civil cases (Law 69/2009 and Legislative Decree 150/2011), and the reform of the appeal and cassation procedure (Law 134/2012). See M. Taruffo, 'Recent and Current Reforms of Civil Procedure in Italy' in N. Trocker and V. Varano (eds), *The Reforms of Civil Procedure in Comparative Perspective*, Giappichelli, Turin 2005.

33 The parallel reform of the criminal process is set by Law 134/2021, GU 4 October 2021, no. 237.

34 The reform of the national justice system is an essential component of the comprehensive Italian national resilience and recovery plan (*Piano Nazionale di Ripresa e Resilienza*, PNRR), which was adopted in April 2021 in order to benefit from the EU Recovery and Resilience Facility, the massive financial programme linked to the NEXTGenerationEU, established in order to back the recovery of the European economy after the Covid-19 pandemic. For Italy, the plan involves over €190 billion (of which over €120 are long-term loans, and €70 are grants). For a description of the actions and priorities of the Italian PNRR see 'Piano Nazionale di Ripresa e Resilienza', <https://www.governo.it/sites/governo.it/files/PNRR.pdf>.

35 Law of 26 November 2021, no. 206. See Servizio studi, Camera dei deputati, XVIII Legislatura, *Riforma del processo civile*, 29 July 2022; Senato della Repubblica e Camera dei deputati, XVIII Legislatura, *Riforma del processo civile*, Dossier A.C. 3289, 18 October 2021. The first proposal for a comprehensive reform was made in 2018, and was later merged as a horizontal/structural reform within a wider plan related to the general reforms to be introduced in accordance with the national plan for the EU recovery fund (*Piano Nazionale di Ripresa e Resilienza*, PNRR, approved by the EU in May 2021), for the period from 2021–26. In order to back the reform of the judicial process, the law strengthens the role of a special body, the Ufficio del processo (process bureau, established in 2012), with significant financial and human resources (lawyers, but also other professionals, such as informatic and organisation analysts), which will help disposing the backlog and restructuring the working of the courts, fostering teamwork. A specific Ufficio del processo is established for the Cassazione, which will help monitor the amount and types of cases, provide legal research and assist the judges in their work.

The required delegated legislation (*decreti legislativi*) defining the details of the scope and content of the reform, entailing several sensitive policy choices,[36] had to be adopted by the Government by 24 December 2022. This objective was met by the coalition government led by Mario Draghi (former President of the European Central Bank) in October 2022, amid significant political pressure, due to the fact that in July 2022, the Government had to resign after failing to ensure sufficient backing in Parliament. Elections for the new Parliament took place in September 2022, and a new right-wing coalition government headed by Giorgia Meloni was formed.[37] Just weeks before the new government took office, the Draghi government enacted the legislative decrees implementing the reform.[38]

The decree on civil justice covers many issues, such as the simplification of the civil process at first instance, appeal at second instance and cassation, special procedures, ADR, the use of technology in the process, as well as funding and human resources.

The most important rules of the reform impacting on the issue of judicial precedent in private law are those concerning appeals (*impugnazioni*, Article 1(8–10)).[39] For the court of appeal (Article 1(8)), the reform aims at

---

36 The new rules will amend the Code of Civil Procedure, the Civil Code and several related statutes. A very important and innovative element of the law is the comprehensive reform of the judicial process for family, personal and juvenile matters, establishing a single judge and procedure. Also the rules on *esecuzione forzata* (execution), tax courts and procedures (*giustizia tributaria*), and labour disputes are extensively reformed. At first instance, the reform establishes a single judge in the tribunali (tribunale in composizione monocratica) as the standard composition, and simplifies and expedites the procedure (which is the same for the single judge in the tribunal and the Justices of the Peace). Finally, the 2021 reform establishes a committee for the monitoring of efficiency of civil justice (Comitato tecnico-scientifico per il monitoraggio sull'efficienza della giustizia civile), having advisory and supportive tasks, overseeing the statistical data concerning the disposal of the backlog of cases and the average duration of the judicial cases. The reforms require a complex task of coordination, which is entrusted to the delegated legislation enacted by the Government.

37 The draft of the legislative decree was approved by the Government on 28 July 2022 (together with a parallel text for the reform of the criminal process), and it was presented by the Government to the competent parliamentary commissions for their mandatory opinion on 2 August 2023.

38 Legislative Decree 149/2022, GU 17 October 2022, no. 243, SO no. 38; another legislative decree was approved concerning criminal justice. The law on the budget (*legge di bilancio*) for 2023 (Law of 29 December 2022, no. 187, Art. 1, c. 380) has modified the transitory regime for the application of the reform, anticipating the date of 28 February 2023, instead of 30 June 2023, as initially established. The new rules apply to judicial proceedings brought after that date, while pending ones continue to be subject to the previous rules.

39 An important reform is introduced in case of contrast between an Italian judicial decision and a decision of the European Court of Human Rights: if the latter renders a decision which is in conflict with a previous Italian judicial decision, the parties can ask for the *revocazione* (annulment) of the Italian decision, which will be granted if alternative remedies, such as compensation, are insufficient to protect the rights infringed. This novelty only concerns decisions in civil matters, because in the criminal area the Constitutional Court had already required the revision of the decision.

making the requirements for the appeal clearer and more stringent, modifying the changes introduced in 2012, which have been considered too wide in allowing the parties to raise all kinds of issues, both of law and of facts, for challenging the first-instance decision.[40] Appeals that do not have a reasonable probability of success must be declared inadmissible (through a judgment) by the court of appeal, a requirement that should allow them to limit the number of cases and concentrate on the most relevant ones,[41] although it remains to be seen how the wide notion of 'reasonable probability' will be interpreted.

For the Cassazione (Article 1(9)), the fundamental aim of the new rules is to ensure a higher level of coherence and predictability of its case law, and to shorten the duration of the process. To this end, a new simplified and expedited procedure is devised for appeals that are '*inammissibili, improcedibili, manifestamente infondati*', i.e. inadmissible (for lack of required elements), unproceedable (in case of inaction of the parties), or manifestly unfounded. This novelty entails the elimination of the special section of the Cassazione having the task to filter inadmissible cases (so-called '*sezione-filtro*', Sezione VI, established in 2009), entrusting the corresponding power to all the sections (*sezioni semplici*), which will apply a uniform expedited procedure (*rito camerale*, currently regulated by Articles 380bis and 380bis1 of the CPC).[42]

The more complex and long procedure of a public hearing (*udienza pubblica*) is reserved only for the most important cases involving issues of law which are particularly relevant and are essential to guarantee a coherent interpretation of the law (Article 375 of the CPC). The way in which the Cassazione will define the boundaries between the two types of cases will be crucial, with significant effects on its work and on its case law.

Moreover, case law uniformity is pursued also by a new instrument, called *rinvio pregiudiziale* (preliminary ruling), through which a lower judge (*giudice*

---

40 See Legislative Decree 83/2012, reforming Arts. 342 and 434 of the CPC. With the new reform, a fundamental role is played by the *giudice istruttore* (judge of the preliminary hearing), who can decide to allow a decision *in absentia* of the defendant, propose a conciliation to the parties, allow evidence, and set the hearing in front of the court. The court directs and controls the action of the judge, and can integrate or modify his/her decision.

41 The reform abolishes the previous system of selection (*filtro in appello*, 'filtering'), established by Law 134/2012. With the new rules the Court of Appeal can suspend the execution (*esecuzione*) of the judgment appealed if it considers that the appeal is likely to succeed, or if there is a risk of a serious and irreparable prejudice if the judgment is implemented.

42 At the basis of this reform lies the fact that the '*sezione-filtro*' has proven unable to perform efficiently the task that was entrusted to it. See G. Costantino, above n. 21, pp. 244–46. The expedited and simplified procedure of the *rito camerale* adopted by the reform corresponds to that of Art. 380bis1 of the CPC (introduced by Law 197/2016) and envisages a decision in the form of a decree (*ordinanza*), without the intervention of the parties; see M. Acierno, P. Curzio and A. Giusti (eds), *La cassazione civile*, Cacucci, Bari 2020. Moreover, the decision can be only concisely motivated and immediately deposited and made public (although the court can have up to 60 days for drafting and publishing it). Waiver by the parties of their appeal is also facilitated. The appeal for cassation must state in a concise and clear manner the material facts of the case and the reasons that justify the request.

di merito, either of first instance or appeal) can ask the Cassazione to rule on an issue of law that is unclear or disputed. Through this new mechanism, lower judges can, after having allowed the parties to be confronted on the merits ('*contraddittorio*'), submit to the Cassazione an issue of law, suspending the case. This procedure is allowed if the issue is particularly relevant and has not been previously addressed by the Cassazione, it poses significant difficulties of interpretation, and is potentially relevant for a high number of cases. If the preliminary question is considered admissible, it will be decided by the Cassazione (either in the competent *sezione*, or by the Sezioni unite) in a public hearing. The decision is binding for the referring judge, but it will clearly have a wider effect as a leading precedent, signalling the relevance of the decision. While it remains to be seen how this mechanism will be used, both by lower judges and the Cassazione, it must be underlined that it will further reinforce the trend to formulate precedents in a highly abstract and theoretical way, leaving the factual aspects of the precedent in the background.[43]

2. A BRIEF HISTORY OF PRECEDENT IN PRIVATE LAW

Because of the influence of the declaratory theory of case law, implying that judges do not make the law but merely interpret and apply it, for a long time there have been few comprehensive studies analysing the role of judicial precedent in Italian law. The first important endeavour was undertaken by a scholar (who was also an important comparatist), Gino Gorla, who, in the 1960s and 70s, published several works[44] on the role of judicial precedents in Italy, both from a historical and a structural perspective. Historically, he showed that the highest courts (*Rote*) of the states existing before the unification of the Italian state in 1861 had the power to establish judge-made rules, and actively did, similarly to what happened in many other European systems. After the unification of the country, the French legal model was generally adopted, with a heavy emphasis on statutory law as the main source of law, due to its democratic nature, and the

[43] See L. Antoniolli, 'Il ruolo dei precedenti giudiziari nel diritto italiano e la nomofilachia della Cassazione – Spunti critici sul nuovo rinvio pregiudiziale interpretativo' in A. Chizzini, D. Abraham, N. Andrews, C. Silvestri, R. Stürner and V. Varano (eds), *Processo civile e Costituzione – Un omaggio a Nicolò Trocker*, Giuffrè, Milan, 2023, pp. 113–36.

[44] Many of his contributions are now collected in G. Gorla, *Diritto comparato e diritto comune europeo*, Giuffrè, Milan 1981. See also G. Gorla, 'Precedente giudiziale' in *Enciclopedia giuridica Treccani*, vol. XXIII, Istituto della Enciclopedia italiana, Rome, 1990, pp. 13 and following. In the 1950s Gorla took part as the Italian reporter to the 'Common core of the formation of contract', a project led by Rudolph Schlesinger at Cornell University, leading to the publication of a major book on Italian contract law (G. Gorla, *Il contratto*, Giuffrè, Milan 1955), applying the case method and a law in action approach. Gorla insisted on the need to reform legal education and training in order to foster the skills and awareness to the factual dimension of law, opposing the tendency to abstraction and theory.

related idea of the judge as a mere 'mouth of the law' ('*bouche de la loi*'). This radically changed the role of case law.

This new conception also led to a structural change in the style of the judicial decisions and of the law reporting system. What mattered were not judicial precedents as such, but rather the legal rules that judicial cases applied. For this reason, the facts of the case are less crucial today, and are mostly only cursorily explained in the decisions and in the law reports (*raccolte di giurisprudenza*). This means that the Italian law reports, and in particular the *Raccolte di massime* of the Cassazione (or Massimario), which collect the rules decided by the supreme court, are structurally and functionally different from the law reports of the common law countries.

After Gorla, other scholars were highly critical of this system and the mental habit of abstraction that underpins it, which makes it hard to find the true *ratio decidendi* of each case and consequently to make correct use of judicial precedents as a source of law. The work by Gorla was followed by an intense debate in the 1980s about the role of case law, particularly in the area of private law, which was started by an important legal journal, *Contratto e impresa*,[45] established in 1985 by Francesco Galgano, a prominent commercial scholar. It focused on the need to guarantee legal certainty and foreseeability, which was challenged by an ever-growing flood of conflicting judicial decisions, and to balance it with the need of flexibility and equity, in line with the rapid evolution of social, cultural and economic conditions.[46]

In the following decades, the debate focused more generally on the crisis of justice, particularly of civil justice, the structural dimension of which threatens the stability of the whole Italian legal system, where the role of precedents is an issue inextricably connected to the working of the machinery of justice.[47]

3. NATURE OF JUDICIAL PRECEDENTS

The need to find the right balance between legal certainty and predictability with flexibility and equity, is a shared feature of all legal systems in all times. Yet, this requirement has a dynamic nature, which implies that the actual balance changes

45 See 'Otto voci sul precedente giudiziario' (1988) *Contratto e impresa*.

46 See M. Bin, above n. 5, pp. 21–26; F. Galgano, 'Il precedente giudiziario nell'esperienza nazionale' (1988) *Contratto e impresa* 504 (and following): '*La legge, nel senso pieno dell'espressione, è ormai una specie alquanto rara, e la funzione di adeguamento del diritto ai mutamenti della realtà è sempre più largamente svolta dal giudice. ... E tuttavia non siamo attrezzati – nè culturalmente, nè tecnicamente – per lavorare compiutamente sulla giurisprudenza ... una scienza, o più modestamente una tecnica dell'interpretazione del prodotto giudiziario è da noi tutta da fondare*'.

47 See S. Chiarloni, above n. 5.

in different systems and times. Therefore, the value of judicial precedents must be discussed and established considering the specific features of each legal system.

The analysis of the nature of judicial precedents in Italian law must start from the premise that formally they are not considered binding, but only persuasive. This statement must be explained in the context of the Italian judicial process and its specificities. Having analysed the way in which precedents are set by judicial decisions and then reported in Italy, the focus can move to the elements of precedents that are relevant for the evolution of Italian law.

Michele Taruffo, the author of many authoritative works on civil justice and case law, has classified judicial precedents according to several dimensions.[48] The institutional dimension relates to the organisation of justice of each legal system, which deeply influences case law and the establishment, value and treatment of precedents; in particular, the vertical effects of judicial precedents (i.e. the effects concerning lower and higher courts in the judicial structure) can work only if there is a clear hierarchy of courts;[49] this also affects its horizontal dimension, i.e. the value of a judicial precedent for a subsequent case decided by a judge at the same hierarchical level, or even by the same court deciding a similar case.

The objective dimension of judicial precedents concerns the analysis of their effects, i.e. of their capacity to influence subsequent decisions; this involves the distinction between *ratio decidendi* and *obiter dicta*, where the latter (which are defined in negative terms as everything that is not the *ratio*) have only persuasive effects. In Italy, as in most civil law systems, even *rationes decidendi* do not have binding effects, yet the distinction is still relevant. It must be underlined that the fundamental distinction between *ratio decidendi* and *obiter dicta*, and between binding and persuasive precedents, gives only very general and superficial information on the content, role and impact of judicial precedents. In fact, it is not a strict rule: the capacity to influence or even decide subsequent cases is determined by many factors, which makes establishing the value of a precedent a complex assessment that varies on a continuum, rather than a black and white threshold: the level of the court, the time of the decision (old or new), the changes in the background social phenomena regulated by the law, the existence of conflicting decisions, etc. all affect the value of precedents.

---

48 See M. Taruffo, 'Dimensione del precedente giudiziario' (1994) *Riv. trim. dir. proc. civ.* 411 (and following). For an important analysis of case law, see W. Bigiavi, *Appunti sul diritto giudiziario*, Studi Urbinati, Urbino 1933, pp. 88–116, 1934, pp. 1–65, now published in M. Bin (ed), *Appunti sul diritto giudiziario*, CEDAM, Padua 1989.

49 This means that, for example, federal systems that have multiple judicial systems, as in the United States, have a looser structure of judicial precedents; see U. Mattei, *Stare decisis*, Giuffrè, Milan 1988. The same happens where there are several systems of courts related to specific legal areas (criminal, civil, administrative, constitutional, etc.), as in Italy and Germany, and there is no mechanism, or only loose ones, for harmonising their case law and solving conflicts.

A structural feature of great importance for judicial precedents in Italy is linked to the fact that decisions are taken by the whole court, also in the case of a panel court: there is only one decision of the court, rather than several concurring opinions. Moreover, judges cannot file dissenting opinions: while they can dissent with the decision of the majority of the panel, there is no 'external' relevance of this dissent, which remains a purely internal matter of the court; the decision of the majority becomes the only decision of the whole court. This makes judicial decisions more 'abstract', in the sense that the contribution of individual judges in them is not visible, which strengthens the bureaucratic nature of judicial decision-making. At the same time, the fact that there is only one judgment is important in the case of appellate courts and the Court of Cassation, which, as a rule, work in panels composed by several judges: having only one decision of the whole court, with no concurring or dissenting opinions, makes it easier to analyse the decisions and distil their *ratio*.

Another element whose impact is crucial in shaping the content and effects of judicial precedents, in Italy as in all legal systems, is the style of judicial decisions (and their technical language).[50] Decisions of Italian judges are often long and use highly technical and complex language. This is the case also for the Cassazione, whose long and complex decisions have been sometimes termed '*sentenze-trattato*' (treaty-decisions), with numerous lengthy and sometimes obscure arguments which make them difficult to read and understand, and make the task of deriving their *ratio* and its separation from the *obiter dicta* particularly difficult.[51] These lengthy arguments do not usually relate to the facts of the case, but rather are a theoretical analysis of the legal issues involved in the case. This approach is in its turn fostered by the complexity of both the statutory framework and of the case law interpreting it, leading to a sort of loophole: the more complex, confused and incoherent the statutory rules, the more complex, confused and incoherent their interpretation by case law is. At the same time, this kind of judicial reasoning often looks like that of doctrinal works, in spite of the fact that, according to the law, citation of scholars in judicial decisions is banned.[52] As a consequence, Italian judicial decisions, and also their *massime*,

---

50 See Universita di Ferrara, *La sentenza in Europa: Metodo, tecnica e stile*, CEDAM, Padua 1988.

51 In fact, the length and complexity of the arguments does not mean that the reasoning is complete and transparent, also in relation to the criteria applied in the judgments concerning value choices. See M. Bin, 'Funzione uniformatrice della Cassazione e valore del precedente giudiziario' (1988) *Contratto e impresa* 545 (and following); M. Taruffo, 'La fisionomia della sentenza in Italia' (1986) *Riv. trim. dir. proc. civ.* 458 (and following); G. Gorla, 'Lo stile delle sentenze, Testi commentati' (1968) *Quad. Foro it.* c. 389.

52 Art. 118 of the preliminary rules of the Civil Code states that in the reasons for a judicial decision ('*motivazione della sentenza*'), any citation of legal doctrine must be avoided ('*In ogni caso deve essere omessa ogni citazione di autori giuridici*'). This is in line with a positivistic attitude, whereby only statutory law (together with legal principles and equity) is a sound basis for judicial decisions. See below Section 4.

tend to have a highly abstract, technical and bureaucratic character, often using rhetorical stereotyped expressions and legalese jargon, which can make the work of lawyers hard, and feels obscure and remote to lay readers.[53]

The structural dimension of a precedent concerns its elements that are taken into account in the decision of subsequent cases. In the Italian legal system, as discussed, what matters is usually not a single precedent, but rather the line of cases that apply the same rule. In Italian law, precedents are generally referred to as a line of cases that have a strong persuasive effect (*giurisprudenza costante*), both by other courts, law reporters, scholars and lawyers in general. Consequently, any change is usually defined in terms of *revirement*, rather than overruling (which in its proper meaning refers to the change of the decision of a specific case).[54] Moreover, in Italian law, due to the extremely high number of cases decided by the courts, particularly the Cassazione, cases of conflicting precedents are very frequent. Conflicts can be synchronic, i.e. they take place at the same moment in time through clashing decisions of different courts or panels, or diachronic, i.e. they are due to subsequent decisions that are decided in an incompatible way; in this second case, they may relate to a wilful change of case law or not. In fact, in case of conflict it is necessary to distinguish 'real' conflicts, i.e. cases where judges disagree on how to solve a certain type of case, from unintentional conflicts, i.e. conflicts that are due to the uncertain state of precedents and the impossibility for the judge to align with a clear judge-made law, because there is a plethora of scattered and incoherent decisions. This can lead to judicial chaos, where decisions are not amenable to any line of decisions, and consequently it proves impossible for subsequent judges to follow precedents. In this case, the judge will simply pick up the choice that he or she considers most reasonable or expedient and will point rhetorically to this precedent as 'the' right one, a situation that is far from rare in the Italian legal systems.

The statement of the *ratio decidendi* is made by a subsequent interpreter of the decision (another judge, or the lawyer that is tasked with the law reporting), not by the judge/s deciding the case. This activity involves a significant (although not unlimited) margin of discretion in establishing the level of abstraction or specificity of the decision and carving out the essential elements. The scope

---

53 This sense of obscurity and self-referentiality, coupled with the dysfunctionality of the machinery of justice, fosters a sense of distrust among the general public in the judiciary, undermining its prestige and role as a fundamental component of the democratic system. For an early discussion, see V. Denti, 'Il processo come alienazione' (1976) *Sociologia del diritto* 149 (and following).

54 There is an important difference between overruling and distinguishing: the latter, which is a very important mechanism in judge-made law systems, implies that any judicial decision must state the material facts on which it is based: the subsequent decision can move away from the previous one by stating that the material facts are different. This allows a different decision to be made, while leaving the old precedent standing. In Italy, where material facts are not comprehensively reported, it is harder to apply this technique.

of this discretion depends on how clearly and precisely the statutory rules to be applied are worded, and on how clearly the material facts are spelled out, providing a pool of factual elements from which the *ratio* can be distilled. This is not a mechanical exercise, but rather a bounded discretionary activity, which allows for a significant amount of flexibility. While this discretion is unavoidable and necessary, it needs to be checked by requiring a standard of rationality and transparency in the process of extraction. This is particularly important in the case of the Massimario, reporting the case law of the Cassazione, which is a crucial instrument for the system of judicial precedents in Italian law.

This shows the mutual relation between judicial precedents and law reports: a solid system of judicial precedents can only exist if there is a reliable system of law reporting. In Italy, where the *massime* only state the legal rule, with no comprehensive reference to the material facts of the case,[55] they cannot lead to a fully-fledged system of judicial precedents. Consequently, all the complex legal techniques used for interpreting and applying judicial precedents (such as the distinction *ratio/obiter*, distinguishing and overruling) are radically different in this setting. This alters the nature of judicial decisions, which are the solutions of a legal problem concerning a specific factual situation, and blurs the distinction with statutory rules, which are meant to have a general and abstract scope.

4. HOW TO IDENTIFY A LEGAL RULE IN A PRECEDENT

The establishment of a precedent is related to the duty to state the reasons in all judicial decisions (Article 111(6) of the Constitution): the judge must explain the arguments that have led to the decision (both the material facts and the applicable rules), and explain, if this happens, the reasons for refusing the application of previous case law in case the social circumstances require a *revirement* in the judicial interpretation of the law.[56] Moreover, Article 118 '*disposizioni di attuazione del codice di procedura civile*' (implementing rules of the CPC), requires judicial decisions not only to state the reasons both in relation to the material facts and the legal rules, but also allows reference to be made to previous case law ('*precedenti conformi*').[57]

---

55 According to M. Taruffo, 'La Corte di cassazione e la legge' in M. Taruffo, *Il vertice ambiguo: Saggi sulla cassazione civile*, above n. 25, the tendency to stress the abstract nature of the interpretation given by the Cassazione in a judicial case is due to the emphasis given to the role of giving a correct ('exact') interpretation of statutory rules as such (*ius constitutionis*), rather than to the decision in relation to specific facts (*ius litigationis*). This is connected to the formalistic and positivistic approach, based on the idea of judicial syllogism and a strictly deductive method.

56 M. Taruffo, *La motivazione della sentenza civile*, CEDAM, Padua 1975.

57 Interestingly, the rule prohibits courts from referring to legal doctrine ('*autori giurdici*'), a requirement (not always followed in practice) that is also related to a formal conception of legal sources, from which doctrine is excluded.

The age of precedents does not have a univocal impact on their value: old precedents are frequently cited, even if they date back many decades, when they have established an important new rule or interpretation, particularly when they have been decided by higher courts. Another relevant element concerns the continuing existence of the rules applied in the precedents: if the statutory framework has remained fundamentally stable, old precedents continue to be applicable; if, on the other hand, legislation has radically changed, this affects the relevance of precedents and their pattern of citation and use. Also, extra-legal factors can influence the enduring value of judicial decisions: if social, economic, or cultural circumstances have significantly changed, they tend to diminish the precedential value of old decisions. In general, the extremely large body of judicial decisions and the relative instability of the statutory framework of the Italian legal system tend to downplay the use of old precedents in favour of a wider use of more recent decisions, which, as discussed, are usually cited as a line of cases (*giurisprudenza consolidata*), although specific precedents are also cited and analysed when they are particularly important for the issue at stake in the decision.

A crucial rule in Italian law concerning the role of case law and judicial precedents of the Cassazione is Article 65 of the judicial order (*Testo unico dell'ordinamento giudiziario*) of 1941, which states that the Cassazione, as the supreme court, ensures the exact compliance and the uniform interpretation of the law ('*l'esatta osservanza e l'uniforme interpretazione della legge*') as well as the unity of national objective law ('*l'unità del diritto oggettivo nazionale*').[58] This rule is based on two fundamental principles: legal certainty (*certezza del diritto*) and equality of citizens under the law (*uguaglianza dei cittadini di fronte alla legge*, Article 3 of the Constitution). The concept of 'legal unity' is particularly relevant for the role of the Cassazione as the court whose case law (and precedents) should be followed, both by lower courts and by the Cassazione itself. This role is also confirmed by the Constitution: Article 111(7) rules that any final judicial decision (*sentenza*) and decisions affecting personal freedom can be challenged in front of the Cassazione for violation of the law ('*violazione di legge*').[59]

---

58 The Law on the Judiciary of 1941 (Royal Decree 12/1941) was modelled on the previous one of 1923. Although some influence from the fascist ideology can be detected in the emphasis on a hierarchical structure, governmental control over the public prosecutor, and the sanctioning power of the Ministry of Justice over judges, by and large the structure of the legislation is in line with the pre-existing nineteenth century liberal one. After the establishment of a democratic regime, and the enactment of the 1948 Constitution, it has been modified several times but never completely repealed, in spite of the clash of values underpinning the two legal documents.

59 Final decisions of the administrative courts (Consiglio di Stato) and auditing courts (Corte dei Conti) can be challenged in front of the Cassazione only for matters related to the scope of the jurisdiction of the courts (*conflitti di giurisdizione*): Art. 111(9) of the Constitution.

Therefore, the Cassazione has a functional duty to guarantee a uniform interpretation of the law, which also implies the duty to ensure uniformity of the case law interpreting statutory law.[60] While this does not amount to a principle of *stare decisis*,[61] because judges neither have a legal obligation to follow legal precedents nor is there any sanction in case of departure from precedents, it is still an obligation having a legal nature, not merely an ethical rule of judicial behaviour.[62]

The Ufficio del massimario della Corte suprema di cassazione is the body that is responsible for the drafting, collection and publication of the *massime*. It was established in 1941 by the law on the judiciary (*Testo unico sull'ordinamento giudiziario*, Article 68), and is staffed by judges[63] who systematically scrutinise all decisions of the Cassazione (both judgments and decrees). The focus of this activity is on the legal rules and principles applied in the case formulated in an abstract way, rather than being structurally referred to the material facts.[64] This activity allows the identification of the *orientamenti* (trends) of the case law of the Cassazione, which bear the strongest persuasive precedential value. Yet, the fact that the *massime* are usually referred only to the legal rule but not to the material facts of the case (the so-called *massime astratte*), besides limiting the precedential value of the decision, also implies a risk that the rule that is formulated in the *massima* will actually not be the one that was applied for deciding the case, and

---

60 See G. Gorla, *Diritto comparato e diritto comune europeo*, above n. 44, pp. 515 and following; S. Chiarloni, 'In difesa della nomofilachia' (1992) *Riv. trim. dir. proc. civ.* 123 (and following), critically writes of 'mass justice' which no longer fulfils its institutional tasks, asking himself rethorically '*quale mai possa essere l'autorevolezza di un organo giurisdizionale posto al vertice dell'organizzazione giudiziaria e composto tuttavia di parecchie centinaia di giudici, che offre sul mercato tutto e il contrario di tutto*', producing a case law that is '*confusa, insicura, insicura, oscillante, a volte addirittura caotica*'.

61 As for examples in the English House of Lords before the Practice Statement 1966 [1966] 1 WLR 1234.

62 In the 1970s and 1980s, many judges and some scholars advocated a more open and flexible approach to judicial precedents, arguing that the Corte suprema di cassazione does not have a legal duty to establish coherence and certainty of case law, but rather to foster some form of convergence emerging dialectically from the interaction between it and lower judges, through a bottom-up approach, in line with a rapidly changing and plural society. Yet, this approach significantly underrated the problems of a plethoric, unstable and conflicting case law, and downplayed the costs that are imposed on citizens and institutions alike. See V. Denti, 'A proposito di Corte di Cassazione e nomofilachia' (1986) V *Foro it.* 417 (and following).

63 A first embryonic body for monitoring the precedents of the Cassazione was established in 1924. For a brief historical overview, see G. Amoroso, 'Nomofilachia e massimario' in *L'ufficio del Massimario e del Ruolo della Corte di cassazione: il presente che guarda al passato per pensare al futuro*, 12 April 2017, Corte di cassazione, Rome.

64 See ibid.: '*Nella redazione delle massime, si mira ad isolare il principio di diritto enunciato (non meramente applicato) dal provvedimento massimato che va a comporre ... il quandro degli orientamenti della giurisprudenza di legittimità. La massima tende a rappresentare sinteticamente il principio affermato nel provvedimento massimato e, solo se necessario, ne riproduce anche la ratio*' (p. 5).

has consequently a misleading character (the so-called *massima mentitoria*),[65] being only an *obiter*, rather than the *ratio*. Since subsequent decisions often refer only to the *massima*, rather than accessing the whole case in order to derive the *ratio*, it is the first that actually becomes a precedent for future cases, while the second can become virtually unknown to subsequent decision-makers and interpreters.

Until the 1980s, the publication of the *massime* was made in monthly reports; subsequently, an electronic retrieval system (*Italgiure*)[66] was introduced by the electronic documentation centre (Centro elettronico di documentazione, CED) of the Cassazione, which is nowadays the main source of information on its case law.[67]

For each *massima*, it specifies whether there are similar precedents (*conformi*, CONF) or conflicting ones (*difformi*, DIFF); a special expression (CERTALEX) is employed only for the *massime* that state a consolidated case law.[68] The Massimario is now testing a system having a dynamic character and evolving according to subsequent decisions, labelled 'CERTANET', which indicates that the decision has been repeatedly followed in a recent period.[69]

Over time, the number of decisions of the Cassazione that are '*massimate*' has been significantly reduced: while in 1985 the process of '*massimazione*' involved around 4,000 decisions out of a total of around 6,500 (i.e. around two-thirds of all decisions), in 2016 there have been around 4,500 *massime* for over 27,000 decisions (i.e. less than a fifth).[70] This means that while the number of decisions has steadily increased, the number of *massime* has remained relatively stable and even decreased. This has a major impact on judicial precedents, because it implies that the Ufficio del massimario selects the cases that are going to have precedential value, discarding the others. The policy implications of this selection process, which is performed without analytically specifying the detailed selection criteria, which should be open to scrutiny, are generally overlooked.

---

65 See R. Sacco, 'La massima mentitoria' in G. Visintini (ed), *La giurisprudenza per massime e il valore del precedente*, CEDAM, Padua 1988, pp. 51 and following. For a less negative assessment of the quality of the *massime* see S. Chiarloni, 'Efficacia del precedente giudiziario e tipologia del contrasti di giurisprudenza' (1989) *Riv. trim. dir. proc. civ.* 118, 124 (and following).

66 See *ItalgiureWeb* <http://www.italgiure.giustizia.it/>. *Italgiure* currently contains approximately 510,000 *massime* and 400,000 decisions in civil matters.

67 The database is freely accessible for courts, and for a fee to private subjects. The website of the court offers a free service of information on recent decisions (<https://www.cortedicassazione.it/corte-di-cassazione/it/recentissime_corte.page>), as well as a yearly review on its case law.

68 This signals to the parties that an appeal to the Cassazione requesting a different decision is likely to be rejected as inadmissible, according to Art. 360bis1 of the CPC.

69 G. Amoroso, 'Il progetto Certanet nel sistema Italgiure della Corte di cassazione' in D. Dalfino (ed), *Scritti dedicati a Maurizio Converso*, TrE-Press, Rome, 2016, p. 24.

70 The number of *massime* which signal a deviation from precedents (*annotazione di difformità*) is 91 in 1985, and 123 for 2016, but it is not clear whether this reflects a similar trend, or if it is the result of a different filtering system. See G. Amoroso, above n. 63, p. 6.

Lower courts' decisions are selectively published in legal journals (but often with *omissis* on facts) and in online databases. In general, the possibility of using digital databases for search and retrieval has radically changed the working method of lawyers, with a much greater ease of searching and a significant saving of time. While finding cases and precedents is now definitely easier, the problem of how to select them remains, and is actually made even more, acute. Informatics and artificial intelligence (of which machine learning is the most recent and advanced development) are radically changing many features of law. This is a phenomenon whose impact is difficult to assess, due to its recent, sweeping and rapidly changing features, but it is surely going to be pervasive and fundamental, not only for information retrieval, but also for its processing and use in judicial decision-making.[71]

5. MANDATE AND IMPORTANCE TO CREATE PRIVATE LAW

Legal certainty and predictability are particularly relevant in private law because citizens and businesses need to know which rules apply to their transactions and relationships, in order to plan and carry out their actions. To ensure them, legal systems must have both clear and consistent statutory law, and a clear and coherent interpretation and application of it by case law. Among the areas of private law where case law has played a crucial role, one can mention tort law (for example, in regard to liability for environmental damage, liability of public bodies towards private individuals, injuries due to traffic accidents, liability for access and use of data, etc.) and family law (for example, in relation to the rights of children of same-sex couples, the right to bear maternal surname, protection of vulnerable parties in family relations, etc.) as areas that have been deeply influenced and shaped by judge-made law. The reasons for the essential role of case law are manifold: the need to fill statutory gaps, new emerging social needs, the slowness of the legislative process, poor drafting and conflicts of statutory provisions, among other elements. And while the lawmaker is often lagging behind in adjusting and updating the legal system to new needs and problems, particularly when this entails taking decisions in politically highly sensitive and controversial sectors, judges are bound to take up the cases that parties lodge. This means that it is exactly the most problematic and controversial cases that get to the courts, and the latter have to, for good or bad, come up with reasonable decisions based on the existing legal rules and principles. It is for this reason

71 For a discussion of some critical issues see H.-W. Micklitz, O. Pollicino, A. Reichman, A. Simoncini, G. Sartor and G. De Gregorio (eds), *Constitutional Challenges in the Algorithmic Society*, Cambridge University Press, Cambridge 2022.

that, while from a theoretical and formal point of view case law is not considered a source of law under Italian law, in fact any lawyer will immediately turn to case law to understand how any legal issue is solved. This applies to all legal sectors and is crucial also in private law.

Due to this complex situation, the Italian legal system is under stress in guaranteeing legal certainty and predictability also of case law, and the previous paragraphs have analysed the critical elements that affect the capacity of the machinery of justice to produce a functioning body of case law in the area of private law.

The most recent statistical data concerning the workload of the Cassazione in civil matters are truly impressive and are essential to understand the context in which judicial precedents operate. The latest report of the Cassazione civile of January 2022 shows a discouraging picture:[72] in 2021 there were over 31,000 cases lodged, after a peak of over 38,000 cases lodged in 2019. The number of cases decided in 2021 was over 40,000, with a sharp increase (around 40%) from the previous years, where around 30,000 cases were decided. Of the cases decided, roughly two-thirds were lodged one or two years before (58% in 2021; it was 49% in 2020); around a fifth (18%) were lodged five to six years before, and one in ten (9%) more than six years before. Pending cases are over 111,000, with a trend that is decreasing, but which remains well over 100,000 cases in the last five years. The average duration of the process is approximately three and a half years (around 1,300 days), with a similar trend in the previous years (and never falling below three years in the last decade, except slightly so in 2012). Of all the cases decided, around a third (29.8%) have been rejected, a comparable percentage (28.8%) have been successful, and approximately a quarter have been declared inadmissible (24.5%).

The picture emerging from these data is daunting: over 30,000 cases decided each year, of which one third (i.e. around 10,000) are considered inadmissible, with three times more cases pending, with an average duration of over three years.

These numbers can only be read in terms of a structural crisis: first of all, as the maxim says, 'justice delayed is justice denied',[73] and second, no court

---

72 Cassazione civile, *Annuario statistico 2021*, 5 January 2022 <https://www.cortedicassazione.it/cassazione-resources/resources/cms/documents/AG2022_ANNUARIO_civile-2021.pdf> provides extensive data for 2021, and selective comparative data from 2012. In the same year, the Cassazione penale (criminal cassation) reported roughly comparable data, except for pending cases (where the backlog of the Cassazione civile is around four times larger than the Cassazione penale): over 46,000 cases lodged, over 47,000 cases decided, over 23,000 cases pending; see Cassazione penale, *Annuario statistico 2021*, 18 January 2022.

73 The systematic violations of individual rights due to the excessive duration of judicial cases has been a major source of litigation at the European Court of Human Rights for the violation of the right to a reasonable duration of the process (Art. 6 of the European Convention on Human Rights), which has led to a plethora of decisions granting damages to parties that won their case in Strasbourg, and to the enactment of specific legislation to this end (Law 89/2001 and subsequent amendments in 2012 and 2015).

can work effectively with such a heavy load and backlog of cases. In the case of the Cassazione, this impacts not only on the working of the court, but also on its ability to work as the highest court tasked to establish a coherent and predictable case law (the '*funzione nomofilattica*'): a court that has to decide around 30,000 cases a year (twice as many if the workload for criminal cases is taken into account) cannot produce strong judicial precedents, not even a solid '*giurisprudenza consolidata*'.[74] The ongoing reform of civil justice aims to reverse this trend and reinstate the Cassazione as the highest court that ensures coherence, correctness and predictability, through the strengthening of filtering mechanisms and the new preliminary reference procedure.[75] Nevertheless, the final content of the reform is not yet defined, and its impact will have to be tested in the practice of the courts.

6. CONCLUDING REMARKS

The evolution and current state of Italian case law is influenced by several important factors. Italy is part of the civil law system, and this is reflected both in the way in which case law is set in the hierarchy of sources of law, and in the structural features of its machinery of justice. Yet, some of its most relevant characteristics, particularly some of the dysfunctional ones, are peculiar to the Italian legal system: the astonishing number of cases decided by the supreme court, the Cassazione, and the inefficiencies and delays in the work of the courts, have hardly a parallel in other European countries.

These elements influence the way in which judicial precedents are made and the way in which they are applied also in the area of private law. This contribution has analysed the peculiar and relevant role played by the so-called *massime* of the Cassazione, and also the shortcomings of the way in which they are formulated, which focuses on legal issues, rather than on the material facts. Yet, the *massime* are a crucial source of law in practice, no matter what their intrinsic quality is, because they are cited, used, and applied by lawyers and judges, and therefore have *de facto* precedential value. In a system where the highest court decides thousands of cases each year, this is simply necessary and unavoidable. While it is unthinkable to get rid of the instrument of *massime*, which are vital for legal practice, their drafting and quality should be improved.[76]

---

74 By comparison, the Italian Constitutional Court (which is composed of 15 judges) decides less than 300 cases a year (an average of around 270 in the last five years): see Corte costituzionale, *Relazione sull'attività della Corte costituzionale nel 2021*, 7 April 2022 <https://www.cortecostituzionale.it/annuario2021/pdf/Relazione_annuale_2021.pdf>.

75 See above Section 1.2.

76 See G. De Nova, 'Sull'interpretazione del precedente giudiziario' (1986) *Contratto e impresa* 779 (and following). The same point was raised several decades ago. See P. Calamandrei, 'La funzione della giurisprudenza nel tempo presente' (1955) *Riv. trim.*

The activity of extracting judicial precedents is not a mechanical one, and it requires comprehensive and reliable information through law reporting, as well as legal skills and craftmanship. It is a creative, but not arbitrary, activity that is influenced by a complex web of factors, whose interaction and balance needs to be carefully assessed.

This issue is inextricably connected to the wider context of the reform of civil justice. After decades of criticism and piecemeal reforms, a new effort for a major reform is underway, centred on the need to simplify, rationalise, and speed up civil justice, and to put the Cassazione back at the heart of case law, strengthening its role in leading case law and guaranteeing legal certainty and uniformity. It is noteworthy that this is not only a national priority, but also a fundamental requirement from the EU, which has made the disbursement of the large recovery fund to Italy conditional also on the reform of civil (and criminal) justice. Its enactment and implementation will be crucial for its future evolution, although at this stage it is impossible to foresee its impact.

A comprehensive change of civil justice must also involve a structural change in the training and recruitment of judges, fostering a less bureaucratic and a more pragmatic attitude, as well as a change of the selection and practice of lawyers, emphasising the aspects related to legal ethics.[77] More generally a systematic change of the situation requires a radical change of mentality of all stakeholders involved: judges, lawyers,[78] and parties alike. The increasing popular mistrust of the judiciary is a sign of a deep social malaise that needs to be comprehensively and effectively addressed.[79]

---

dir. proc. civ. 262; Redenti, 'I nostri tesmoteti, ovvero le "massime consolidate" della Corte Suprema' (1949) *Riv. trim. dir. proc. civ.* 121.

77 See M. Taruffo, above n. 11, pp. 353–58; S. Chiarloni, above n. 5, advocates a general reform and merge of the access and training both of judges and lawyers, focused on practical training and skills. A partial reform in this direction has been introduced with the establishment in 1999 (Decree 537/1999) of the Scuole di specializzazione per le professionali legali (SSPL, Schools for the legal professions).

78 One of the problems affecting the class of practicing lawyers is their excessive number: in spite of a long and complex process for entering the bar, in 2021 there were almost 250,000 lawyers enrolled (with a steady growing trend which has stopped only in 2021; in 2008 there were around 150,000), significantly more than in most European countries, also those belonging to the civil law tradition; see Consiglio Nazionale Forense (CNF), *Statistiche anno 2021*, 2021 <https://i2.res.24o.it/pdf2010/Editrice/ILSOLE24ORE/QUOTIDIANI_VERTICALI/Online/_Oggetti_Embedded/Documenti/2022/04/27/Avvocati_Cnf_statistiche.pdf>. S. Chiarloni, above n. 5, uses harsh words: 'The increasing number of lawyers has caused the profession to assume an unpleasantly parasitic aspect. … If one has only a few cases, it is necessary to make them last as long and cost as much as possible. Such a situation also contributes to the judicial burden' (p. 277). This problem is an old one: see the criticism by P. Calamandrei, 'Troppi avvocati' in P. Calamandrei, *Opere giuridiche*, Naples 1966, pp. 65 and following.

79 Over two decades ago, S. Chiarloni criticised 'the progressive decay of the administration of justice to levels which are intolerable in a civilized country': S. Chiarloni, above n. 5, p. 269. Since then, the situation has, if anything, worsened.

Finally, it must be kept in mind that Italian law, also its case law, does not live and develop in isolation: it is part of a wider legal web which influences it and is influenced by it. The most important framework in which Italian law is set is the European Union, which over time has increasingly focused on the judiciary as a fundamental building block of the European legal system and the rule of law. But the scope of judicial relations is actually wider and involves national and international systems in a global web, where the working methods are connected and mutually influenced. Ensuring a sound and effective justice system, of which case law and judicial precedent in private law matters are a fundamental component, is therefore not only a national goal, but an aim that should be pursued through a shared transnational effort.

PRECEDENT IN RUSSIAN PRIVATE LAW

Roman Zykov

1. LEGAL SYSTEM

1.1. SOURCES OF LAW

The Russian legal system is a civil law system conceptually based on statutes and codes. The statutory provisions are rather abstract and require interpretation when they are applied to a particular legal relationship or in a court case.

Being a federal state, the Russian legal system comprises federal and regional statutes and codes. The Constitution of the Russian Federation (the Constitution)[1] draws a fundamental borderline between the competence of the federal and regional authorities. A more detailed division of powers is provided by federal agreements between the Russian Federation and its regions. For example, civil, criminal, tax, customs, land, forestry, water resources, inland

[1] Arts. 11, 71, 72 and 73 of the Constitution.

water transportation, and civil and criminal procedure matters are regulated at the federal level. Centralised regulation of fundamental matters under federal legislation creates a homogeneous legal environment in all regions of the Russian Federation and consequently, as will be discussed further below, a rather unified application of law by Russian courts.

The statutory law regulates nearly all spheres of activities and is regularly supplemented and amended by the legislator. In those fields where there is less or no statutory regulation, sub-laws fill the gap.

A large part of Russian legal acts are sub-laws enacted by the state executive bodies and other state organs.

Although there is no statutory definition of the hierarchy of sources of law, it is accepted doctrinally[2] that the sources of law form the following hierarchy:

1. the Constitution;
2. ratified international treaties;
3. federal constitutional laws; and
4. federal codified laws (codes) and federal laws.

Sub-laws form the following hierarchy:

1. Decrees of the President of the Russian Federation, Resolutions of the State Duma (a lower chamber of the State Assembly), instructions of the Central Bank of the Russian Federation, and instructions of the Central Elections Committee;
2. Resolutions of the Russian Government; and
3. sub-laws enacted by the federal executive bodies.

Case law is secondary and subordinate to statutory law, except for the decisions of the Constitutional Court of the Russian Federation. Suffice to say at this stage, only binding interpretations of the law are given by the Constitutional Court of the Russian Federation, which may also abolish some legislative norms that are incompatible with the Constitution and, without a doubt, represent a source of law.

Although, case law plays an important role in the Russian legal system, its place among other sources of law is still a subject of debate. Formally speaking, the Russian legal system does not recognise case law as a source of law. In practice, however, the courts routinely rely on other decided cases to explain how they have arrived at their decisions.

The decisions of the Supreme Court of the Russian Federation, and (before 2014) of the Supreme Arbitrazh Court of the Russian Federation

---

[2] V.A. Tolstik, *The Hierarchy of Sources of Russian Law*, Nizhny Novgorod 2022.

(Sup Arb Ct RF),[3] arguably represent a source of law, albeit it is still a matter of debate, which will be further explained in this contribution.

To some extent, business custom is also recognised as a source of law, for example by the Civil Code of the Russian Federation (CC RF):

> As a custom shall be deemed a rule of behavior which has taken shape and is widely applied in some sphere of business or other kinds of activities, and which has not been stipulated by legislation, regardless of whether it has or has not been fixed in any document.[4]

And:

> In cases when the relations, stipulated in Items 1 and 2 of Article 2 of the present Code are not directly regulated by legislation or by an agreement between the parties, while the custom that would apply to them does not exist, and if this is not in contradiction with their substance, the civil legislation shall be applied, which regulates similar relations (the analogy of the law).[5]

1.2. THE RUSSIAN COURT SYSTEM IN BRIEF

Due to the federal structure of the Russian Federation, the Russian court system includes the following courts:

a. federal courts:
   i. the Constitutional Court of the Russian Federation (Const Ct RF);
   ii. the Supreme Court of the Russian Federation (Sup Ct RF); and
   iii. first, appeal and cassation instances of the courts of general jurisdiction and commercial (arbitrazh) courts;
b. the Constitutional Courts of the regions; and
c. the magistrate judges (*mirovoi sud*).

The courts have different specialisations and can be grouped into:

a. constitutional courts (federal and regional);
b. courts of general jurisdiction (federal courts and magistrate judges); and
c. commercial (arbitrazh) courts.

---

3 '*Arbitrazh*' is the system of state commercial courts and should not be confused with 'arbitration', being an independent third-party dispute resolution mechanism that is based on the agreement between the parties. See R. Zykov, 'Arbitration in Russia' (Ch. 25) in T.P. Asanti, *Corporate Counsel's Guide to Doing Business in Russia*, 2nd ed., Thomson West, Minnesota, USA, 2008, p. 849.

4 Art. 5 of the CC RF.

5 Art. 6 of the CC RF.

This contribution will focus only on the system of commercial (arbitrazh) courts and the Sup Ct RF as the highest instance above them. But the conclusions, with some caveats, should also apply to the federal courts of general jurisdiction.

The system of commercial courts comprises the following levels:

a. courts of the first instance;
b. courts of appeal;
c. courts of cassation; and
d. the Sup Ct RF.

Procedural rules for the courts of general jurisdiction are laid down in the Civil Procedure Code of the Russian Federation, dated 14 November 2002, No. 138-FZ (CPC RF). Procedural rules for commercial courts are laid down in the Arbitrazh (Commercial) Procedure Code of the Russian Federation, dated 24 July 2002, No. 95-FZ (APC RF). It shall be noted that the term '*arbitrazh*' refers to resolving disputes in the state commercial (arbitrazh) courts in Russia, as opposed to commercial arbitration, which is referred to as '*arbitration*' or '*tretejskij sud*'.

1.3. TYPES OF JUDICIAL DECISIONS

There are four types of court decisions: orders (*prikaz*), judgments (*reshenie*), resolutions (*postanovlenie*), and rulings (*opredelenie*).[6]

Decisions of the courts of first instance are issued in the form of:

a. judgments – decisions on the merits;
b. orders – in certain types of cases; and
c. rulings – on procedural issues or enforcement of judgments or arbitral awards.

Decisions of appellate and cassation instances are issued in the form of:

a. resolutions; and
b. rulings – on procedural issues or enforcement of judgments or arbitral awards.

Decisions of the Sup Ct RF are held in the form of:

a. rulings for cassation appeals; and
b. resolutions in cases where the Sup Ct RF acts as a supervisory instance.

6 Art. 15(1) of the APC RF.

c. In addition, the Sup Ct RF issues information letters together with overviews of cases (*obzor praktiki*) for the unified application of the law by the courts of all instances.

2. A PRECEDENT

2.1. EXISTENCE OF A PRECEDENT

As follows from the above, only some of the judicial decisions contain holdings on the issues of the law, and presumably, only such decisions may theoretically create a precedent.

The Sup Ct RF is the supreme judicial body for civil, economic, criminal, administrative, and other cases, which carries out judicial supervision over the activities of lower courts and provides explanations on the issues decided in other cases.[7]

The Presidium of the Sup Ct (Sup Ct RF [Presidium])[8] acts as a supervisory instance for the individual resolutions of the Sup Ct RF (for example, the resolutions of the Sup Ct RF when it acts as the court of first instance or appeal in specific cases, or in its collegiums as the highest court instance) to ensure uniformity of case law. An application for a supervisory action may be filed by the parties to the dispute, or third parties whose interests are impacted by the respective court decisions, by the Chairman or Deputy Chairman of the Sup Ct RF, or in some cases by the General Prosecutor. A Supreme Court judge reviews the application and decides whether to transfer the case to the Presidium or not. If the Sup Ct RF judge refuses to transfer the case to the Presidium, the Chairman or Deputy Chairman of the Sup Ct RF may disagree with such a decision and nevertheless transfer the case to the Sup Ct RF [Presidium].

As a result, the Sup Ct RF [Presidium] passes a resolution in which it may:[9]

a) confirm the decision of the first, appeal or cassation instances and dismiss the application for supervision;
b) quash entirely or in part the decision of the first, appeal or cassation instances and refer the case back to the respective court. The Sup Ct RF [Presidium] may also require that the case be tried by different judges;

---

7 Art. 126 of the Constitution.

8 Pursuant to Art. 7.1(1) of Federal Constitutional Law No. 3-FKZ dated 5 February 2014 On the Supreme Court of the Russian Federation (Sup Ct RF Law). Also prior to 2014, the Presidium of the Sup Arb Ct RF before it merged with Sup Ct RF (Sup Arb Ct RF [Presidium]) which was governed then by a separate law.

9 Art. 308.11 of the APC RF.

c) quash entirely or in part the decision of the first, appeal or cassation instances and leave the supervisory appeal without consideration or dismiss the case;
d) quash entirely or in part the decision of the first, appeal or cassation instances and decide the case without referring it back to the lower instances, in the event the lower courts incorrectly applied (or interpreted) the law; or
e) dismiss the application for supervision without consideration of the merits.[10]

The resolutions of the Sup Ct RF [Presidium] are binding *inter partes*, however, they have also an *erga omnes* (towards all) legal effect, because the court interprets and applies statutory law to individual cases to achieve uniform application of the law by all courts. Therefore, it can be argued that the resolutions of the Sup Ct RF [Presidium] amount to a so-called 'declaratory precedent' because they apply already existing statutory norms or principles of law to particular facts of the case and create a binding rule based on the interpretation of such norms and principles.

As a result, when trying cases with similar facts, lower courts accurately follow the resolutions of the Sup Ct RF [Presidium]. Consequently, if a lower court decision contradicts the courts' uniform interpretation and application of the law set out by the Sup Ct RF [Presidium], this may serve as a basis for quashing the decision on appeal.

Furthermore, some decisions of the Sup Ct RF may retroactively reopen for trial the existing decisions of lower courts. In a landmark resolution of the Sup Arb Ct RF, the Court ruled that if its resolution forms a position on a particular matter and if it explicitly permits so, such resolutions may serve as a ground for reopening the already concluded proceedings in the lower courts, even in unrelated cases.[11] Such supervisory resolutions of the Sup Ct RF also will most likely be followed by lower courts. This is because the reopening of a case demonstrates the importance of its outcome to the development of case law, and therefore it will likely be treated by lower courts as a rule they need to follow in similar cases. If seeking an analogy in common law, this tool somewhat resembles the concept of '*overruling*'. Such a resolution of the Sup Ct RF may alter the existing courts' practice or introduce a new interpretation of law concerning a subject matter.

Another form of 'creating' guidance by the Sup Ct RF is the resolutions of the Plenum of the Sup Ct RF (Sup Ct RF [Plenum]).[12]

---

10 This may be done due to procedural or formalistic deficiencies of the application for supervision, such as lack of form, lack of a person's authority to lodge the application with the court, missed application deadlines, etc.

11 Resolution of the Sup Arb Ct RF [Plenum] No.14 dated 14 February 2008.

12 Also prior to 2014 by the former Plenum of the Supreme Commercial (Arbitrazh) Court of the Russian Federation before it merged with Sup Ct RF (Sup Arb Ct RF [Plenum]) which was governed then by a separate law.

When a critical mass of decisions of lower courts on a particular issue accrues, the Sup Ct RF [Plenum] embarks on the analysis of the decided cases to guide lower courts on how to apply certain provisions of the law for achieving their uniform application.[13] The resulting document is called a resolution of the Sup Ct RF [Plenum].

There are some examples of resolutions issued by the Sup Ct RF [Plenum] concerning commercial matters, titled: On some aspects related to the application of the provisions of the CPC RF on limitation periods;[14] On the application by courts of selected provisions of Section I Part I of the Civil Code;[15] On the application of the general part of the Civil Code concerning conclusion and interpretations of agreements;[16] On some aspects of the resolution of disputes arising out of suretyships;[17] and On the application of Article 9.1 of the Russian Bankruptcy law.[18] As can be seen, the resolutions of the Sup Ct RF [Plenum] focus on particular aspects of law based on the analysis of the prevailing practice in the area.

As noted above, the resolutions of the Sup Ct RF [Plenum] comprise overarching guidance on how lower courts shall uniformly apply the law. Consequently, the resolutions issued by the Sup Ct RF [Plenum] have a persuasive effect as regards clarifying to the lower courts how to apply the law in certain classes of cases, however, being of a more abstract nature, such resolutions are unlikely to form a precedent in the strict sense.

In cases where the court practice is not certain or contradictory, the resolutions of the Sup Ct RF [Plenum] are commonly relied on and followed by the lower courts. However, there is no explicit statutory rule about the binding effect of the resolutions made by the Plenum. The Arbitrazh (Commercial) Procedure Code (APC RF) only suggests that commercial courts may, in the reasoning parts of their decisions, rely on the resolutions of the Sup Ct RF [Plenum].[19] Although there is not a similar procedure stipulated in the Civil Procedure Code (CPC RF), nevertheless, there is a resolution of the Sup Ct RF [Plenum] that encourages lower courts to take into account the decisions of the supreme instance, including the resolutions of the Sup Ct RF [Plenum] that provide abstract guidance on how to apply statutory procedural and substantive norms.

Because of the more general scope and language of the resolutions of the Sup Ct RF [Plenum], conceptually they may not be treated as a precedent,

---

13 Art. 5.3(1) of the Sup Ct RF Law.
14 Resolution of the Sup Ct RF [Plenum] No. 43 dated 29 September 2015.
15 Resolution of the Sup Ct RF [Plenum] No. 25 dated 23 June 2015.
16 Resolution of the Sup Ct RF [Plenum] No. 49 dated 25 December 2018.
17 Resolution of the Sup Ct RF [Plenum] No. 45 dated 24 December 2020.
18 Resolution of the Sup Ct RF [Plenum] No. 44 dated 24 December 2020.
19 Art. 170.4 of the APC RF.

because they are not a result of deciding a case with a unique set of facts. The resolutions have a much broader effect and *de facto* represent the law-making function of the judiciary, and are very instrumental when it comes to the interpretation of the abstract provisions of the statutory law, especially when the latter is not clear in its provisions. In terms of the legal style, the resolutions of the Sup Ct RF [Plenum] can be compared to an academic commentary on the statutory legal norms. Metaphorically, the Sup Ct RF [Plenum] puts flesh on the bones of the abstract statutory norms.

As rightfully noted by the last Chairman of the Sup Arb Ct RF (merged with the Sup Ct RF in 2014), 80% of tax cases that reach the Sup Arb Ct RF were related to the fact that the provisions of the Russian Tax Code had many inconsistencies and sometimes were not clear.[20]

Unlike the resolutions of the Sup Ct RF, the decisions of the first-instance, appellate and cassation courts are less valuable. However, when there is a great body of similar decisions on the same subject, this can serve as evidence of the common judiciary views concerning a particular legal matter, provided that there has not been a settled position of the higher courts on the legal matter. This hypothesis can be demonstrated by references to various empirical studies, which will be discussed further below.

As noted above, there is no explicit rule that precedents represent a source of law in Russia. However, the rising role of precedent was recognised by the then Chairman of the Sup Arb Ct RF, who in 2010 made a programme speech titled 'Speaking of precedents' where he noted that:

> Already now we evidence the increasing interest in the published decisions on the Internet. However, not just a publication is important for the law of precedent, but a thorough analysis of legal positions expressed in the decided cases. A deep analysis of the existing case law is required to identify similar cases.[21]

Furthermore, on 30 June 2020, the Sup Ct RF [Plenum] issued two resolutions in relation to the application of the APC RF to the cases reviewed by the appellate and cassation instances.[22] In particular, the Sup Ct RF [Plenum] noted that in the process of reviewing the correctness of application by the courts of first and appellate instances of procedural and substantive laws, higher courts must analyse whether the conclusions in the decisions of the lower courts comply with the rulings and resolutions of the Sup Ct RF [Plenum] and Sup Ct RF [Presidium].

---

20 *Kommersant*, 17 July 2006.

21 A.A. Ivanov, 'Speaking of precedents' (2024) <https://law-journal.hse.ru/2010--2/27303076.html>.

22 Resolution of the Sup Ct RF [Plenum] No. 12 dated 30 June 2020, and Resolution of the Sup Ct RF [Plenum] No. 13 dated 30 June 2020.

The Sup Ct RF [Plenum] said that:

> [Item 28, paragraph 5:] When reviewing the correctness of the application by the courts of the first and appellate instances of the norms of substantive and procedural law, the court of cassation under Article 170(4) APC RF must establish whether the conclusions of the [lower] courts correspond to the practice of application of legal norms, determined by the resolutions of the Sup Ct RF [Plenum] and resolutions of the Sup Arb Ct RF [Plenum] that still have remained in force ...
>
> [Item 30, paragraph 7:] Other cases with similar facts may be submitted by a party as evidence confirming its position and the correctness in the application of substantive and procedural laws by the courts of first and appellate instances.[23]

These resolutions reinforced the thesis of some legal commentators that because lower courts are guided to and in fact must follow the legal positions expressed by the Sup Ct RF (and, before 2014, by the Sup Arb Ct RF), this gives rise to the acceptance of the doctrine of precedent in Russia.[24]

Some of the commentators went on to say that although the decisions of the supreme instance in Russia do not constitute a primary source of law, the unified practice of courts applying the primary sources of law (statutes, codes, etc.) *de facto* creates the norms of the secondary sources of law. Such a symbiosis between the statutory norms and case law is necessitated by the generally abstract nature of the provisions of the primary sources of law inherent to the continental legal systems. Therefore, in circumstances when the primary sources of law are so linguistically abstract that they inevitably require interpretation by courts, court decisions may arguably create a secondary source of law.

Eventually, stability, transparency, and predictability of law is a paramount principle. On the contrary, it is unlikely that legal vagueness, uncertainty, and loopholes may assist the law in achieving its main goals, hence the important role of courts in assuring the uniform application of the law, which is carried out by way of legal interpretation of statutes or even by filing legal uncertainty by introducing pragmatic and sometimes novel solutions. Indeed, when one puts abstract legal concepts established by statutes into practical application, the outcome may not be what was initially envisaged by the legislator. There is nothing unusual in the fact that after the approbation of abstract statutory norms by courts, the statutory norms may require amendments and sometimes even the introduction of new provisions to comply with the reality, based on the settled case law.

---

[23] Resolution of the Sup Ct RF [Plenum] No. 13 dated 30 June 2020.

[24] S.L. Saveliev, *Precedent in Russia: Unification potential of the practice of the Presidium of the Supreme Arbitrazh Court of the Russian Federation*, Statute, Moscow 2020, p. 102.

Finally, at a more fundamental level, the idea of case law being a source of law may derive from the principle of equality or egalitarianism, which proclaims that everyone shall be equally protected by the law.[25] To enjoy the same degree of protection by law, legal norms must be applied in a predictable, just, and comprehensible manner. In practical terms, this principle binds the courts to apply the law uniformly and consistently, and therefore this cornerstone principle expects the courts to confer their decisions on a similar subject matter with one another.

2.2. THE EMPIRICAL VIEW ON RELEVANCE OF THE SUP CT RF RESOLUTIONS

In a recent empirical study of the resolutions of the Sup Arb Ct RF [Presidium] (which existed until 2014 and was succeeded by the Sup Arb Ct RF) the author argues that the resolutions formed vertical and horizontal precedents, declaratory precedents, and even *contra legem* (when the court's interpretation of a statutory rule contradicts the initial meaning of the rule), creative precedent, and overruling precedents.[26]

The empirical study compared the effect of the resolutions of the Sup Arb Ct RF [Presidium] on the decisions of lower courts on various subject matters. In particular, the author demonstrated that before a resolution of the Sup Arb Ct RF [Presidium] on a particular subject matter, there was no uniform practice and the decisions of lower courts had different, even opposing outcomes. However, after the Sup Arb Ct RF [Presidium] passed a resolution on a subject matter, the lower courts started deciding the cases on the subject matter uniformly.

The study reviewed cases related to such subject matters as service agreements, payment of real estate rent, trademarks, unilateral withdrawal from commercial agreements, lease agreements, purchase of land, the rights of companies' directors, reduction of statutory penalties in commercial agreements, unjust enrichment, rights of investors concerning real estate, tariffs for heating, suretyship, powers of attorney for procedural court actions, damages arising out of moral harm, and others.

Although the functions of the Sup Arb Ct RF [Presidium] were transferred to the Sup Ct RF [Presidium] in 2014, it can be argued that the conclusions made in the study are true also today in respect of the Sup Ct RF [Presidium].

---

25 A.G. Vishnevsky, 'Unity in application of law by courts as a means of ensuring the supremacy of law' (2002) 11 *Pravo* 8.

26 ibid., S.L. Saveliev, above n. 24, pp. 97–98.

2.3. THE EMPIRICAL VIEW ON RELEVANCE OF LOWER COURT DECISIONS

While the concept of precedent is discussed and nearly accepted at the highest judiciary level, there has been no certainty whether and to what extent the lower courts' decisions contribute to the development of the precedent in Russia.

One of the possible ways to measure the impact of such case law on the overall court practice would also be through an empirical study. Notably, in 2021 such a study was made under the auspices of the Institute for the Rule of Law in Russia under the title of '"Same Point of Law": Citations of [Precedent] Cases in Commercial Courts'[27] (Citations of Precedent Study).

It should be noted that the wide use of case law became possible after: (a) the introduction of commercial legal databases, such as www.consultant.ru, www.garant.ru, and others in the late 1990s; and (b) the introduction of the commercial courts' decisions database in 2004. The databases of decisions are publicly available and are easy to work with, because a legal researcher may search cases through references to the provisions of statutory law and other court decisions. Digitalisation of case law virtually welcomed legal practitioners and judges to search for guidance in the existing decisions of courts even from other regions and levels of the judiciary system. The existence of publicly available case law databases in Russia is, in itself, a great achievement because it improves the courts' transparency and makes case law accessible to everyone. That was a giant leap towards, *de facto*, the acceptance of case law as a source of law by the state courts.

Coming back to the Citations of Precedent Study, the authors used one of the existing case law databases and reviewed 6,948,904 random court decisions of different instances entered between 2009–19 comprising 31% of all commercial cases for that period (except bankruptcy cases).

The Citations of Precedent Study revealed that overall, the reviewed court decisions contained 1,595,711 references to other cases. Assuming that a precedent means something that represents an established practice, the authors extracted only those court decisions that were referred to in more than three other decisions. As a result, there were 280,138 referenced decisions left. Even more interesting is that the wording 'a similar legal position', referring to the cases with similar outcomes, was used by the courts 42,000 times.

Furthermore, the study revealed that 84% of references were made to the decisions of the Sup Ct RF and Sup Arb Ct RF, which, in the current author's view, may speak in favour of acceptance of the concept of a vertical *stare decisis* by Russian courts.

---

27 D.A. Saveliev, '"Same Point of Law": Citations of [Precedent] Cases in Commercial Courts' (2021) <https://enforce.spb.ru/images/analit_zapiski/saveliev_links_to_cases.pdf>.

Finally, the Citations of Precedent Study identified a dozen cases that were referenced in as many as 1,000–10,000 other cases. These precedents are related to: the burden of proof of *bona fide* actions of company directors; the proportionality of liability for breach of contract; unfair terms in the state procurement contracts; joint liability of municipal bodies; evaluation of land plots, etc.

In the current author's view, the results that were achieved by the Citations of Precedent Study provide irrefutable evidence that the decisions of Russian commercial courts of different instances and geographical locations comprise a system of legal authority that is routinely used by legal practitioners and judges.

Another example of the empirical study of Russian case law was carried out by the Russian Arbitration Association about the court rulings on the recognition and enforcement of foreign arbitral awards under the United Nations (New York) Convention on the Recognition and Enforcement of Foreign Arbitral Awards 1958 in 2017 (the NYC Study).[28]

The NYC Study revealed that it has been a common practice that the courts routinely rely on the rulings of other Russian courts of all instances on the subject matter. The NYC Study permitted the working group to identify the common positions of Russian courts on certain aspects of the application of Article V of the New York Convention, from which the courts usually do not depart in their rulings. It was concluded that such stability makes case law predictable, the court decisions transparent, and, as a result, increases reliability of the legal system in the eyes of foreign parties entering into commercial contracts with their Russian counterparties. It was concluded that from previously being formalistic and inconsistent, the case law on the application of the New York Convention had become more uniform in the past two decades. There were several reasons for that, one of which, arguably, is consistent guidance and explanation on the application of the Convention through the resolutions of the Sup Ct RF (and previously the Sup Arb Ct RF).

Since its first report in 2018, the working group on the NYC Study continued its study of cases on Article V of the New York Convention and has already analysed cases for the period between 2018–20. As a general observation, Russian courts continue to rely on the existing decisions when trying cases under Article V of the New York Convention.

To the current author's knowledge, there have been other statistical studies of Russian case law, which mostly came to the same conclusion, i.e. that there is a tacit understanding between judges that it is not only instrumental but also

---

28 R. Zykov (ed), *Recognition and Enforcement of Foreign Arbitral Awards in Russia and Former Soviet States*, Kluwer Law International, 2021, pp. 195–206.

important to reference the decisions of other judges (and not only supreme justices) in similar cases to ensure the stability and predictability of case law.

Importantly, reliance on the existing case law has also become a part of court advocacy, especially in commercial cases. Legal counsel commonly invoke court decisions on analogous cases in their legal briefs and court applications. It has become almost a professional rule that a trial lawyer must validate his or her position by extensively relying on case law to substantiate a pleaded legal argument. As a sign of the importance of case law and consequently its uniform citation mainly in the English language proceedings abroad, the Russian Arbitration Association produced 'The Russian Guide to Legal Citation 2021' (RGLC 2021).[29] The RGLC 2021 is a style guide for Russian legal acronyms and citations that are widely used in foreign arbitral and court proceedings and English language publications. It was developed to assist lawyers, scholars, judges, law students, paralegals, and others to uniformly reference Russian laws, codes, cases, names of courts, and other state bodies.

As to the use of legal doctrine in parties' submissions to the courts, i.e. the practice of referring to scholarly writings, textbooks, etc., it has almost seized to exist in recent years. Perhaps this is because there exists a rather comprehensive body of court decisions on various subject matters. Only on rare occasions, when a subject matter has not been discussed in other decided court cases, the parties may want to refer to scholarly writings to be able to support their legal argument in court. However, it is quite common for the scholars to refer in their works to the courts' practice, and more specifically to the resolutions of the Sup Ct RF [Plenum] and [Presidium].

To conclude this section, the statistical studies have demonstrated that the Russian judiciary routinely revert to the existing court decisions by expressing references to other cases in their rulings. Furthermore, the use of analogous court decisions in support of their positions has also become a common feature of the legal profession for litigation lawyers, as it has been in common law jurisdictions already for a long time.

3. RESOLUTIONS OF THE SUPREME COURT [PRESIDIUM]

3.1. SELECTION OF CASES BY THE SUP CT RF [PRESIDIUM]

As noted above, when a case is brought before the Sup Ct RF, the latter may finally resolve the case in the Sup Ct RF [Presidium] if the case has a precedential

29 R. Zykov (ed), 'The Russian Guide to Legal Citation 2021' (2021) <https://arbitration.ru/upload/iblock/e5b/The-Russian-Guide-to-Legal-Citation-2021.pdf>.

value. For the benefit of this contribution, it will be useful to understand how the Sup Ct RF [Presidium] identifies cases that require its decisions.

Each year hundreds of thousands of commercial cases are tried by Russian courts: only a fraction of them reach the Sup Ct RF and only a handful of cases reach the Supt Ct RF [Presidium].

When a case is filed with the Supt Ct RF, a sole supreme justice reviews the case and decides whether the case is important for uniformity of the courts' practice.

Generally speaking, there are several criteria for a case to be escalated to the Sup Ct RF [Presidium]:

- if the existing case law is fundamentally wrong and requires revision;
- if the existing case law is controversial and requires uniformity;
- if the anticipated developments in the case law require a proactive reaction of the Sup Ct RF [Presidium] for uniformity; or
- if the existing position of the Sup Ct RF requires revision.

These, by all means, are not exhaustive criteria, but are certainly the most important. Naturally, it is always at the discretion of the supreme justice who reviews the case to decide which case can be passed on to the Sup Ct RF [Presidium].

In exercising its filtering function, the Supreme Court justice describes the reasons for the decision to transfer a case to the Sup Ct RF [Presidium] or not.

3.2. *OBITER DICTA* AND *RATIO DECIDENDI* IN THE SUPT CT RF [PRESIDIUM] RESOLUTIONS

The resolutions of the Sup Ct RF [Presidium], among other case identifiers, such as the parties, date and place, name of the judge, etc., shall include the reasons and conclusions of the Sup Ct RF [Presidium] in a particular case.[30]

Over the past decade, there has been some criticism that the decisions of the Sup Ct RF [Presidium] were rather casuistic and concise. However, the situation has been gradually changing and the court's decisions have become more elaborate when it comes to explaining the law and mistakes that were made by the lower courts. As noted above, commercial courts only rarely refer to scholarly writings and probably never to the preparatory works of the legislator that precede the enactment of laws. At the same time, the courts increasingly refer to other court decisions in support of their conclusions.

---

30 Art. 308.12 of the APC RF (an identical provision is found in Art. 391.13 of the CPC RF).

Although it is formally not recognised, as a matter of actual content, the resolutions of the Sup Ct RF [Presidium] include both *ratio decidendi* and *obiter dicta*.

Ratio decidendi is a Latin term that means the reason for deciding. In the cases decided by the Sup Ct RF [Presidium], *ratio decidendi* is found in the reasoning part of the resolutions.

Obiter dictum is an observation by the court on a legal question suggested in a case but not arising in such a manner as to require a decision.

In practice, the Sup Ct RF [Presidium] (like other courts) has never stated that a particular statement in a decision forms a *ratio decidendi* or an *obiter dictum*. There is no legal tradition or even legal terminology to identify and distinguish these parts. However, both elements can be deducted from the texts of the decisions.

Although there is no legally defined test for which part is which, this author finds it acceptable to use the so-called 'Wambaugh's Inversion Test': if excluding a particular statement from the decisions, would the decision have become different? If the answer is 'yes', then that statement is a critical part of the decision and is, therefore, *ratio decidendi*. The rest of the court's reasonings would be *obiter dictum*.

One way to distinguish a *ratio decidendi* is the language of a resolution of the Sup Ct RF [Presidium]. Empirically, the following categories of reasoning in the court decisions that could assist in identifying a *ratio decidendi* can be listed. The court may:

- give an interpretation of a legal norm, a legal term, or a legal concept (hereinafter jointly referred to as the 'legal norm');
- explain how a legal norm applies in general;
- explain how a legal norm applies (or does not apply) to a particular relationship or a dispute at hand;
- point out what legal criteria must be present for a legal norm to apply (or not to apply); and
- point out what factual circumstances must be present for a legal norm to apply (or not to apply).

Although these examples are by no means exhaustive, they may give an idea of how to extract a *ratio decidendi* from the text of a resolution.

Another way to distinguish a *ratio decidendi* in the resolutions of the Sup Ct RF [Presidium] would be to seek the cases in which the Sup Ct RF [Presidium] refers to its previous resolutions in analogous cases.

Furthermore, if a reference in a resolution of the Sup Ct RF [Presidium] is made to its previously decided case and is made along the language categories listed above, it will most likely be identified as a *ratio decidendi*.

3.3. DISSENTING OPINIONS

The decisions taken by a collegium of judges in commercial cases (also in the lower court instances) are made by a majority vote.[31] A judge who does not concur with the majority in part or entirely shall nevertheless sign the decision but may provide a dissenting opinion.

A dissenting opinion shall not disclose information related to the judges' deliberations or individual positions of judges in the case or otherwise disclose the judicial deliberations when handing down court decisions.

The dissenting opinions are included in the record, however they are not announced together with the decision and mostly are not published. However, it is common practice that the court informs the parties that there has been a dissenting opinion in the case.

This linguistic uncertainty of Article 20 of the APC RF has opened a debate on whether a dissenting opinion nevertheless may be published. In practice, there have been a handful of dissenting opinions published by the judges, however, it has not become common practice. It is unlikely that the situation will change in the forthcoming future.

Although the dissenting opinions, being purely a minority view on a subject matter, do not create the *ratio decidendi*, with some caveats they may be considered as an *obiter dictum*. This is so because it is always important to understand the logic of a court decision in the context of pros and cons which were discussed during deliberations. In such circumstances, a different view that has been expressed by a judge could complete the jigsaw puzzle of the court decisions and give a better understanding of the context.

As explained by the Supreme Court Justice Elena Peisikova, it is important to permit judges to express their alternative views, and the other judges in the collegium, although disagreeing with the dissent, treat them with respect.[32]

A similar opinion was expressed by Justice Gadzhiev of the Russian Constitutional Court who opined that society is genuinely interested in the nature and depth of the legal discussions that occur between the judges when they decide cases.[33] In this light, it can be concluded that the supreme justices recognise the importance of maintaining the institute of dissenting opinions in Russia.

Historically, there have been numerous examples when dissenting opinions in different jurisdictions expressed views that were quite ahead of their time. As time passed, some of them became the basis for new overruling precedents.

---

31 Art. 20 of the APC RF.

32 E. Peisikova, 'It is important to have dissenting opinions' (11 March 2022) <https://rapsinews.ru/publications/20220311/307787038.html>.

33 'Resolution of the Constitutional Court of the Russian Federation No. 12-П, dated 17 June 2004' (2004) 4 *Vestnik of the Constitutional Court of the Russian Federation* 88.

Therefore, it is important to record all alternative points of view and explore alternative positions when developing new case law.

4. CONCLUDING REMARKS

There seems to be a universal understanding that statutory law, being abstract, does not always produce uniformity and predictability. In such circumstances, precedents enable the statutes to be applied in a uniform and predictable manner. Because a precedent allows for a swifter reaction to the rapidly changing world than any statute ever could, the balancing role of the precedent makes it a vital part of the legal system.

While there is no official acceptance and even definition of precedent in Russia, in practice, the advocates and courts routinely resort to the previously decided cases in support of their legal positions and conclusions. It can be presumed that the role of precedents in Russia will grow, which ultimately may lead to formal legal recognition of the concept of precedent.

PRECEDENT IN SOUTH AFRICAN PRIVATE LAW

Leo Boonzaier

1. A GENERAL INTRODUCTION TO LEGAL PRECEDENT

The South African legal system is of comparative interest for two main reasons. The first is that it is a mixed legal system, blending civilian and common-law elements.[1] The second is that in the mid-1990s, when the racist and authoritarian system of apartheid was replaced by full democracy, the country enacted a famously ambitious Constitution.[2] Both these features have important implications for the role of judicial precedent in South Africa, as this contribution to the volume will discuss. This contribution introduces the country's doctrine of precedent in Section 1. and sketches its historical background in Section 2. Sections 3. and 4. discuss the mechanics of the doctrine's operation. Sections 5. and 6. situate the role of precedent in a wider geographical, theoretical, and methodological context. The main themes are summarised in the conclusion.

South Africa adheres to a doctrine of judicial precedent (or *stare decisis*) on the same broad model as England and Wales and other common law jurisdictions.[3] The South African doctrine of precedent arose in the early nineteenth century through judicial custom. For over 150 years, it had no statutory or constitutional authorisation. However, the courts have recently held that respect for precedent is an incident of the rule of law,[4] which is one of the founding values of the new Constitution.[5]

South African law has never been codified. The bulk of the country's private and commercial law (and much of its public law) was and still is contained in judicial decisions.[6] Accordingly, case law is highly respected, and legal education in South Africa shares the hallmarks of other common law systems, namely that it 'is founded on the primacy of the decided cases', and its 'heroes … are

1 R. Zimmermann and D. Visser (eds), *Southern Cross: Civil Law and Common Law in South Africa*, Clarendon Press, Oxford 1996; C.G. van der Merwe, J. du Plessis, M. de Waal, R. Zimmermann and P. Farlam, 'The Republic of South Africa' in V.V. Palmer (ed), *Mixed Jurisdictions Worldwide: The Third Legal Family*, 2nd ed., Cambridge University Press, Cambridge 2012.

2 Constitution of the Republic of South Africa 1996.

3 The classic study of the doctrine of precedent in South Africa, and still the most detailed, is H.R. Hahlo and E. Kahn, *The South African Legal System and Its Background*, Juta & Co Ltd, Cape Town 1968, Ch. VII, which was preceded by a series of articles by Kahn in the 1967 *South African Law Journal*. For more recent overviews, see F. du Bois (ed), *Wille's Principles of South African Law*, 9th ed., Juta & Co Ltd, Cape Town 2007, pp. 76–92; M. Wallis, 'Courts and Tribunals' in *The Law of South Africa*, 3rd ed., vol. 10, LexisNexis, Durban 2017, paras. 520–28.

4 See Section 6.1. below.

5 Constitution 1996, s. 1(c). The Constitution also refers on several occasions to 'the common law' and the courts' duty to develop it (see e.g. ss. 8(3), 39(2), 39(3), and 173), which implicitly recognises judicial law-making.

6 Details are given in Section 5.1. below.

the outstanding judges'.[7] The characteristic methods of South African lawyers would thus be immediately familiar to lawyers from England and the wider Commonwealth. At the same time, civilian inflections remain evident, as a result of the Roman-Dutch substrate upon which English principles were overlaid.[8] Most relevantly here, the South African approach to *stare decisis* is less rigid than the English one. In particular, horizontal precedent in South Africa has always been qualifiedly, rather than absolutely, binding.[9]

South African legal culture is often stereotyped as 'formalist' and deferential to historical and posited sources. However, these commitments have come under pressure following the enactment of the new Constitution, which aims to 'transform' the legal system, including the common law. Familiar tensions between legal certainty and flexibility, and between formal and substantive reasoning, have therefore acquired a new urgency.[10]

2. A BRIEF HISTORY OF PRECEDENT IN SOUTH AFRICA

This section discusses the history of *stare decisis* in South Africa. The doctrine's origin and early history must be understood in light of the contest between the Roman-Dutch and English common law traditions, which is the subject of Section 2.1. Section 2.2. is about the emerging effects of South Africa's new Constitution.

2.1. A MIXED LEGAL SYSTEM

The South African legal system has a distinctive history.[11] The Dutch East India Company ruled the Cape Colony from 1652–1795. It brought with it Roman-Dutch law, comprised mainly of Dutch scholars' commentaries on Roman sources. This became the general law of the Cape, and thence of the other three colonies that would later make up the Union of South Africa.[12]

---

7 J. Dainow, 'The Civil Law and the Common Law: Some Points of Comparison' (1966) 15 *American Journal of Comparative Law* 419, 428–29.

8 See Section 2.1. below.

9 See Section 3.2.1. below.

10 See Sections 3.2.2. and 6.2. below.

11 See for more detail, H.R. Hahlo and E. Kahn, above n. 3, Ch. XII; C.G. van der Merwe, J. du Plessis, M. de Waal, R. Zimmermann and P. Farlam, above n. 1, pp. 95–118.

12 The classic study is J.W. Wessels, *History of the Roman-Dutch Law*, African Book Co, Grahamstown 1908. See too E. Fagan, 'Roman-Dutch Law in Its South African Historical Context' in R. Zimmermann and D. Visser (eds), above n. 1.

During the Napoleonic Wars, however, Britain took occupation of the Colony (since the Dutch were allied to Britain's enemy, Revolutionary France), first temporarily and then, in 1806, permanently. This meant that the Colony was removed from civilian influence just as the codification movement was being consummated in Europe; hence Roman-Dutch law, though it was superseded by civil codes on its native continent, survived, anomalously, at the southern tip of Africa.

On the other hand, since the Cape Colony was then integrated into the British Empire, which over the next 100 years would rise to its zenith, South Africa's legal system began to acquire English characteristics. Though the new colonial government preserved the substantive Roman-Dutch law, it overhauled the court system in a Charter of Justice enacted in 1827. Court proceedings were to be conducted in English, judges and practitioners had to be trained in England, and litigants had the right of appeal to the Privy Council. Predictably in this new context, South Africa's lawyers and judges were strongly inclined to draw inspiration from English law, which contained a 'storehouse of precedents' of 'extraordinary richness';[13] these were also more accessible, univocal, and attuned to modern problems than the Roman-Dutch writings.[14] Hence, in time, by an organic rather than obligatory process, English rules and principles were steadily overlaid upon South Africa's civilian substrate.[15]

The most important legacy of the common law, for the purposes of this contribution, is a doctrine of judicial precedent on broadly the English model. Shortly after 1827, when the colonial government rationalised the court structure, the Cape Supreme Court began relying on its previous decisions.[16] Its doing so was hampered, however, by the absence of law reports. The first of these appeared in 1857, and they became regular only in 1882.[17] The first express judicial endorsement of the doctrine of precedent was in 1880, when Chief

---

13 P.Q.R. Boberg, 'Oak Tree or Acorn? – Conflicting Approaches to Our Law of Delict' (1966) 83 *South African Law Journal* 150, 171.

14 J. Wessels, 'The Future of Roman Dutch Law in South Africa' (1920) 37 *South African Law Journal* 265, 276.

15 See further, on this process of 'reception', R. Zimmermann, 'Roman Law in a Mixed Legal System: The South African Experience' in R. Evans-Jones (ed), *The Civil Law Tradition in Scotland*, Stair Society, Edinburgh 1995, pp. 47–52.

16 E. Kahn, 'The Rules of Precedent Applied in South African Courts' (1967) 84 *South African Law Journal* 43, 45. The earliest case usually cited is *In re Taute* (1830) 1 Menz 497. Before 1827, any such practice would have been impossible since the courts did not produce written judgments.

17 See for details S.D. Girvin, 'Law Reporting: Menzies Reports, Precedent and Legal Sources at the Cape Colony in the Nineteenth Century' (1995) 63 *Legal History Review* 103; also R. Zimmermann and D. Visser, 'South African Law as a Mixed Legal System' in R. Zimmermann and D. Visser (eds), above n. 1, pp. 15–19.

Justice de Villiers, the dominant judicial figure of the late nineteenth century,[18] wrote in *R v. Strydom*:

> I think it is a sound rule to adhere to, that when once the Court has laid down certain principles, if they are not found to be in direct opposition to the provisions of the law, for the Court to abide them.[19]

He repeated similar sentiments in later decisions,[20] locating the value of *stare decisis* in both 'expediency' and 'justice', i.e. protecting the parties' expectations.[21] It was also made clear that courts lower in the hierarchy were bound by the Supreme Court's decisions.[22] A similar approach took hold in the other colonies that would later form South Africa.[23]

Roman and Roman-Dutch writers had also seen some value in courts respecting their prior decisions.[24] And it has been claimed that a doctrine of precedent was familiar to African customary law[25] (that is, South Africa's indigenous system of law, which the colonial authorities consistently marginalised).[26] But it is widely accepted that the doctrine of precedent that in fact emerged in the practice of the South African courts in the nineteenth century, and in which prior decisions are not only persuasive but formally binding,[27] is a product of English influence.[28] Indeed, it has been described as 'surely the greatest'[29] and 'the most significant and lasting'[30] contribution of English law to South Africa, and still constitutes 'probably the most significant connection between South African law and

---

18 'Lord De Villiers CJ: An Appreciation' (1921) 37 *Law Quarterly Review* 473; E.A. Walker, *Lord de Villiers and His Times: South Africa, 1842–1914*, Constable & Co, London 1925.

19 *R v. Strydom* (1880) 1 SC 60, 61.

20 *Marsh v. Makein* (1882) 2 SC 104.

21 *Jacobson v. Nitch* (1890) 7 SC 174, 178.

22 *Marsh*, above n. 20, 106.

23 H.R. Hahlo and E. Kahn, above n. 3, p. 241.

24 J.G. Kotzé, 'Judicial Precedent' (1917) 34 *South African Law Journal* 280, 280–87; H.R. Hahlo and E. Kahn, above n. 3, pp. 217–21.

25 H.R. Hahlo and E. Kahn, above n. 3, p. 216.

26 See R. Zimmermann and D. Visser, above n. 17, pp. 12–15; and for comprehensive treatment C. Himonga and T. Nhlapo (eds), *African Customary Law in South Africa*, Oxford University Press Southern Africa, Cape Town 2014.

27 Compare the three 'ideal models' of precedent discussed in N. MacCormick, 'The Significance of Precedent' (1998) *Acta Juridica* 174, 181–82. South Africa clearly adopts the third, 'formally binding model'.

28 J.G. Kotzé, above n. 24, 311; H.R. Hahlo and E. Kahn, above n. 3, p. 242; *Fellner v. Minister of the Interior* 1954 (4) SA 523 (A), 529E; *Trade Fairs and Promotions (Pty) Ltd v. Thomson* 1984 (4) SA 177 (W), 184A.

29 O.D. Schreiner, *The Contribution of English Law to South African Law; and the Rule of Law in South Africa*, Juta & Co Ltd, Cape Town 1967, p. 11.

30 H. Scott, 'The Death of Doctrine? Private Law Scholarship in South African Today' in J. Basedow, H. Fleischer and R. Zimmermann (eds), *Legislators, Judges, and Professors*, Mohr Siebeck, Tübingen 2016, p. 226.

Anglo-American law'.[31] South African courts have regularly drawn upon judicial and scholarly writing about the English doctrine of precedent to illuminate their own.[32]

The doctrine was never applied as rigidly in South Africa, however, as it was in England (where even horizontal precedent was, until 1966, absolutely binding).[33] In 1835, the Cape Supreme Court refused to follow a judgment it had given two years before, on the basis that it was 'wrong' and 'a bad decision'.[34] Thereafter, the courts of the colonies, and then of the Union of South Africa, consistently maintained that horizontal precedent was qualifiedly, rather than absolutely, binding.[35] Many reasons have been offered for this difference from the approach that prevailed in England. To begin with, the English and South African legal systems were never formally linked, and so the hardening of the doctrine of judicial precedent that took place in England from 1898–1944 simply passed South Africa by.[36] Another reason is that, during the colonial era, an appeal lay from the Cape courts to the Privy Council, which was not bound by its own precedents;[37] hence it was natural that South Africa's domestic appellate courts would adopt a similar position.[38] Third, and most fundamental, is the country's mixed legal heritage.[39] When South African courts began to lay down precedents, they did so atop an established civilian substrate. Hence there was not the same need, as there was in England, to stand firmly by past decisions: Roman-Dutch law already provided a comprehensive set of principles.[40] Moreover, these principles provided a standard against which a judicial precedent could be considered wrong[41] – it might have misunderstood,

---

31 C.G. van der Merwe, J. du Plessis, M. de Waal, R. Zimmermann and P. Farlam, above n. 1, p. 142.

32 See e.g. *Fellner*, above n. 28, 537A–37D, 538B–38D (discussing the work of Arthur Goodhart, *Halsbury's*, and *Young v. Bristol Aeroplane Co Ltd* [1944] KB 718); *Trade Fairs*, above n. 28, 184H–85C (discussing the work of Rupert Cross and Glanville Williams); *Pretoria City Council v. Levinson* 1949 (3) SA 305 (A), 316–17 (discussing Goodhart, *Halsbury's*, and *Tidy v. Battman* (1934) 103 LJKB 158).

33 Compare J. Cartwright's contribution, elsewhere in this volume.

34 *Wylde v. Wylde* (1835) 1 Menz 269.

35 *Collett v. Priest* 1931 AD 290, 297, 301; *Bloemfontein Council v. Richter* 1938 AD 195, 232; *Harris v. Minister of the Interior* 1952 (2) SA 428 (A), 452–55.

36 The unyielding approach taken in *London Tramway Co v. London CC* [1898] AC 375 was therefore quickly rejected in South Africa: *Motan v. Transvaal Government* 1904 TS 404, 413.

37 R. Cross and J.W. Harris, *Precedent in English Law*, 4th ed., Clarendon Press, Oxford 1991, pp. 22–24.

38 *Fellner*, above n. 28, 530E–30F.

39 ibid., 529G; H.R. Hahlo and E. Kahn, above n. 3, p. 243; F. du Bois, above n. 3, p. 77.

40 Compare A.L. Goodhart, 'Precedent in English and Continental Law' (1934) 50 *Law Quarterly Review* 40, 61–62 (drawing a similar contrast between English and continental legal systems).

41 H. Scott, above n. 30, p. 227.

misrepresented, or otherwise been at odds with the old authorities – in which case there was much pressure to reverse it.[42]

This sort of objection was, on occasion, levelled against the system of judicial precedent as a whole. Since the old authorities were being buried under a pile of precedents, which were often heavily influenced by English law, some commentators felt the Roman-Dutch system would lose its vitality unless drastic action were taken, such as its being codified.[43] These calls for codification were not taken up. Yet periodic irruptions of 'purist' sentiment, enflamed by emergent Afrikaner nationalist politics, would continue for much of the twentieth century.[44] These were embodied, most notoriously, in the figure of L.C. Steyn, Chief Justice from 1959–71, who sought to extirpate English influence on the law of South Africa, including by overturning decades-old lines of judicial authority on the basis that they had misunderstood the true Roman-Dutch position.[45] But even Steyn was committed to the doctrine of precedent;[46] these episodes only showed that, on certain issues, he had an exceptional readiness to find the precedents to be clearly wrong. Again, some academic commentators went further, railing against the system of precedent on the basis that it stifles characteristic Roman-Dutch methods,[47] but these views now seem quaintly idiosyncratic.[48]

In sum, a cohesive doctrine of precedent on broadly the English model has endured in South Africa, notwithstanding occasional criticism, for approaching 200 years. To be sure, South Africa's civilian heritage remains visible in judicial reasoning: even in the final years of the twentieth century and into the twenty-first, some judges drew directly upon Roman and Roman-Dutch

---

42 On this basis, precedents were overturned, e.g. in *Hare v. Trustee of Heath* (1884) 3 SC 32, 33; *Halse v. Warwick* 1931 CPD 233. See also *Dukes v. Marthinusen* 1937 AD 12, 23. To be sure, this consideration was not always decisive; some judges held that standing by precedents was more important than according with the old authorities. The tendentious statement of Corbett JA in *Du Plessis NO v. Strauss* 1988 (2) SA 105 (A), 150F that 'South African case law should not be permitted to override the law of Holland' is criticised in E. Fagan, above n. 12, p. 44, and is not typical. See further below n. 50.

43 J.F. v. O, 'Some Remarks on the Study of Roman-Dutch Law' (1893) 10 *Cape Law Journal* 205, 214; J. Wessels, above n. 14, 282–84.

44 For a useful overview see C.G. van der Merwe, J. du Plessis, M. de Waal, R. Zimmermann and P. Farlam, above n. 1, pp. 203–11.

45 E. Cameron, 'Legal Chauvinism, Executive-Mindedness and Justice: LC Steyn's Impact on South African Law' (1982) 99 *South African Law Journal* 38, 43–52; E. Fagan, above n. 12, pp. 60–64; E. Zitzke, 'The History and Politics of Contemporary Common-Law Purism' (2017) 23 *Fundamina* 185.

46 *R v. Sibiya* 1955 (4) SA 247 (A).

47 J.C. de Wet, 'Gemene Reg of Wetgewing?' (1948) 11 *Tydskrif vir Hedendaagse Romeins-Hollandse Reg* 1, 15, describing *stare decisis* as 'the most pernicious' (*verderflikste*) doctrine that South Africa's courts had imported from England.

48 See e.g. Coetzee J's riposte to de Wet in *Trade Fairs*, above n. 28, 184C–84E. According to C.G. van der Merwe, J. du Plessis, M. de Waal, R. Zimmermann and P. Farlam, above n. 1, pp. 132–33, *stare decisis* has long been accepted by judges even 'of civil law orientation' and dissenting voices were 'soon silenced'.

sources to justify their decisions.[49] But this is not typical, and would usually be accepted as legitimate only interstitially, i.e. when the precedents are silent, conflicting, or otherwise indeterminate.[50] The primary significance of Roman-Dutch principles nowadays is that they have been *absorbed into* South African precedents, and no longer compete with them.[51] And so, despite the importance of the South African legal system's mixed heritage, its core methodology, which centres on the parsing of decided cases, would be instantly familiar to lawyers elsewhere in the Anglosphere.[52]

2.2. CONSTITUTIONAL TRANSFORMATION

Of perhaps more palpable relevance to current judicial practice than South Africa's Roman-Dutch substrate is its new Constitution, which was enacted, as mentioned,[53] in 1996.[54] It is a paradigm of so-called 'aspirational constitutionalism',[55] seeking not to entrench the *status quo* but to 'transform' the legal system in order to undo the legacy of apartheid.[56] No part of the legal system is unaffected: the Constitution makes explicit that all law is subject to it,[57] whether legislative or judge-made, and must accord with constitutional

---

49 The most infamous example is *Bank of Lisbon and SA Ltd v. De Ornelas* 1988 (3) SA 580 (A), discussed in A.P.H. Cockrell, 'Adjudication Styles in South African Private Law' (1993) 56 *Tydskrif vir Hedendaagse Romeins-Hollandse Reg* 590, 594–95; R. Zimmermann, above n. 15, pp. 69–74. See also *Janse van Rensburg v. Grieve Trust CC* 2000 (1) SA 315 (C); *Linvestment CC v. Hammersley* 2008 (3) SA 283 (SCA).

50 Only occasionally do South African courts go further and upset a settled line of derived precedents through 'the device of stating that it does not accord with Roman-Dutch law': D. Visser, 'Daedalus in the Supreme Court: The Common Law Today' (1986) 49 *Tydskrif vir Hedendaagse Romeins-Hollandse Reg* 127, 137. Notably, South African courts have upheld precedents even when they are found to have misunderstood Roman-Dutch law, as in *Horowitz v. Brock* 1988 (2) SA 160 (A), 186–87.

51 *Paulsen v. Slip Knot Investments 777 (Pty) Ltd* 2015 (3) SA 479 (CC) and *Jordaan v. City of Tshwane Metropolitan Municipality* 2017 (6) SA 287 (CC) are therefore typical: Roman-Dutch writers are consulted, but only prefatorily, to illuminate a rule that had long since been accepted into South African case law.

52 See for a complementary assessment, A.J.G.M. Sanders, 'The Characteristic Features of Southern African Law' (1981) 14 *Comparative and International Law Journal of Southern Africa* 328.

53 See above n. 2.

54 This 'final' Constitution was preceded, however, by the Interim Constitution Act 200 of 1993, which came into force on 27 April 1994, marking the start of the transition to constitutional democracy.

55 K.L. Scheppele, 'Aspirational and Aversive Constitutionalism: The Case for Studying Cross-Constitutional Influence through Negative Models' (2003) 1 *International Journal of Constitutional Law* 296.

56 K.E. Klare, 'Legal Culture and Transformative Constitutionalism' (1998) 14 *South African Journal on Human Rights* 146. See too *S v. Makwanyane* [1995] ZACC 3, para. 261.

57 Constitution 1996, s. 2.

values,[58] and that not only organs of state, but also private persons, are bound by constitutional rights.[59] The shift to a system of constitutional supremacy with strongly reformist ambitions has provided a powerful stimulus to the legal system that all lawyers and judges have had to reckon with. Yet the Constitution's full impact is contested and still emerging. Moreover, one should not overlook the Constitution's preservative elements.

On the one hand, then, the Constitution states that '[a]ll law that was in force when the new Constitution took effect, continues in force',[60] an obvious and necessary concession to legal certainty and continuity. Moreover, the courts have many times insisted that *stare decisis* remains valid and important in the new legal order, and indeed sourced it in the Constitution's founding values.[61] On the other hand, the new Constitution mandates vigorous law reform in manifold areas. Relevantly here, courts have a duty to develop the common law to remove any inconsistency between it and the Constitution.[62] They must do this not only where the common law infringes a constitutional right,[63] but also where the common law fails to bear out the Bill of Rights' underlying values. This follows from the Constitution's now-famous Section 39(2), which provides:

> When interpreting any legislation, and when developing the common law or customary law, every court, tribunal or forum must promote the spirit, purport and objects of the Bill of Rights.

Courts are therefore obliged, even where no enumerated constitutional right has been contravened, to remove any divergence between the common law and the 'objective normative value system' that underlies the Constitution.[64] And courts must sometimes consider developing the common law even where the parties themselves have not.[65]

Though South Africa's courts have always had the power to develop the common law, these are far-reaching obligations, sourced in the country's

---

58 s. 39(2).

59 s. 8, which expressly recognises 'direct horizontal application'. See further H. Cheadle and D. Davis, 'The Application of the 1996 Constitution in the Private Sphere' (1997) 13 *South African Journal on Human Rights* 44.

60 Schedule 6 ('Transitional Arrangements'), s. 2(1).

61 See for details Section 6.1. below.

62 See generally *Thebus v. S* [2003] ZACC 12, paras. 24–28.

63 s. 8(2) and (3).

64 *Carmichele v. Minister of Safety and Security* [2001] ZACC 22, para. 54. As comparative lawyers will recognise, this phrase (a translation of '*objektive Wertordnung*') was borrowed from Germany's *Lüth* judgment: 1 BvR 400/51, BverfG 7, 198 (1958). For criticism of *Carmichele*'s reading of s. 39(2), see A. Fagan, 'The Secondary Role of the Spirit, Purport and Objects of the Bill of Rights in the Common Law's Development' (2010) 127 *South African Law Journal* 611.

65 *Carmichele*, above n. 64, paras. 36, 39.

basic law, that now compel its more regular exercise. Their normative force is especially great because of the obvious need to transform South African society after the ravages of apartheid, as well as the esteem enjoyed, at least among some segments of the legal profession and judiciary, by the new Constitution and its associated human rights culture. Seeking to defend common law rules that derive from the apartheid era is, of course, less appealing. Indeed the question was raised, in the run-up to the transition, whether the common law should be scrapped, so that post-apartheid lawmakers could start from a 'clean slate'.[66] But instead, a pragmatic compromise was struck:[67] the pre-existing common law would remain in force, but would now require a comprehensive 'constitutional audit'.[68] A related compromise resulted in the creation of a new judicial body: alongside the old Appellate Division (renamed the Supreme Court of Appeal), which was seen as illegitimate and unduly complacent during apartheid, a new Constitutional Court was created to act as the Constitution's key custodian.[69]

It bears emphasis that these changes are highly relevant even in private law.[70] As mentioned, the Bill of Rights expressly applies to 'all law', as well as to disputes between private parties[71] – and it does so precisely because its drafters wanted to ensure that all parts of the legal system, including the so-called private sphere, are subjected to constitutional oversight. The Constitutional Court, despite its name, is a court of general jurisdiction.[72] It has expressly denied that there are parts of the legal system beyond constitutional purview,[73] and held that 'virtually all issues … are, ultimately, constitutional', which affects how courts should approach them 'from the outset'.[74] Private law disputes are

66 A. Sachs, 'The Future of Roman Dutch Law in a Non-Racial Democratic South Africa: Some Preliminary Observations' (1992) 1 *Social & Legal Studies* 217, 219 (ultimately rejecting this view). See too N. Cloete, 'Codification and Stare Decisis in a New South African Legal Order' (1991) 16 *Journal for Juridical Science* 58 (arguing that the common law should be replaced by a civil code).

67 See for details R. Spitz and M. Chaskalson, *The Politics of Transition: A Hidden History of South Africa's Negotiated Settlement*, Witwatersrand University Press, Witwatersrand 2000, Ch. 14.

68 *Rivett-Carnac v. Wiggins* 1997 (3) SA 80 (C), 87. The judge responsible for this phrase has, in prolific extra-curial writing, defended an especially far-reaching vision of constitutional transformation: see, e.g. D.M. Davis and K. Klare, 'Transformative Constitutionalism and the Common and Customary Law' (2010) 26 *South African Journal on Human Rights* 403.

69 See further R. Spitz and M. Chaskalson, above n. 67, Ch. 11; H. Corder and J. Brickhill, 'The Constitutional Court' in C. Hoexter and M. Olivier (eds), *The Judiciary in South Africa*, Juta & Co Ltd, Cape Town 2014.

70 In South Africa there has never been so deep a distinction between public law and private law as there is in, say, France. A unitary court system, in the manner of England and Wales, applies both.

71 See above nn. 57–59.

72 See further Section 3.1. below.

73 *Pharmaceutical Manufacturers Association of South Africa: In re Ex Parte President of the Republic of South Africa* [2000] ZACC 1, para. 44. See also *De Lange v. Presiding Bishop of the Methodist Church of Southern Africa for the time being* [2015] ZACC 35, paras. 69–86.

74 *Jordaan*, above n. 51, para. 8.

no exception.[75] This is perhaps most obvious in the case of property law, since property rights are constitutionally protected,[76] as is the right to housing.[77] In addition, the Court's key judgment interpreting Section 39(2) was a case of delictual liability for a negligent omission (albeit by a state defendant);[78] it has also held that the application of the requirements of vicarious liability raises constitutional issues,[79] as do the rules of factual causation.[80] The law of defamation, to take another example, is constitutional throughout, since it seeks to balance the plaintiff's right to reputation and the defendant's right to freedom of expression.[81] The Court has also held many times that constitutional values are at stake in contractual disputes,[82] including ones between large for-profit corporations.[83] The law of succession also raises constitutional issues, often because of its allegedly discriminatory consequences.[84] All disputes, in sum, regardless of subject matter, can be, and often are, subordinated to the characteristic methods of constitutional adjudication.[85]

South Africa's post-apartheid legal order is thus eye-catching and unusual. Central to it is an urgent project of large-scale change, but one that must take place within a stable rule-governed order, led by the courts.[86] Naturally this has implications for the relative balance between legal certainty and legal change,

---

75 Examples of the 'constitutionalisation' of private law are discussed in C.G. van der Merwe, J. du Plessis, M. de Waal, R. Zimmermann and P. Farlam, above n. 1, pp. 173–74, 186–95.

76 Constitution 1996, s. 25.

77 s. 26.

78 *Carmichele*, above n. 64. Consistently with the 'Diceyan approach' that is well-known in England, the South African law of delict applies a single set of rules to determine the liability of both public and private defendants.

79 *K v. Minister of Safety and Security* [2005] ZACC 8.

80 *Lee v. Minister of Correctional* Services [2012] ZACC 30.

81 *Khumalo v. Holomisa* [2002] ZACC 12. The right to freedom of expression is expressly protected in s. 16 of the Constitution. The right to reputation enjoys protection via the right to dignity in s. 10.

82 *Barkhuizen v. Napier* [2007] ZACC 5; *Beadica 231 CC v. Trustees for the time being of the Oregon Trust* [2020] ZACC 13.

83 *Everfresh Market Virginia (Pty) Ltd v. Shoprite Checkers (Pty) Ltd* [2011] ZACC 30; *Fujitsu Services Core (Pty) Ltd v. Schenker South Africa (Pty) Ltd* [2023] ZACC 20. Sometimes, as in *Barkhuizen*, above n. 82, the constitutional issue arises because a contract term allegedly infringes a party's constitutional right. But sometimes the relevant constitutional value identified by the Court is simply the value of fairness: compare *Everfresh*, paras. 22–25, 48.

84 *Bwanya v. Master of the High Court, Cape Town* [2021] ZACC 51. See also *King NO v. De Jager* [2021] ZACC 4, which invalidated a private testamentary trust on the grounds that it was unfairly discriminatory.

85 The 1996 Constitution is therefore a paradigmatic example of what M. Kumm calls a 'total constitution': 'Who Is Afraid of the Total Constitution? Constitutional Rights as Principles and the Constitutionalization of Private Law' (2006) 7 *German Law Journal* 341. Kumm is discussing the German *Grundgesetz*, but its characteristic features are shared (and perhaps pushed further) by South Africa's Constitution, which it heavily influenced.

86 For more on the balance between judicial and parliamentary law-making, see Section 5.1. below.

and has resulted in certain modifications of the doctrine of *stare decisis*, which are detailed in Section 3.2.2. Other effects of the Constitution upon judicial reasoning, discussed in Section 6.2., are more subtle. As the characteristic methods of constitutional rights adjudication have spread across the legal system, traditional private law methods, in which precedents stand central, have arguably been displaced.

3. NATURE OF PRECEDENT

The South African doctrine of precedent can be given the following preliminary statement: a court is bound to follow a decision of a court higher in the hierarchy, unless it was made *per incuriam*, and a court is bound to follow its own previous decision, unless it is clearly wrong.[87] This statement presupposes an account of the hierarchy of South African courts, which is provided in Section 3.1. Thereafter, in Sections 3.2. to 3.4., the binding effect of a precedent is discussed in detail. This discussion takes for granted that a binding precedent exists and has been identified; the issue of how to identify the binding component of a decision, namely its *ratio decidendi*, is postponed to Section 4.

3.1. THE COURT STRUCTURE[88]

The Constitutional Court, as mentioned, is South Africa's highest court.[89] The inaptly named Supreme Court of Appeal (SCA) sits one rung below it in the hierarchy. Both are generalist appeal courts. The country also has several High Court 'divisions', whose jurisdiction is defined territorially.[90] The SCA hears appeals from the High Courts,[91] and the Constitutional Court hears appeals

---

87 Compare H.R. Hahlo and E. Kahn, above n. 3, p. 243.

88 The discussion in this section is streamlined and, in some respects, simplified. See for comprehensive treatment M. Wallis, above n. 3.

89 This has been the case since 2013. Between 1995 and 2013, the Constitutional Court enjoyed co-equal status with the Supreme Court of Appeal, with their respective jurisdictions determined by subject matter: the Constitutional Court was the apex court in 'constitutional' matters, and the SCA was the apex court in non-constitutional ones. In virtue of the Constitution Seventeenth Amendment Act (which came into force in 2013), however, the Constitutional Court became the apex court in all matters, even non-constitutional ones; and the two courts' names have become misnomers: the Constitutional Court does not hear only constitutional matters, and the SCA is no longer supreme. See further C. Hoexter, 'The Structure of the Courts' in C. Hoexter and M. Olivier (eds), above n. 69, pp. 16–17.

90 The High Courts' respective territorial jurisdictions were subject to some historical quirks, but in essence they correspond to the country's provinces. See M. Wallis, above n. 3, para. 480.

91 Superior Courts Act 10 of 2013, s. 16.

from the SCA (and occasionally from a High Court directly).[92] A typical private law matter will therefore commence in the High Court and may ascend through two levels of appeal.[93] The SCA will, with minor exceptions, hear any appeal with 'a reasonable prospect of success'.[94] For the Constitutional Court to hear a further appeal, the threshold is higher; it hears only 'arguable points of law of general public importance',[95] a test borrowed from the Supreme Court of the United Kingdom.[96] As mentioned, the Court regularly decides cases in contract, delict, and property law,[97] and on occasion in more technical areas like mortgages and trusts.[98] But it hears only a small fraction of the cases filed with it,[99] with the result that most rules of South African private law are laid down by the SCA (and its predecessor, the Appellate Division).

The picture so far is readily understood. Complexities arise, however, from the fact that each of the High Courts sits in different configurations.[100] Civil matters at first instance are heard by a single judge. But appeals from a single judge's decision may be heard by a 'Full Court' comprising three judges. Hence there are, in effect, two layers of the judicial hierarchy within each High Court.[101]

The Constitutional Court is bound (horizontally) by its own decisions, but not by those of any other court. The SCA is bound (vertically) by the Constitutional Court's decisions and (horizontally) by its own decisions, but not by those of the High Courts. A Full Court is bound (vertically) by decisions of both the Constitutional Court and the SCA, and (horizontally) by other decisions of a Full Court in its division. A single judge sitting in the High Court is bound

---

92 The Constitution 1996, s. 167(3)–(7). The Constitutional Court may also act as a court of first instance, but only very exceptionally.

93 South Africa has a number of specialist courts, such as the Equality Court, Labour Court, Labour Appeal Court, and Competition Appeal Court. These are not discussed further. They operate according to substantially the same rules of precedent as the country's generalist courts.

94 Superior Courts Act 2013, s. 17.

95 Constitution 1996, s. 167(3)(b)(ii). There are many additional complexities, discussed in M. Wallis, above n. 3, para. 471.

96 UK Supreme Court Practice Direction 3, para. 3.3.3.

97 See above nn. 75–84.

98 *Absa Bank Ltd v. Moore* [2016] ZACC 34.

99 N. Ally and L. Boonzaier, 'The Constitutional Court's Efficiency: Statistics from the Mogoeng Era, 2010–2021' (2022) 12 *Constitutional Court Review* 317, 332. Though comprehensive data on the point is not available, it seems fairly clear that private law cases, and especially ones raising technical points of commercial and corporate law, are filed with and heard by the Court much less often than public law ones.

100 Superior Courts Act 2013, ss. 14, 16; M. Wallis, above n. 3, para. 481.

101 Further complexities arise from the fact that the High Courts have appellate jurisdiction in respect of the magistrate's courts, but these are not considered in this contribution. Magistrate's courts do not themselves create precedents, but are bound, as one might expect, by decisions of superior courts: M. Wallis, above n. 3, para. 528. Also ignored are the complexities discussed in M.J. Oelschig, J.R. Midgley and A.J. Kerr, 'Stare Decisis in Provincial and Local Divisions' (1985) 102 *South African Law Journal* 370.

(vertically) by the Constitutional Court, SCA, and Full Court decisions within his or her own division, and (horizontally) by other single-judge decisions within his or her division. High Courts are not bound by the decisions of other High Court divisions, whether given by a single judge or a Full Court. This last-mentioned rule – that *stare decisis* at High Court level operates 'on a purely provincial basis'[102] – is usually traced to the fact that, before South Africa was unified in 1910, its territory contained four distinct political entities, each of whose courts were independent from those of the others, and that the mutual independence of these colonial-era courts was passed down to the High Courts, their descendants.[103]

Each of these textbook rules is, in practice, soft-edged; precedents often influence later courts' reasoning even when they are not strictly binding. For example, the appellate courts, though never required to do so, have many times refused to depart from High Court decisions of long standing on which citizens have relied.[104] And High Courts in one division, though not strictly bound by precedents set in another division, tend to regard them as highly persuasive, particularly because of the value of having a uniform rule that applies throughout the country.[105]

3.2. THE BINDINGNESS OF PRECEDENT

Supposing a court is bound by a precedent, what does that entail? As will be explained in Section 4.1., only the *ratio decidendi* of a case is binding, and not *obiter dicta*. This section discusses the binding force of a case's *ratio*, assuming it exists and has been identified. Although any court may of course 'distinguish' a precedent, i.e. determine that the facts of the instant case are relevantly different and therefore do not fall within the precedent, this power is not considered further in this section.[106]

3.2.1. *General Principles*

The *ratio* of a case is 'absolutely' or 'fully' binding on courts lower in the hierarchy than the court that decided it. In other words, where a lower court

102 *National Chemsearch (Pty) Ltd v. Borrowman* 1979 (3) SA 1092 (T), 1100E.

103 H.R. Hahlo and E. Kahn, above n. 3, p. 254; M. Wallis, 'Whose Decisis Must We Stare?' (2018) 135 *South African Law Journal* 1, 3–5. Wallis argues that the rule may now need to be changed, in line with a rationalisation of the High Court system that took place in 2013, but that complexity will not be discussed here.

104 Several examples are cited in H.R. Hahlo and E. Kahn, above n. 3, p. 250, fn. 15.

105 *Halse*, above n. 42, 239; *National Chemsearch*, above n. 102, 1100E–00F, discussed in C.G. van der Merwe, J. du Plessis, M. de Waal, R. Zimmermann and P. Farlam, above n. 1, p. 137.

106 But see Section 4.3. below.

is faced with a precedent that is not distinguishable, it must follow it. There is only one exception, namely where the decision was given *per incuriam* ('through lack of care'), in other words in ignorance of applicable law.[107] The *per incuriam* exception is rarely used, and perhaps for that reason its boundaries remain obscure.[108] Clearly a decision that defies a relevant statute falls within the exception,[109] as does a decision that defies a vertically binding precedent,[110] but courts have occasionally stretched the exception's scope beyond this.[111]

The horizontal effect of a precedent is qualified (or 'presumptive')[112] rather than absolute. This is because a precedent may be departed from where a court of equal status considers it to be 'clearly wrong'.[113] This exception to the horizontal bindingness of precedent has a long history, having been applied consistently by the colonial courts before the creation of South Africa and by both the High Courts and the Appellate Division after Union.[114] In the post-apartheid era, the High Courts,[115] SCA,[116] and Constitutional Court[117] have accepted many times that the 'clearly wrong' exception continues to apply.

This exception sets a deliberately stringent test.[118] Whether a decision is clearly wrong is 'not a matter of personal preference, mere disagreement, misgivings, doubt, let alone whim'.[119] Rather, a court is bound by its own

---

107 'A decision is given *per incuriam* where the attention of the court was not drawn to relevant authority': M. Wallis, above n. 3, para. 520, fn. 6. In South Africa *incuria* are used primarily as an exception to *vertical* precedent, which appears to differ from its main function in England: S. Ryan, 'The Balance between Certainty and Flexibility in Horizontal and Vertical Stare Decisis' (2015) 132 *South African Law Journal* 230, 236.

108 Compare E. Kahn, 'Judgments *Per Incuriam* and the Doctrine of Precedent' (1955) 72 *South African Law Journal* 404; F. du Bois, above n. 3, p. 89.

109 *Trade Fairs*, above n. 28, 185E; H.R. Hahlo and E. Kahn, above n. 3, pp. 243, 245.

110 *R v. Nxumalo* 1939 AD 580; H.R. Hahlo and E. Kahn, above n. 3, p. 253.

111 See e.g. *Sealandair Shipping & Forwarding v. Slash Clothing Co (Pty) Ltd* 1987 (2) SA 635 (W), which treats a decision as *per incuriam* because it had based itself upon a prior judgment that it interpreted wrongly. This approach is criticised in *Mofokeng v. General Accident Versekering Bpk* 1990 (2) SA 712 (W); M. Dendy, 'A Cavalier Approach to Stare Decisis' (1988) 105 *South African Law Journal* 411. A point of particular contention is whether a decision that fails to apply a relevant provision of the Bill of Rights is for that reason *per incuriam*: see further below n. 175.

112 F. du Bois, above n. 3, p. 87.

113 See most recently *Bwanya*, above n. 84, para. 46; *Makhala v. S* [2022] ZASCA 19, para. 115 and authorities cited there.

114 This was discussed in Section 2.1. above. Additional examples are *R v. Faithfull and Gray* 1907 TS 1077, 1081; *R v. Jansen* 1937 CPD 294, 297; *S v. Tarajka Estates (Edms) Bpk* 1963 (4) SA 467 (T), 470A.

115 e.g. *Hall v. S* [2021] ZAWCHC 231, para. 48.

116 e.g. *Patmar Explorations (Pty) Ltd v. Limpopo Development Tribunal* [2018] ZASCA 19; *Makhala*, above n. 113.

117 See further Section 3.2.2.3. below.

118 *Turnbull-Jackson v. Hibiscus Coast Municipality* [2014] ZACC 24, para. 72; *Bwanya*, above n. 84, para. 46.

119 *Bwanya*, above n. 84, para. 46.

decision unless it was based upon a 'manifest oversight or misunderstanding', 'palpable mistake', or 'fundamental departure from principle'.[120] Hence 'a deviation from previous decisions should not be undertaken lightly'.[121] The bar is particularly high where the court is considering whether to depart from a long line of decisions on which citizens have relied.[122] On the other hand, the courts have said that 'a judge must not be faint-hearted, and when he is morally convinced that justice requires a departure from precedent he will not hesitate to do so',[123] and that the exercise of this power ensures that South African law remains a 'virile, living system'[124] and avoids the excessive rigidity of the English approach.[125]

A precedent grounded upon public policy is more vulnerable than others, since it is recognised that public policy changes over time.[126] And where a decision was made on an issue that was not properly argued, the courts are much more willing to overrule it.[127] Finally, although any majority opinion is officially as binding as any other,[128] those written by highly esteemed judges seem, in practice, to carry greater force.[129]

3.2.2. *The Impact of the Constitution*

The 1996 Constitution raised new questions about the binding force of precedent, which some commentators anticipated would 'undergo [a] fundamental overhaul'.[130] This was for two main reasons. First, as discussed in Section 2.2., the new Constitution has powerful ambitions to transform South African law, including the common law, after the end of apartheid.

---

120 *Richter*, above n. 35, 232; *Patmar Explorations*, above n. 116, para. 3.

121 *Media 24 Ltd v. SA Taxi Securitisation (Pty) Ltd* [2011] ZASCA 117, para. 34.

122 *Harris*, above n. 35, 454A–54B; *Horowitz*, above n. 50, 186H.

123 *National Chemsearch*, above n. 102, 1101D–01E.

124 ibid., 1101C. The quoted phrase derives from *Pearl Assurance Co. v. Union Government* [1934] AC 570 (PC), 579 (Lord Tomlin).

125 See again *Fellner*, above n. 28, 529–32.

126 *Roffey v. Catterall, Edward & Goudré (Pty) Ltd* 1977 4 SA 494 (N), 506, quoting *Nordenfelt v. Maxim Nordenfelt Guns and Ammunition Co Ltd* [1984] AC 535 (HL), 553–54.

127 *Faithfull*, above n. 114, 1081; *Harris*, above n. 35, 453, 471. Although South African courts have suggested that the *per incuriam* exception applies in respect of horizontal precedent (*Harris*, above n. 35, 471E–71F), it is subsumed by the 'clearly wrong' exception and therefore has limited practical utility: E. Kahn, above n. 108, 406–07.

128 See Section 4.2. below.

129 See e.g. *Botha v. Soocher* 1941 TPD 245, 247.

130 S.A. Jazbhay, 'Stare Decisis: Are Courts Bound Thereby in the Interpretation of the Interim Constitution?' (1996) *De Rebus* 37; also A. Henderson, 'Defeating the Justification of Iniquitous Opinion: The Role of Stare Decisis in the Adjudication of Constitutional Disputes' (1996) *De Rebus* 469; N. MacCormick, above n. 27, 174–78. See further the discussion in W.J. Hosten et al, *Introduction to South African Law and Legal Theory*, 2nd ed., Juta & Co Ltd, Cape Town 1995, pp. 501–02 and authorities cited there.

Since *stare decisis* of course requires courts to leave the existing law intact, the question arose whether the doctrine might have to be weakened in the new regime. Second, and more controversially, it is sometimes felt that a true commitment to constitutional supremacy requires courts to be guided solely by the Constitution, and thus to depart from precedents that, in their view, interpret or apply it wrongly.[131]

3.2.2.1. The Vertical Bindingness of Precedents Post-Dating the Constitution

There were some eye-catching early skirmishes, shortly after the enactment of the Constitution, about whether SCA decisions interpreting and applying it were binding on the High Courts. Clearly the SCA was higher in the judicial pecking order than the High Courts. And yet some High Court judges, attracted to the strong form of constitutional supremacy just mentioned, held that they were empowered to depart from an SCA precedent if they considered it to be 'inconsistent with decisions of the Constitutional Court' – even where those decisions predated, and were taken into account in, the judgment of the SCA.[132] But this drew a sharp rebuke from the Constitutional Court, which held in *S v. Walters* that the doctrine of *stare decisis* remains valid and important in the constitutional era and that the High Court judge was 'bound to accept the authority and the binding force of applicable decisions of higher tribunals', 'however much he may personally have had his misgivings about it'.[133] It is true, as the Court noted, that Section 39(2) of the Constitution requires all courts to develop the common law in line with the Bill of Rights. But this duty is itself constrained by the doctrine of precedent: lower courts are not therefore licensed to depart from common law rules created by the SCA.[134]

---

131 This idea is perhaps most familiar from the United States Supreme Court: see e.g. *Graves v. New York* 306 US 466 (1939), 491–92, per Frankfurter J ('the ultimate touchstone of constitutionality is the Constitution itself, and not what we have said about it'); *Burnet v. Coronado Oil & Gas Co.* 285 US 393 (1932), 410, per Brandeis J.

132 *S v. Walters* 2001 (10) BCLR 1088 (Tk), especially at paras. 13, 19, and 22, which rejects the authority of *Govender v. Minister of Safety and Security* 2001 (4) SA 273 (SCA), a unanimous SCA judgment handed down five weeks earlier. This was not the general view of the High Courts, however: see *Shabalala v. Attorney-General, Transvaal; Gumede v. Attorney-General, Transvaal* 1995 (1) SA 608 (T), 618G–18H; *Bookworks (Pty) Ltd v. Greater Johannesburg Transitional Metropolitan Council* 1999 (4) SA 799 (W), 810H–11D.

133 *Ex parte Minister of Safety and Security: In Re S v. Walters* 2002 (4) SA 613 (CC), paras. 60–61. This holding clearly covers the situation in which a single High Court judge is confronted by a precedent laid down by a Full Court in the same division. See further *Shabalala*, above n. 132, 618F–18G, quoted with apparent approval in *Walters*, para. 58.

134 A related but conceptually distinct question is whether a post-constitutional decision that did not consider the Constitution at all is binding on a lower court, or instead *per incuriam*. See below n. 175.

3.2.2.2. The Vertical Bindingness of Precedents Pre-Dating the Constitution

Walters related to the binding force of precedents laid down during the constitutional era. The more difficult question, which *Walters* left open,[135] was whether precedents established *before* the transition to democracy were entitled to continued deference. Could a High Court, for example, overrule an apartheid-era precedent of the Appellate Division on the basis that it was inconsistent with the new Constitution? A number of High Court judges decided that they did have this power, and, on the basis of it, had departed even from unanimous Appellate Division decisions given just a few years, or months, earlier.[136] Predictably, these judgments generated immediate controversy: some hailed their approach as bearing out the Constitution's transformational promise,[137] but others condemned it for imperilling legal certainty and failing to respect the established common law.[138]

A favourable view was taken by the High Court judge in *Strydom v. Afrox Healthcare Ltd*,[139] which involved the judicial power to invalidate unjust or unfair contract terms. He held that *stare decisis*, since it entails that lower courts would have to 'blindly follow' a common law approach adopted 'many years ago', 'is not consonant with the provisions of section 39 of the Constitution'.[140] On appeal, this attracted a sceptical response from the SCA,[141] which gave a detailed account of the vertical bindingness of pre-constitutional decisions. It held that one must distinguish three situations:

1. First is 'the situation where the High Court is convinced that the relevant rule of the common law is in conflict with a constitutional provision',[142] most obviously, a particular constitutional right. In this situation, the High Court is not only empowered but 'obliged to depart from the common law'.[143] After all, '[t]he Constitution is the supreme law and where a rule of law conflicts with it, the rule must yield'.[144]

135 *Walters*, above n. 133, para. 61.

136 See especially *Gardener v. Whitaker* 1995 (2) SA 672 (E) and *Holomisa v. Argus Newspapers Ltd* 1996 (2) SA 588 (W), both of which rejected the authority of *Neethling v. Du Preez; Neethling v. Weekly Mail* 1994 (1) SA 708 (A).

137 *Rivett-Carnac*, above n. 68, 87–88; *Buthelezi v. South African Broadcasting Corporation* 1997 (12) BCLR 1733 (D), 1738H–38J; *Bookworks*, above n. 132, 810G.

138 *Bogoshi v. National Media Ltd* 1996 (3) SA 78 (W); *McNally v. M&G Media (Pty) Ltd* 1997 (4) SA 267 (W), 276; D. van der Merwe, 'Constitutional Colonisation of the Common Law: A Problem of Institutional Integrity' (2000) *Tydskrif vir die Suid-Afrikaanse Reg* 12, 14.

139 *Strydom v. Afrox Healthcare Ltd* [2001] JOL 8434 (T).

140 ibid., 10.

141 *Afrox Healthcare Bpk v. Strydom* 2002 (6) SA 21 (SCA), paras. 26–30. All translations from the original Afrikaans are the author of this contribution's own.

142 ibid., para. 27.

143 ibid.

144 ibid.

2. 'The second possible situation', according to *Afrox*, 'is where the pre-constitutional decision of [the Appellate Division] was based on considerations such as the *boni mores* or public policy', and 'the High Court is of the opinion that, taking into account constitutional values, the decision no longer accurately reflects the *boni mores* or public policy'.[145] In such a case, the High Court is again 'obliged' to depart from the decision.[146] This does not violate *stare decisis*, the SCA held, because it has long been accepted that public policy and societal norms are not static;[147] courts are, therefore, relatively free to update precedents based upon community attitudes that have since changed.[148] The clearest examples of this second situation are pre-constitutional precedents of the Appellate Division that had refused to confer common law recognition upon Islamic marriages (which were unlawful according to discriminatory apartheid legislation), and from which the High Court was now justified in departing.[149] This situation presumably also encompasses pre-constitutional precedents that tested whether a discriminatory testamentary provision[150] or contract term[151] is contrary to public policy.
3. The third and final situation identified by *Afrox* is one in which, although neither of the first two obtains, the High Court is convinced that, 'in light of section 39(2) [of the Constitution], the common-law rule in question must be changed in order to promote the spirit, purport and objects of the Constitution'.[152] Here, unlike in the first two situations, 'the principles of *stare decisis* remain valid and the High Court is not permitted by section 39(2) to depart from the decisions of [a higher court], whether pre- or post-constitutional'.[153] The SCA held that this cautious approach was justified by the benefits of *stare decisis*, which must be balanced against the need for reform; to allow judges to depart from precedents on the basis of their contestable judgments about constitutional values 'would inevitably lead to a lack of uniformity and certainty'.[154]

---

145 ibid., para. 28.
146 ibid.
147 Compare above n. 126.
148 *Afrox*, above n. 141, para. 28.
149 *Afrox* gives *Ryland v. Edros* 1997 (2) SA 690 (C) and *Amod v. Multilateral Motor Vehicle Accidents Fund* 1999 (4) SA 1319 (SCA) as examples. Its third example is *Carmichele*, above n. 64, which is discussed in the text at below n. 155.
150 *Minister of Education v. Syfrets Trust Ltd NO* 2006 (4) SA 205 (C).
151 The High Court in *Afrox* itself (above n. 139) clearly saw the issue before it in this way, citing to similar effect *Stembridge v. Stembridge* [1998] 2 All SA 4 (D); *Mort NO v. Henry Shields-Chiat* 2001 (1) SA 464 (C), 475D–75E.
152 *Afrox*, above n. 141, para. 29.
153 ibid.
154 ibid., para. 30. See also para. 32 (rejecting the use of 'values' as though they are legal rules).

Afrox is an attempt to moderate the Constitution's effect upon *stare decisis*. Though the SCA grants that lower courts have the power to depart from pre-constitutional precedents in situations 1 and 2, its holding on the third situation was, in context, the crucial one, since Section 39(2) had unmistakably become the main portal used to 'constitutionalise' the common law. In *Carmichele*,[155] decided one year earlier, the Constitutional Court gave an expansive reading to that very section and urged the High Court to use it to change the common law of delict as it had been laid down by the Appellate Division pre-constitutionally.[156] *Afrox* seeks, in effect, to confine *Carmichele*'s approach to instances where the Appellate Division precedent at issue was based expressly upon public policy or the *boni mores* (situation 2), although there is no suggestion of this limitation in the *Carmichele* judgment itself. *Afrox* has, therefore, been widely condemned by academics.[157] Even if its approach is taken at face value, however, the Constitution has created one new exception to the vertical bindingness of precedent (situation 1) and endorsed and underscored one old one (situation 2); moreover, the Court is in these situations not merely permitted but obliged to depart from precedent. These are significant developments, tilting the scales away from legal certainty and towards reform.

3.2.2.3. Horizontal Precedent in the Constitutional Era

As already explained in Section 3.2.1., horizontal precedent has always been only qualifiedly binding in South Africa. Hence there is nothing new in the idea, which *Walters* confirmed post-constitutionally, that High Courts and the SCA may depart from their own prior precedents if they are 'clearly wrong'.[158] The larger question was how the newly created Constitutional Court would approach its own precedents.[159] Some suggested that adopting a traditional model of *stare*

---

155 Above n. 64.

156 The High Court judgments cited, above n. 136, which *Afrox* does not mention, had also relied on s. 39(2) (or rather its equivalent in the Interim Constitution, namely s. 35(3)).

157 S.D. Woolman and D. Brand, 'Is There a Constitution in This Courtroom? Constitutional Jurisdiction after Afrox and Walters' (2003) 18 *SA Public Law* 37; G. Devenish, 'The Doctrine of Precedent in South Africa' (2007) 28 *Obiter* 1, 16; F. du Bois, above n. 3, p. 91, fn. 162; I. Currie and J. De Waal, *Bill of Rights Handbook*, 6th ed., Juta & Co Ltd, Cape Town 2013, p. 66. *Afrox*'s discussion has been cited by the Constitutional Court, though without endorsing its analysis on the crucial point: see *Daniels v. Campbell NO* 2004 (5) SA 331 (CC), para. 82, fn. 115; *Camps Bay Ratepayers and Residents Association v. Harrison* [2010] ZACC 19, para. 29, fn. 41. Arguably it does not reflect the practice of the High Courts.

158 *Walters*, above n. 133, paras. 58–60. The High Courts and SCA had adopted this view some years before: *Shabalala*, above n. 132, 618D; *Robin Consolidated Industries Ltd v. Commissioner for Inland Revenue* 1997 (3) SA 654 (SCA), 666F–66G. To be sure, the Constitution's norms and values now provide additional and arguably more forceful grounds upon which an earlier decision may be found to be clearly wrong: see further F. du Bois, above n. 3, pp. 92–99.

159 See A. Rycroft, 'The Doctrine of Stare Decisis in Constitutional Court Cases' (1995) 11 *South African Journal on Human Rights* 587 and authorities cited, above n. 130.

decisis would be too inhibiting, since the Court was tasked with driving forward rapid legal development. But the Court held in one of its early decisions that '[t]he sound jurisprudential basis' for the doctrine of *stare decisis* 'is no less valid [in constitutional adjudication] than is generally the case'.[160] It has since affirmed the doctrine of precedent's importance many times,[161] and indeed said that fidelity to precedent has special importance to a court in its position:

> A highest court of appeal – and this Court in particular – has to be especially cautious as far as adherence to or deviation from its own previous decisions is concerned. … [A] single source of consistent, authoritative and binding decisions is essential for the development of a stable constitutional jurisprudence and for the effective protection of fundamental rights. This Court must not easily and without coherent and compelling reason deviate from its own previous decisions, or be seen to have done so.[162]

The Court has confirmed that its own duty to stand by its prior decisions has the same incidence as the long-standing doctrine.[163] And so, while some suggested *stare decisis* would have to yield to the demand for post-apartheid law reform, the Constitutional Court has, in relation to its own precedents, taken a quite different view: its precedents are a crucial means by which a secure post-apartheid legal order is constructed.[164]

The Court has accepted that it may depart from its own precedents when they are 'clearly wrong'.[165] Strikingly, however, the Court has never, in its 29-year existence, exercised this power.[166] It has instead tried to avoid direct conflict with

---

160 *Certification of the Amended Text of the Constitution of the Republic of South Africa, 1996* [1996] ZACC 24, para. 8.

161 e.g. *Van der Walt v. Metcash* [2002] ZACC 4, para. 39; *Walters*, above n. 133, paras. 56–61; *Daniels*, above n. 157, paras. 94–96; *Gcaba v. Minister for Safety and Security* [2009] ZACC 26, paras. 58–62; *Camps Bay Ratepayers*, above n. 157, paras. 28–30; *Turnbull-Jackson*, above n. 118, paras. 54–58; *Ruta v. Minister of Home Affairs* [2018] ZACC 52, para. 21; *Bwanya*, above n. 84, para. 46.

162 *Gcaba*, above n. 161, para. 62. The SCA, too, has held that *stare decisis* is especially important at 'this tender stage of our legal development' and that failures to follow precedent may cause 'detriment to public faith in constitutional processes': *True Motives 84 (Pty) Ltd v. Mahdi* [2009] ZASCA 4, para. 102; *De Kock NO v. Van Rooyen* [2004] ZASCA 136, para. 18.

163 *Turnbull-Jackson*, above n. 118, para. 57 provides a succinct summary. Presumably the Court's precedents would have no binding force at all if decided *per incuriam*: compare *Jacobs v. S* [2019] ZACC 4, paras. 97–105, in which a minority opinion appears to take this view (though it is doubtful that the decision discussed there was indeed *per incuriam*).

164 Compare *Mistry v. Interim National Medical and Dental Council* [1998] ZACC 10, para. 3; J. Brickhill, 'Precedent and the Constitutional Court' (2010) 3 *Constitutional Court Review* 79, 104.

165 *Turnbull-Jackson*, above n. 118, para. 57.

166 J. Brickhill, above n. 164, 80. Since Brickhill's article appeared in 2010, the Court has confronted its prior precedents in some high-profile cases, notably *Turnbull-Jackson*, above n. 118, and *Bwanya*, above n. 84, but in both cases denied that its precedent was clearly wrong.

its prior judgments by interpreting them narrowly and by creative acts of distinguishing – seemingly because the Court fears a loss of legitimacy if it were to acknowledge it has erred, or if trusted constitutional precepts were suddenly reversed. Of course, strained and unpredictable reinterpretations of prior decisions may themselves produce uncertainty, confusion, and perhaps a loss of legitimacy; in due course the Court may require express flexibility to adapt constitutional law to changing conditions.[167] At the time of writing, however, the Court continues to procure the necessary flexibility indirectly and *ad hoc*.[168]

3.3. THE TEMPORAL OPERATION OF PRECEDENTS

The orthodox position is that South African courts do not have the power to create a 'purely prospective' precedent, i.e. one that will not be applied to the case before the court, but only to future cases.[169] Nor is it possible for a court to apply a precedent to cases that have already been concluded. In criminal matters, however, the Constitutional Court has been willing 'in rare cases' to set a precedent that is prospective only.[170] In civil contexts, concerns about non-retrospectivity are less pressing,[171] but in principle the courts might see fit to use the same power there.[172]

---

167 J. Brickhill, above n. 164, 100–09.

168 See again *Bwanya*, above n. 84, a case about the rights of unmarried life partners in the law of succession. In it, the Court reached the opposite outcome from its fiercely criticised judgment in *Volks NO v. Robinson* [2005] ZACC 2, but puzzlingly did not hold *Volks* to be clearly wrong. Instead, the Court held it was entitled to take a different view because *Volks* was based partly on factual questions and because the Court now had additional information before it. See for further discussion J. Brickhill, 'Constitutional Law' (2022) 3 *Yearbook of South African Law* 239, 266–69.

169 H.R. Hahlo and E. Kahn, above n. 3, p. 250; *Du Plessis v. De Klerk* [1996] ZACC 10, para. 65. In this respect, as *Du Plessis* explains, 'our courts have followed the practice of the English courts' (which is critiqued in R. Cross and J.W. Harris, above n. 37, pp. 228–32).

170 *Masiya v. Director of Public Prosecutions* [2007] ZACC 9, paras. 47–57, 74.6. The Court justified this in terms of s. 172(1)(b) of the Constitution, which allows a court, when making a declaration that law or conduct is inconsistent with the Constitution, to 'limit the retrospective effect of the declaration of invalidity'.

171 Constitution 1996, s. 35(3)(l), which was relied upon in *Masiya*, above n. 170, prohibits the retroactive creation of criminal offences.

172 In *Du Plessis*, above n. 169, a civil law defamation dispute (though one with a distinctive constitutional dimension), the Court suggested at paras. 66–67 that there may be good reason to depart from past judicial practice and set a prospective precedent. See too K. O'Regan, 'Change v Certainty: Precedent under the Constitution' (2001) 14(1) *Advocate* 31, 32. More recently, the Court in *Stratford v. Investec Bank Ltd* [2014] ZACC 38 used s. 172(1)(b) to limit the retrospective effect of a declaration that it made about the proper meaning of a legislative provision. The effect of this is arguably to create a purely prospective precedent, though the Court did not style it in this way.

3.4. FAILURES TO FOLLOW PRECEDENT

Of course, courts sometimes fail to follow relevant precedents. Naturally this tends to 'incur the wrath of the appellate tribunal'.[173] The legal consequences of the error must also be determined.[174] Where a court has overlooked a binding precedent of a higher court, then its decision is *per incuriam* and will have no binding effect in future cases.[175] Where a court has ignored a precedent of its own, views differ about the consequences. One view, which has been endorsed by both the High Courts and the Appellate Division, is that a future court should follow whichever of the two decisions it considers correct.[176] Another view, which enjoys limited support within the Constitutional Court, is that the later decision should be disregarded in favour of the first.[177] But at other times, the Court has implied, dubiously, that in the event of an inconsistency between two of its decisions the later of them is authoritative.[178]

Following the creation of the Constitutional Court at the top of the judicial hierarchy in 1995, the prospect of conflicting vertical precedents has increased.[179] High Courts are strictly bound by both Constitutional Court precedents and SCA precedents, and so are left in a dilemma if the two are in conflict – as, on occasion, they have been.[180] These conflicts can become fraught, particularly

---

173 *Trade Fairs*, above n. 28, 185. Examples are *De Kock*, above n. 162, para. 18; *Ruta*, above n. 161, paras. 21–22. Others are given in C.G. van der Merwe, J. du Plessis, M. de Waal, R. Zimmermann and P. Farlam, above n. 1, pp. 140–41. It should be noted, however, that on rare occasions, and despite the official rules of precedent, lower courts have defied a vertically binding precedent that they considered to be badly mistaken and been vindicated on appeal. An early example is *Faithfull*, above n. 114, discussed in H.R. Hahlo and E. Kahn, above n. 3, p. 241. Two more recent examples are *Van der Merwe Burger v. Munisipaliteit van Warrenton* 1987 (1) SA 899 (NC) and *MEC for the Department of Welfare v. Kate* [2006] ZASCA 49, both of which are discussed (and praised) in G. Devenish, above n. 157, 9–13, 20–21.

174 A decision that ignores binding precedent remains valid and effectual *inter partes*: *Trade Fairs*, above n. 28, 185. The discussion in the text is about the precedential effect of the decision.

175 See above n. 110. In the constitutional era, some High Court judges have occasionally used an expanded reading of the *per incuriam* exception to justify their refusal to be bound by an SCA decision, reasoning that the SCA decision was incompatible with the Constitutional Court's understanding of the Constitution: see again *Kate*, above n. 173; *Walters*, above n. 132, is arguably open to a similar interpretation. This stretching of the exception is questionable (compare *Bookworks*, above n. 132, 809C–09D), since in these sorts of cases the SCA had expressly considered, rather than overlooked, the higher authority in question, and because the High Courts' powers to develop the common law under constitutional impetus are regulated by other means.

176 *R v. Sillas* 1959 (4) SA 305 (A), 311 (endorsing the view in *Young*, above n. 32).

177 This seems to be the implication of the minority opinion in *Jacobs*, above n. 163.

178 *Gcaba*, above n. 161, para. 77.

179 This possibility existed in the pre-constitutional era, since a single High Court judge might face conflicting precedents of a Full Court and of the Appellate Division, but was rare.

180 The main example is in the law of contract, where the SCA and Constitutional Court have taken different views about the extent to which courts have a common law discretion to

because of the tension between the two courts that is discussed below in Section 6.2.

4. HOW TO IDENTIFY A LEGAL RULE IN A PRECEDENT

This section considers the principles for identifying the binding part of a precedent, in other words its *ratio decidendi*, and how it – as well as the non-binding parts – features in the reasoning of later courts.

4.1. FINDING THE *RATIO DECIDENDI*

South African courts distinguish the *ratio decidendi* of a case from *obiter dicta*, only the former of which is binding.[181] *Ratio decidendi* 'means "the reason of or for the decision" and the "decision" means the order of [the] court'.[182] Identifying the *ratio* can be difficult. The words used in the court's reasoning are highly relevant but not determinative;[183] the question is what principle the court took to justify its decision,[184] not the words in which it expressed it.[185] The applicable criteria appear from the Appellate Division's canonical judgment in *Pretoria City Council v. Levinson*,[186] where Schreiner JA held that 'the reasons given in a judgment' form part of its *ratio* provided:

> (a) that they do not appear from the judgment itself to have been merely subsidiary reasons for following the main principle …
> (b) that they were not merely a course of reasoning on the facts … and
> (c) (which may cover (a)) that they were necessary for the decision, not in the sense that it could not have been reached along other lines, but in the sense that along the lines actually followed in the judgment the result would have been different but for the reasons.[187]

---

control unfair terms. The resulting conflict, which saw both the SCA and the Constitutional Court complaining that its precedents were being defied, is discussed in D. Hutchison, 'From Bona Fides to Ubuntu: The Quest for Fairness in the South African Law of Contract' (2019) *Acta Juridica* 99; E. Cameron and L. Boonzaier, 'Venturing beyond Formalism: The Constitutional Court of South Africa's Equality Jurisprudence' (2020) 84 *Rabels Zeitschrift für ausländisches und internationales Privatrecht* 786, 818–34.

181 *Fellner*, above n. 28, 537A–37D; *Camps Bay Ratepayers*, above n. 157, para. 30.

182 *Fellner*, above n. 28, 537D.

183 *Daniels*, above n. 157, para. 33.

184 *Collett*, above n. 35, 302.

185 Compare J. Gardner, 'Some Types of Law' in D.E. Edlin (ed), *Common Law Theory*, Cambridge University Press, Cambridge 2007, pp. 67–70.

186 *Levinson*, above n. 32.

187 ibid., 317.

Schreiner JA's account is widely respected and still routinely cited.[188] His last condition, (c), has received the most attention. Its 'necessity' or 'but for' test, though orthodox, is not without problems. One of them is that it struggles to deal with cases of overdetermination, i.e. where a court's judgment decides two (or more) issues, each of which is capable on its own of justifying the result it reached. Since each of the two bases is sufficient for the result, neither is necessary, and hence Schreiner JA's formulation implies that neither is capable of forming part of its *ratio* – an outcome generally regarded as unsatisfactory and at odds with judicial practice.[189] The Constitutional Court, faced with this problem in *Turnbull-Jackson v. Hibiscus Coast Municipality* in 2014,[190] held that *Levinson*'s condition (c) should, in such cases, be viewed with caution, and that the principle used by the court to support each basis of its decision forms part of the *ratio* provided it is 'central to the resolution of the issue under consideration'.[191]

If reasons given in a judgment 'were merely subsidiary', as stated in condition (a), they do not form part of its *ratio*. As Schreiner JA indicates, this may simply be the obverse of their not being 'necessary' in terms of condition (c). The treatment of these parts of the court's reasoning is discussed further in Section 4.4. below.

Condition (b) turns on the elusive distinction between statements of law and reasoning 'on the facts'.[192] Factual findings by a court plainly set no precedent.[193] It is sometimes said that the application of an accepted principle of law is also necessarily a matter of fact,[194] but this may be too simple. First, the scope of an accepted principle is sometimes settled, or extended, *by* its application in a contentious case, and accordingly the act of application changes the law.[195]

---

188 See e.g. R. Cross and J.W. Harris, above n. 37, p. 75.; *True Motives*, above n. 162, para. 103; *Turnbull-Jackson*, above n. 118, para. 61; *Atholl Developments v. Valuation Appeal Board, City of Johannesburg* [2015] ZASCA 55, para. 6.

189 Compare *Camps Bay Ratepayers*, above n. 157, para. 30.

190 *Turnbull-Jackson*, above n. 118.

191 ibid., para. 62. The decision is discussed in P. Olivier, 'Deriving the Ratio of an Over-Determined Judgment: The Law after *Turnbull-Jackson v. Hibiscus Coast Municipality*' (2016) 133 *South African Law Journal* 522. Though the Court does not say it, presumably the 'issue under consideration' must itself have been one that was not merely subsidiary, but rather one it was duty-bound to decide.

192 H.R. Hahlo and E. Kahn, above n. 3, p. 260. Parallel debates have taken place in respect of the Constitutional Court's jurisdiction and the running of prescription, both of which turn partly on the law–fact distinction: see respectively E. Cohen, 'The Jurisdiction of the Constitutional Court' (2021) 11 *Constitutional Court Review* 433, 464–70; *Mtokonya v. Minister of Police* [2017] ZACC 33, paras. 38–45. Hence, despite the fact that South Africa does not use juries, the law–fact distinction is important.

193 *R v. Wells* 1949 3 SA 83 (A), 87–88.

194 *Phoebus Apollo Aviation CC v. Minister of Safety and Security* [2002] ZACC 26, para. 9 and authorities cited there.

195 *K*, above n. 79, paras. 16–17 (discussing the application of the 'course and scope' test for vicarious liability).

Second, determinations made through the application of a settled legal test may themselves have precedential force. Where a court decides that a defendant's conduct in a delictual action is wrongful, for example, it applies a settled test,[196] but clearly sets a precedent when doing so.[197] On the other hand, a determination that the defendant's conduct was negligent does not set a precedent, since it is too closely bound up with the facts of the instant case to provide useful guidance to future courts.[198] The determination that conduct is (or is not) contrary to public policy is often understood in the same way,[199] though the better view may be that it does set a precedent, but one vulnerable to being overruled if public policy changes.[200]

Though not clear from *Levinson*, a 'proposition assumed to be correct for the purpose of disposing of the case',[201] including but not limited to a proposition conceded by the parties,[202] is not part of the case's *ratio*. In sum, therefore, the *ratio decidendi* of a case comprises pronouncements on matters of law, made by the court after due consideration, that were necessary for the outcome reached in the case or, at least, central to an issue that the court was bound to decide.

4.2. JUDGMENTS WITH MULTIPLE OPINIONS

Well-known complexities arise when multiple opinions have been given in a case that was decided by more than one judge.[203] Then it must be determined which of the views, if any, constitutes the case's *ratio decidendi*. 'The basic principle here', as F. du Bois explains, 'is that the majority rules'.[204] The *ratio* is comprised, in other words, of the principles for the decision endorsed by a majority of the judges who sat on the case. It may derive from: a single opinion that determines the order of the court and is concurred in by all judges who support that order; a single opinion that is concurred in by only some judges who support the court's order (but a sufficient number to form a majority of the court);[205] or two (or more) opinions which, though neither is expressly concurred in by a majority, endorse substantially the same legal principles, which can thus be said

196 See canonically *Minister van Polisie v. Ewels* 1975 (3) SA 590 (A).

197 *Telematrix (Pty) Ltd v. Advertising Standards Authority SA* [2005] ZASCA 73, para. 15.

198 *Kruger v. Coetzee* 1966 (2) SA 428 (A), analysed in A. Fagan, 'The Confusions of K' (2009) 126 *South African Law Journal* 156, 187. See also *Wells*, above n. 193, 87–88.

199 See the authorities cited in F. du Bois, above n. 3, p. 85, fn. 115.

200 Compare the rule discussed in the text, above n. 126.

201 *Kaplan v. Incorporated Law Society, Transvaal* 1981 (2) SA 762 (T), 788, citing *Baker v. The Queen* (1975) 3 All ER 55 (PC), 64.

202 *R v. Nkala* 1961 (4) SA 177 (FC), 181; *Shenker v. Levy* 1997 (4) SA 260 (W), 265.

203 See for detailed treatment H.R. Hahlo and E. Kahn, above n. 3, pp. 272–76.

204 F. du Bois, above n. 3, p. 86.

205 It is not sufficient that there is agreement by a majority of the judges who supported the court's order: *Fellner*, above n. 28.

to enjoy the majority's support. The last-mentioned possibility is particularly important for eras in which the practice of the appeal courts was that each judge would write his or her own opinion.[206] If no principle carries the support of the majority, the case sets no precedent.[207] But a narrow majority decision is just as binding as a unanimous one.[208] A judge who dissented from the majority decision is no less bound than any other to respect its precedential effect in future cases.[209]

4.3. HOW FAR DOES A PRECEDENT EXTEND?

Precedents feature in South African judges' legal reasoning in much the same way that they do in Anglo-American law.[210] The identification of a precedent requires inference and interpretation, on which there is often much room for reasonable disagreement,[211] not least because the principle applied by the precedent court can be stated at many degrees of generality.[212] A large part of common law reasoning is therefore argumentation about the precedent's scope, and, relatedly, the distinguishing of that precedent if it is thought to be overbroad in its application to the case at hand. As in other common law jurisdictions, any South African court may distinguish any precedent it encounters, regardless of its provenance.[213] The power is, in this sense, far-reaching. But, on the other

---

206 This was the practice of the pre-Union appeal courts and of the Appellate Division for the first decades of its existence. The practice is nowadays different in both the SCA and Constitutional Court, which aim, in the absence of a clear difference of opinion, to give single majority opinions. See, for relevant recent discussion by a justice of the Constitutional Court, O. Rogers, '"I Beg to Differ": Are Our Courts Too Agreeable?' (2022) 139 *South African Law Journal* 300.

207 *Fellner*, above n. 28. Plurality opinions, though they may be considered persuasive, are therefore not binding.

208 *Fellner*, above n. 28, 538D.

209 The practice of 'persistent dissent', in other words, 'is not the South African way': H.R. Hahlo and E. Kahn, above n. 3, pp. 281–82. This approach remains valid in the Constitutional Court, but see, for an apparent exception, the persistent dissents by Jafta J in *MEC for Health, Eastern Cape v. Kirland Investments (Pty) Ltd* [2014] ZACC 6; *Merafong City Local Municipality v. AngloGold Ashanti Ltd* [2016] ZACC 35; *Department of Transport v. Tasima (Pty) Ltd* [2016] ZACC 39.

210 For a useful South African discussion see F. du Bois, above n. 3, pp. 81–84, which draws upon the analyses in J. Raz, 'Law and Value in Adjudication' in J. Raz, *The Authority of Law*, Oxford University Press, Oxford 1979; N. MacCormick, *Legal Reasoning and Legal Theory*, Clarendon Press, Oxford 1994.

211 F. du Bois, above n. 3, p. 83.

212 See again J. Gardner, above n. 185, pp. 68–69. To be sure, any valid precedent or statement of the reason for a decision necessarily possesses *some* degree of generality, going wider than the instant case: F. Schauer, 'The Generality of Law' (2004) 107 *West Virginia Law Review* 217, 230–31.

213 The power to distinguish, being a trite aspect of judicial custom, is rarely discussed by courts, but see *Daniels*, above n. 157, paras. 94–104; *Bwanya*, above n. 84, para. 155. Some illustrations are offered in F. du Bois, above n. 3, p. 82, fn. 99.

hand, the modifications that the later court may make are limited: its act of narrowing the precedent must leave unaffected the result of the case in which it was laid down.[214]

It is an equally common feature of South African judicial practice that precedents, even when their binding force does not reach the instant case, may be extended to that case by analogy.[215] Precedents thus have a 'radiating effect' beyond the cases strictly within their scope.[216] Countless examples can be found,[217] and the benefits of reasoning by 'principled analogy' from past cases are sometimes applauded.[218] Arguably South African lawyers, because of the influence of civilian modes of thought, are more inclined towards this process of abstraction, in search of coherent general principles, than those in other common law jurisdictions.[219] But a court's willingness to extend a precedent by analogy must be tempered by the recognition that 'a case is only authority for what it actually decides'[220] and may have been 'intended by the [precedent] court to be confined to its particular facts'.[221] In addition, the courts have suggested that reasoning by analogy with past cases has disadvantages relative to direct engagement with underlying values.[222]

4.4. *OBITER DICTA*

In South Africa, as elsewhere, 'it is trite that the binding authority of precedent ... does not extend to *obiter dicta* or what was said "by the way"'.[223] An *obiter dictum*

214 See for classic analysis J. Raz, above n. 210, pp. 185–89.
215 ibid., pp. 201–06.
216 F. du Bois, above n. 3, p. 84.
217 *Syfrets*, above n. 150, paras. 23–26 extends the approach to public policy that had been taken in contract law cases to the realm of testamentary trusts. Several examples of analogical reasoning in Constitutional Court cases are discussed in C. Rautenbach and L. du Plessis, 'The Constitutional Court of South Africa' in A. Jakab, A. Dyevre and G. Itzcovich (eds), *Comparative Constitutional Reasoning*, Cambridge University Press, Cambridge 2017, pp. 557–58.
218 A. Price, 'The Contract/Delict Interface in the Constitutional Court' (2014) 25 *Stellenbosch Law Review* 501, approved in *Masstores (Pty) Ltd v. Pick n Pay Retailers (Pty) Ltd* [2016] ZACC 42, para. 32.
219 This is the respect in which the views of J.C. de Wet, discussed above n. 47, proved enduring. Compare R. Zimmermann and C. Hugo, 'South African Legal Scholarship in the 20th Century: The Contribution of JC de Wet (1912–1990)' in J. du Plessis and G. Lubbe (eds), *A Man of Principle: The Life and Legacy of J.C. de Wet*, Juta & Co Ltd, Cape Town 2013.
220 *Jurgens v. Volkskas Bank Ltd* 1993 (1) SA 214 (A), 221G, quoting *Quinn v. Leathem* [1901] UKHL 2, [1901] AC 495 (HL), 506.
221 *Jurgens*, above n. 220, 221H.
222 *H v. Fetal Assessment Centre* [2014] ZACC 34, para. 47. After all, reasoning by analogy with an existing precedent produces a sound argument only if the precedent is itself justified: see again J. Raz, above n. 210, p. 204.
223 *Camps Bay Ratepayers*, above n. 157, para. 30.

is a remark that was 'not necessary for the [court's] decision',[224] in other words, one that does not satisfy *Levinson*'s condition (c).[225] Even a lower court, then, is not bound by a remark of this kind, no matter how carefully considered.[226] Despite this, *obiter dicta* are far from irrelevant.[227] South African courts have said many times that *obiter dicta*, especially those of an esteemed judge, 'may be of potent persuasive force' and that lower courts should be very slow to depart from them.[228] There are well-known instances in which a lower court has conscientiously decided that a remark is *obiter* and should not be followed, only to be overturned, and sometimes rebuked, on appeal.[229] And indeed the SCA has said that it, too, 'will not lightly depart from a view previously expressed by it, particularly by five of its members sitting together, even if expressed *obiter*'.[230] Unsurprisingly, then, many examples can be given of courts refusing to depart from *obiter dicta*, citing the value of stability and the need to protect the expectations that have grown up around them.[231] They can also provide a useful means for appeal courts to signal the direction of future developments.[232] Indeed some of the best-known developments in South African private law began in this way, such as the strict liability of media defendants in defamation[233] and the allowance of an Aquilian action for pure economic loss.[234] *Dicta* therefore play an important role in legal development despite their officially non-binding status.

5. PRECEDENT IN WIDER CONTEXT

This section considers three other issues relating to the doctrine of precedent: first, the law-making power of judges, set against the role of the legislature; second, the role of legal scholars; and third, the relevance of foreign precedents.

---

224 *R v. Nkwali* 1925 AD 578; *R v. Crause* 1959 (1) SA 272 (A), 281; *De Kock*, above n. 162, para. 17.

225 See Section 4.1. above.

226 *Petersen v. Jajbhay* 1940 TPD 182, 185; *True Motives*, above n. 162.

227 Compare H.R. Hahlo and E. Kahn, above n. 3, pp. 270–72.

228 *Turnbull-Jackson*, above n. 118, para. 56.

229 See e.g. *Collett*, above n. 35, as well as *Levinson*, above n. 32, itself. A more recent example is *True Motives*, above n. 162, which was criticised in *Turnbull-Jackson*, above n. 118.

230 *Steenkamp v. South African Broadcasting Corporation* 2002 (1) SA 625 (SCA), para. 12.

231 e.g. *Dhlomo v. Natal Newspapers (Pty) Ltd* 1989 (1) SA 945 (A), 952.

232 The appeal court might also wish to signal its approval (or disapproval) of a development undertaken at High Court level: H.R. Hahlo and E. Kahn, above n. 3, p. 271.

233 *SAUK v. O'Malley* 1977 (3) SA 394 (A).

234 *Administrateur Natal v. Trust Bank van Afrika Bpk* 1979 (3) SA 824 (A). On the other hand, *Hamman v. Moolman* 1968 (4) SA 340 (A) held *obiter* that delictual liability should not be extended to the pre-contractual context, which was regarded as 'the clearest affirmation of judicial policy' and followed by lower courts (*Latham v. Sher* 1974 (4) SA 687 (W), 695H–96A; see also *Du Plessis v. Semmelink* 1976 (2) SA 500 (T). 502H–03F), but was later disavowed by the Appellate Division itself.

5.1. JUDICIAL LAW-MAKING AND THE LEGISLATURE

As is by now apparent, all of South Africa's 'superior courts', i.e. its High Courts, Supreme Court of Appeal, and Constitutional Court,[235] set precedents and thus create law. Its 'inferior courts', i.e. its magistrate's courts and some other similar tribunals, do not.[236] The superior courts' law-making power extends to all areas of law, not limited by subject matter.[237] As mentioned in Section 4.1., some judicial determinations are so fact-sensitive that they are not treated as setting a precedent.[238] But, these determinations apart, there is no enquiry on which judicial law-making is foreclosed.

That judges have these law-making powers is widely understood and not controversial; many famous judicial statements can be found attesting to their importance.[239] South African judges provide written reasons, often fairly lengthy, which focus on the issues of legal principle (as well as their application to the facts before them), and parsing these judgments is central to legal practice. In the constitutional era, the courts' valuable role in reforming the common law has gained still further prominence.[240]

Though the Constitutional Court has recognised that 'the major engine for law reform should be the legislature and not the judiciary',[241] it is relatively rare for courts to disclaim responsibility for developing the law on this basis.[242] Certainly, the courts still regard themselves as the primary custodians of large swathes of private law. The South African law of delict, for example, has seen only

---

235 This is also true of specialist courts equivalent in status to the High Court or SCA: see above n. 93.

236 Above n. 101.

237 Predictably, however, courts' power to create or expand criminal prohibitions is highly constrained: see e.g. *Sibiya*, above n. 46, 256H.

238 See above n. 198. The classic example is the determination that a defendant behaved negligently.

239 Classic statements are *Blower v. Noorden* 1909 TS 890, 905: *O'Callaghan NO v. Chaplin* 1927 AD 310, 327. And see again above n. 5 in relation to the Constitution's implicit recognition of judicial law-making.

240 The courts' power to develop the law is enshrined in s. 173 of the Constitution, and their duty to do so, especially in terms of s. 39(2), is much discussed: see e.g. *Carmichele*, above n. 64.

241 *Carmichele*, above n. 64, para. 36.

242 But see *MEC for Health and Social Development, Gauteng v. DZ obo WZ* [2017] ZACC 37. Naturally, South Africa's project of court-led constitutional transformation discussed in Section 2.2. above may be critiqued on the basis that it expects too much of the judiciary (and indeed of legal processes in general) and gives it too much power relative to the governmental branches. For discussion of this problem, see e.g. J. Fowkes, 'Relationships with Power: Re-imagining Judicial Roles in Africa' in C.M. Fombad, *Separation of Powers in African Constitutionalism*, Oxford University Press, Oxford 2016. Post-constitutional South Africa was famously condemned as a 'juristocracy' in R. Hirschl, *Towards Juristocracy: The Origins and Consequences of the New Constitutionalism*, Harvard University Press, Cambridge (Massachusetts) 2009.

very limited legislative intervention,[243] and the expansion of liability over the course of the twentieth and early twenty-first centuries was driven exclusively by the courts.[244] Similarly, the general principles of the South African law of contract still derive from the common law,[245] albeit that far-reaching consumer legislation was enacted in 2008.[246] Throughout South African history, significant legislative interventions have taken place affecting land rights,[247] but the judge-made rules of property law, built by judges atop Roman and Roman-Dutch sources, remain vibrant and indispensable.[248] The courts thus play an active role in legal development and do not wait to take their cue from the legislature.[249] They have acknowledged, however, that judicial law-making is 'incremental' and 'fact-driven', and that sweeping or fundamental changes are best left to the legislature.[250] The areas that have seen the most extensive statutory interventions, perhaps unsurprisingly, are those such as company law, labour law, and the administration of estates.[251] Even where legislation attempts to govern an area

---

243 See the Apportionment of Damages Act 34 of 1956 (which regulates the defence of contributory negligence and contributions amongst joint wrongdoers) and the Road Accident Fund Act 56 of 1996 (which, in respect of injuries caused by road traffic accidents, replaces the common law delictual claim with a claim against a state compensation fund).

244 For valuable discussion of the growth of negligence liability, see D. Hutchison, 'Aquilian Liability II (Twentieth Century)' in R. Zimmermann and D. Visser (eds), above n. 1. The development of the *actio iniuriarum* has not been so unidirectional, but it is again striking that the developments have been exclusively judicial: see J.M. Burchell, 'The Protection of Personality Rights' in R. Zimmermann and D. Visser (eds), above n. 1.

245 R. Zimmermann and D. Visser (eds), above n. 1, Chs. 5–9; L.F. Van Huyssteen, G.F. Lubbe, M.F.B. Reinecke and J. du Plessis, *Contract: General Principles*, 6th ed., Juta & Co Ltd, Cape Town 2020.

246 Consumer Protection Act 68 of 2008 (and see too the National Credit Act 34 of 2005, which regulates consumer credit agreements). Even here, it is perhaps revealing that the South African courts have continued to develop and apply their own principles by which to regulate unfair contract terms, largely impervious to the statutory instruments. See for discussion D. Hutchison, above n. 180; E. Cameron and L. Boonzaier, above n. 180, 818–34.

247 For the colonial and apartheid history, see T.W. Bennett, 'African Land – A History of Dispossession' in R. Zimmermann and D. Visser (eds), above n. 1. In the early constitutional era, important changes were introduced by legislation to strengthen the land rights of those previously disadvantaged: see especially the Extension of Security of Tenure Act 62 of 1997 and the Prevention of Illegal Eviction from and Unlawful Occupation of Land Act 19 of 1998.

248 R. Zimmermann and D. Visser (eds), above n. 1, Chs. 20–25; A. Pope and E. du Plessis, *The Principles of the Law of Property in South Africa*, 2nd ed., Oxford University Press Southern Africa, Cape Town 2020.

249 See too the many examples discussed in C.G. van der Merwe, J. du Plessis, M. de Waal, R. Zimmermann and P. Farlam, above n. 1, pp. 167–203.

250 *Masiya*, above n. 170, para. 31; *Mighty Solutions CC t/a Orlando Service Station v. Engen Petroleum Ltd* [2015] ZACC 34, para. 44.

251 For example, the Labour Relations Act 66 of 1995 and the Companies Act 71 of 2008 attempt to regulate their respective subject areas almost comprehensively. See for historical treatment of these and related areas R. Zimmermann and D. Visser (eds), above n. 1, Chs. 12–15.

of law comprehensively, however, it is recognised that large bodies of judicial precedent are necessary to interpret and operationalise it.[252]

5.2. THE ROLE OF LEGAL SCHOLARS

South Africa has a rich history of legal scholarship.[253] For one thing, its system of private law was founded upon the writings of the Roman-Dutch jurists.[254] More relevantly in the present day, writings by academics based at the many South African law schools,[255] legal practitioners, and other commentators play a significant role in both systematising and criticising the courts' decisions. Scholars sometimes criticise courts for breaching the duties imposed by *stare decisis*: they may have failed to follow a relevant precedent, treated as *obiter* what is in fact *ratio*, and so on.[256] But the role of scholars is not only 'reactive';[257] they have also made major contributions to the course of legal development.[258] Accordingly, South African courts refer to academic writing 'as a matter of course',[259] free of the inhibitions that once prevailed in England. However, the views of modern writers (as opposed to the Roman-Dutch jurists of old) are always weighed on their merits and accepted only if persuasive; 'no one has suggested that their views are a formal source of law'.[260] It is often said, in summary, that the status of legal writing in South Africa 'lies somewhere between' its status in the legal systems of England, on the one hand, and of continental Europe, on the other.[261] While South African law professors do not enjoy the exalted status of French or German jurists, it is easy to name many scholars whose impact on legal development has been profound.

---

252 In doing so, courts sometimes invoke case law that they developed prior to the enactment of the statute, and will presume that the statute does not depart (or departs to the most limited extent possible) from the common law: see *Glen Anil Finance (Pty) Ltd v. Joint Liquidators, Glen Anil Development Corp Ltd* 1981 (1) SA 171 (A), 181–82 and authorities cited there.

253 R. Zimmermann and D. Visser, above n. 17, pp. 11–12, 19–30; E. Kahn, 'The Role of Doctrine and Judicial Decisions in South African Law' in J. Dainow (ed), *The Role of Judicial Decisions and Doctrine in Civil Law and in Mixed Jurisdictions*, Louisiana State University Press, Baton Rouge 1974, pp. 245–54; H. Scott, above n. 30.

254 See above Section 2.1.

255 J.B. Kaburise, 'The Structure of Legal Education in South Africa' (2001) 51 *Journal of Legal Education* 363.

256 See, for a small sample, M. Dendy, above n. 111; A. Fagan, above n. 198, 159–78; S. Ryan, above n. 107.

257 H. Scott, above n. 30, p. 227.

258 Examples are provided in E. Kahn, above n. 253, pp. 245–54; H. Scott, above n. 30, pp. 227–31.

259 F. du Bois, above n. 3, p. 112.

260 E. Kahn, above n. 253, p. 245. But see H. Scott, above n. 30, pp. 227–34, who charts a strand of civilian influence which causes even some modern-day treatise writers to claim for themselves a higher status.

261 E. Kahn, above n. 253, pp. 249–50; also H. Scott, above n. 30, p. 227.

5.3. FOREIGN PRECEDENTS

Foreign precedents are persuasive, but not binding, in South Africa. But behind this innocuous general statement lie several complexities.[262] As already mentioned, South African law was greatly influenced by English law, especially in the second half of the nineteenth century, as judges found it useful to rely on the extensive body of case law emanating from Britain, then the colonial power.[263] Even well into the twentieth century, South African judges were often influenced, to a perhaps objectionable extent, by English precedents, including in areas with a rich Roman-Dutch pedigree.[264] And in certain enclaves, where statutes had either expressly incorporated English case law or were modelled upon English enactments, English precedents enjoyed a heightened status, and were indeed for a certain period formally binding. Hence the South African law of evidence and company law have a particularly strong connection with English law.[265]

Yet there were also countervailing tendencies. Because of South African law's Roman-Dutch substrate, and because of the relatively fraught relationship with the British Empire, English precedents were (outside of the enclaves just mentioned) never formally binding in South Africa in the way that they were in other dominions. There was also, as discussed, a strong counter-reaction to English influence, particularly amongst Afrikaner judges and scholars.[266] Occasionally, judges have said they should be guided by the laws of other systems that, like South Africa, 'have been touched by the greatness of the Roman law'.[267]

---

262 See for excellent in-depth treatment, F. du Bois and D. Visser, 'The Influence of Foreign Law in South Africa' (2003) 13 *Journal of Transnational Law and Contemporary Problems* 593.

263 See Section 2.1. above. For general surveys of the extent of English influence, see O.D. Schreiner, above n. 29; B. Beinart, 'The English Legal Contribution in South Africa: The Interaction of Civil and Common Law' (1981) *Acta Juridica* 7.

264 See e.g. D. Hutchison, above n. 244, arguing that South African decisions on wrongfulness in delict were pivotally impacted (though often without acknowledgment) by developments in England.

265 See respectively H.R. Hahlo and E. Kahn, above n. 3, pp. 258–60; C.G. van der Merwe, J. du Plessis, M. de Waal, R. Zimmermann and P. Farlam, above n. 1, pp. 150–51, 162–63. The formal linkage of South African law of evidence with England's ended in 1961, when South Africa left the Commonwealth. A separate issue is the status of decisions of the Privy Council on matters of South African (or Roman-Dutch) law, which until 1950 were binding in South Africa: H.R. Hahlo and E. Kahn, above n. 3, p. 244. But South African appeals to the Privy Council were not numerous.

266 See above nn. 44–47.

267 *Government of the Republic of South Africa v. Ngubane* 1972 (2) SA 601 (A), 609. Celebrated instances in which the South African courts have opted for the civilian approach, rather than following the English case law, are *Cape Town Municipality v. Paine* 1923 AD 207, *Perlman v. Zoutendyk* 1934 CPD 151, and *Maisel v. Van Naeren* 1960 (4) SA 836 (C).

The 1996 Constitution and its surrounding ethos exposed South African law to comparative influence of a new kind.[268] The drafting of the constitutional text was heavily influenced by comparative examples, especially the German *Grundgesetz*, and when the South African Bill of Rights jurisprudence was in its infancy the Constitutional Court drew readily upon foreign case law.[269] This is expressly licensed by the new Constitution, Section 39(1)(c) of which provides that courts 'may consider foreign law'. Now that South Africa's constitutional jurisprudence has matured, however, the courts refer to foreign judgments less often, but comparative surveys do appear when they are confronted by a particularly novel or difficult problem,[270] including in private law.[271] The most common comparators have been the major Anglophone jurisdictions, like Canada, England and Wales, and the United States, as well as Germany,[272] but on occasion the Constitutional Court has sought to learn from jurisdictions elsewhere in Africa.[273] Again, this practice is not systematic, and often accompanied by cautions.[274]

6. PRECEDENT IN LEGAL THEORY AND CULTURE

As made clear in the previous sections, South Africa has a virile system of judge-made common law. Its precedents now stretch back in an unbroken line to 1827 and continue to form the essential substrate of most areas of private law. This

268 J. De Waal, 'A Comparative Analysis of the Provisions of German Origin in the Interim Bill of Rights' (1995) 11 *South African Journal on Human Rights* 1; D.M. Davis, 'Constitutional Borrowing: The Influence of Legal Culture and Local History in the Reconstitution of Comparative Influence: The South African Experience' (2003) 1 *International Journal of Constitutional Law* 181; F. du Bois and D. Visser, above n. 262, 625–57.

269 C. Rautenbach, 'South Africa: Teaching an "Old Dog" New Tricks? An Empirical Study of the Use of Foreign Precedents by the South African Constitutional Court (1995–2010)' in T. Groppi and M.-C. Ponthoreau (eds), *The Use of Foreign Precedents by Constitutional Judges*, Hart Publishing, Oxford 2013.

270 See for recent discussion E. Cameron and L. Boonzaier, above n. 180, 834–38.

271 A famous example is the endorsement of the third-party effect (*Drittwirkung*) of constitutional rights, particularly in the law of delict: see *Du Plessis*, above n. 169; *Carmichele*, above n. 64. The use of comparativism also extends to private law matters that are less obviously constitutional, such as those in *H*, above n. 222; *DE v. RH* [2015] ZACC 18. In *Makate v. Vodacom (Pty) Ltd* [2016] ZACC 13, the Constitutional Court relied (or perhaps over-relied) on English cases to understand the doctrine of estoppel, which was imported into South African law from England.

272 C. Rautenbach, above n. 269, pp. 197–202.

273 See for example *DE v. RH*, above n. 271, paras. 33–36 (noting, however, the difficulties of doing comparative research on African law).

274 In *H*, above n. 222, paras. 28–31, the Court repeated certain well-known cautions about relying too slavishly upon foreign sources to understand South Africa's own law. Justice Kriegler's earlier complaints about relying upon comparative law are quoted in E. Cameron and L. Boonzaier, above n. 180, 834–35.

section considers two residual matters: first, the perceived value of precedent; and second, the way precedents feature in South Africa's changing legal culture.

6.1. THE VALUE OF *STARE DECISIS*

Many statements can be found in South African legal history of the doctrine of precedent's value and importance. Perhaps the classic expression is from Hahlo and Kahn's landmark work on *The South African Legal System and Its Background*, published in 1968 and still regularly cited by the courts:[275]

> The maintenance of the certainty of the law and of equality before it, [and] the satisfaction of legitimate expectations, entail a general duty of judges to follow the legal rulings in previous judicial decisions. The individual litigant would feel himself unjustly treated if a past ruling applicable to his case were not followed where the material facts were the same. … [The doctrine of precedent] enables the citizen, if necessary with the aid of practising lawyers, to plan his private and professional activities with some degree of assurance as to their legal effects; it prevents the dislocation of rights, particularly contractual and proprietary ones, created in the belief of an existing rule of law; it cuts down the prospect of litigation; it keeps the weaker judge along right and rational paths, drastically limiting the play allowed to partiality, caprice or prejudice, thereby not only securing justice in the instance but also retaining public confidence in the judicial machine through like being dealt with alike.[276]

More recently, the Constitutional Court in *Van der Walt v. Metcash* reasserted the role of equality (or 'uniformity' in the treatment of similar cases),[277] which is both a founding value[278] and a justiciable right[279] in the new Constitution. It also drew a connection between *stare decisis* with the rule of law[280] – also a founding value[281] – which South African courts have repeated many times.[282] Without the doctrine of precedent, they have said:

> there would be no certainty, no predictability and no coherence. The courts would operate in a tangle of unknowable considerations, which all too soon would become vulnerable to whim and fancy. Law would not rule.[283]

275 *Walters*, above n. 133, para. 57; *Gcaba*, above n. 161, para. 58; *Camps Bay Ratepayers*, above n. 157, para. 28; *Turnbull-Jackson*, above n. 118, para. 54.
276 H.R. Hahlo and E. Kahn, above n. 3, pp. 214–15.
277 Above n. 161, para. 39.
278 Constitution 1996, s. 1(a).
279 s. 9.
280 *Van der Walt*, above n. 161, para. 39.
281 s. 1(c).
282 *Daniels*, above n. 157, para. 94; *Gcaba*, above n. 161, paras. 61–62.
283 *True Motives*, above n. 162, para. 100.

'To deviate' from the doctrine, they have also said, 'is to invite legal chaos'.[284]

Thus, South African courts have defended the importance of the doctrine in familiar ways and rooted them in the fundamental commitments of the constitutional scheme. In other respects, however, *stare decisis*, and the doctrinal reasoning which it complements, have recently come under pressure, as discussed in the following section.

6.2. PRECEDENTS AND LEGAL CULTURE

South African legal culture is a distinctive blend of civilian and common law elements, and one which is congenial, broadly speaking, to *stare decisis* and its associated doctrinal methods. The civilian historicist approach, German conceptualism, and the English lawyer's attachment to rule-based adjudication have combined, despite their differences, to produce a culture in which texts and formal legal sources are, in general, highly respected, and where legal reasoning, especially in private law, is regarded as autonomous and desirably apolitical.[285] True, courts have, at crucial moments in South African legal history, opted for tests that are relatively abstract, flexible, and discretionary, on the basis that this is more consonant with the Roman-Dutch tradition than the more strict and rule-based approach followed in England.[286] Nevertheless, it is a commonly accepted generalisation that South African legal culture is, at base, 'formalistic'.

Importantly, however, this feature is nowadays typically regarded as a problem, with the new Constitution requiring a shift to reasoning that is more 'substantive'.[287] That courts must consider abstract values and norms when they are construing a new constitution's open-ended rights guarantees may seem obvious. But the point should not be underestimated. First, as mentioned in

---

284 *Camps Bay Ratepayers*, above n. 157, para. 28.

285 For useful discussions of these aspects of South African legal culture, particularly in private law, see A.P.H. Cockrell, above n. 49; A.J. van der Walt, 'Tradition on Trial: A Critical Analysis of the Civil-Law Tradition in South African Property Law' (1995) 11 *South African Journal on Human Rights* 169; H. Scott, above n. 30. See too M. Chanock, *The Making of South African Legal Culture 1902–1936: Fear, Favour and Prejudice*, Cambridge University Press, Cambridge 2001.

286 See above nn. 219 and 267.

287 See A.P.H. Cockrell, 'Rainbow Jurisprudence' (1996) 12 *South African Journal on Human Rights* 1, which applies the analytical framework of P.S. Atiyah and R.S. Summers, *Form and Substance in Anglo-American Law: A Comparative Study of Legal Reasoning, Legal Theory, and Legal Institutions*, Clarendon Press, Oxford 1987, to South Africa at the time of the constitutional transition. Cockrell's thesis has been embraced by many others, including, notably, the judges of the Constitutional Court: J.C. Froneman, 'Legal Reasoning and Legal Culture: Our "Vision" of Law' (2005) 16 *Stellenbosch Law Review* 3; P. Langa, 'Transformative Constitutionalism' (2006) 17 *Stellenbosch Law Review* 351, 357; C. O'Regan, 'From Form to Substance: The Constitutional Jurisprudence of Laurie Ackermann' (2008) *Acta Juridica* 1. See too K.E. Klare, above n. 56, whose rejection of 'high formalism' has been influential.

Section 2.2., the South African Constitution is very far-reaching: its normative effect is 'pervasive' and 'must be felt throughout the common law', including in core areas of private law.[288] Second, the distrust of formal reasoning is sourced in South African history, and not limited to Bill of Rights adjudication. Quiescence in the application of unjust laws was considered the defining vice of South Africa's judges during apartheid.[289] And so, in the new era, the Constitutional Court has held that judges must openly acknowledge the norms and values that they take to justify their decisions, and not defer to the authority of legal rules.[290] This is required both so that courts remain alive to the possibility that the law may require improvement in light of the Constitution,[291] and so that judges' reasoning remains accountable and does not 'render inarticulate' the normative premises that animate their decisions.[292] The Constitutional Court has, therefore, emphasised that not only the creation but also the application of doctrinal tests, including in private law, must involve express regard to the normative values that underlie them.[293]

These changes are not logically incompatible with *stare decisis*. But it is also not surprising, in this climate, that the Court tends to reason from first principles, or indeed from broad statements about the values that the Constitution allegedly aims to foster, rather than parsing the decided cases.[294] In addition, it emphasises the benefits of 'flexibility' and doing justice on a case-by-case basis, preferring to avoid the adoption of fixed rules in the first place.[295]

Unsurprisingly, not everyone welcomes this approach. The Court's arguable neglect of traditional legal values, like certainty and the curtailment of judicial discretion, has often been criticised.[296] According to one influential study, the

---

288 *K*, above n. 195, paras. 15, 17.

289 The classic essay is J. DUGARD, 'The Judicial Process, Positivism and Civil Liberty' (1971) 88 *South African Law Journal* 181.

290 *K*, above n. 195, paras. 22–23. See too *H*, above n. 222, para. 42.

291 As A.P.H Cockrell puts it, 'the past will no longer justify itself, but must now be justified in terms of a commitment to substantive constitutional values': A.P.H. COCKRELL, 'Studying Legal History in South Africa: The Lesson of Lot's Wife' (1997) *Zeitschrift für Europäisches Privatrecht* 436, 441.

292 *K*, above n. 195, para. 23 (which evokes O. W. Holmes's famous proto-realist remark in *Lochner v. New York* 198 US 45 (1905), 76). See to similar effect *H*, above n. 222, paras. 22–23.

293 *K*, above n. 195, para. 22 (discussing the common law 'course and scope' test for vicarious liability).

294 S. WOOLMAN, 'The Amazing, Vanishing Bill of Rights' (2007) 124 *South African Law Journal* 762. And see A.P.H. COCKRELL, above n. 287; I.J. KROEZE, 'Doing Things with Values: The Role of Constitutional Values in Constitutional Interpretation' (2001) 12 *Stellenbosch Law Review* 265.

295 Two well-known examples are *Lee*, above n. 80, and *Botha v. Rich NO* [2014] ZACC 11, which controversially urged a flexible approach to the determination of factual causation in delict and to the availability of contractual remedies respectively.

296 e.g. J. LEWIS, 'The Constitutional Court of South Africa: An Evaluation' (2009) 125 *Law Quarterly Review* 440.

Court's strategy 'of speaking in values' has granted it 'the licence to decide each case as it pleases, unmoored from its own precedents'; it thus 'sits as a court of equity', rather than one of law.[297] Another academic commentator has asked whether South African law is witnessing 'the death of doctrine', as private law decisions at the highest level 'are not … justified according to any rule of general application'.[298] But perhaps the Court's most prominent critics are the judges of the Supreme Court of Appeal,[299] which, for 85 years, was the country's highest court, until in 1995 the Constitutional Court displaced it.[300] The SCA's own approach shows a greater attachment to established doctrine and rule-based decision-making.[301] It often draws accusations, in turn, of formalism and complacency from those who had hoped for a more thoroughgoing revamp of the pre-constitutional common law.[302] There is thus a rivalry, at times unseemly, between two visions of adjudication, and between the country's two appellate courts.[303]

The overall picture is therefore contested and not easily summarised. Broadly speaking, it may be said that precedent-based adjudication and doctrinal private law enjoy a hospitable environment in South Africa but face some interesting new rivals.

7. CONCLUDING REMARKS

This contribution has explained the nature of the South African doctrine of precedent. Its two main themes were the following.

First, the country's approach is a product of its mixed legal heritage. The South African doctrine of precedent derives from England's and shares its main features. This includes the distinction between vertical and horizontal precedent and between *ratio decidendi* and *obiter dicta*. But the Roman-Dutch setting into

---

297 S. Woolman, above n. 294, 763. Two of the authors' three main examples are in private law, namely *Barkhuizen*, above n. 82, which dealt with contract law; and *NM v Smith* [2007] ZACC 6, which applied the *actio iniuriarum*.

298 H. Scott, above n. 30, p. 245.

299 e.g. L.T.C. Harms, 'Judging under a Bill of Rights' (2009) 12 *Potchefstroom Electronic Law Journal* 1, 20; C. Lewis, 'The Uneven Journey to Uncertainty in Contract' (2013) 76 *Tydskrif vir Hedendaagse Romeins-Hollandse Reg* 80; M. Wallis, 'Commercial Certainty and Constitutionalism: Are They Compatible?' (2016) 133 *South African Law Journal* 545; F.D.J. Brand, 'The Role of Good Faith, Equity and Fairness in the South African Law of Contract: A Further Instalment' (2016) 27 *Stellenbosch Law Review* 238.

300 Officially, this took place only in 2013: see again above n. 89. Prior to that, the two courts had co-equal status, but in practice the Constitutional Court, the apex court in 'constitutional matters', was able to manoeuvre itself into the leading role.

301 Compare *Brisley v. Drotsky* [2002] ZASCA 35, paras. 21–25; *Afrox*, above n. 141, para. 32.

302 e.g. D.M. Davis and K. Klare, above n. 68.

303 See again above n. 180 and authorities cited there.

which it was brought has left it with certain peculiarities. The most important is that the doctrine is less strict than in England, particularly because horizontal precedent in South Africa has never been absolutely binding. The civilian legacy has had other relevant impacts, but these are mostly of historical interest; they have not lastingly disrupted the coherent and well-settled rules of *stare decisis*. Legal reasoning in the country, which focuses upon the interpretation, application, and distinguishing of the decided cases, would therefore be instantly familiar to lawyers elsewhere in the Anglo-American world.

The second main theme has been the stimulus provided by the 1996 Constitution. This envisaged major changes to all aspects of the legal system that was inherited from apartheid. Accordingly, the binding effect of vertical precedent was weakened in respect of pre-constitutional precedents. In respect of post-constitutional precedents, however, no changes were made. And the Constitutional Court, newly established in 1995, has embraced the doctrine of precedent, and indeed fulsomely refused to overrule its own decisions. At the same time, the Constitution has triggered certain changes to adjudication styles in South Africa, which may have served to decentre precedent-based reasoning from the exalted status it enjoyed hitherto. But these last-mentioned effects of the Constitution are subtle, contested, and by and large still emerging.

In sum, therefore, South Africa's doctrine of precedent, though clearly modelled on England's, bears the eclectic imprint of other sources, and has sought to strike the balance, in a perhaps unusually fraught context, between stability and change.

PRECEDENT IN SWEDISH PRIVATE LAW

Christina RAMBERG

1. A GENERAL INTRODUCTION TO LEGAL PRECEDENT

1.1. SOURCES OF SWEDISH LAW

Swedish law does not belong to the common law or the civil law legal families. It is in a legal family of its own, together with the law of Denmark, Finland, Iceland and Norway. This Nordic legal family is a mix between common and civil law. Although Swedish lawyers perceive themselves as closer to civil law – mainly the German legal family – Sweden lacks a coherent all-encompassing civil code. Its statutes are fragmentary and non-hierarchal. Many of the private law rules are 'unwritten law', i.e. not codified in statutes.

Sweden lacks legislation on the sources of law. Legal scholars and courts generally agree that precedents from the Supreme Court are a source of law.

Whether there is any hierarchy among various sources of law is disputed, but everyone agrees that after statutory law, precedents and preparatory statutory works are important sources of law.

1.2. THE SWEDISH COURT SYSTEM

Sweden has two supreme courts, one for criminal, private and procedural law, and another for administrative law. Specialist courts deal with certain areas or matters of law. For example, labour law disputes are resolved by a special court. This contribution will only refer to the Swedish Supreme Court (for criminal, private and procedural law), as the Swedish Supreme Court for Administrative law is not relevant for this volume.

In Sweden, only cases from the Supreme Court are precedents. Sweden does not give decisions by the (non-final) lower courts any function as precedents. The lower court judges do not perceive themselves as creating law or as providing guidance, instead they focus only on solving the individual case at hand. However, it has become increasingly common for disputing parties and legal scholars to refer also to lower court cases as they are now easily retrievable through various private legal databases. Such references to lower court cases are generally merely seen as illustrations and not as sources of law.

It is easier to get access to the courts of appeal (the stage before the supreme court) after a private law decision by the district court (the first-instance court) when it is likely that the district court has applied the law inaccurately, *inter alia* by deviating from supreme court precedents.[1]

---

[1] Ch. 40 s. 14 of the Procedural Act 1942.

Sweden effectively limits the number of precedents by allowing only very few cases to be decided and referred by the Supreme Court. For a case to be admitted to the Supreme Court, it basically needs to address an uncertain legal question on which guidance is needed. The Swedish Supreme Court for private law matters reports only about 20–30 private law cases each year. Due to the rather few precedents in Swedish private law, it is feasible to accomplish coherence among precedents.

Sweden has easily accessible records of all Supreme Court decisions.[2]

A precedent by the Supreme Court is normally decided by five Supreme Court judges. They are allowed to have dissenting opinions and it is quite frequent to see these. The Supreme Court, in rare instances, makes plenum decisions, i.e. decisions where all 16 Supreme Court judges participate.

The Supreme Court provides quite extensive reasonings in its awards. The explanations for which rules the Supreme Court applies and the basis for such rules are nowadays often transparently described in the reasonings. Formerly, the reasonings were short without reference to the applied legal rules. The change of style in the reasonings has been gradual and was fully implemented around the year 2000.[3]

2. A BRIEF HISTORY OF PRECEDENT IN PRIVATE LAW

Precedents had strong importance in medieval times and were still important in the seventeenth century. Thereafter followed a period of hostility against precedents by some scholars, inspired by Montesquieu's theories on the distribution of powers, who complained about the courts' lack of coherent application of the law. Despite this, the Constitution, from 1809, made clear that the Supreme Court could issue general Explanations of the Law (*lagförklaringar*) detached from an individual case. This was abolished in 1974.

Precedents have been gaining increasing importance in Swedish law ever since the late nineteenth century. The change has been gradual without any legislative reform. The tasks of the Supreme Court have been reformed by many small steps. It has gradually moved from being an openly available court for appeals to, in 1971, only admitting cases which address legally uncertain questions where the Supreme Court's guidance is of relevance to the general public.

The Swedish Supreme Court has in recent years indicated that it gives increased importance to precedents. This is demonstrated in the Supreme

---

2 Högsta Domstolen, 'Avgöranden' (2024) <https://www.domstol.se/hogsta-domstolen/avgoranden/>, and *lagen.nu* <https://lagen.nu>.

3 M. Jarnesand, 'Hogsta Domstolen och Enhetligheten' (2023) Stockholm University Doctoral dissertation, Ch. 13.4.5.

Court's reasonings by more frequent references to and discussions about previous cases.[4]

Also, Swedish legal scholars are paying increasing attention to precedents as a source of law, and they no longer refer to precedents merely for the purpose of providing illustrations. A reason for the increased scholarly interest is that the cases are now easily accessible and searchable in databases.

The main reason for the increasing importance of precedents in Sweden is the need for certainty and predictability in legal matters that are not solved by statutory law, either because there is a lack of statutory law (a gap) or because the statute is of a general nature, referring to concepts such as 'fair', 'fundamental', 'reasonable', 'negligence', 'gross', etc.[5]

In recent times, it has been more common in the legal literature to openly admit that the law is uncertain, instead of trying to hide uncertainties by pretending that the legal rules are all-encompassing and clear. This is probably also a reason why the more vague source of case law has gained importance compared to elaborate exegetic interpretations of statutory law.

3. THE NATURE OF PRECEDENT

There is no statutory law regarding the binding nature of precedents in Sweden. According to the Procedural Act (Chapter 54, Sections 10 and 11 of the Procedural Act), the Supreme Court's task is to *provide guidance for the application of law*. It is not clear from the Act what guidance means or to what extent the guidance is binding. The legislator has been intentionally vague in this respect. The preparatory works to a minor legislative reform note that case law has become an increasingly important source of law, without specifying how precedents are important.[6]

In effect, the binding nature of precedents is determined by the Supreme Court itself. The Swedish Supreme Court has not made any general proclamation about the binding nature of its decisions.[7] But in a case regarding the liability for appeal court judges who actively decided against a precedent, the Supreme Court stated:[8]

---

4 C. Ramberg, *Prejudikat som rättskälla i förmögenhetsrätten*, Wolters Kluwer, Stockholm 2017, Ch. 11.2. Approximately four out of five Supreme Civil Court cases have references to precedents, see M. Derlén and J. Lindholm, 'Judiciell aktivism eller prejudikatbildning?' *SvJT* 2016 p. 143.

5 U. Bernitz, 'Bättre rättskällor: Reflexioner över lagboken, rättsfallssamlingarna, betänkandena och departementspromemoriorna' *SvJT* 1976 p. 81; C. Ramberg, above n. 4, Ch. 8.8.

6 SOU 1986:1, pp. 71 and following.

7 C. Ramberg, above n. 4, Ch. 5.

8 NJA 1994, p. 194 (translation by the author of this contribution).

> Even though lower courts are not bound by precedents from the Supreme Court, the precedents are of great importance in determining if a court has committed a wrong or negligence in its application of the law. At the same time, the courts must be given room to develop the law. Consequently, a court ought to be given some possibility to deviate from some earlier case law. Anyhow, the State cannot become liable for damages if a court has provided realistic reasons for why it applies the law different from the Supreme Court.

This Supreme Court statement is rather vague and provides only limited understanding of the nature of precedents. Nevertheless, the Supreme Court perceives itself as *bound to take precedents into account*. Consequently, precedents have effect and are relevant as a Swedish source of law.

Even though precedents are not formally binding, they have a strong influence *de facto*. It is difficult to quantify to what extent precedents are effective, and whether they are binding, guiding, persuasive or merely illustrations. There are only limited – although growing – discussions about to what extent precedents are binding.

It has been said in Sweden that precedents are only *persuasive*, but their status is in practice stronger.[9] Some argue that precedents are not *dictating* but *guiding* the courts. Others argue that precedents, although not formally *binding*, are in practice *followed*. Some say that precedents are binding *pro tanto*, i.e. preliminarily binding.[10] The exact meanings of these terms and descriptions are unclear.[11]

It is not clear whether precedents qualify as legal rules (*rättsregler*), as they are not absolutely binding and furthermore sometimes are not sufficiently generalised. Precedents create norms and rules, but whether they are to be defined as legal rules, non-legal rules or principles is disputed.[12]

The Swedish Supreme Court is increasingly providing references to precedents and nowadays explains more in detail how its decisions relate to earlier cases. This indicates that the Supreme Court itself perceives precedents as an increasingly important source of law.

---

9 C. Ramberg, above n. 4, p. 54; Folke Schmidt, 'Domaren som lagtolkare' in *Festskrift tillägnad Professor, Juris och Filosofie Doktor Nils Herlitz vid hans avgång från professorsämbetet den 30 juni 1955*, Norstedt, Stockholm 1955; T. Bergquist, quoted in *SvJT* 1947 pp. 285 and following; L.A.E. Hjerner, *Om Rättsfallstolkning*, Juristförlaget, Stockholm 1981, pp. 46 and 23; B. Lehrberg, *Praktisk juridisk metod*, Institutet för bank- och affärsjuridik, Uppsala 2001, p. 102.

10 P. Asp, 'Skäl, slut och skiljaktighet – noteringar kring svensk prejudikatlära' *SvJT* 2021 p. 444; with reference to S. Kagan, *The Limits of Morality*, Clarendon Press, Oxford 1989, p. 17.

11 T. Gregow, 'Obiter dictum. Något att uppmuntra eller motarbeta?' (2015–16) 1 *Juridisk Tidskrift* 36; J. Lind, 'Högsta domstolen och frågan om doktrin och motiv som rättskälla' (1996–97) 2 *Juridisk Tidskrift* 352; S. Strömholm, 'En svensk prejudikatlära: behov och möjligheter' *SvJT* 1984 pp. 923 and following.

12 C. Ramberg, above n. 4, Ch. 8.2.

It is natural for Swedish judges to take precedents into account in parallel with other sources of law, such as statutory law and preparatory works. Judges take precedents into account for two reasons: they perceive the Supreme Court as authoritative, and they are concerned about the coherent application of the law. For these two reasons, judges apply the law in harmony with the Supreme Court's decisions even when they consider the Supreme Court to be wrong. Also, the Swedish Supreme Court judges perceive themselves as somehow bound by its own precedents. This is, *inter alia*, demonstrated by dissenting judges in subsequent cases following the former majority, although they still believe that the former majority applied the law incorrectly.[13]

A Swedish judge is expected to *note* relevant precedents, to *analyse* the precedents, and to *relate* to the precedent by either following it, distinguishing it, or openly deviating from it. Furthermore, judges are expected to *explain* in their reasoning which rule a precedent entails and to provide an explanation for deviations from that rule (comply or explain).

There are no examples of sanctions against judges who deviate from precedents.[14] In theory, a judge who deviates from precedents can be deemed to have committed a crime (malpractice) but hitherto there are no such instances. The above-mentioned Supreme Court case (NJA 1994 p. 194) concerned damages from appeal court judges for deviating from a precedent. The Swedish Supreme Court did not impose any liability for damages on the judges as they had referred to criticism against the precedent in the legal literature as reasons for why they deviated from the rule in the precedent.

Also, legal counsels are required to take note of precedents when giving advice to clients. If they fail to do so, they risk being liable for damages due to breach of contract.[15] Most legal counsel would also refer to precedents when arguing a case in front of the court, although some refrain from doing so and instead rely on the court's ability to find relevant precedents (*jura novit curia*).

The Supreme Court functions by updating the law in order for it to be in harmony with societal needs in a more flexible way than statutory law. The Supreme Court's law-making enables continuous adaptations to societal realities and to bridge ideological incongruences between the law and society. It furthermore adds vitality to the statutory law's old branches by developing the law for situations unforeseen when the statutory law was enacted.

The borderline is not sharp between, on the one hand, interpreting existing law and, on the other hand, developing new law. The reason is partly due to different understandings about whether statutory law is complete or contains

---

13 See cf. the Swedish Supreme Court cases NJA 1978 p. 992 compared with NJA 1988 p. 521, and NJA 1986 p. 579 compared with NJA 1987 p. 777.

14 See C. Ramberg, above n. 4, Ch. 5.2.

15 Supreme Court case NJA 2021 p. 129.

gaps and, if gaps are accepted, what constitutes a gap. The distinction between interpretation of law and developing new law is, however, not of practical importance in Sweden as there is no prohibition against judges' law-making.

It is not preferred in Sweden to be too tightly bound by precedents, as it would prevent the Supreme Court from adapting the law appropriately. The interest of adaptation is hard to reconcile with the interest of predictability.[16] The Swedish Supreme Court strives towards balancing these two interests. An unjust legal rule will sooner or later be amended either by statutory law or by precedents. An amendment by precedents is often gradual and slow. It typically starts by creating exemptions that gradually turn into an opposite main rule. The interest of fair and appropriate legal rules explains why law based on precedents needs to be reinterpreted, distinguished, and deviated from.

4. HOW TO IDENTIFY A LEGAL RULE IN A PRECEDENT

4.1. INTRODUCTION

Sweden does not have statutory law explaining how to use and interpret precedents, nor is there any such express guidance by the Swedish Supreme Court. Instead, guidance can be found by analysing how the Supreme Court actually acts in relation to precedents. Such analyses have been, until now, uncommon in the Swedish legal literature.[17]

The Swedish Supreme Court does not have any consistent method of interpreting precedents, although there seems to be a growing awareness of the need to develop a coherent approach to precedents. There are often references to precedents in the Swedish Supreme Court's reasonings without any explanation as to how the precedents are relevant. It has become more common for the Swedish Supreme Court to analyse precedents and to explain how precedents differ from the present case, although it is still rare to see any in-depth analysis of the facts in the precedent for the purpose of comparing it with the present case. Only in a few scattered cases does the Swedish Supreme Court make specific considerations about the factual and legal issues for the purpose of comparing precedents with the case under examination. Supreme Court judges occasionally make statements clarifying their opinions of the holding of the case, which sometimes shed light on how precedents are relevant.[18]

---

16 M. Jarnesand, above n. 3, Ch. 12.5.6.

17 C. Ramberg, above n. 4, Ch. 10; L. Heuman, *Metoder för rätttillämpning och lagtolkning*, Jure, Stockholm 2018.

18 See C. Ramberg, above n. 4, Chs. 11.2.1 and 11.5.

There is no consensus in the Swedish legal literature on how to identify legal rules in precedents. Swedish judges have an ambition to explain from where they find support for their decisions, be it in statutory law, preparatory works, precedents, or legal literature. As there is a generally high degree of trust in Swedish judges, there is very limited criticism against the lack of clear methods for interpreting precedents.

The focus of Swedish legal scholars' analyses of precedents is generally on the substantive issues and the outcome. It is less common to see an in-depth analysis of the methods to use for identifying rules in precedents. There is, however, an increase in the studies of precedent with efforts to create methods on how to use precedents.[19]

Swedish lawyers do not have any theory on how to identify landmark cases or *stare decisis* and generally do not give any such names to cases. Nevertheless, some cases gain more importance than others as they are more often referred to by the Supreme Court and in the legal literature to support conclusions about the law.

There is a common understanding that the identification of legal rules in precedents is not a logical exercise in the strict rational sense. Accordingly, there is no Swedish literature on deductive (syllogism) or inductive methods for interpreting precedents.[20]

Quite often arguments are based on analogies, particularly when analysing whether a precedent is analogous to a later case. The discussion in Sweden on the weaknesses of analogous reasonings is scarce and generally such analyses are, to a large extent, unaware of these weaknesses.[21]

There is a consensus by Swedish scholars that precedents are not suitable for providing *e contrario* guidance. Despite this, there is an example where the Supreme Court has made reference to a precedent and used it as an argument *e contrario*.[22]

Swedish scholars are generally not interested in which Supreme Court judge participated in the decision. And it is not *comme il faut* to teleologically search for what an individual judge had in mind when making the decision, although there are occasional exemptions.[23]

---

19 C. Ramberg, above n. 4, Ch. 1, with references; J. Nergelius, 'Prejudikat(o)bundenhet inom den konstitutionella rätten' *SvJT* 2017 p. 783; K. Calissendorff, 'Plenum och skiljaktigheter – vad ska det vara bra för?' *SvJT* 2017 p. 795; M. Mellqvist, 'Förmögenhetsrättsliga prejudikat – en nödvändig rättskälla' *SvJT* 2017 p. 805.

20 C. Ramberg, above n. 4, Chs. 9.2 and 9.3; A. Lindhagen, 'Om motivering av dom' *SvJT* 1947 pp. 322 and 325.

21 C. Ramberg, above n. 4, Ch. 9.4.

22 The Supreme Court case NJA 2007 p. 86, C. Ramberg, above n. 4, Ch. 9.5.

23 For example, the Supreme Court case NJA 2007 p. 663.

4.2. THE STYLE OF THE SWEDISH SUPREME COURT'S REASONINGS

The Supreme Court has gradually changed the style of its reasonings. Formerly, the reasonings were short and it was generally impossible to understand what the outcome was based on. There were only rarely references to sources of law and no explicit explanations of *ratio legis* (the *pro et contra* for a certain rule).[24]

Nowadays, the Supreme Court makes efforts to thoroughly explain the legal situation and to demonstrate how the legal rules apply to the case at hand. Regularly the Supreme Court makes extensive references to analogous statutory law, preparatory works, precedents, and legal literature. It is also common to see the court openly making free evaluations of a rule's suitability and weighing opposing societal interests against each other. The reasonings in modern precedents regularly explain how the applied rule fits into the legal system and how it relates to other statutory law and older precedents. Some Swedish legal scholars argue that such suitability reasonings undermine the Supreme Court's authority.[25] Others argue that suitability reasonings increase the importance of precedents and also make it easier to determine whether the precedent is still relevant after a period of societal change.[26]

This change of style has, in itself, worked to increase the importance of precedents in Sweden, as the modern style provides explicit guidelines that can be easily applied to many subsequent situations. Furthermore, the new transparent style of reasonings increases the Supreme Court's legitimacy as the public is able to understand and approve the Court's wisdom.

4.3. THE LEVEL OF GENERALISATION – DISTINGUISHING THE CASE

There is little Swedish debate or interest in methods for generalisation from an individual case to other similar cases. There is hardly any discussion to what extent it is allowed or suitable to generalise from an individual case to another case. Some scholars interested in the matter seem to agree with Anglo-American and French scholars who criticise theories on generalisation of precedents for being transcendental ('*la superstition du cas*').[27]

---

24 See A. Jarnesand, above n. 3, Ch. 13.4.5, on the development of the style of reasoning.

25 S. Strömholm, above n. 11, pp. 923 and following.

26 P. Asp, above n. 10; C. Ramberg, above n. 4, p. 323.

27 M.S. Moore, 'Precedent, Induction and ethical generalization' in L. Goldstein, *Precedent in Law*, Oxford University Press, New York, 1987, p. 196; S.J. Burton, 'Professor MacCormick's claim regarding universalization in law' (14–16 December 1984) Conference on Reason in Law, Bologna, and S.J. Burton, *An Introduction to Law and Legal Reasoning*, Little Brown, Boston 1985; G. Christie, 'Objectivity in the Law' (1969) 78 *Yale Law Review* 1311; E. Levi,

Only rarely does the Supreme Court explain how a case is different from an earlier precedent or why it is similar.[28] In most cases, however, there are no explanations as to why the Supreme Court refers to an earlier precedent. And when the Supreme Court develops the law in relation to an earlier precedent – by expanding a rule or making an exemption – it is often not clear what circumstances were decisively different in the two cases.[29] There are examples where the Supreme Court distinguishes a case from a precedent. Sometimes the distinguishing is clearly explained (as in the Supreme Court case NJA 2016 p. 1057).

The Swedish Supreme Court sometimes implicitly indicates that a case is not intended to be extensively generalised by stressing the particularities of the case.

Swedish lawyers are not trained in how to distinguish or generalise from earlier precedents, and it is quite rare to see such analyses in pleadings. There is a slightly increased interest for the art of distinguishing, which can be seen in both the universities' law programmes and in practice.

4.4. *OBITER DICTA* AND *RATIO DECIDENDI*

4.4.1. Generally on Obiter Dictum and Ratio Decidendi

It is rare to find Swedish commentators pointing to *obiter dictum*. Many Swedish legal scholars argue that the distinction between *ratio decidendi* and *obiter dictum* is irrelevant.[30] Some disagree.[31] The reason why the distinction is not perceived as important is probably because the Supreme Court often follows its own *obiter dicta*. There are only very few examples where the Supreme Court openly states that a statement in a precedent was *obiter dictum* and produces a rule contrary to the *obiter dictum*, cf. the Supreme Court case NJA 2013 p. 242. However, in that case the Supreme Court explained that the *obiter dictum* was illogical which demonstrates that the Supreme Court was unwilling to ignore the statement without a special reason. It is more common that the Supreme Court follows *obiter dicta* in earlier precedents.[32]

'An Introduction to Legal Reasoning' (1948) 15 *University of Chicago Law Review* 501, and E. Levi, 'The Nature of Judicial Reasoning' in S. Hook (ed), *Law and Philosophy*, New York University Press, New York 1964; R. Stone, 'Ratiocination not rationalization' (1965) 74 *Mind* 463, and R. Stone, 'The compleat wrangler' (1966) 50 *Minnesota Law Journal* 1001; J. Wisdom, *Philosophy and Psychoanalysis*, Barnes & Noble, New York 1969; R. Cross and J.W. Harris, *Precedent in English Law*, 4th ed., Clarendon Press, Oxford 1991, p. 26; see also S. Strömholm, above n. 11. See however, C. Ramberg, above n. 4, Ch. 10.

28 cf. the Supreme Court case NJA 2016 p. 799 for distinguishing and NJA 2016 p. 962 for not distinguishing. See C. Ramberg, above n. 4, p. 194.

29 C. Ramberg, above n. 4, pp. 196 and following.

30 C. Ramberg, above n. 4, Chs. 10.2 and 11.9; P. Asp, above n. 10.

31 C. Ramberg, above n. 4, Chs. 10.2 and 11.9.

32 See examples, C. Ramberg, above n. 4, Ch. 11.9.6. See also A. Jarnesand, above n. 3, Ch. 13.4.3.

It is likely that the distinction between *ratio decidendi* and *obiter dicta* will become more important as the Supreme Court, for the last ten to 20 years, has increasingly made statements that are clearly *obiter dicta*. Before the millennium, the Supreme Court's reasonings were often casuistic, short and closely related to the facts of the actual case. Nowadays, the Supreme Court has changed its style and in almost every case demonstrates an ambition to provide general guidance relevant for situations that are quite different from the facts of the individual case.

4.4.2. Obiter as General Statements in the Supreme Court's Reasonings

The Swedish Supreme Court's modern reasonings often have a paragraph where the relevant legal situation is generally described, detached from the facts in the individual case, although still in close connection with them. Very often the descriptions refer to non-statutory law and establish 'new' law. Such general descriptions are sometimes broad enough to be *obiter dicta* and can be ignored or distinguished in later cases.[33]

The binding nature of general statements by the Supreme Court is not clear. As too general statements of law may go beyond the Supreme Court's mandate to decide the individual case, they do not provide any strong binding effect, at least not theoretically.[34] Only very few question whether the Supreme Court has a mandate to provide such general rules and whether it is suitable to consider all aspects of a general rule.[35] In practice, many practitioners and scholars seem to treat the Supreme Courts' general statements as binding law. The reason is probably that there is great trust in the Supreme Court judges' wisdom and a thirst for predictability in the many uncertain areas of Swedish private law.

4.4.3. Statements that the Supreme Court Admit are Obiter Dicta and Hypothetical Obiter Dicta

Sometimes the Supreme Court's reasoning clarifies that a statement is superfluous. This happens when the Supreme Court provides examples that are not relevant in the case at hand. The Supreme Court may then describe a

---

33 B. Bengtsson, 'Domare och lagstiftare i samverkan och konflikt' in U. Göransson, T. Håstad and Å. Frändberg (eds), *Festskrift till Stig Strömholm*, Iustus, Uppsala 1997, p. 109; C. Ramberg, above n. 4, p. 286; P. Westberg, 'Prejudikattolkningens ABC' in A. Numhauser-Henning (ed), *Festskrift till Anna Christensen*, Juristförlaget i Lund, Lund 2000, p. 583.

34 L.A.E. Hjerner, above n. 9, pp. 17 and 46; P. Westberg, above n. 33, p. 596. Jan Andersson provides examples of such *obiter dicta* in company law (J. Andersson, 'Högsta Domstolens prejudikatfunktion och bruket av obiter dicta' (2008) I *Stockholm Centre for Commercial Law Yearbook* 11, 11 and 30 and following).

35 C. Ramberg, above n. 4, pp. 181 and following.

situation and state that 'this question needs not be determined by the Court'.[36] Such statements are important as they indicate that there is reason not to make too broad generalisations from the precedent. However, there is uncertainty as to the binding nature of answers provided by the Supreme Court to questions that it need not address.

The Supreme Court sometimes states rules for other situations than the situation at hand (hypothetical *obiter dicta*). The purpose of this is probably to provide guidance for future cases with similar facts. As an example of a hypothetical *obiter dictum*, the Supreme Court in NJA 2014 p. 892 stated what liability a company board member would have had if he had been seriously ill. The board member in the case at hand was not ill at all. What is the binding effect of the Supreme Court's statement regarding seriously ill board members? Some argue that the statement *obiter dictum* has as much value as statements *ratio decidendi*. Others argue that the statement *obiter dictum* has less value, since the Supreme Court did not get a chance to hear all arguments in relation to seriously ill board members.[37]

4.5. DECISIONS WITH DISSENTING OPINIONS

Most cases from the Supreme Court are unanimous, that is to say all five Supreme Court judges deciding on a case agree to the outcome and to the reasons for the outcome. In such cases, they make one common statement. Dissenting opinions are allowed and appear in about 20% of the private law cases. A dissenting opinion is noted, and the dissenting judge provides special reasonings as an appendix to the award. A dissenting judge may dissent to the outcome and reasonings or agree on the outcome but dissent with respect to the reasoning. Sometimes two judges are dissenting together in one common dissenting opinion or dissenting separately with two separate reasonings. It also happens, but only very rarely, that the two judges (the majority) provide one reasoning, and that one judge dissents with respect to the reasoning, and that two judges dissent with respect to the outcome and reasoning ('2-2-1 decisions'). Other combinations are also possible.

The Supreme Court itself generally makes references to precedents with dissenting opinions without noting that it is not a unanimous decision, which indicates that dissenting opinions are irrelevant.[38] However, sometimes dissenting opinions may indicate that something is changing in society and

---

36 The Supreme Court cases NJA 2012 p. 953 and NJA 2010 p. 709.

37 C. Ramberg, above n. 4, p. 290.

38 In rare instances, the Supreme Court makes a reference to a dissenting opinion and then appears to treat it as something in parallel to legal literature, cf. the Supreme Court cases NJA 2013 p. 1190 and NJA 2016 p. 900.

point to an increased probability that the precedent may become extensively distinguished in the future or that a future deviation from the precedent is likely. Sometimes, however, the transparently different opinions instead increase the importance of the precedent as the Supreme Court's majority openly discussed and carefully considered various possible rules and ultimately chose one.

In the Swedish legal literature, various conclusions are made as to whether precedents with dissenting opinions have less importance than unanimous precedents.[39] The legal literature often analyses dissenting opinions when criticising the Supreme Court's reasonings *de lege ferenda*, i.e. arguing that the precedent is inaccurate (*per incuriam*) or ought to have been differently formulated.

4.6. DECISIONS IN PLENUM

The Supreme Court normally decides cases with five Supreme Court judges. Some cases are decided in plenum (by all 16 judges). Decisions in plenum are very rare. They are made only when there is reason to deviate from an earlier precedent or when the case concerns a matter of particular importance.[40]

It is disputed in the Swedish legal literature whether decisions in plenum are more important than ordinary precedents. An argument for giving plenum

---

39 P. Asp, above n. 10; K. Calissendorff, G. Lambertz and S. Lindskog, 'Tillägg till Högsta domstolens avgöranden, samt något om skiljaktigheter' *SvJT* 2012 p. 313 at p. 317, K. Calissendorff (fn. 3) pp. 795 and following, and T. Håstad, 'Om skiljaktiga meningar' in T. Andersson and B. Lindell, *Festskrift till Per Henrik Lindblom*, Iustus, Uppsala 2004, pp. 303, 309 and following; G. Bergholtz and A. Peczenik, 'Precedent in Sweden' in N. MacCormick, R.S. Summers and A.L Goodhart, *Interpreting Precedents*, Routledge, London 1997, p. 302; A. Peczenik, *Juridikens metodproblem: rättskällelära och lagtolkning*, Almqvist & Wiksell, Stockholm 1974 p. 133. See also B. Bengtsson, above n. 33, p. 116; S. Strömholm, above n. 11; L. Heuman, 'Högsta domstolens prejudikatnedbrytande verksamhet' in *Festskrift till Per Olof Bolding*, Norstedts Juridik, Stockholm 1992, pp. 201, 210 and following. In later writings, Lars Heuman states that well-motivated dissenting opinions may diminish the importance of a precedent (L. Heuman et al, 'Rättspraxis' in *Finna rätt – Juristens källmaterial och arbetsmetoder*, Norstedts Juridik, 2014, p. 159); J. Munck, 'Haltande prejudikat' in J. Gernandt, J. Kleineman and S. Lindskog, *Festskrift till Torkel Gregow*, Norstedts juridik, Stockholm 2010, p. 315; C. Ramberg, above n. 4, Ch. 11.4. T. Gregow, Högsta domstolens rättsskapande verksamhet – några reflektioner, 2011, p. 87, at p. 92 and following; T. Gregow, 'Några synpunkter på frågan om prejudikats bindande verkan' in S. Lindskog, *Festskrift till Gösta Walin*, Norstedts Juridik, Stockholm 2002, p. 105; L.A.E. Hjerner, above n. 9, p. 41; J. Hellner, *Rättsteori*, 2nd ed., Norstedts Juridik, Stockholm 1994, p. 103.

40 G. Bergholtz and A. Peczenik, above n. 39, p. 302; A. Peczenik, above n. 39, pp. 123 and 133; L. Heuman, above n. 39, p. 233; D. Victor, 'Högsta Domstolen och prejudikaten – särskilt på straffrättens område' in P. Asp, *Festskrift till Nils Jareborg*, Iustus, Uppsala 2002; D. Victor, 'Något om domskrivning i högsta instans' in S. Heckscher and A. Eka, *Festskrift till Johan Hirschfeldt*, Iustus, Uppsala 2008, p. 54, at p. 547; C. Ramberg, above n. 4, Ch. 11.3.

decisions more importance as precedents is that many judges expressing the same opinion increases the likelihood that the case will be followed. However, it is – at least in theory – possible for all 16 judges to provide 16 different opinions. It is quite common, with dissenting opinions in plenum decisions.

When analysing how the Supreme Court relates to decisions in plenum, it is quite clear that they are not more important or more binding than ordinary precedents. In practice, the Supreme Court deviates from plenum decisions to the same extent as from normal decisions.[41]

4.7. ADDITIONS (APPENDICES)

A strange phenomenon in Swedish law are Supreme Court judges making a special comment as an addition (appendix) to the reasonings (*tillägg*). These appendices are published after the dissenting opinions (if there are any). They do not form part of the Supreme Court's precedents and they are to be treated as parallel to legal literature.[42] The Supreme Court makes references to additions quite often in the same way as it makes references to other legal literature.

It happens that Supreme Court judges write articles in law journals, but they are generally careful when analysing or criticising their own decisions. Their legal writings are mainly in the format of systematisations (case law overviews) or comments to statutes. Formally, such legal literature is of equal value to writings by legal scholars. But in practice, it is quite clear that legal writings by Supreme Court judges have a very strong influence, at least as long as the authors remain judges in the Supreme Court.

4.8. DEVIATIONS

One aspect of assessing the binding nature of precedents is to what extent deviations are allowed and how deviations are made. Sweden allows deviations from Supreme Court decisions and there is no need for any particular methods

---

41 C. Ramberg, above n. 4, Ch. 11.3.

42 K. Calissendorff, G. Lambertz and S. Lindskog, above n. 39; T. Ingvarsson, 'Tillägg för egen del' in E. Bylander, *Doktrinen i praxis*, Iustus, Uppsala 2013, p. 93; J. Munck, 'Får Gertrud Lennander kommentera rättsfall i vilka hon själv medverkat som domare?' in J. Gernandt, J. Kleineman and S. Lindskog, *Festskrift till Gertrud Lennander*, Jure, Stockholm 2010, pp. 239 and following; J. Lind, 'Recension av Argumentationsformer inom processrätten' (1993–94) 3 *Juridisk Tidskrift* 592, 602, and J. Lind, 'Rättsfallsanalyser – recension eller analys?' (1995–96) 1 *Juridisk Tidskrift* 232, 233; J. Hellner, 'Rättsfallsöversikter i SvJT' *SvJT* 1994 p. 536; J. Kleineman, 'Förutsättningsläran och jura novit curia' (1993–94) 4 *Juridisk Tidskrift* 881, 882 and 892; E. Hedfeldt, 'Något om prejudikat och referat' *SvJT* 1976 p. 493; C. Ramberg, above n. 4, Ch. 11.5.

in order to make a deviation. It is not necessary with a decision including more judges than normal (five) to make a deviation, although the court typically involves all 16 judges (plenum) when it actively puts into question whether to make a deviation.

The Swedish Supreme Court is anxious to satisfy the interest of coherence and, consequently, deviations from earlier precedents are rare. Within the area of private law there is approximately one plenum case every other year.[43]

It is also rare that the Supreme Court makes unintentionally conflicting precedents. It is, however, not uncommon for the Supreme Court to make far-reaching distinguishments of earlier precedents and thereby in reality deviate from the earlier precedent but present the new case in the form of a different situation.[44]

There are many reasons why the Swedish Supreme Court may deviate from a precedent:[45]

1. legislative changes after the earlier precedent (including decisions from the European Court of Justice and the European Court of Human Rights);
2. strong arguments that have been overlooked before;
3. new knowledge;
4. societal changes;
5. change in values;
6. the earlier precedent does not fit in to the legal system; or
7. the earlier precedent is poorly supported (*per incuriam*).

The most common reason for a deviation is that the earlier precedent is outdated due to subsequent legislation or societal change.[46]

When there is reason to make a deviation, the Supreme Court must consider a number of restraining factors:

1. whether the public has adopted to the earlier precedent (the retroactive effect);
2. how strong a need for deviation is;
3. whether the deviation is only of theoretic-academic relevance;
4. whether the change is more appropriately made through legislation;
5. if there are ongoing statutory reforms;
6. whether it is more appropriate to distinguish the case than making a deviation; and

---

43 C. Ramberg, above n. 4, p. 208, fn. 44.

44 L. Heuman, 'Högsta domstolens prejudikatnedbrytande verksamhet', above n. 39, pp. 225 and following. C. Ramberg, above n. 4, Ch. 10.6.3.

45 C. Ramberg, above n. 4, Ch. 10.6; P. Asp, above n. 10.

46 See for example the Supreme Court cases NJA 1994 p. 194, NJA 2009 p. 16 and NJA 2011 p. 843.

7. whether a deviation concerns a deviation from many or few earlier precedents.

Swedish law is generally willing to adapt and salute the interests of flexibility and adaptation to new societal circumstances. Sweden has, for a long period of time, been lucky to have internal and external peace, trust in society, economic growth and safe societal conditions. Such fortunate circumstances in Sweden may be an explanation for why the interests of certainty and foreseeability are less important and that instead the interests of material fairness and adaptation to changes have become more important.

The Supreme Court has sometimes pointed to the need for legal change, but refrained from making the change as it would be more suitable for the legislator to deal with the problem.[47]

One main reason for not making a deviation even when there is a need for legal change is that it would be politically sensitive. When the Supreme Court decided to allow damages from the state to a person who was wrongfully deprived of his citizenship, one dissenting Supreme Court judge argued that it was beyond the Court's mandate to create a rule to this effect without statutory support as it is a politically controversial question.

Another main reason for not making a deviation even when there is a need for legal change is when a deviation would cause unwanted or uncertain retroactive effects. When a rule is laid down in a precedent, there is a fictitious assumption that the rule always existed. When the precedent transparently states that the old rule is now replaced by a new rule, the retroactive effects are often uncertain. When the legislator replaces an old statute with a new statute, the retroactive effects are often solved specifically. The Supreme Court, however, cannot regulate retroactive effects as it only decides over the present dispute, and has no means to state anything about how the deviation (the new rule) affects other parties who may have acted in reliance on the old precedent (the old rule). The Supreme Court has created new rules without contemplating problematic retroactive effects by establishing a wide liability for providers of district heating.[48] In a famous case, the Supreme Court deviated from outdated statutory rules in the Promissory Notes Act from 1936 as they were ill-suited for electronic credit agreements.[49] But there are cases where the Supreme Court has abstained from creating a new rule by referring to the problematic retroactive effects. One example concerns interpretation of wills, where the Supreme Court preferred an 'inappropriate rule' that people had adapted to over an 'appropriate rule'.[50]

---

47 See the Supreme Court cases NJA 2006 p. 662 and NJA 2013 p. 314.

48 The Supreme Court case NJA 1991 p. 720.

49 The Supreme Court case NJA 2010 p. 467.

50 The Supreme Court case NJA 1950 p. 483.

The reasons for deviations are expected to be explained in the courts' reasonings. However, there are cases where the Swedish Supreme Court in fact has deviated from precedents without transparently admitting it.[51]

4.9. THE IMPORTANCE OF OLD PRECEDENTS

The Swedish Supreme Court is rather young, and its role has only gradually developed to become a creator of guiding precedents. Consequently, it is rare to see references to cases older than the 1900s. On average the private law cases referred to are 25 years old, which is some years older than the references by the UK Supreme Court.[52]

Old age may weaken or strengthen the importance of a precedent. An old case may, on the one hand, be a strong precedent when the public has adapted it to during a long period of time. On the other hand, an old precedent may be weak due to societal change or to new statutory law. The impact of societal change is particularly relevant within the area of private law. The means of making business today are in many ways different from a century ago, which puts into question whether it is at all useful to refer to old precedents. But at the same time, it is clear how many businesses have adapted to rules in precedents, and this is a reason in itself to uphold them, particularly when considering that the Supreme Court cannot solve problematic retroactive effects of deviating from an old precedent (see above).

The Supreme Court treats old cases with respect and always considers whether the reasons behind an old precedent are still valid. According to the principle of *cessante ratione sessat lex ipsa*, an old precedent can become obsolete. In effect, by constantly questioning whether there is still reason to uphold old cases, their importance as precedents diminishes and is replaced by a free analysis, not restricted by precedents. It is probably fair to say that the Supreme Court has a (weak) presumption that an old case is binding, but always makes an assessment as to what extent the old precedent is relevant for modern conditions.

Generally, the Supreme Court makes efforts to explain how it relates to old precedents. The Supreme Court case NJA 2016 p. 303 concerned the relevance of two cases of 100 and 88 years old. The legal matter was whether a lessee was entitled to a rent reduction for the period prior to giving notice about the defect to the landlord. The Supreme Court noted:

> although the need for consumer protection has changed over time, the legal situation ought not to be changed. The [old] rule described above is not only well established; there are also good reasons for it.

---

51 C. Ramberg, above n. 4, Ch. 10.6.1.

52 R.P. Caldarone, 'Precedent in operation: a comparison of the judicial House of Lords and the US Supreme Court' (2004) *Public Law* 759, 775; C. Ramberg, above n. 4, p. 305.

5. MANDATE TO CREATE PRIVATE LAW

5.1. FORMAL RULES REGARDING THE JUDGES' MANDATE

Sweden does not have any statutory law directly addressing the judges' powers as lawmakers. The Constitution ensures that court judges are independent by the 1974 Instrument of Government.[53] Apart from that, there is no statutory law on the relationship between the legislator and the courts.

5.2. *DE FACTO* MANDATE

The interpretation and application of law in the Supreme Court's resolution of a particular dispute is a kind of law-making as the decisions have the potential to become recurring norms applicable to future similar situations. In this sense, Swedish Supreme Court judges are lawmakers.[54]

The legislator does not always follow the pace of societal change. This is one reason why judges need to adapt the law by interpreting pre-existing law in the light of new situations. In practice, the Swedish judges must interpret old statutory law whenever it is unclear, which is often the case as the statutory law in many private law areas has not been reformed for many decades. Such creative interpretation is, in reality, judge-made law, even though this is not always formally acknowledged.

Sweden comes from a history where judges were not seen as making law, but as simply applying already-existing law. Despite this, judges have always in practice been lawmakers, and case law has often later become codified in statutes. The Swedish Tort Act of 1972 is an example of judge-made law which legislators have partly turned into statutory law.

According to the *declarative theory*, judges are applying an autonomous legal system which they do not have the right or possibility to influence. Through legal training, the judges have acquired the ability to identify already-existing legal rules. The declarative theory is now abandoned in Sweden.

The *façade theory* allows judges to create law but stresses the importance of judges hiding their law-making from the public. According to this theory, the main purpose of legal reasoning is to establish legitimacy for the legal order. The reasoning should therefore provide an impression that the legal rules are clear and stable. The Swedish Supreme Court sometimes hides its law-making by referring to a seemingly already-existing legal rule instead of

---

53 The Instrument of Government (*Regeringsformen*), Ch. 11, s. 7.

54 cf. B. N. Cardozo, *The Nature of the Judicial Process*, Yale University Press, New Haven 1921, p. 150.

clearly explaining that the court could have chosen to formulate an alternative rule.[55] Some Supreme Court judges have openly stated that they adhere to the façade theory, for instance Supreme Court judge Dag Mattson:[56] 'For legitimacy it is decisive not how power in reality is but how it is generally perceived in society.'

The *transparency theory*, which is predominant nowadays, entails that judges have the mandate to create law in order to fill gaps in statutory law. Or, in other words, judges have the power to create legal rules by clarifying the law when no answer is provided by statutory law. The Supreme Court quite frequently expressly points out that there is no applicable statutory law, and thereby indirectly indicates that it must create law to fill the gap. Such transparent behaviour can be found in some 20% of private law precedents during 2006–15.[57] The Supreme Court's reasonings sometimes openly discuss *pro et contra* for different solutions when the law is uncertain. Generally, transparent law-making is nowadays perceived as a means to increase – not decrease – the Supreme Court's legitimacy.[58]

Every time judges are to decide a legal question, they must consider whether it is suitable to apply a rule restrictively or extensively. This is the same when applying both statutory law and case law. The judges furthermore need to consider whether the rule is obsolete. Such necessary considerations form part of the judges' powers and, consequently, law is always developed by judges.

Nowadays, there is general Swedish agreement that judges make law. The role of judges is perceived as being not only to declare or to expose the meaning of the law, but also to supplement it and to create rules for situations not governed by specific statutory law.[59] Swedish Supreme Court judges admit that their decisions create law, and they do not seem afraid of jeopardising their legitimacy by expressly declaring that they create law.[60]

---

55 C. Ramberg, above n. 4, p. 97, fn. 90.

56 D. Mattson, 'Domarnas makt – domdarrollen i ett nytt rättsligt landskap' *SvJT* 2014 p. 588 at p. 593 (translation by the author of this contribution).

57 C. Ramberg, above n. 4, p. 104, fn. 101.

58 C. Ramberg, above n. 4, p. 104.

59 M. Derlén and J. Lindholm, above n. 4, p. 143; J. Kleineman, 'Från prejudikatinstans till lagstiftare? Högsta domstolens ökade aktivism' (2014–15) 3 *Juridisk Tidskrift* 495; J. Nergelius, 'Domstolar och demokrati – Är det dags för maktdelning?' *SvJT* 2000 p. 545; C. Ramberg, above n. 4, Ch. 8; O. Wiklund, 'Om Högsta domstolens rättsskapande verksamhet – löper domstolen amok?' *SvJT* 2014 p. 336; M. Zamboni, '"Makers" vs. "Markers": Are constitutional courts political or legal actors?' in S. Comtois and K. de Graaf, *On Judicial and Quasi-Judicial Independence*, Eleven International Publishing, The Hague 2013, p. 69.

60 Swedish Supreme Court cases NJA 1994 p. 194; NJA 2009 p. 16; NJA 2011 p. 843; and Justice Stefan Lindskog's opinion in the Swedish Supreme Court case NJA 2012 p. 535.

The former Chairman of the Swedish Supreme Court, Stefan Lindskog, has stated:[61]

> Precedents entail making law. It is not about the court finding something. Instead the court declares what should be, within certain limits of discretion.

The Supreme Court displays various approaches to its role as lawmaker and there is no clear pattern on how it acts in relation to law-making. The willingness among Supreme Court judges to openly acknowledge its law-making function varies, as do the reasons for changing existing law by precedents. One judge may put emphasis on history, another on structure, a third on societal needs, a fourth on formalism, a fifth may be flexible and encompass all views, a sixth stresses the interest of stability, and a seventh the interest of pragmatism. This diversity of views hopefully leads to an appropriate balance.

5.3. DISCUSSION ON THE DISTRIBUTION OF POWERS

Sweden has hesitations about judges' suitability as lawmakers. Judges are generally not well-equipped to make law. The reasons are manifold. First, the facts of cases in the Supreme Court are often peculiar and do not always represent 'normal' problems. Second, the judges are often restrained by how the legal counsels have structured their arguments. Third, the courts do not have the ability to foresee the economic effects for society as a whole and lack national budgetary powers. Fourth, the courts need to make their decisions rather fast and lack the legislator's possibilities to carefully investigate and evaluate various solutions.[62]

There is quite intense debate in Sweden as to the distribution of powers between Supreme Court judges and the Parliament and to what extent the court should exercise its law-making powers.[63] The general understanding in Sweden is that rules emanating from court decisions suffer from a shortage of democracy.[64] This worry is naturally less prominent within the area of private commercial law as compared to more politically controversial areas of law. The

---

61 S. Lindskog, 'Tillitsfullmakten – en replik' *SvJT* 2020 p. 785 at p. 795, (translation by the author of this contribution).

62 C. Ramberg, above n. 4, Ch. 8.10.

63 J. Andersson, above n. 34, p. 11; J. Andersson, 'Olovlig värdeöverföring och koncernbidrag i HD – mekanisk juridisk verkstad eller rättspolitisk designbyrå?' (2016–17) 1 *Juridisk Tidskrift* 124; C. Josefsson, 'Domstolarna och demokratin – Något om syftet med grundläggande rättigheter, europeiseringens konsekvenser och aktivismens baksida' *SvJT* 2015 p. 40; J. Kleineman, above n. 59, 495; F. Wersäll, 'En offensiv Högsta domstol. Några reflektioner kring HD:s rättsbildning' *SvJT* 2014 p. 1.

64 For an introduction to the debate, see O. Wiklund, above n. 59, p. 339.

Swedish Supreme Court does not rule against statutory law (unless it violates the Constitution, EU law or the European Convention on Human Rights) and there are no obvious examples of the Supreme Court abusing its powers.[65] However, lately the Supreme Court has, in several cases, openly deviated from statements in the statutory preparatory works. This is controversial as the preparatory works have traditionally been an important means to establish the 'legislator's intention' to achieve predictability and a coherent application of the law. Apart from the trend that precedents reduce the importance of preparatory works, most debates conclude that the legislator always has the upper hand by its power to change unwanted precedents through new legislation, which the courts must and will follow.[66] Consequently, there is no substantial fear that the increasing importance of precedents provides Swedish judges with excessive powers.

Politically controversial issues may also occur within the area of private law. The Supreme Court case NJA 2002 p. 322 concerned whether a claim should be dismissed when the parties had agreed to pay a constructor black money (tax evasion). The five Supreme Court judges were in disagreement. Their reasonings are transparent and clearly demonstrate the politically controversial issues. They openly admit that their decision will create law. This case is an example of how the Swedish Supreme Court judges avoid hidden political activism by openly admitting that they are making political decisions and that they are careful in doing so. This transparent behaviour is a message to the Parliament that it may reverse the rule if it disagrees with it.

The Parliament has, to a large degree, delegated powers to the Supreme Court within the area of private law by not providing encompassing statutory law and by general wording in the existing statutory law. It is thus uncontroversial that private law develops through precedents.

It is only rarely that the Supreme Court discusses the limits for its power to make law and its relation to the legislator (the Parliament). From the few occasions that the Supreme Court has addressed the issue, it is clear that there are different opinions among the Supreme Court judges about the boundaries for its powers.

The greater expectation there is about a coherent application from the Supreme Court, the larger its power. The Supreme Court can therefore increase its power in the long term by following its own statements in precedents. The more it acts as if it is bound by its own precedents, the more expectation there is of precedents being binding, which in turn leads to the public acting in accordance with the precedents, which ultimately establishes the Supreme Court's powers.

---

65 J. Kleineman, above n. 59, 527.

66 See judge Stefan Lindskog's reasoning in an addition to the Supreme Court case NJA 2012 p. 535 at p. 553; M. Zamboni, above n. 59, p. 69.

6. THE IMPORTANCE OF PRECEDENTS IN PRIVATE LAW

Precedent is an important source of private law in Sweden. The reason is that Sweden does not have a coherent private law code. Instead, Swedish statutory law is incomplete, casuistic, and fragmented. Furthermore, statutory law is generally old, with the exception of consumer law. Therefore, precedents cater for the need for certainty and to foresee the legal effects before making decisions within the area of private law.

General contract law is mainly laid down by precedents, as the Contracts Act is from 1915 with few amendments and only covers some scattered specific matters. The questions of interpretation and construction of contracts, pre-contractual liability (*culpa in contrahendo*) and restitution are wholly determined by case law.

Sales contracts, insurance contracts, agency contracts, the sale and lease of real estate, and various consumer contracts are quite comprehensibly covered by statutory law and, consequently, precedents are less important. Although, of course, guidance from precedents is needed to understand abstract and vague wording in statutes, such as 'material' and 'reasonable'.

Other contracts, such as advice, construction contracts between businesses, credit agreements between businesses, distribution contracts and shareholder agreements are not covered by statutory law. For such contract types, precedents are necessary. Precedents are, however, scarce in many contract types. This is due to the frequent use of arbitration in Swedish domestic commercial contracts. The Swedish Supreme Court has, for the past 15 years, been active and taken every opportunity to provide guidance, particularly within the area of construction contracts. For shareholder agreements and credit agreements business-to-business (B2B) there is, regrettably, no relevant precedent. There are only a few precedents concerning advice and distribution contracts.

Tort law has been covered by statutory law since 1972. The Tort Damages Act was made with the main purpose to codify existing case law. The Tort Damages Act is based on responsibility for negligence and there are many precedents providing concrete guidance as to what constitutes negligence. There are also many cases establishing how to calculate damages (the quantum) for tortious liability as a supplement to statutory law. The precedents preceding the Tort Damages Act 1972 still provide guidance on what constitutes negligence and causality.

Intellectual property law, company law and bankruptcy law are well-covered by statutory law and thus, precedents play a minor, but not unimportant, role.

Labour and employment law are covered by general statutory law but mainly regulated by agreements between the unions and employers' organisations. There are many important precedents from the Supreme Labour Court within this area of private law.

Property law and securities outside real estate are only partly covered by statutory law and to a large extent are created and governed by precedents.

Family law is regulated in statutes on, *inter alia*, marriage, cohabitation and inheritance. Due to societal change, precedents have recently become very important, and the Supreme Court has lately provided quite radical and important precedents within the area of family law.

7. CONCLUDING REMARKS

The main challenge in relation to precedents in Sweden is how to balance, on the one hand, the interest of coherence and predictability and, on the other hand, the interest of flexibility and materially fair outcomes.[67] Many argue that precedents do not create predictability in the same way as statutory law. Against this, some argue that statutory law does not provide any real predictability due to the language either being too general or too casuistic. The conclusion is that predictability is best achieved through a combination of statutory law and precedents.[68]

Swedish private law (outside consumer law) has, *de facto*, become a legal order based on precedents. This is a rather new insight among Swedish lawyers, as the traditional perception was that private law was based on statutory law and that precedents were merely illustrations of the application of law, with only slight relevance as a source of law. Sweden will need to develop and fine-tune methods for using precedents as a source of law. In this respect, Sweden has embarked on an interesting and challenging journey.

---

[67] C. Ramberg, above n. 4.

[68] C. Ramberg, above n. 4, pp. 142 and following.

www.ingramcontent.com/pod-product-compliance
Ingram Content Group UK Ltd.
Pitfield, Milton Keynes, MK11 3LW, UK
UKHW051922100926
8556IPUK00021B/1317

9 781839 705366